SPIDER-GIRL

writer
TOM DEFALCO

pencils
PAT OLLIFFE

inks
AL WILLIAMSON

WITH *SAL BUSCEMA* (FINISHES, ANNUAL)

colors
CHRISTIE SCHEELE

letters
DAVE SHARPE

cover art
PAT OLLIFFE

collection editor
JENNIFER GRÜNWALD

senior editor, special projects
JEFF YOUNGQUIST

director of sales
DAVID GABRIEL

production
JERRY KALINOWSKI

book designer
CARRIE BEADLE

creative director
TOM MARVELLI

editor in chief
JOE QUESADA

publisher
DAN BUCKLEY

AVENGING ALLIES

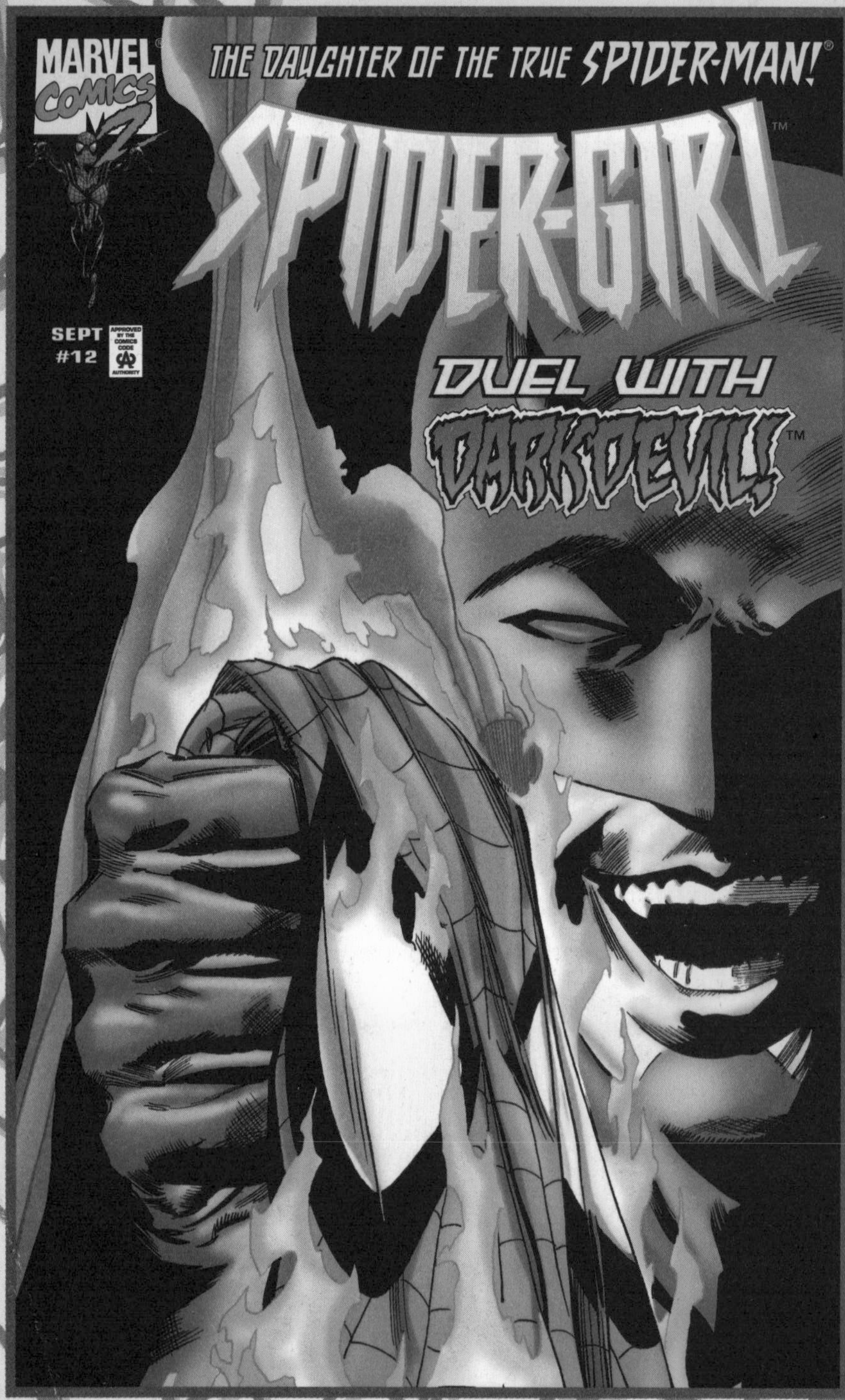
MARVEL COMICS
THE DAUGHTER OF THE TRUE SPIDER-MAN!
SPIDER-GIRL
SEPT #12
APPROVED BY THE COMICS CODE AUTHORITY
DUEL WITH DARKDEVIL!

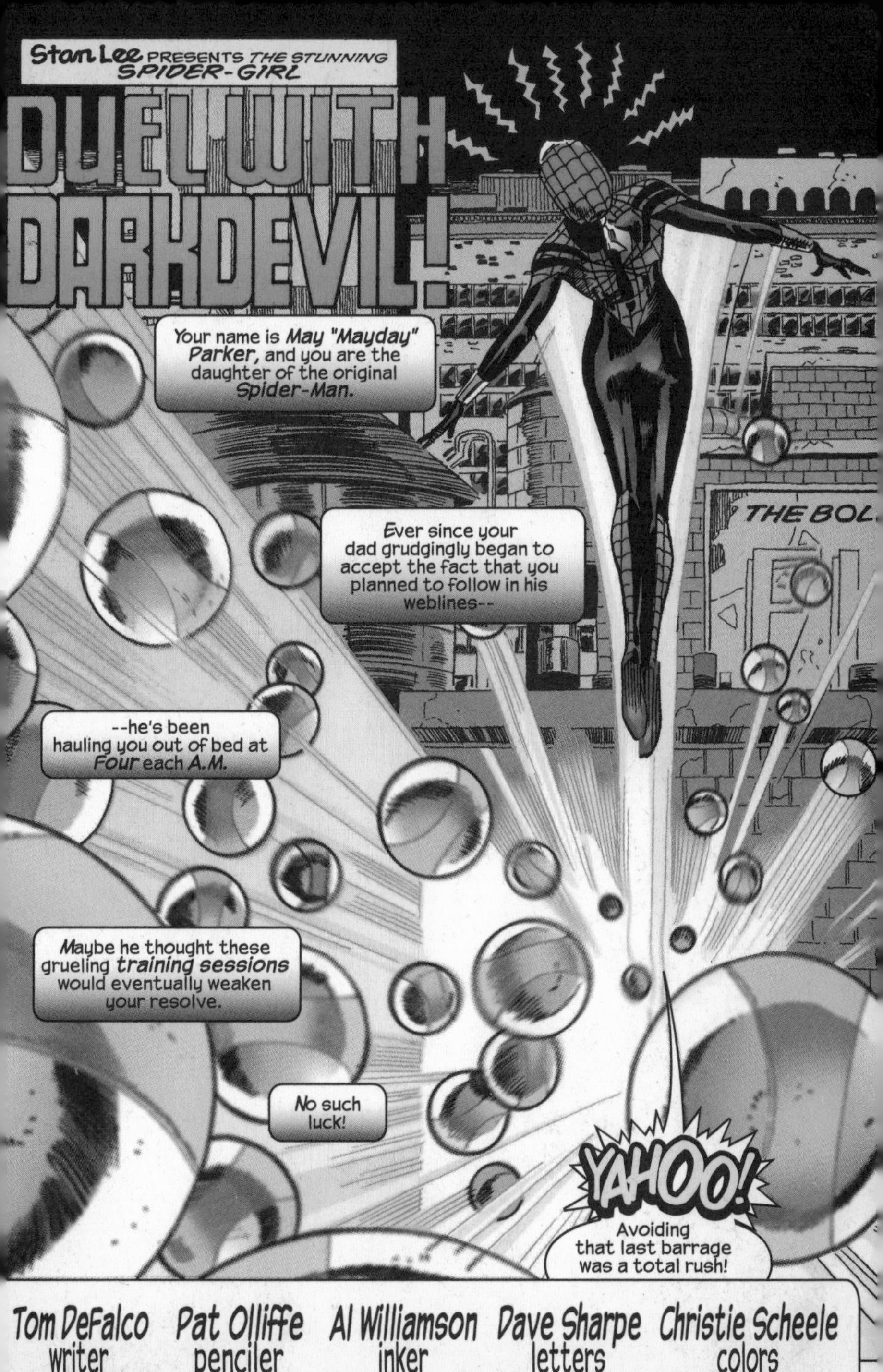
Stan Lee PRESENTS THE STUNNING SPIDER-GIRL
DUEL WITH DARKDEVIL!
Your name is May "Mayday" Parker, and you are the daughter of the original Spider-Man.
Ever since your dad grudgingly began to accept the fact that you planned to follow in his weblines--
--he's been hauling you out of bed at Four each A.M.
Maybe he thought these grueling training sessions would eventually weaken your resolve.
No such luck!
THE BOL
YAHOO!
Avoiding that last barrage was a total rush!
Tom DeFalco writer
Pat Olliffe penciler
Al Williamson inker
Dave Sharpe letters
Christie Scheele colors

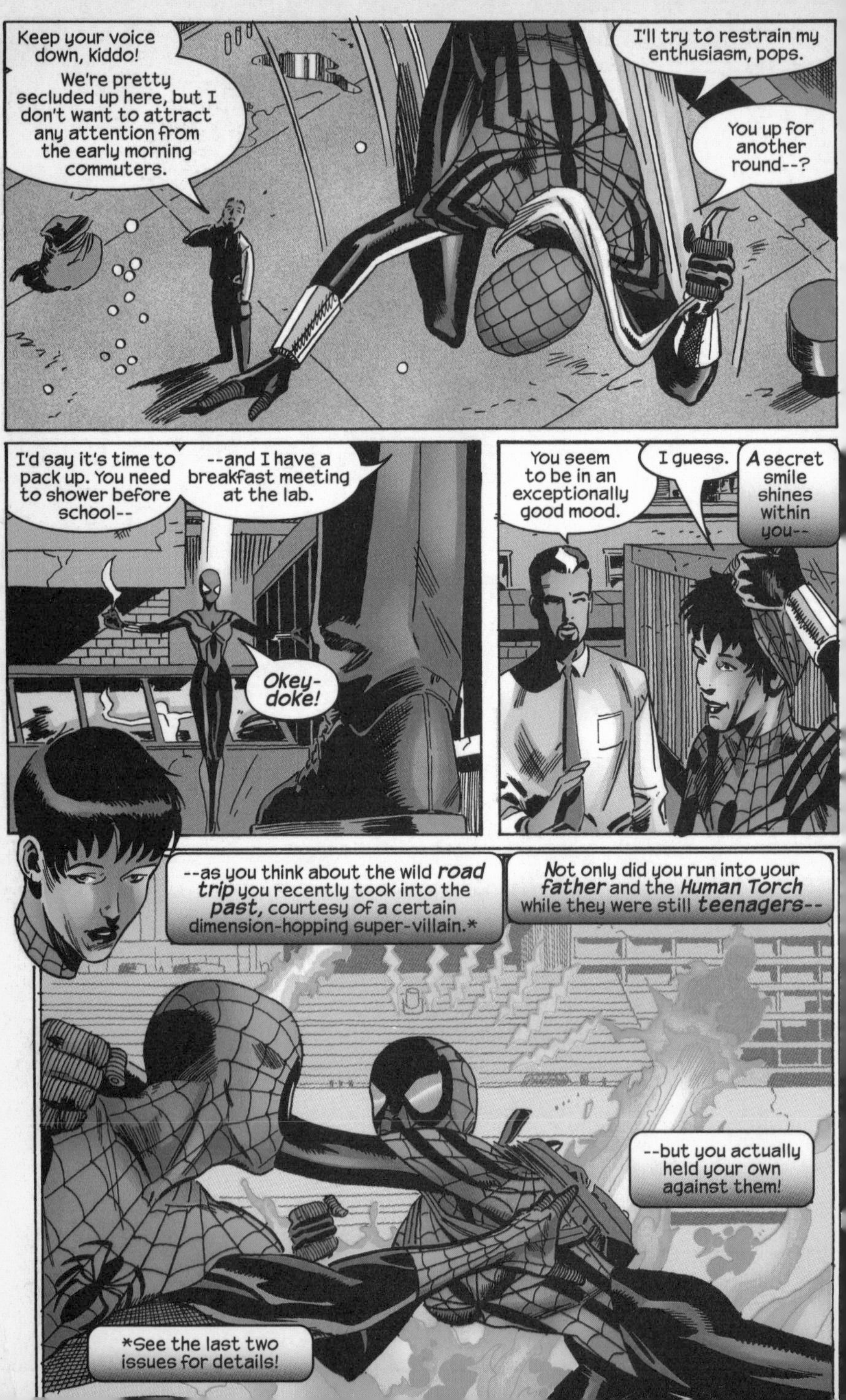
Keep your voice down, kiddo!
We're pretty secluded up here, but I don't want to attract any attention from the early morning commuters.
I'll try to restrain my enthusiasm, pops.
You up for another round--?
I'd say it's time to pack up. You need to shower before school--
--and I have a breakfast meeting at the lab.
Okey-doke!
You seem to be in an exceptionally good mood.
I guess.
A secret smile shines within you--
--as you think about the wild road trip you recently took into the past, courtesy of a certain dimension-hopping super-villain.*
Not only did you run into your father and the Human Torch while they were still teenagers--
--but you actually held your own against them!
*See the last two issues for details!

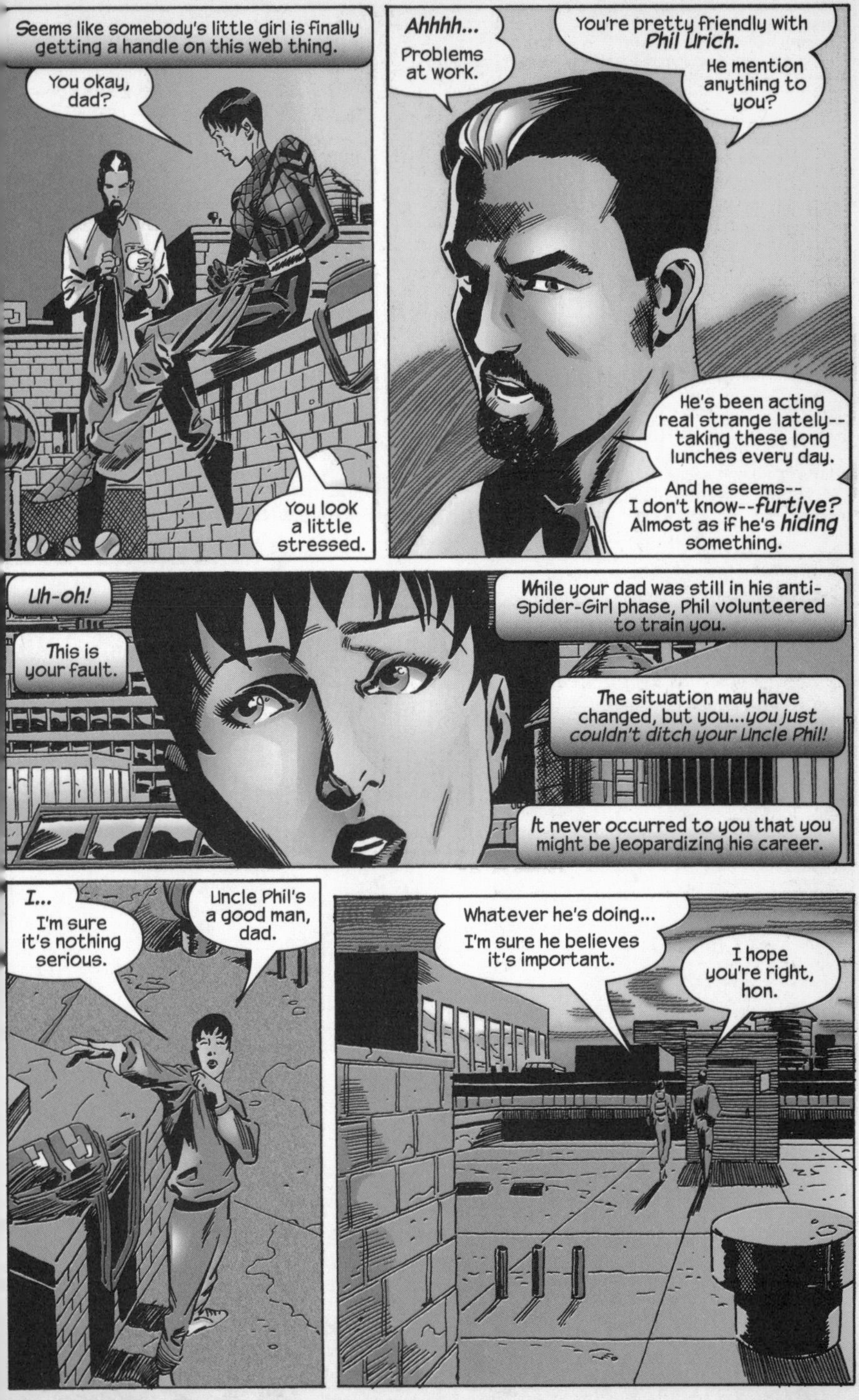

Seems like somebody's little girl is finally getting a handle on this web thing.
You okay, dad?
You look a little stressed.
Ahhhh...
Problems at work.
You're pretty friendly with Phil Urich.
He mention anything to you?
He's been acting real strange lately-- taking these long lunches every day.
And he seems-- I don't know--furtive? Almost as if he's hiding something.
Uh-oh!
This is your fault.
While your dad was still in his anti-Spider-Girl phase, Phil volunteered to train you.
The situation may have changed, but you...you just couldn't ditch your Uncle Phil!
It never occurred to you that you might be jeopardizing his career.
I...
I'm sure it's nothing serious.
Uncle Phil's a good man, dad.
Whatever he's doing...
I'm sure he believes it's important.
I hope you're right, hon.

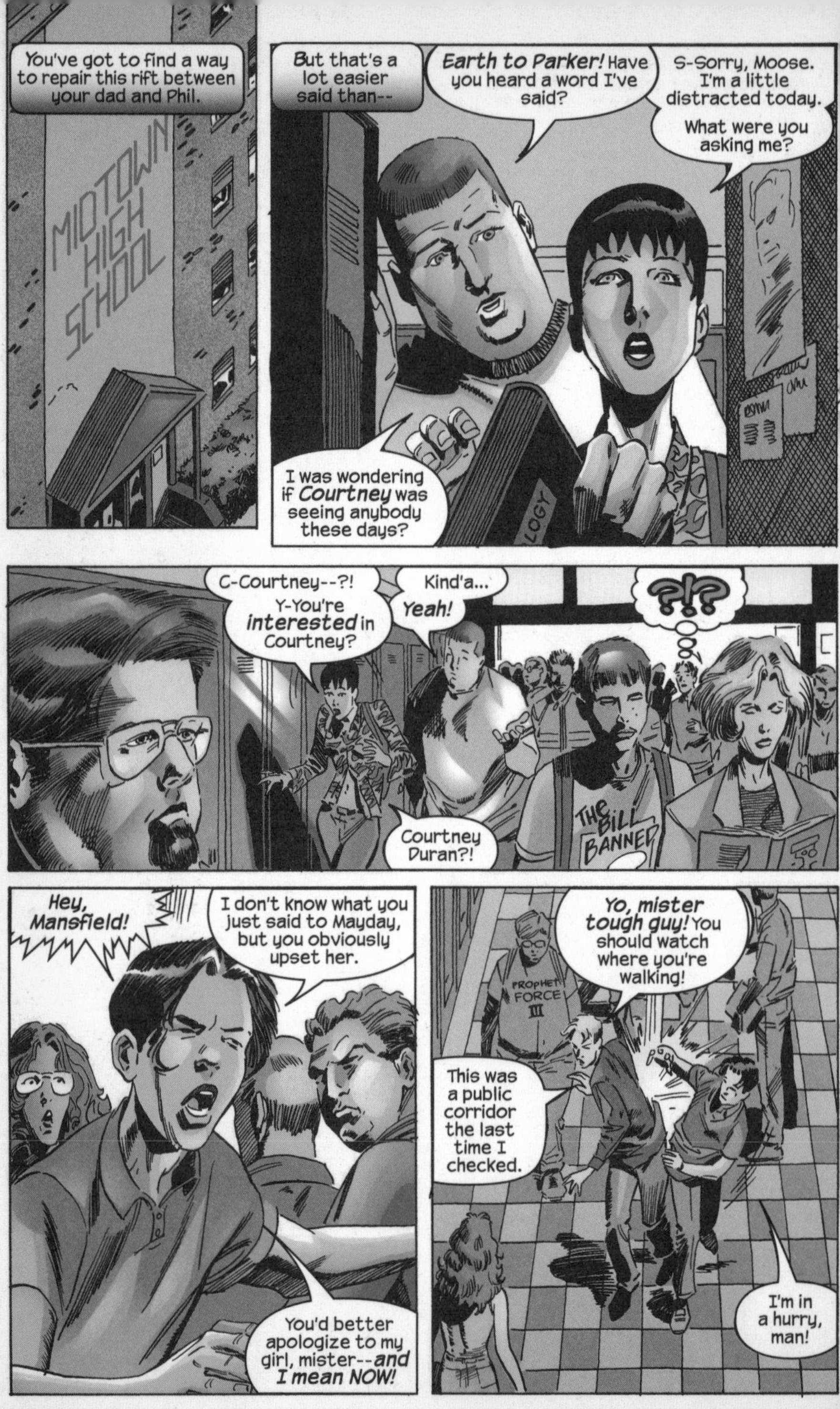
You've got to find a way to repair this rift between your dad and Phil.
MIDTOWN HIGH SCHOOL
But that's a lot easier said than--
Earth to Parker! Have you heard a word I've said?
S-Sorry, Moose. I'm a little distracted today.
What were you asking me?
I was wondering if Courtney was seeing anybody these days?
C-Courtney--?!
Y-You're interested in Courtney?
Kind'a...
Yeah!
?!?
Courtney Duran?!
THE BILL BANNED
Hey, Mansfield!
I don't know what you just said to Mayday, but you obviously upset her.
You'd better apologize to my girl, mister--and I mean NOW!
Yo, mister tough guy! You should watch where you're walking!
PROPHET FORCE III
This was a public corridor the last time I checked.
I'm in a hurry, man!

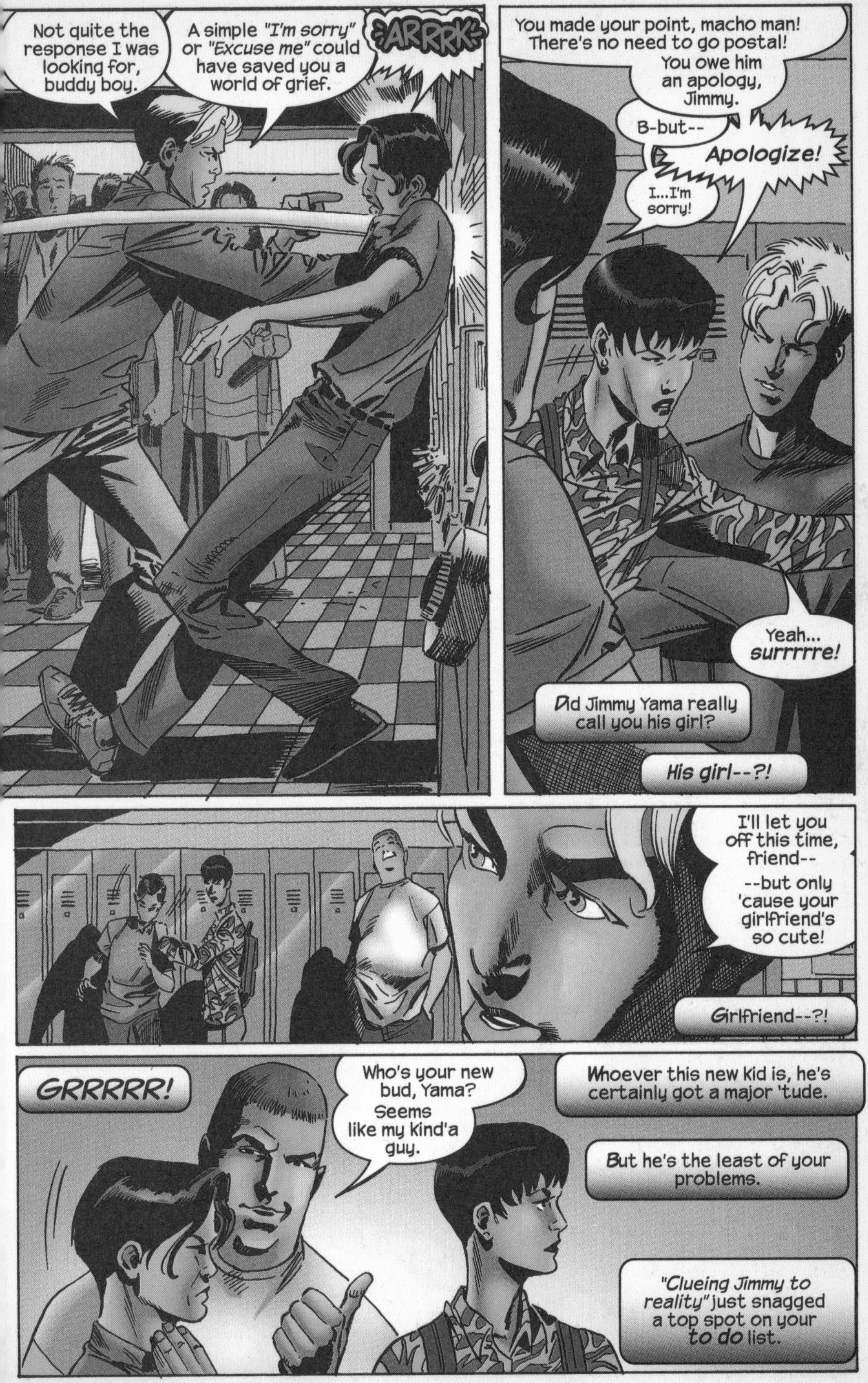
Not quite the response I was looking for, buddy boy.
A simple "I'm sorry" or "Excuse me" could have saved you a world of grief.
ARRRK
You made your point, macho man! There's no need to go postal!
You owe him an apology, Jimmy.
B-but--
Apologize!
I...I'm sorry!
Yeah... surrrrre!
Did Jimmy Yama really call you his girl?
His girl--?!
I'll let you off this time, friend--
--but only 'cause your girlfriend's so cute!
Girlfriend--?!
GRRRRR!
Who's your new bud, Yama? Seems like my kind'a guy.
Whoever this new kid is, he's certainly got a major 'tude.
But he's the least of your problems.
"Clueing Jimmy to reality" just snagged a top spot on your to do list.

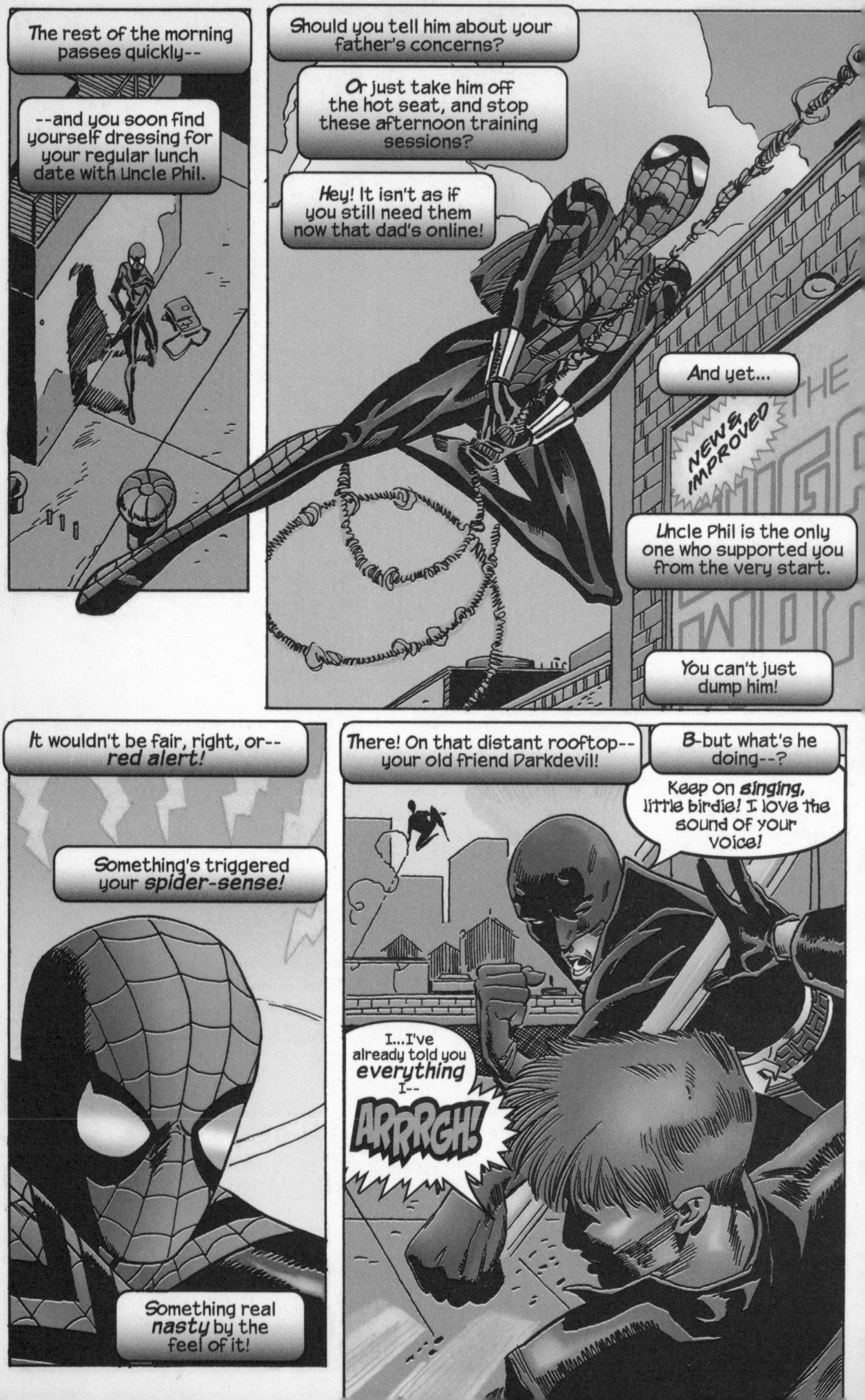

The rest of the morning passes quickly--
--and you soon find yourself dressing for your regular lunch date with Uncle Phil.
Should you tell him about your father's concerns?
Or just take him off the hot seat, and stop these afternoon training sessions?
Hey! It isn't as if you still need them now that dad's online!
And yet...
NEW & IMPROVED
Uncle Phil is the only one who supported you from the very start.
You can't just dump him!
It wouldn't be fair, right, or-- red alert!
Something's triggered your spider-sense!
Something real nasty by the feel of it!
There! On that distant rooftop-- your old friend Darkdevil!
B-but what's he doing--?
Keep on singing, little birdie! I love the sound of your voice!
I...I've already told you everything I--
ARRRGH!

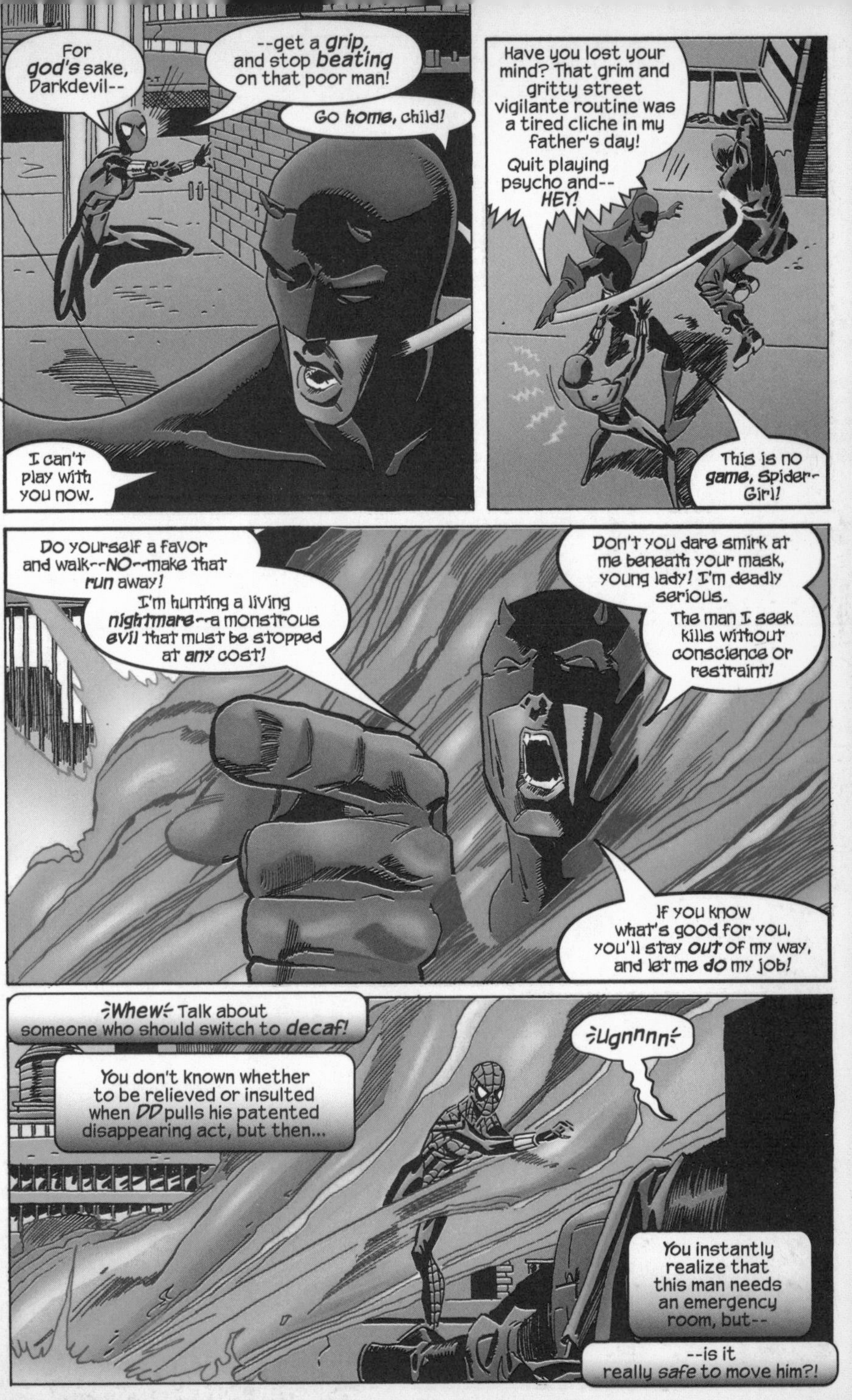

For god's sake, Darkdevil--
--get a grip, and stop beating on that poor man!
Go home, child!
I can't play with you now.
Have you lost your mind? That grim and gritty street vigilante routine was a tired cliche in my father's day!
Quit playing psycho and-- HEY!
This is no game, Spider-Girl!
Do yourself a favor and walk--NO--make that run away!
I'm hunting a living nightmare--a monstrous evil that must be stopped at any cost!
Don't you dare smirk at me beneath your mask, young lady! I'm deadly serious.
The man I seek kills without conscience or restraint!
If you know what's good for you, you'll stay out of my way, and let me do my job!
Whew Talk about someone who should switch to decaf!
Ugnnnn
You don't known whether to be relieved or insulted when DD pulls his patented disappearing act, but then...
You instantly realize that this man needs an emergency room, but--
--is it really safe to move him?!

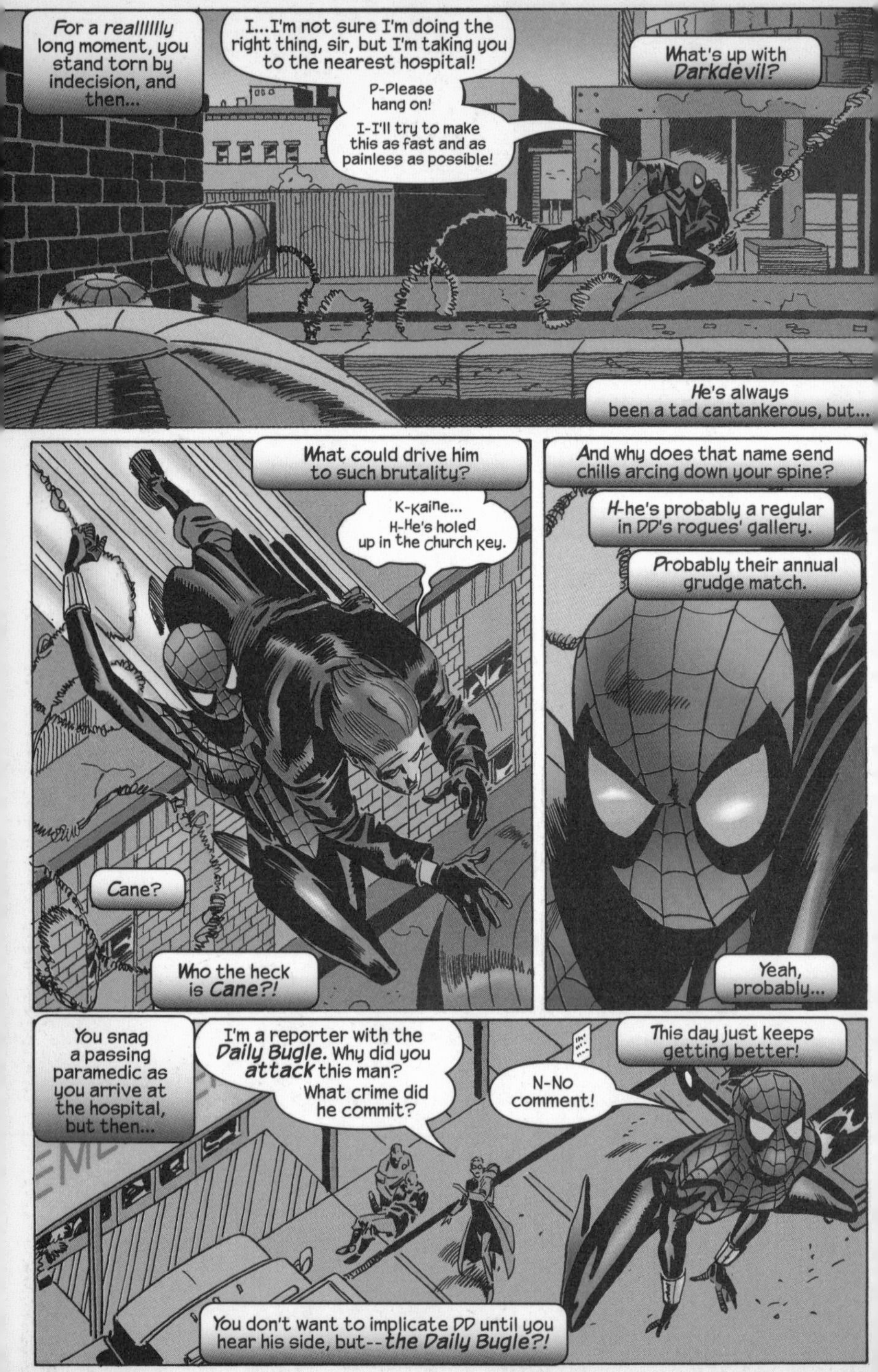

For a reallllly long moment, you stand torn by indecision, and then...
I...I'm not sure I'm doing the right thing, sir, but I'm taking you to the nearest hospital!
P-Please hang on!
I-I'll try to make this as fast and as painless as possible!
What's up with Darkdevil?
He's always been a tad cantankerous, but...
What could drive him to such brutality?
K-Kaine... H-He's holed up in the Church Key.
Cane?
Who the heck is Cane?!
And why does that name send chills arcing down your spine?
H-he's probably a regular in DD's rogues' gallery.
Probably their annual grudge match.
Yeah, probably...
You snag a passing paramedic as you arrive at the hospital, but then...
I'm a reporter with the Daily Bugle. Why did you attack this man?
What crime did he commit?
N-No comment!
This day just keeps getting better!
You don't want to implicate DD until you hear his side, but--the Daily Bugle?!

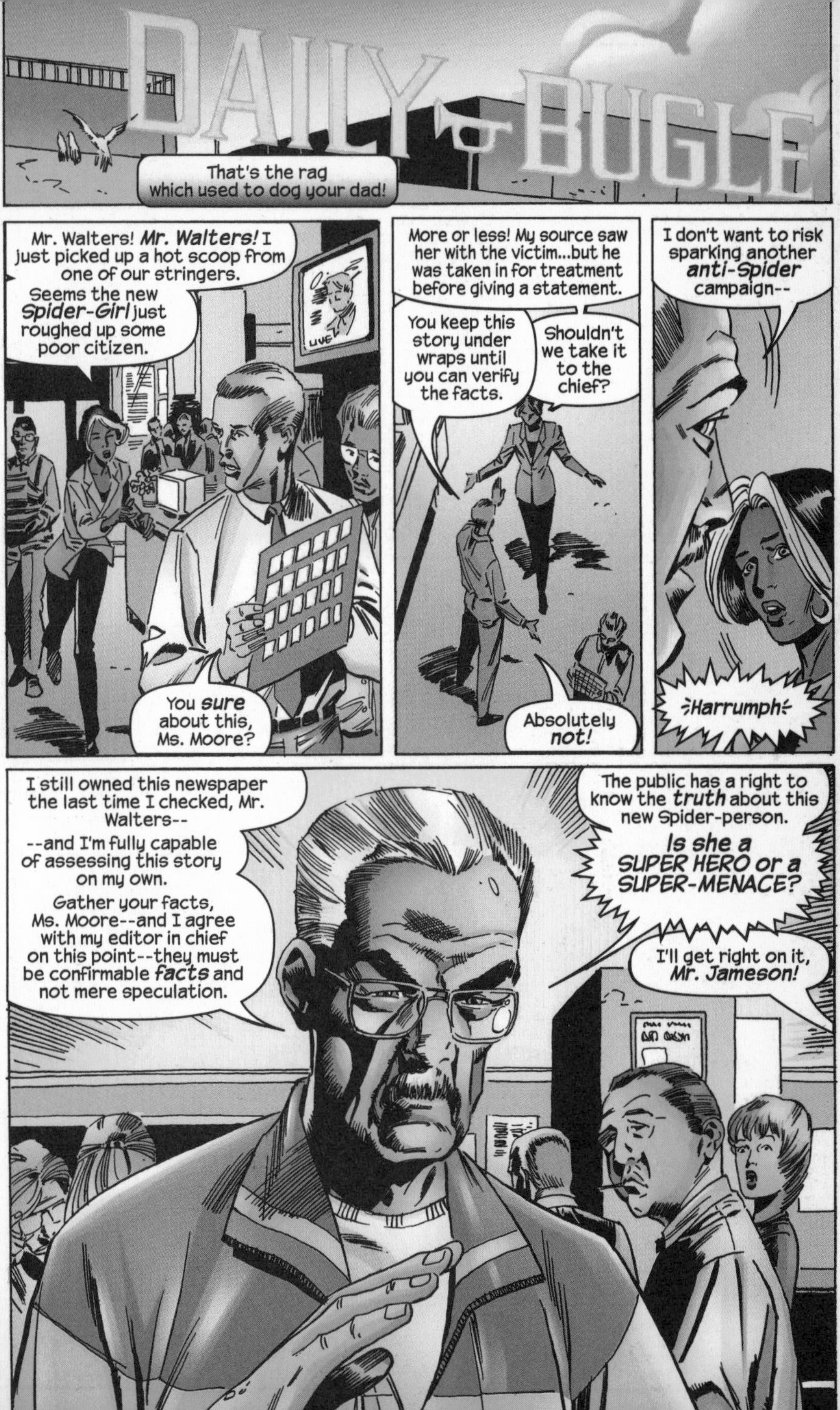

DAILY BUGLE
That's the rag which used to dog your dad!
Mr. Walters! Mr. Walters! I just picked up a hot scoop from one of our stringers.
Seems the new Spider-Girl just roughed up some poor citizen.
You sure about this, Ms. Moore?
More or less! My source saw her with the victim...but he was taken in for treatment before giving a statement.
You keep this story under wraps until you can verify the facts.
Shouldn't we take it to the chief?
Absolutely not!
I don't want to risk sparking another anti-Spider campaign--
Harrumph
I still owned this newspaper the last time I checked, Mr. Walters--
--and I'm fully capable of assessing this story on my own.
Gather your facts, Ms. Moore--and I agree with my editor in chief on this point--they must be confirmable facts and not mere speculation.
The public has a right to know the truth about this new Spider-person.
Is she a SUPER HERO or a SUPER-MENACE?
I'll get right on it, Mr. Jameson!

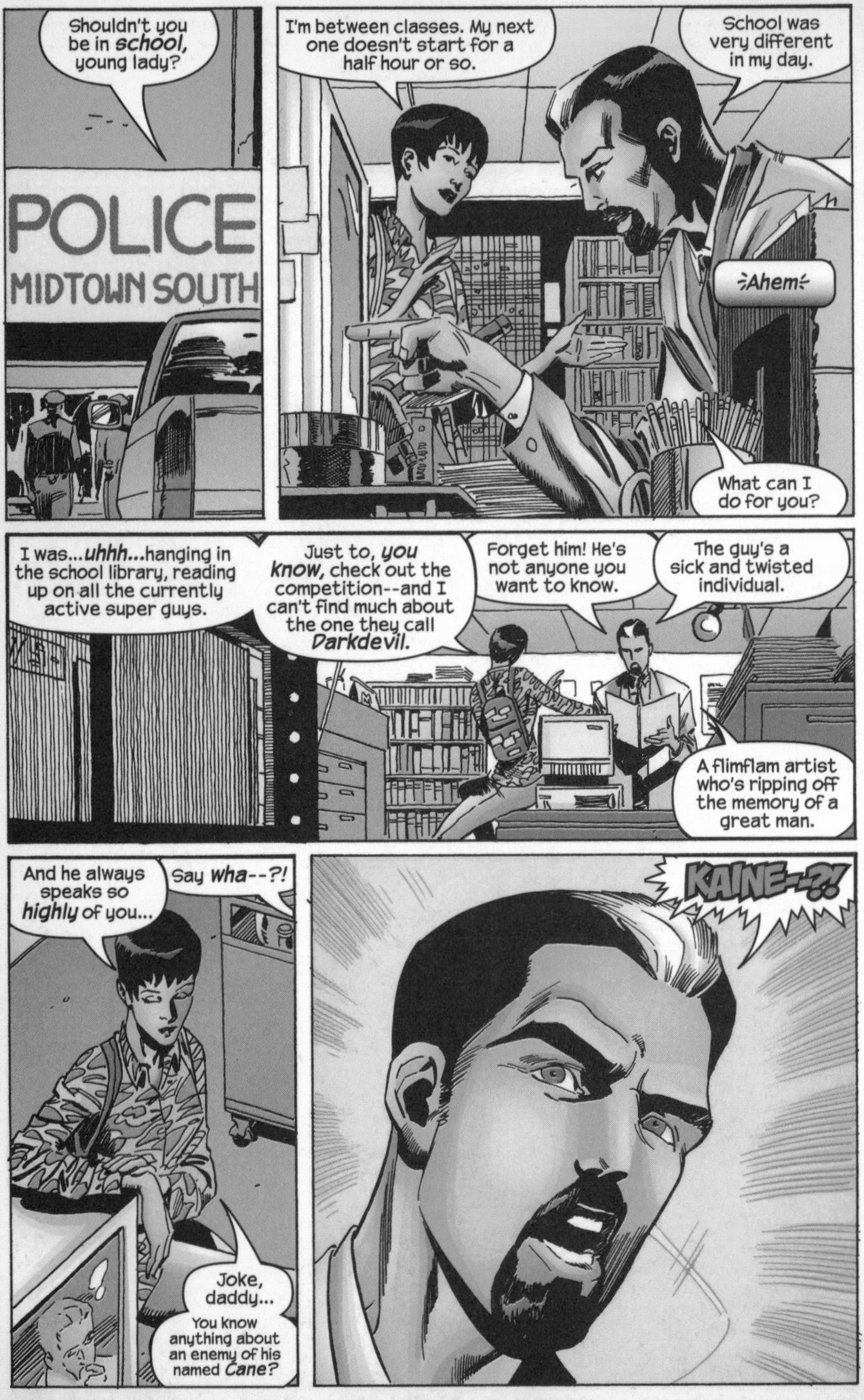
Shouldn't you be in school, young lady?
POLICE
MIDTOWN SOUTH
I'm between classes. My next one doesn't start for a half hour or so.
School was very different in my day.
Ahem
What can I do for you?
I was...uhhh...hanging in the school library, reading up on all the currently active super guys.
Just to, you know, check out the competition--and I can't find much about the one they call Darkdevil.
Forget him! He's not anyone you want to know.
The guy's a sick and twisted individual.
A flimflam artist who's ripping off the memory of a great man.
And he always speaks so highly of you...
Say wha--?!
Joke, daddy...
You know anything about an enemy of his named Cane?
KAINE--?!

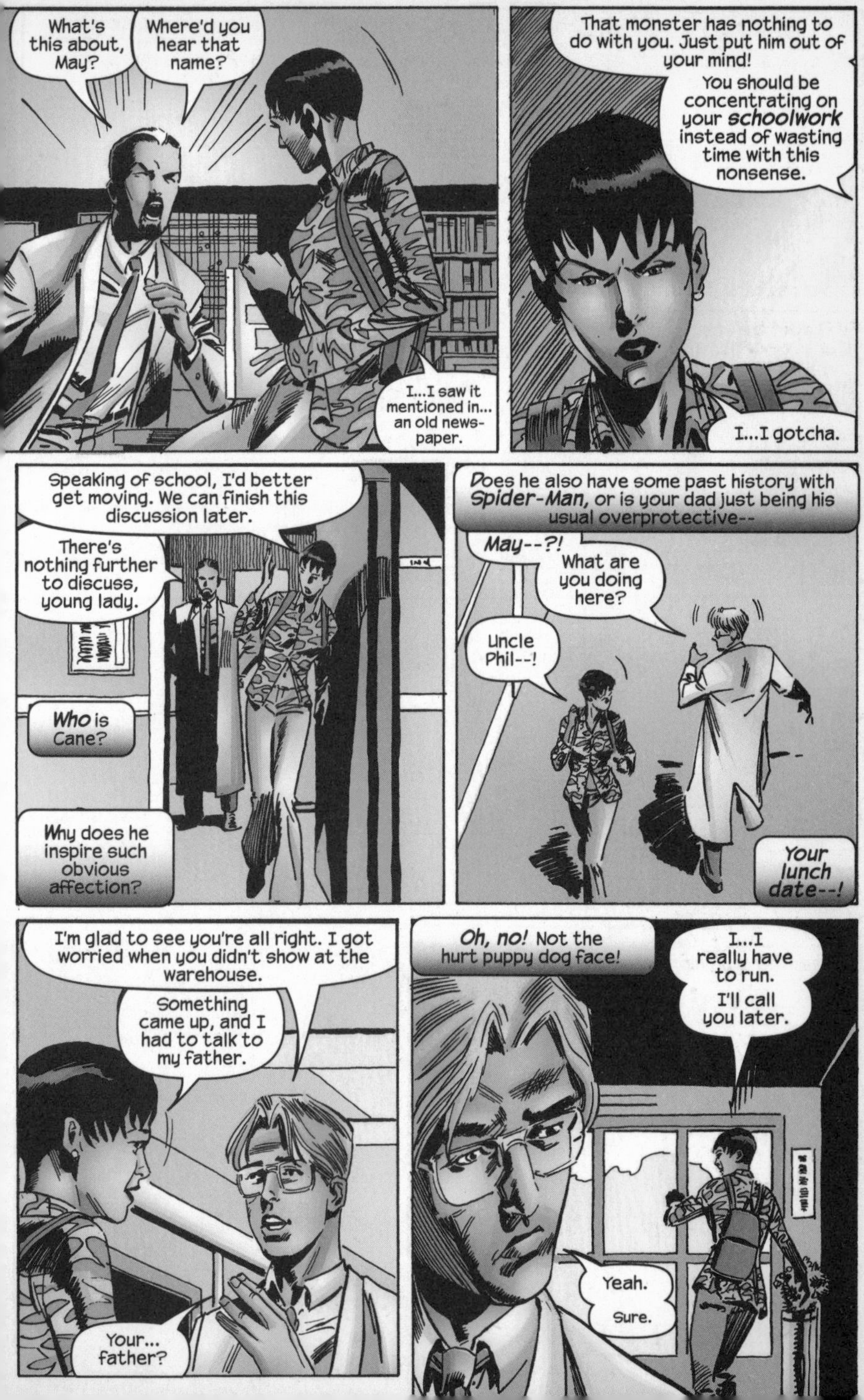
What's this about, May?
Where'd you hear that name?
I...I saw it mentioned in... an old news-paper.
That monster has nothing to do with you. Just put him out of your mind!
You should be concentrating on your *schoolwork* instead of wasting time with this nonsense.
I...I gotcha.
Speaking of school, I'd better get moving. We can finish this discussion later.
There's nothing further to discuss, young lady.
Who is Cane?
Why does he inspire such obvious affection?
Does he also have some past history with *Spider-Man,* or is your dad just being his usual overprotective--
May--?!
What are you doing here?
Uncle Phil--!
Your lunch date--!
I'm glad to see you're all right. I got worried when you didn't show at the warehouse.
Something came up, and I had to talk to my father.
Your... father?
Oh, no! Not the hurt puppy dog face!
I...I really have to run.
I'll call you later.
Yeah.
Sure.

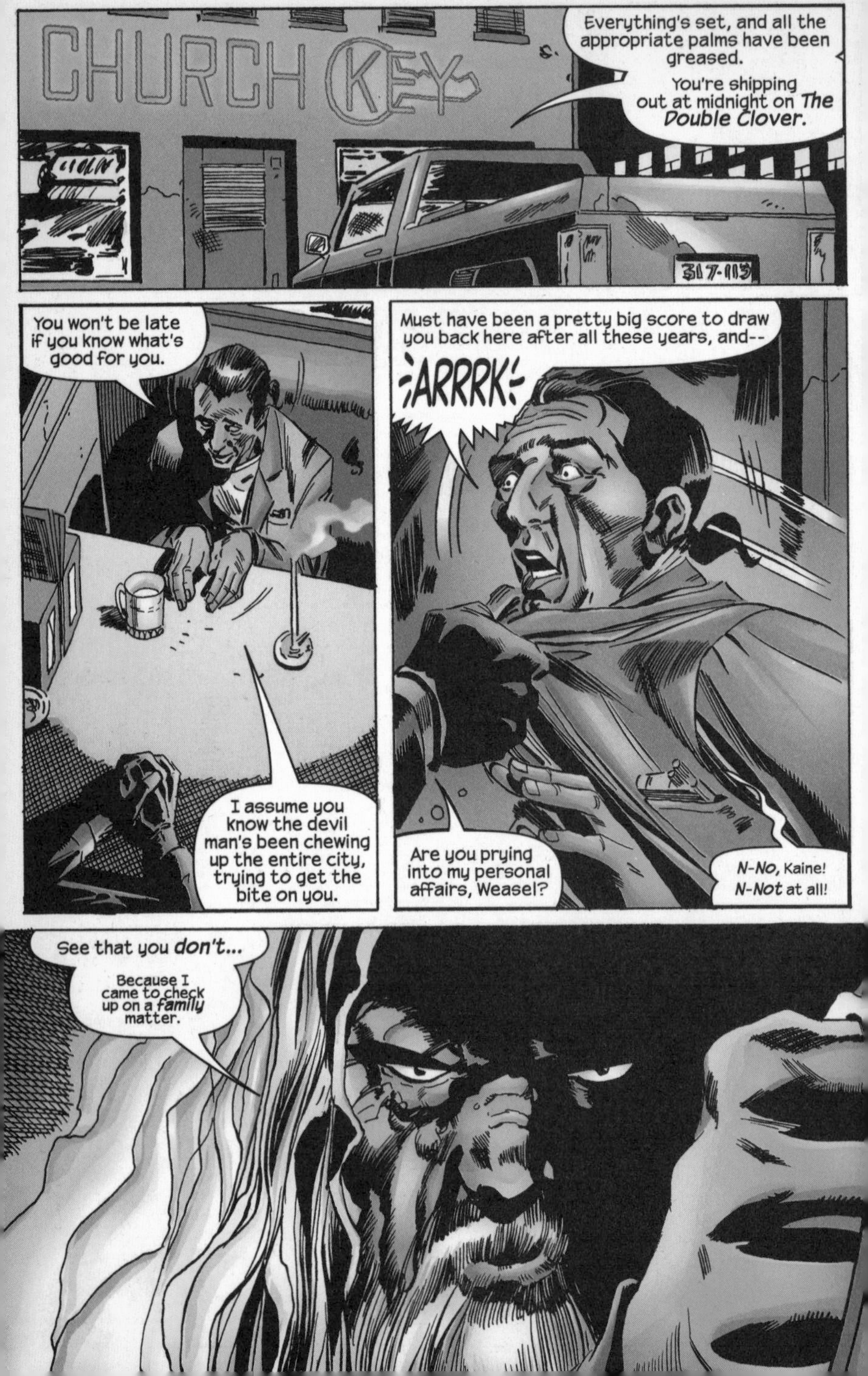
CHURCH KEY
Everything's set, and all the appropriate palms have been greased.
You're shipping out at midnight on *The Double Clover.*
317-113
You won't be late if you know what's good for you.
I assume you know the devil man's been chewing up the entire city, trying to get the bite on you.
Must have been a pretty big score to draw you back here after all these years, and--
ARRRK
Are you prying into my personal affairs, Weasel?
N-No, Kaine! *N-Not* at all!
See that you *don't...*
Because I came to check up on a *family* matter.

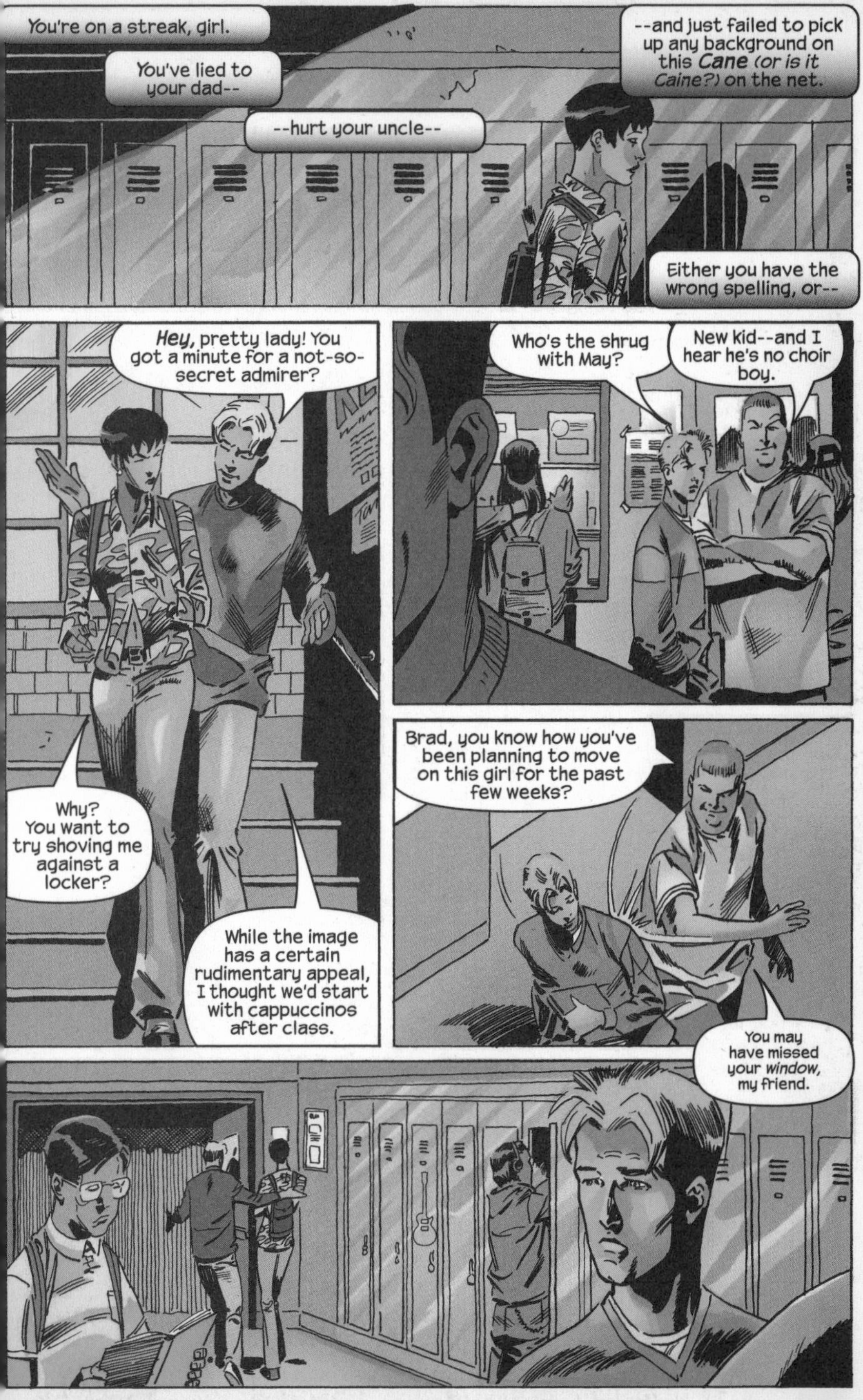

You're on a streak, girl.
You've lied to your dad--
--hurt your uncle--
--and just failed to pick up any background on this *Cane (or is it Caine?)* on the net.
Either you have the wrong spelling, or--
Hey, pretty lady! You got a minute for a not-so-secret admirer?
Why? You want to try shoving me against a locker?
While the image has a certain rudimentary appeal, I thought we'd start with cappuccinos after class.
Who's the shrug with May?
New kid--and I hear he's no choir boy.
Brad, you know how you've been planning to move on this girl for the past few weeks?
You may have missed your *window,* my friend.

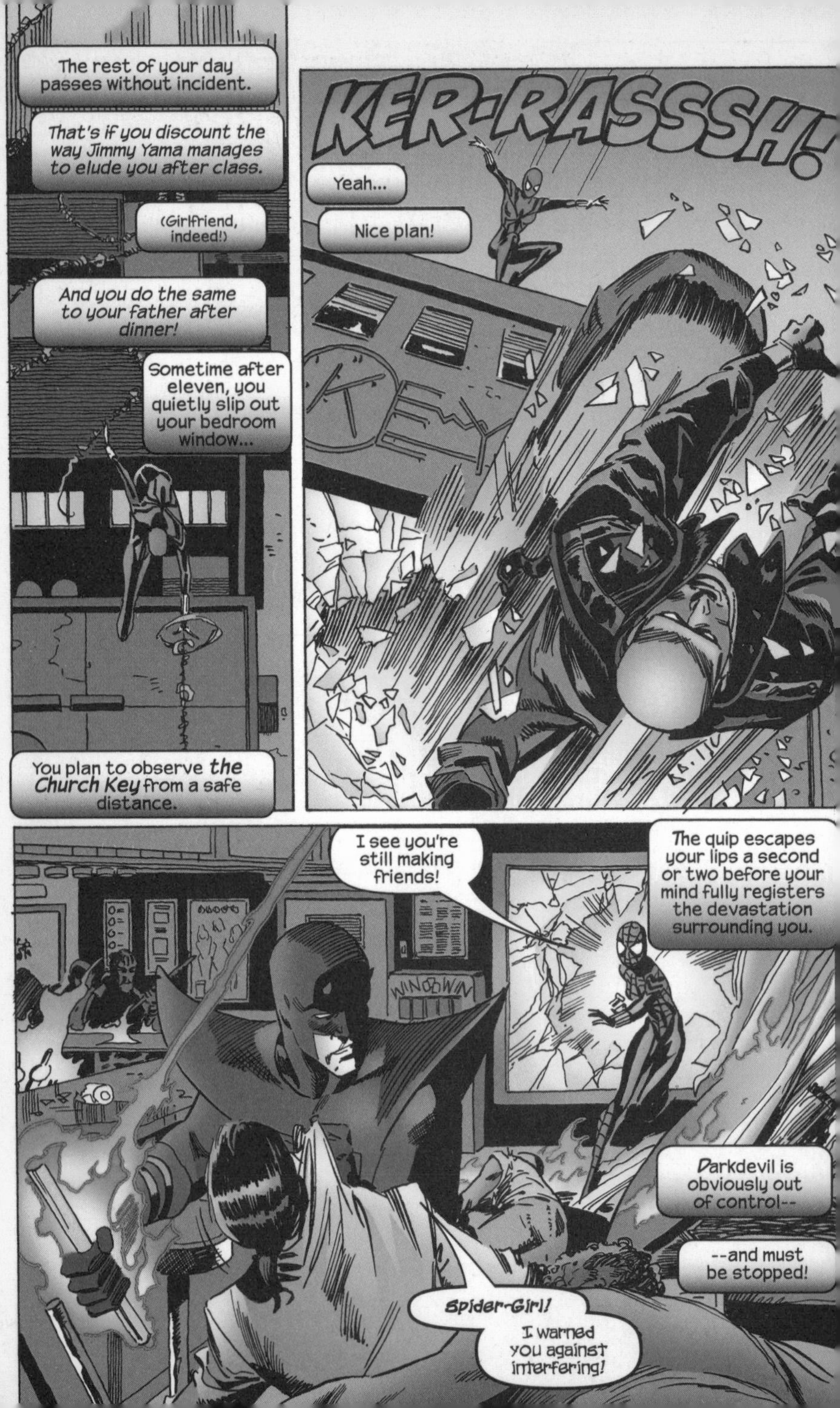

The rest of your day passes without incident.
That's if you discount the way Jimmy Yama manages to elude you after class.
(Girlfriend, indeed!)
And you do the same to your father after dinner!
Sometime after eleven, you quietly slip out your bedroom window...
You plan to observe the Church Key from a safe distance.
KER-RASSSH!
Yeah...
Nice plan!
I see you're still making friends!
The quip escapes your lips a second or two before your mind fully registers the devastation surrounding you.
Darkdevil is obviously out of control--
--and must be stopped!
Spider-Girl!
I warned you against interfering!

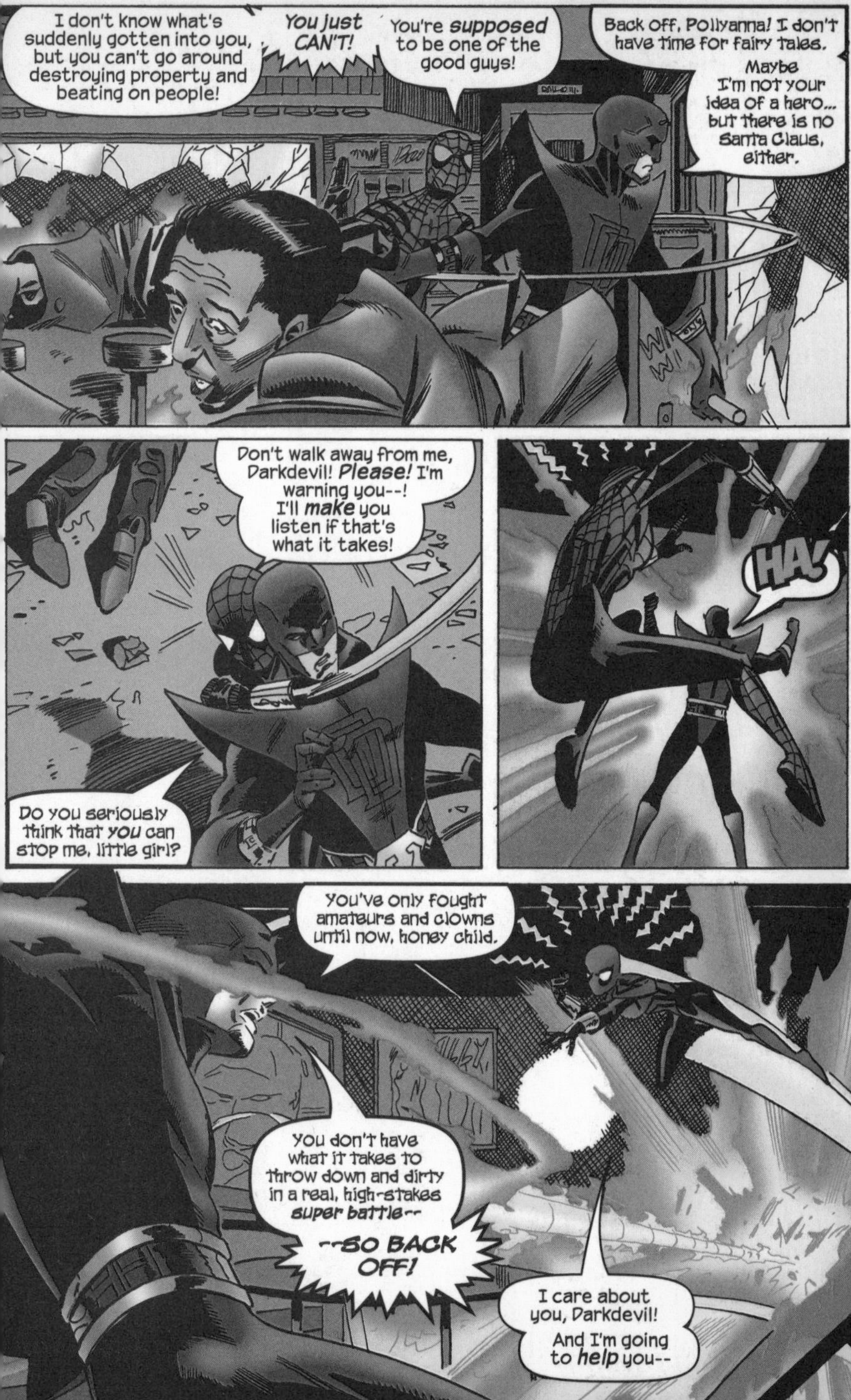

I don't know what's suddenly gotten into you, but you can't go around destroying property and beating on people!
You just CAN'T!
You're supposed to be one of the good guys!
Back off, Pollyanna! I don't have time for fairy tales.
Maybe I'm not your idea of a hero... but there is no Santa Claus, either.
Don't walk away from me, Darkdevil! Please! I'm warning you--! I'll make you listen if that's what it takes!
Do you seriously think that you can stop me, little girl?
HA!
You've only fought amateurs and clowns until now, honey child.
You don't have what it takes to throw down and dirty in a real, high-stakes super battle--
--SO BACK OFF!
I care about you, Darkdevil!
And I'm going to help you--

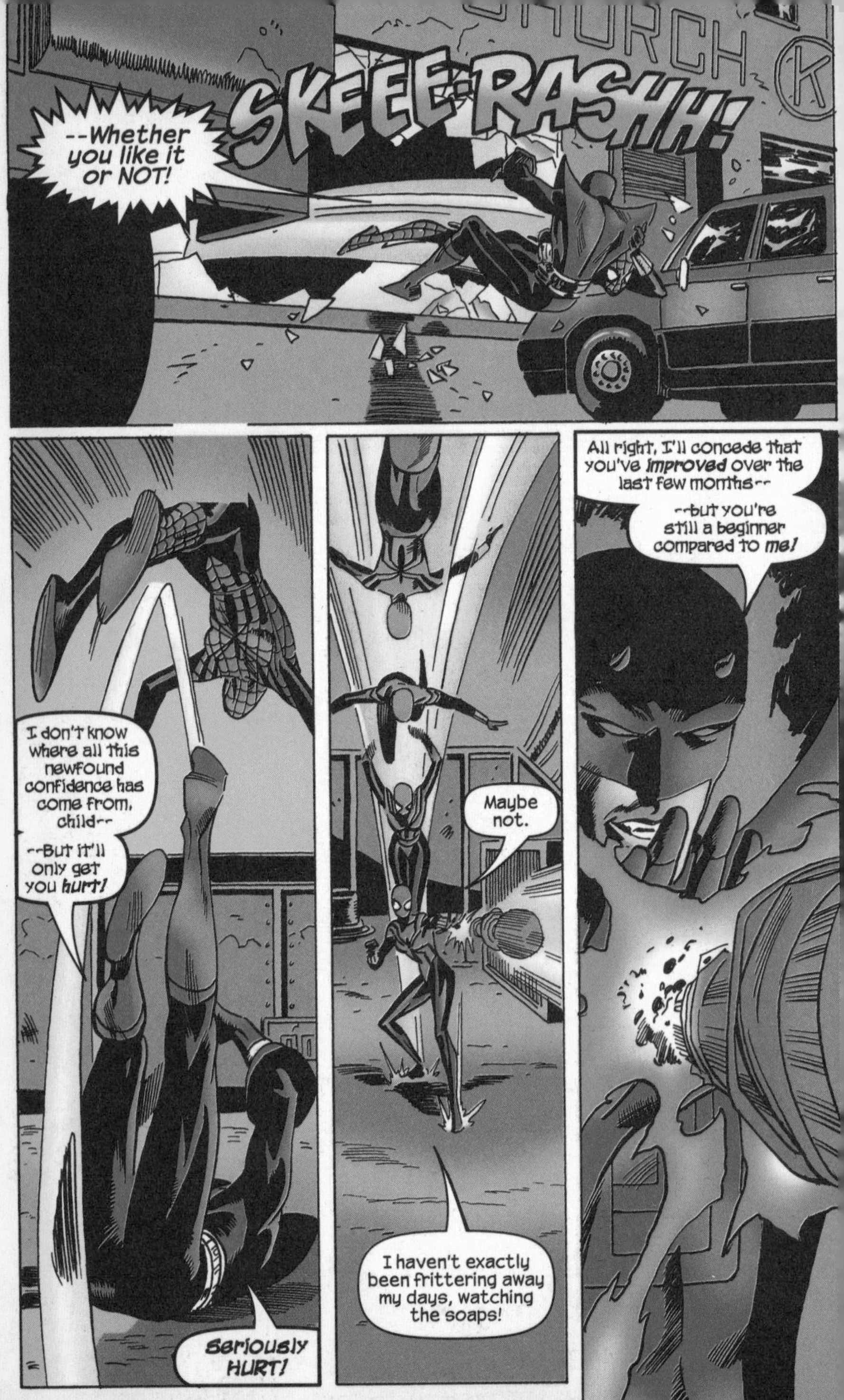
--Whether you like it or NOT!
SKEEE-RASHH!
CHURCH
I don't know where all this newfound confidence has come from, child--
--But it'll only get you hurt!
Seriously HURT!
Maybe not.
I haven't exactly been frittering away my days, watching the soaps!
All right, I'll concede that you've improved over the last few months--
--but you're still a beginner compared to me!

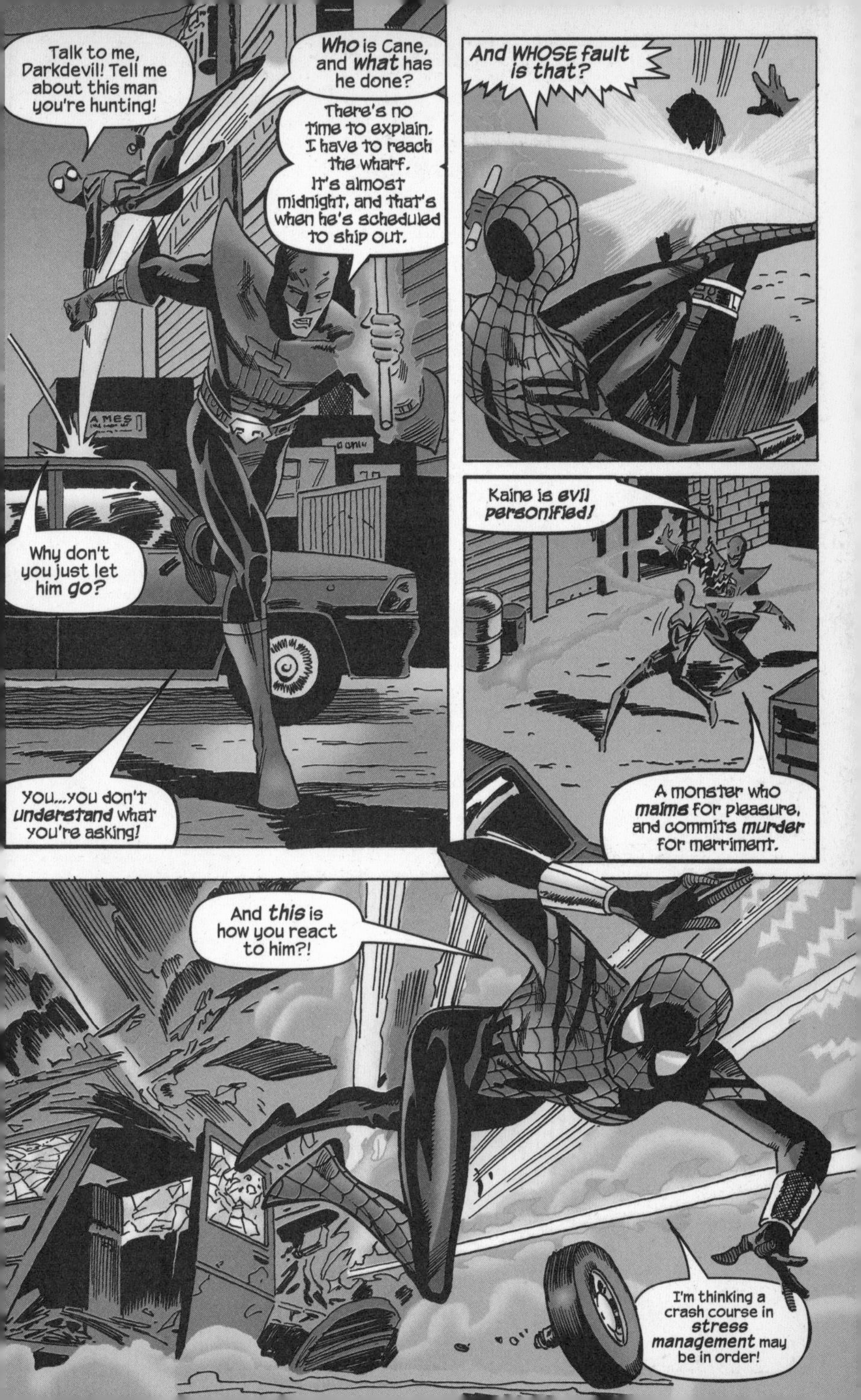
Talk to me, Darkdevil! Tell me about this man you're hunting!
Who is Cane, and what has he done?
There's no time to explain. I have to reach the wharf.
It's almost midnight, and that's when he's scheduled to ship out.
Why don't you just let him go?
You...you don't understand what you're asking!
And WHOSE fault is that?
Kaine is evil personified!
A monster who maims for pleasure, and commits murder for merriment.
And this is how you react to him?!
I'm thinking a crash course in stress management may be in order!

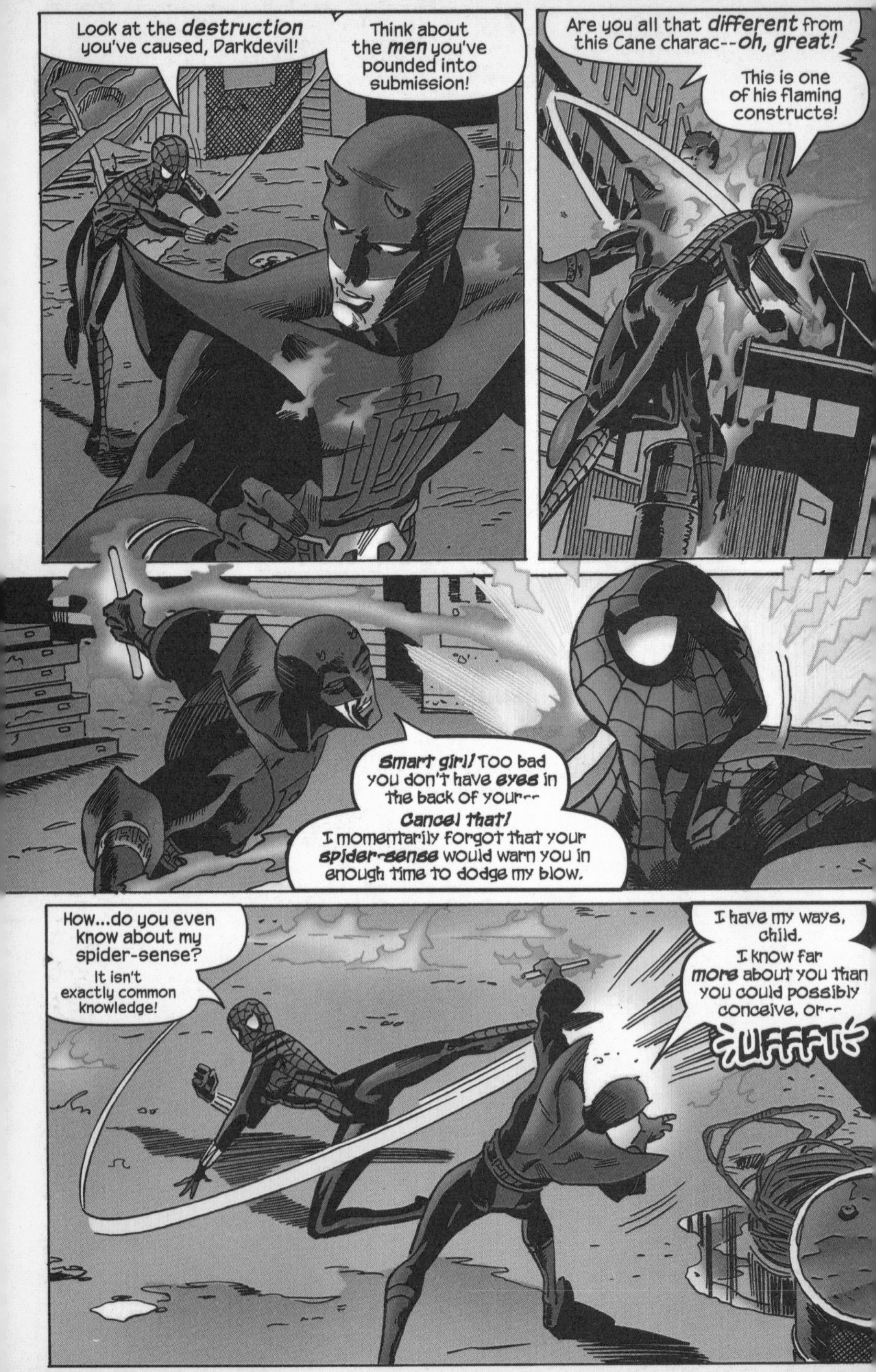

Look at the destruction you've caused, Darkdevil!
Think about the men you've pounded into submission!
Are you all that different from this Cane charac--oh, great!
This is one of his flaming constructs!
Smart girl! Too bad you don't have eyes in the back of your--
Cancel that! I momentarily forgot that your spider-sense would warn you in enough time to dodge my blow.
How...do you even know about my spider-sense?
It isn't exactly common knowledge!
I have my ways, child.
I know far more about you than you could possibly conceive, or--
UFFFT

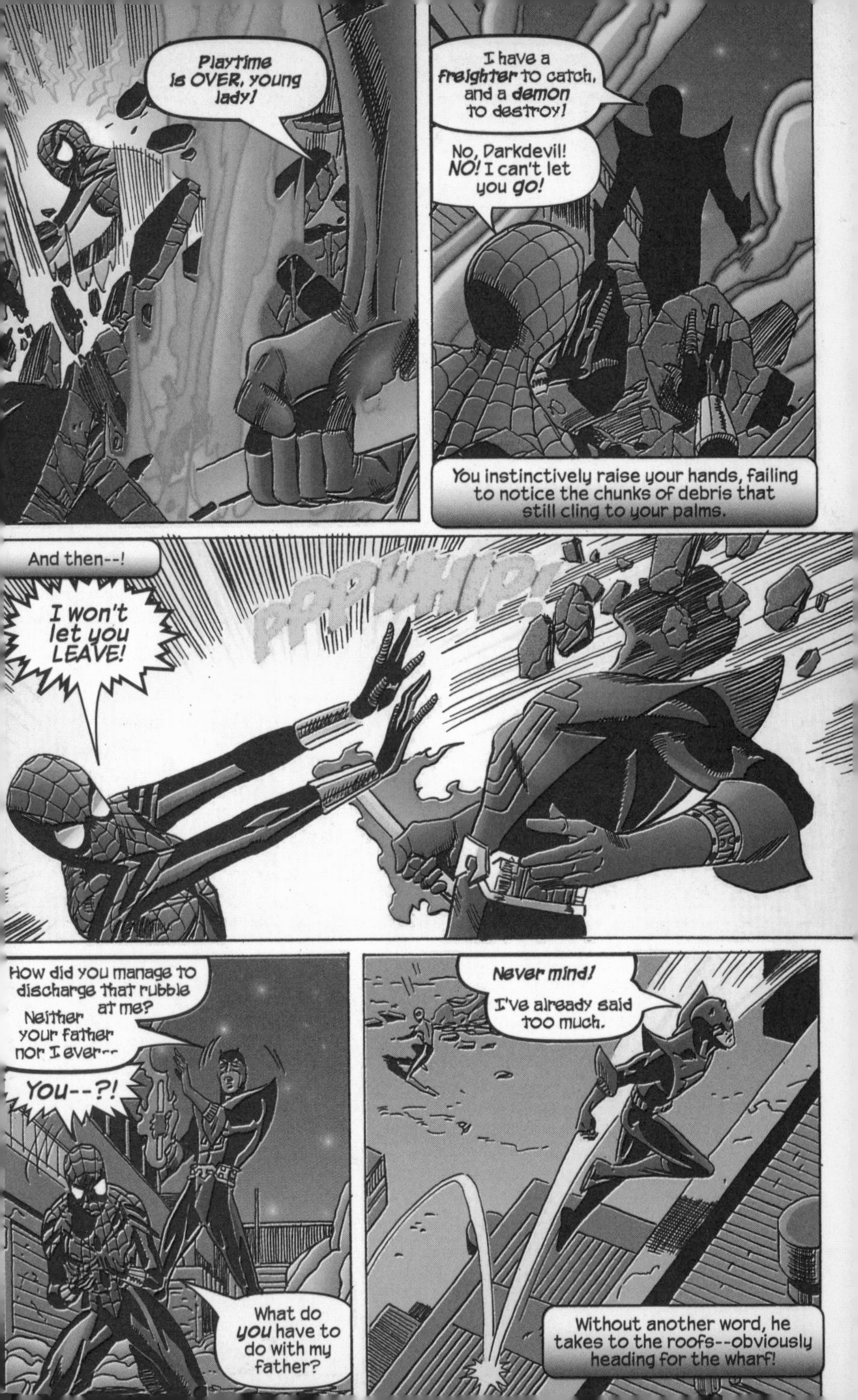
Playtime is OVER, young lady!
I have a freighter to catch, and a demon to destroy!
No, Darkdevil! NO! I can't let you go!
You instinctively raise your hands, failing to notice the chunks of debris that still cling to your palms.
And then--!
I won't let you LEAVE!
PPPWHIP!
How did you manage to discharge that rubble at me?
Neither your father nor I ever--
YOU--?!
What do you have to do with my father?
Never mind!
I've already said too much.
Without another word, he takes to the roofs--obviously heading for the wharf!

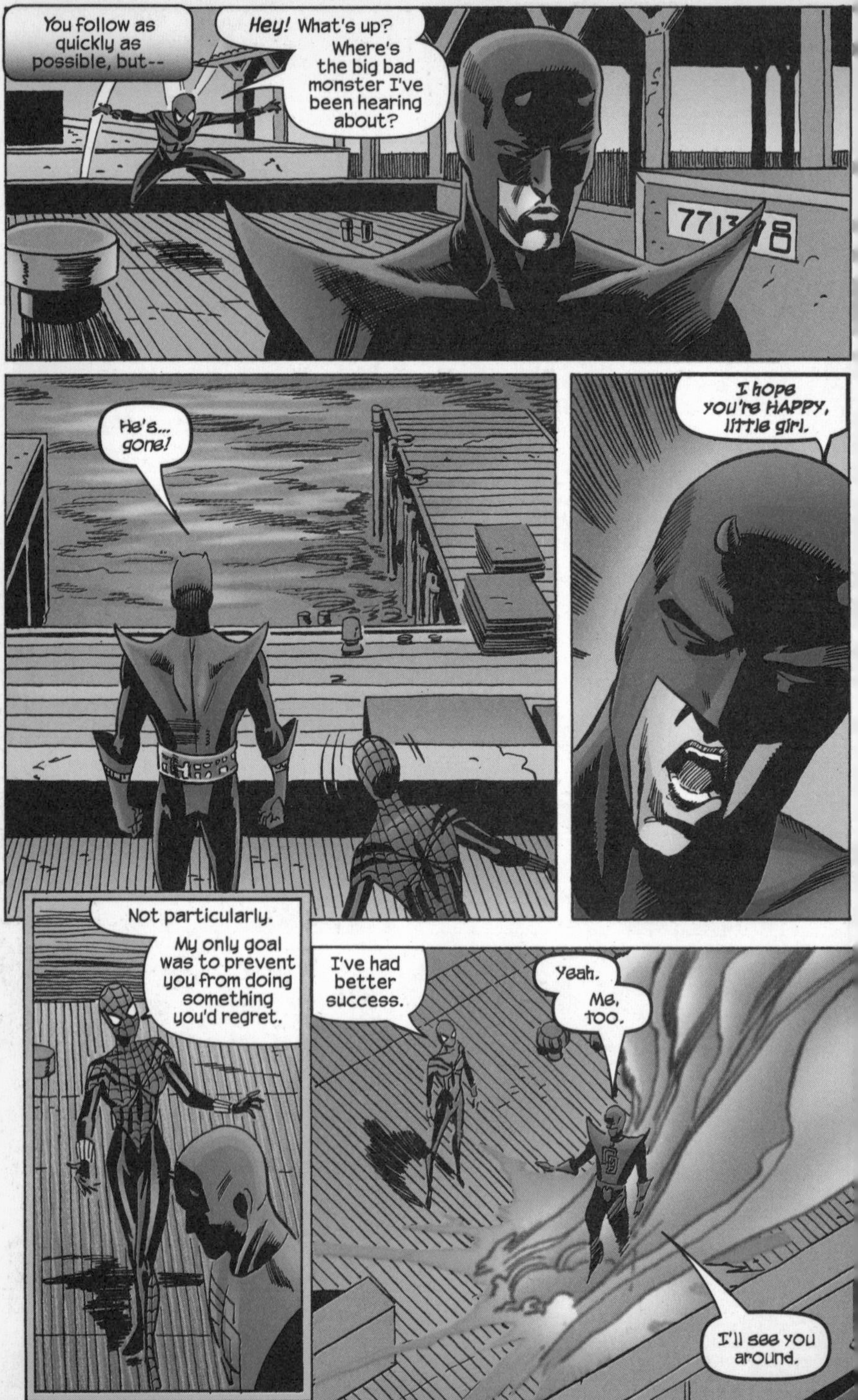
You follow as quickly as possible, but--
Hey! What's up? Where's the big bad monster I've been hearing about?
7713?8
He's... gone!
I hope you're HAPPY, little girl.
Not particularly.
My only goal was to prevent you from doing something you'd regret.
I've had better success.
Yeah.
Me, too.
I'll see you around.

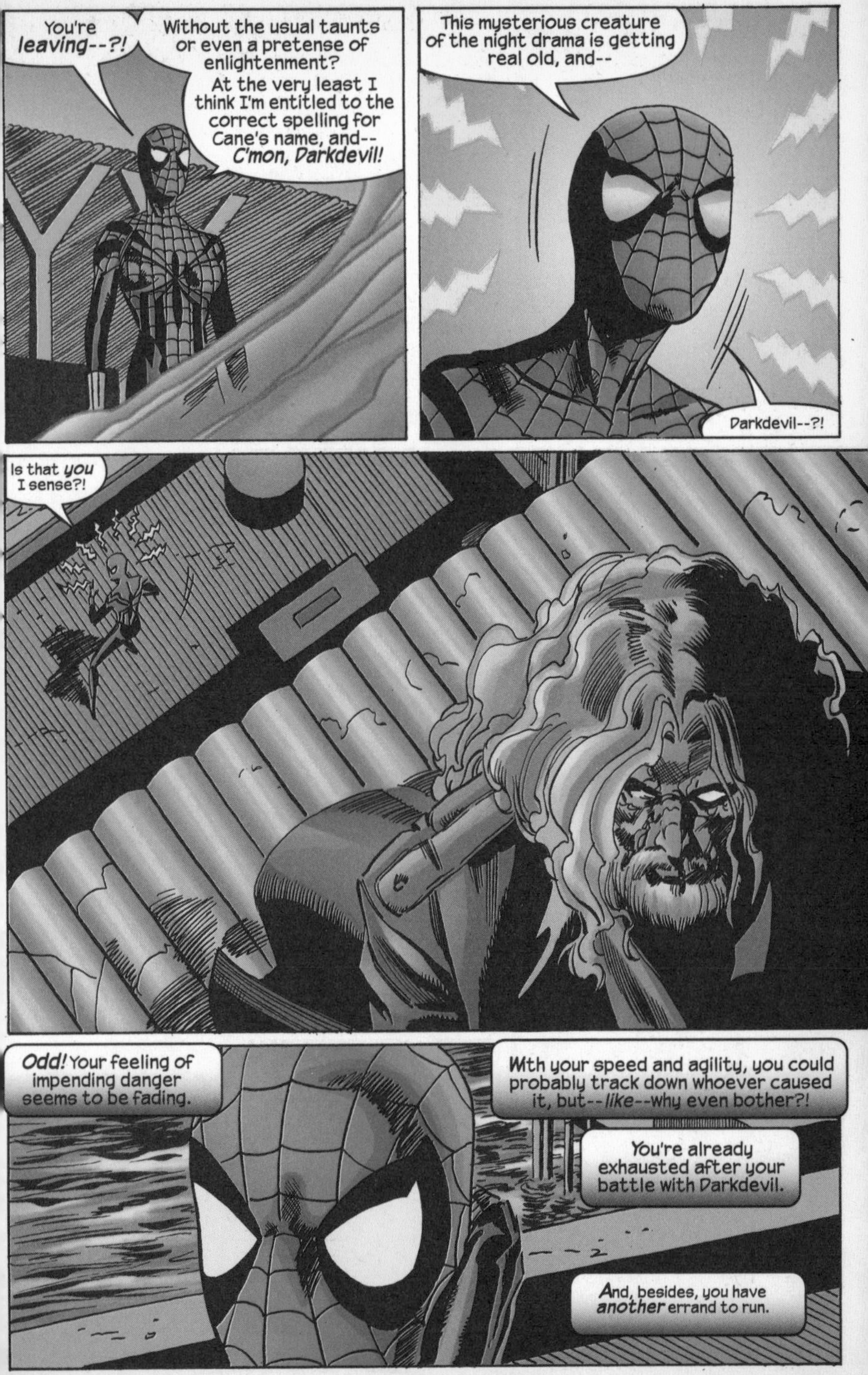
You're leaving--?!
Without the usual taunts or even a pretense of enlightenment?
At the very least I think I'm entitled to the correct spelling for Cane's name, and-- C'mon, Darkdevil!
This mysterious creature of the night drama is getting real old, and--
Darkdevil--?!
Is that you I sense?!
Odd! Your feeling of impending danger seems to be fading.
With your speed and agility, you could probably track down whoever caused it, but--like--why even bother?!
You're already exhausted after your battle with Darkdevil.
And, besides, you have another errand to run.

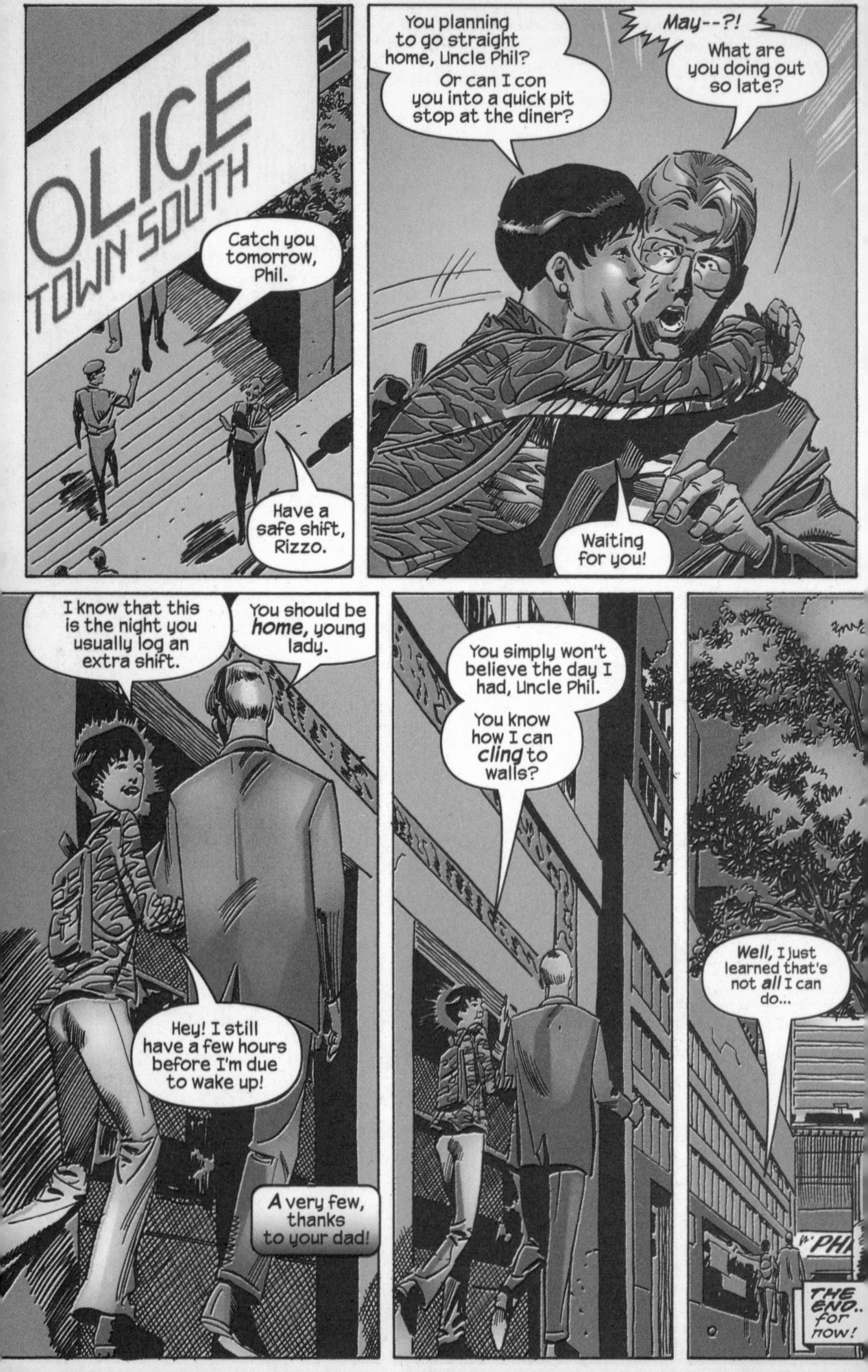

OLICE
TOWN SOUTH
Catch you tomorrow, Phil.
Have a safe shift, Rizzo.
You planning to go straight home, Uncle Phil?
Or can I con you into a quick pit stop at the diner?
May--?!
What are you doing out so late?
Waiting for you!
I know that this is the night you usually log an extra shift.
You should be *home*, young lady.
Hey! I still have a few hours before I'm due to wake up!
A very few, thanks to your dad!
You simply won't believe the day I had, Uncle Phil.
You know how I can *cling* to walls?
Well, I just learned that's not *all* I can do...
THE END... for now!

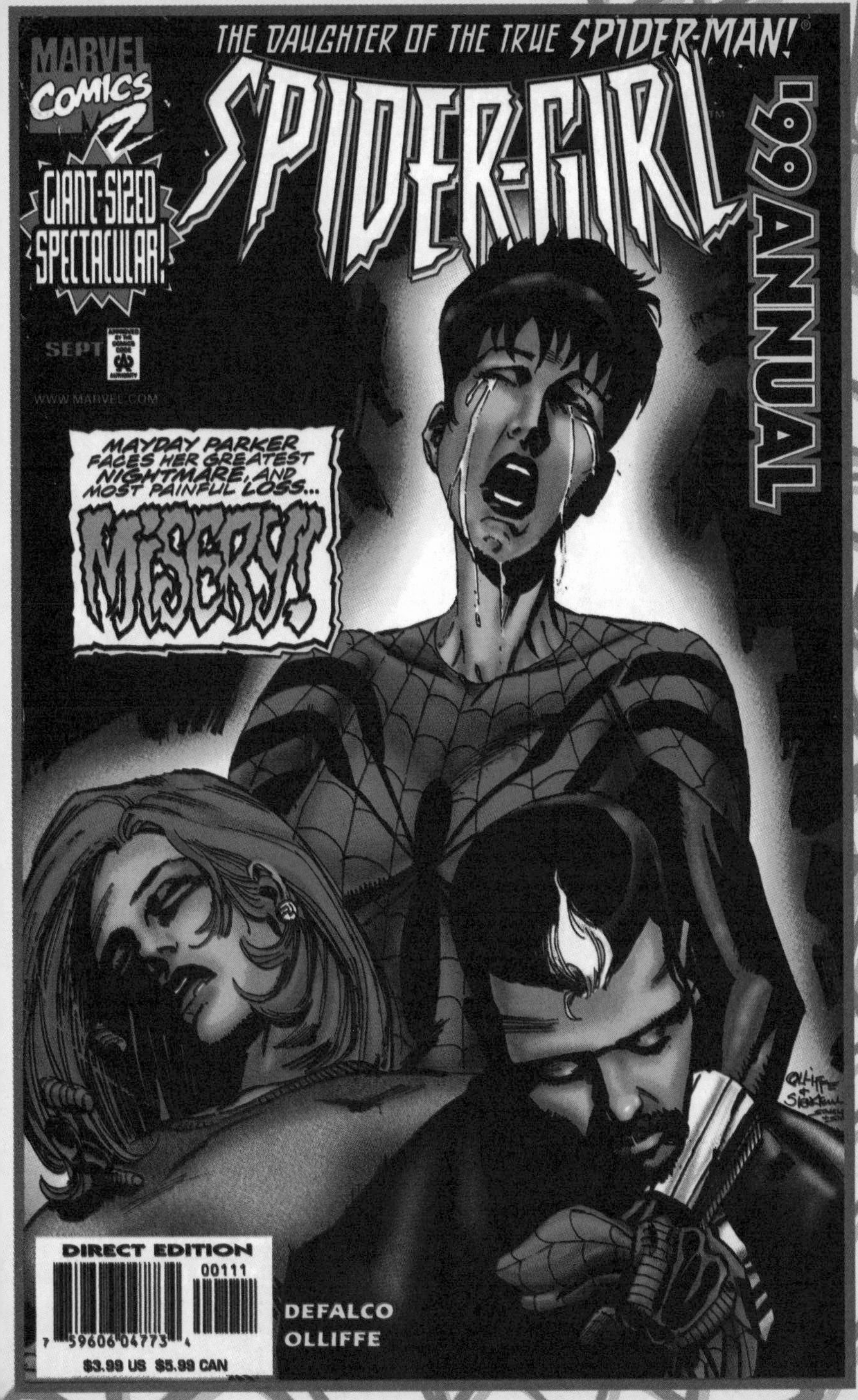

MARVEL COMICS
THE DAUGHTER OF THE TRUE SPIDER-MAN!
SPIDER-GIRL
'99 ANNUAL
GIANT-SIZED SPECTACULAR!
SEPT
WWW.MARVEL.COM
MAYDAY PARKER FACES HER GREATEST NIGHTMARE, AND MOST PAINFUL LOSS...
MISERY!
DIRECT EDITION
00111
7 59606 04773 4
$3.99 US $5.99 CAN
DEFALCO
OLLIFFE

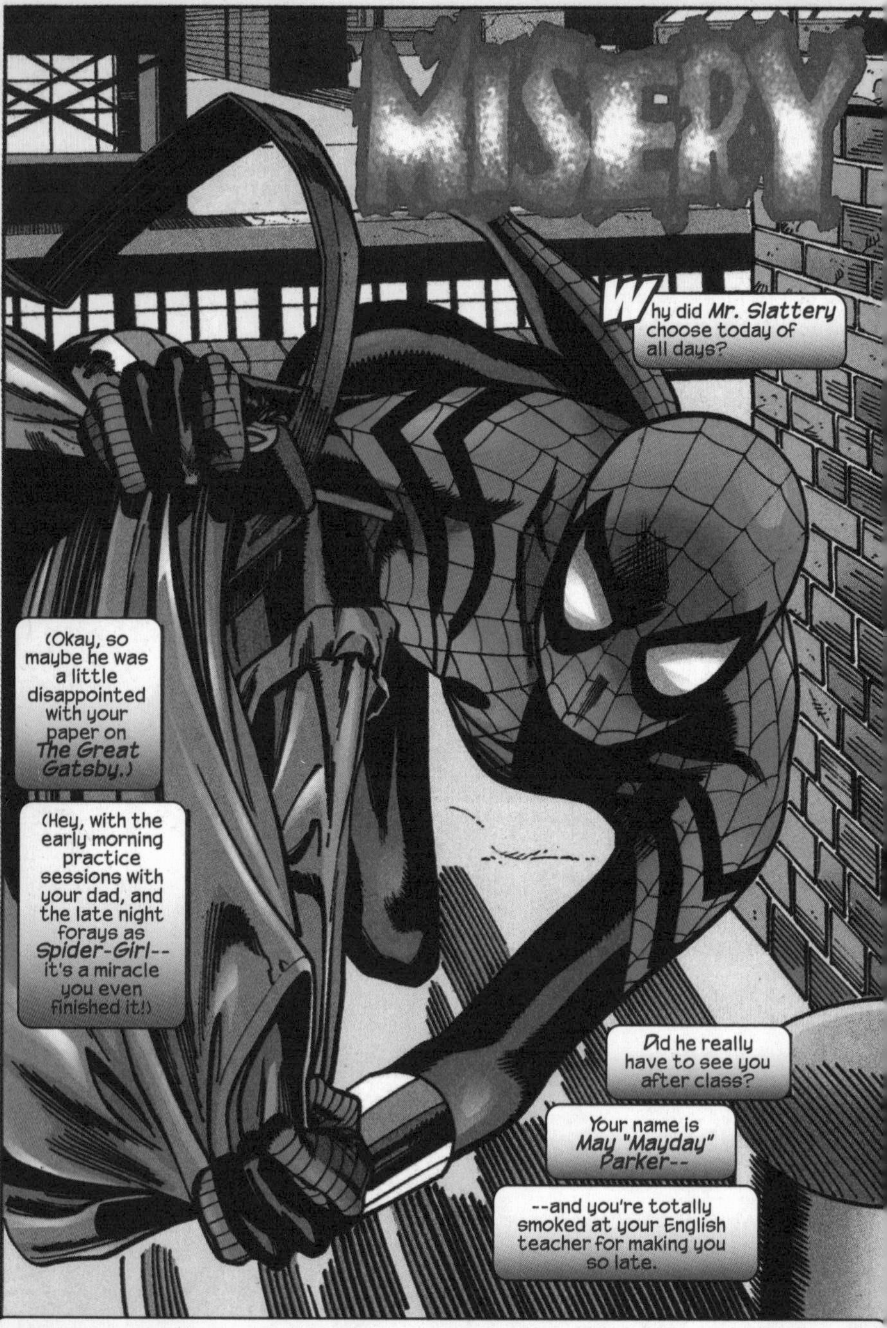
MISERY
Why did Mr. Slattery choose today of all days?
(Okay, so maybe he was a little disappointed with your paper on The Great Gatsby.)
(Hey, with the early morning practice sessions with your dad, and the late night forays as Spider-Girl-- it's a miracle you even finished it!)
Did he really have to see you after class?
Your name is May "Mayday" Parker--
--and you're totally smoked at your English teacher for making you so late.

Ron Frenz story idea | Tom DeFalco writer | Pat Olliffe pencil breakdowns | Sal Buscema finished art | Dave Sharpe letters | Christie Scheele colors

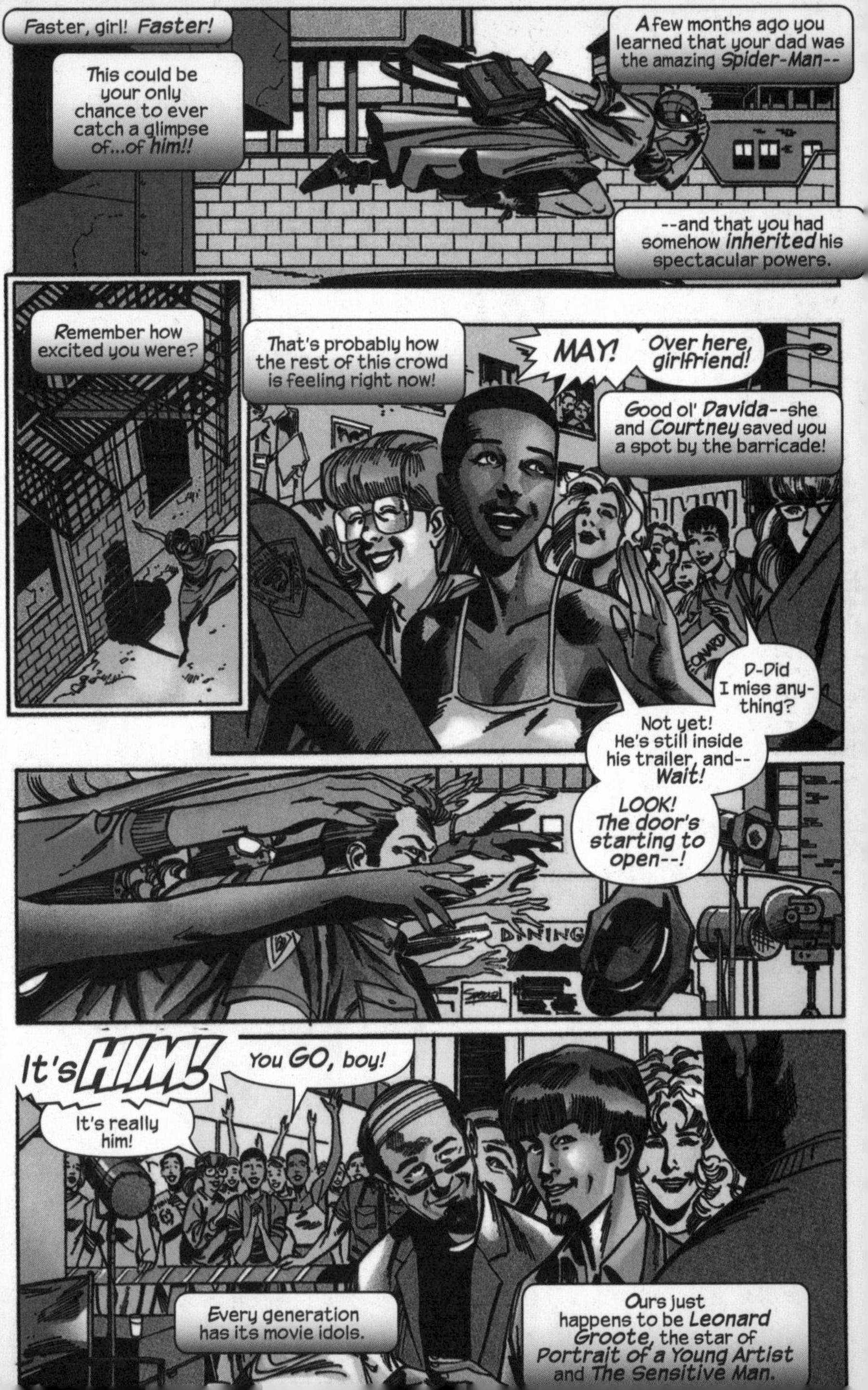
Faster, girl! Faster!
This could be your only chance to ever catch a glimpse of...of him!!
A few months ago you learned that your dad was the amazing Spider-Man--
--and that you had somehow inherited his spectacular powers.
Remember how excited you were?
That's probably how the rest of this crowd is feeling right now!
MAY!
Over here, girlfriend!
Good ol' Davida--she and Courtney saved you a spot by the barricade!
D-Did I miss any-thing?
Not yet! He's still inside his trailer, and-- Wait!
LOOK! The door's starting to open--!
It's HIM!
You GO, boy!
It's really him!
Every generation has its movie idols.
Ours just happens to be Leonard Groote, the star of Portrait of a Young Artist and The Sensitive Man.

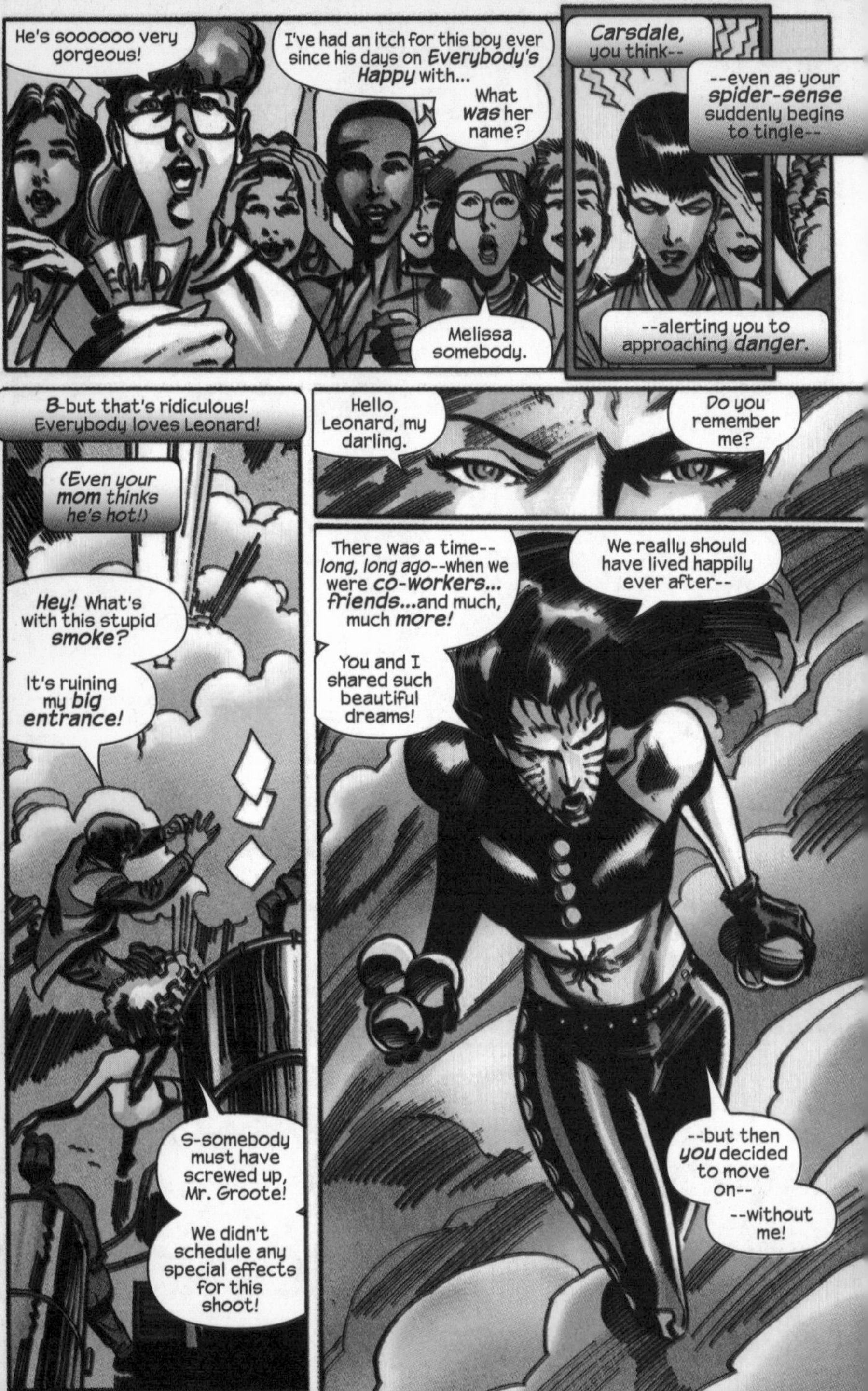
He's soooooo very gorgeous!
I've had an itch for this boy ever since his days on Everybody's Happy with...
What was her name?
Melissa somebody.
Carsdale, you think--
--even as your spider-sense suddenly begins to tingle--
--alerting you to approaching danger.
B-but that's ridiculous! Everybody loves Leonard!
(Even your mom thinks he's hot!)
Hey! What's with this stupid smoke?
It's ruining my big entrance!
S-somebody must have screwed up, Mr. Groote!
We didn't schedule any special effects for this shoot!
Hello, Leonard, my darling.
Do you remember me?
There was a time--long, long ago--when we were co-workers... friends...and much, much more!
You and I shared such beautiful dreams!
We really should have lived happily ever after--
--but then you decided to move on--
--without me!

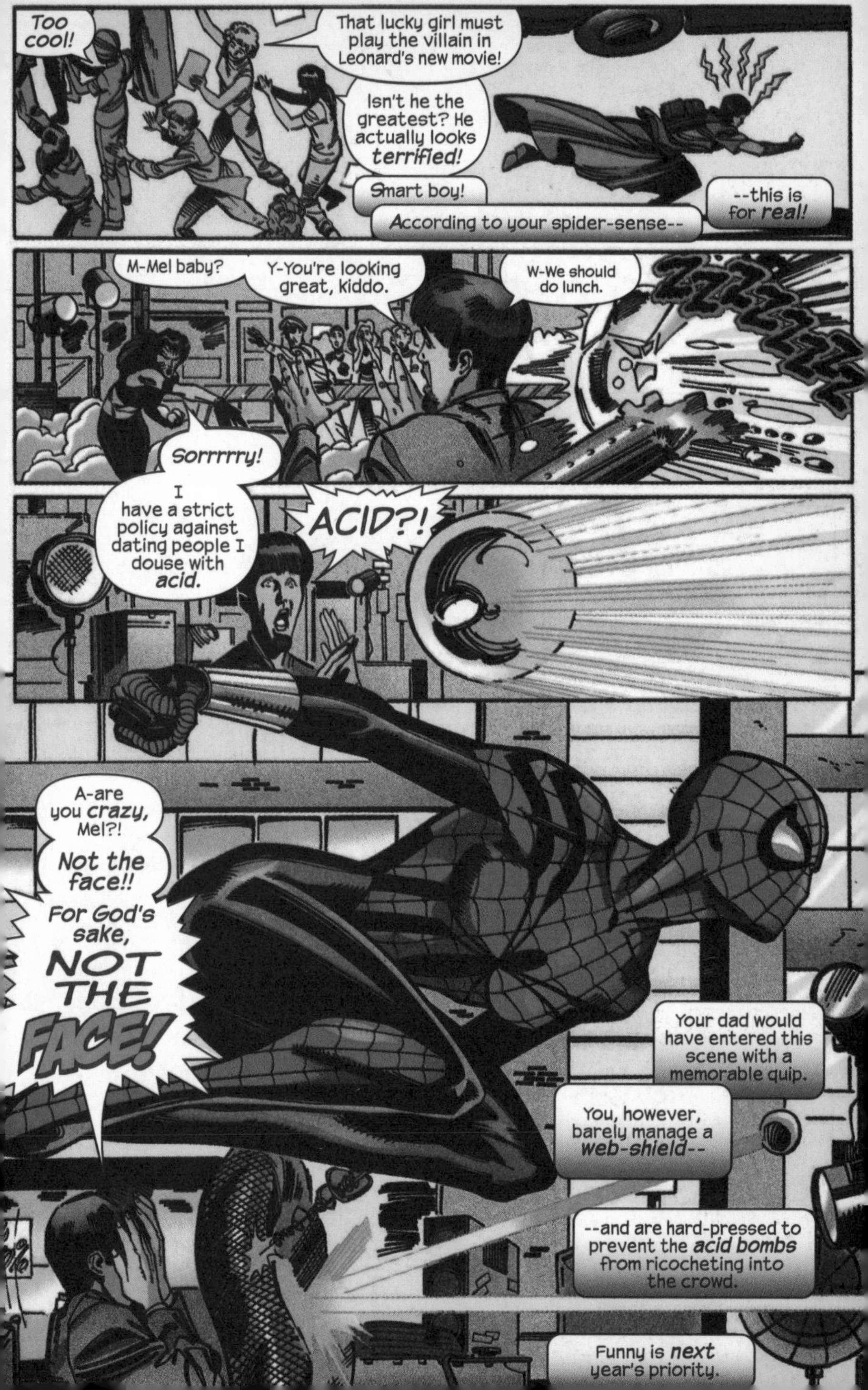
Too cool!
That lucky girl must play the villain in Leonard's new movie!
Isn't he the greatest? He actually looks terrified!
Smart boy!
According to your spider-sense--
--this is for real!
M-Mel baby?
Y-You're looking great, kiddo.
W-We should do lunch.
Sorrrrry!
I have a strict policy against dating people I douse with acid.
ACID?!
A-are you crazy, Mel?!
Not the face!!
For God's sake, NOT THE FACE!
Your dad would have entered this scene with a memorable quip.
You, however, barely manage a web-shield--
--and are hard-pressed to prevent the acid bombs from ricocheting into the crowd.
Funny is next year's priority.

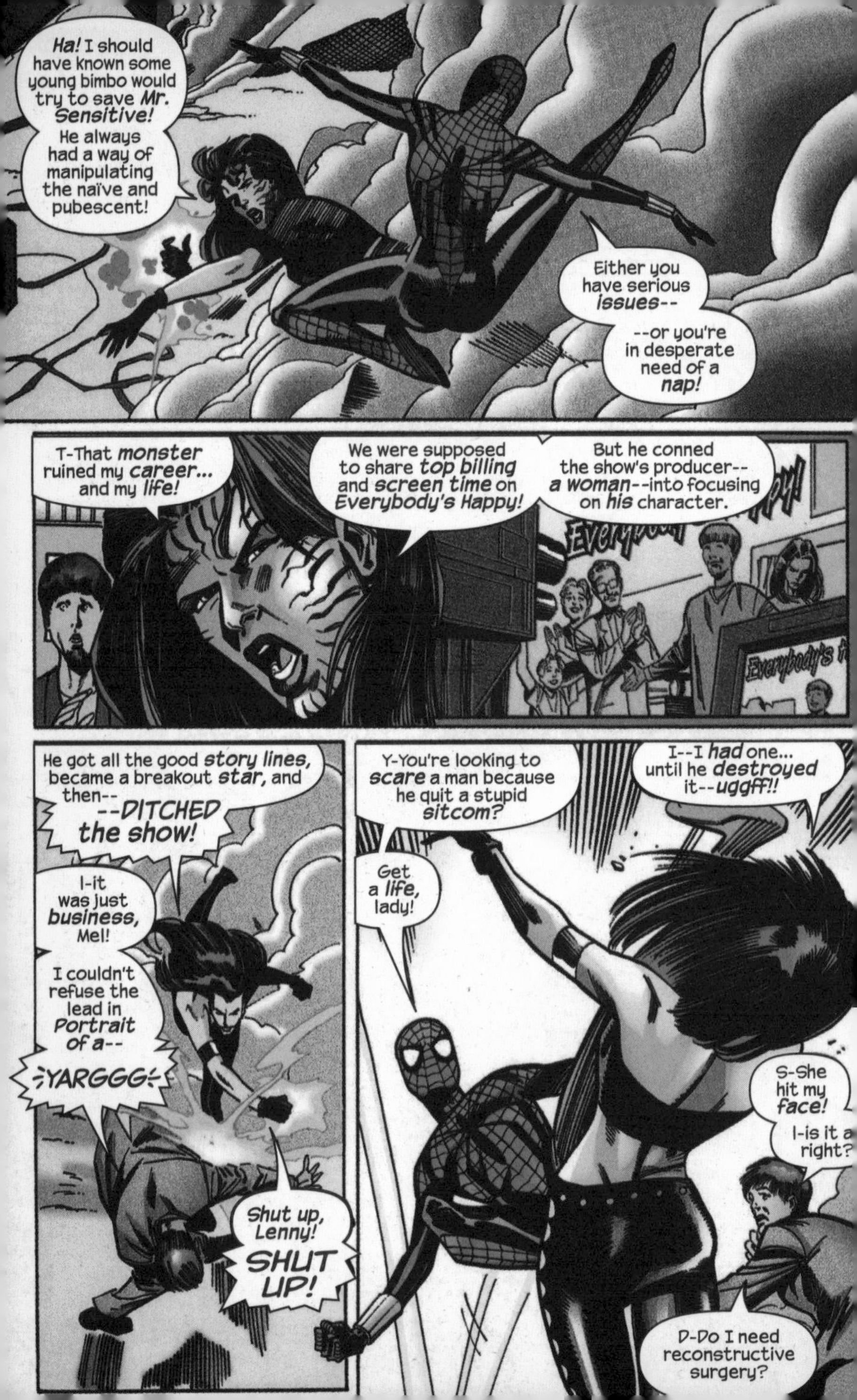
Ha! I should have known some young bimbo would try to save Mr. Sensitive!
He always had a way of manipulating the naïve and pubescent!
Either you have serious issues--
--or you're in desperate need of a nap!
T-That monster ruined my career... and my life!
We were supposed to share top billing and screen time on Everybody's Happy!
But he conned the show's producer-- a woman--into focusing on his character.
He got all the good story lines, became a breakout star, and then--
--DITCHED the show!
I-it was just business, Mel!
I couldn't refuse the lead in Portrait of a--
YARGGG
Shut up, Lenny!
SHUT UP!
Y-You're looking to scare a man because he quit a stupid sitcom?
Get a life, lady!
I--I had one... until he destroyed it--uggff!!
S-She hit my face!
D-Do I need reconstructive surgery?

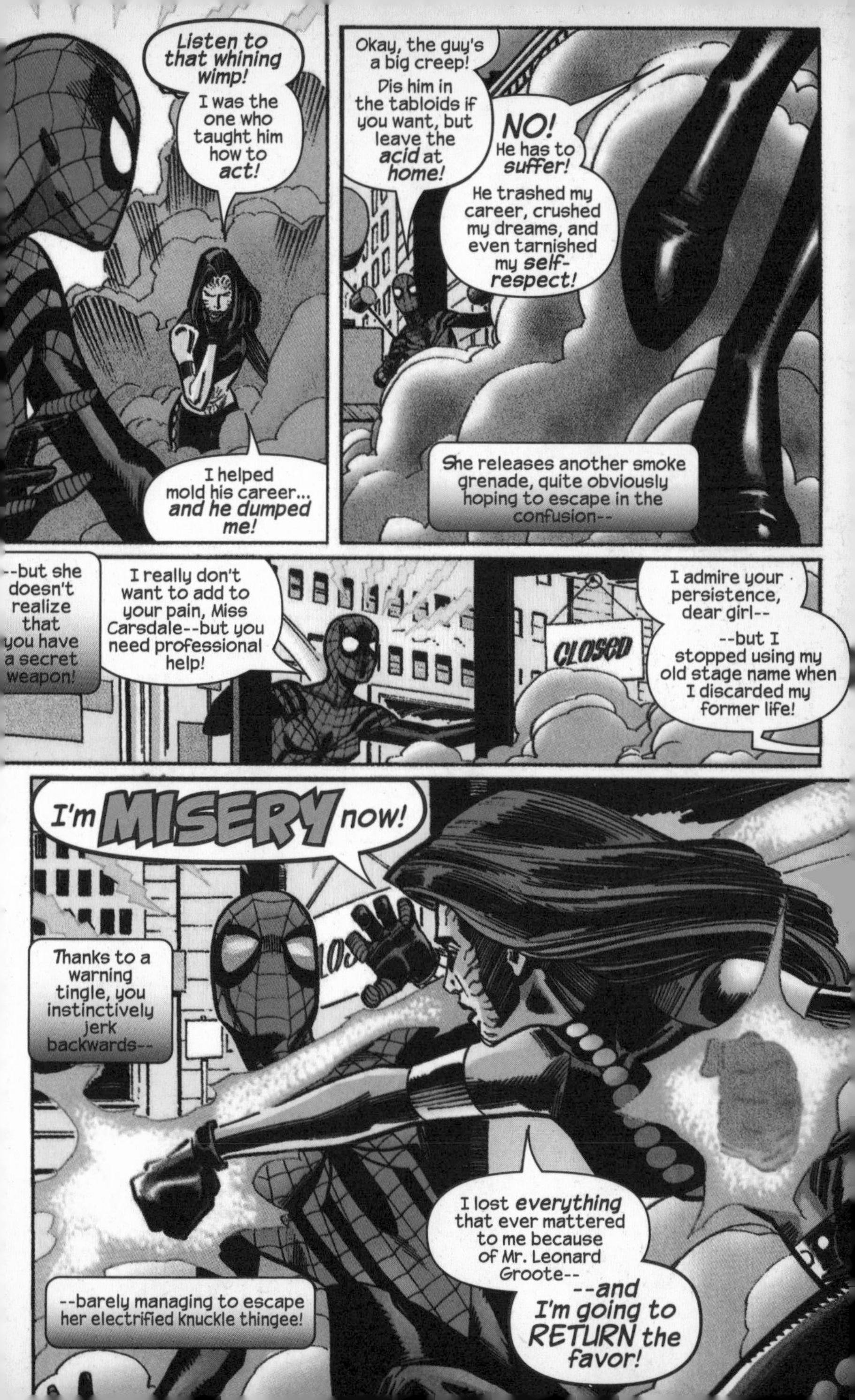
Listen to that whining wimp!
I was the one who taught him how to act!
I helped mold his career... and he dumped me!
Okay, the guy's a big creep!
Dis him in the tabloids if you want, but leave the acid at home!
NO! He has to suffer!
He trashed my career, crushed my dreams, and even tarnished my self-respect!
She releases another smoke grenade, quite obviously hoping to escape in the confusion--
--but she doesn't realize that you have a secret weapon!
I really don't want to add to your pain, Miss Carsdale--but you need professional help!
CLOSED
I admire your persistence, dear girl--
--but I stopped using my old stage name when I discarded my former life!
I'm MISERY now!
Thanks to a warning tingle, you instinctively jerk backwards--
--barely managing to escape her electrified knuckle thingee!
I lost everything that ever mattered to me because of Mr. Leonard Groote--
--and I'm going to RETURN the favor!

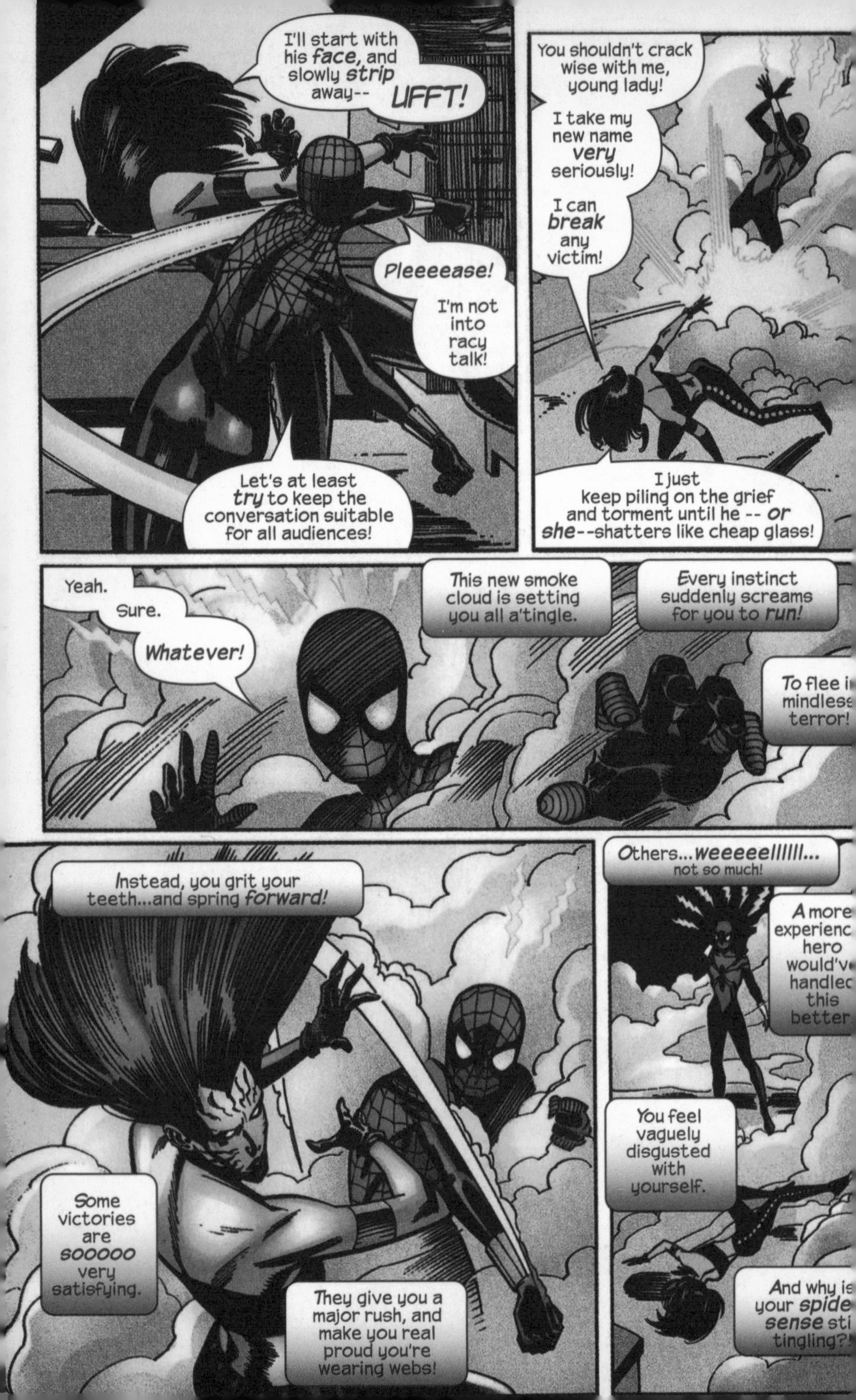

I'll start with his face, and slowly strip away-- UFFT!
Pleeeease!
I'm not into racy talk!
Let's at least try to keep the conversation suitable for all audiences!
You shouldn't crack wise with me, young lady!
I take my new name very seriously!
I can break any victim!
I just keep piling on the grief and torment until he -- or she--shatters like cheap glass!
Yeah.
Sure.
Whatever!
This new smoke cloud is setting you all a'tingle.
Every instinct suddenly screams for you to run!
To flee i mindless terror!
Instead, you grit your teeth...and spring forward!
Some victories are sooooo very satisfying.
They give you a major rush, and make you real proud you're wearing webs!
Others...weeeeelllllll... not so much!
A more experienc hero would'v handlec this better
You feel vaguely disgusted with yourself.
And why is your spide sense sti tingling?

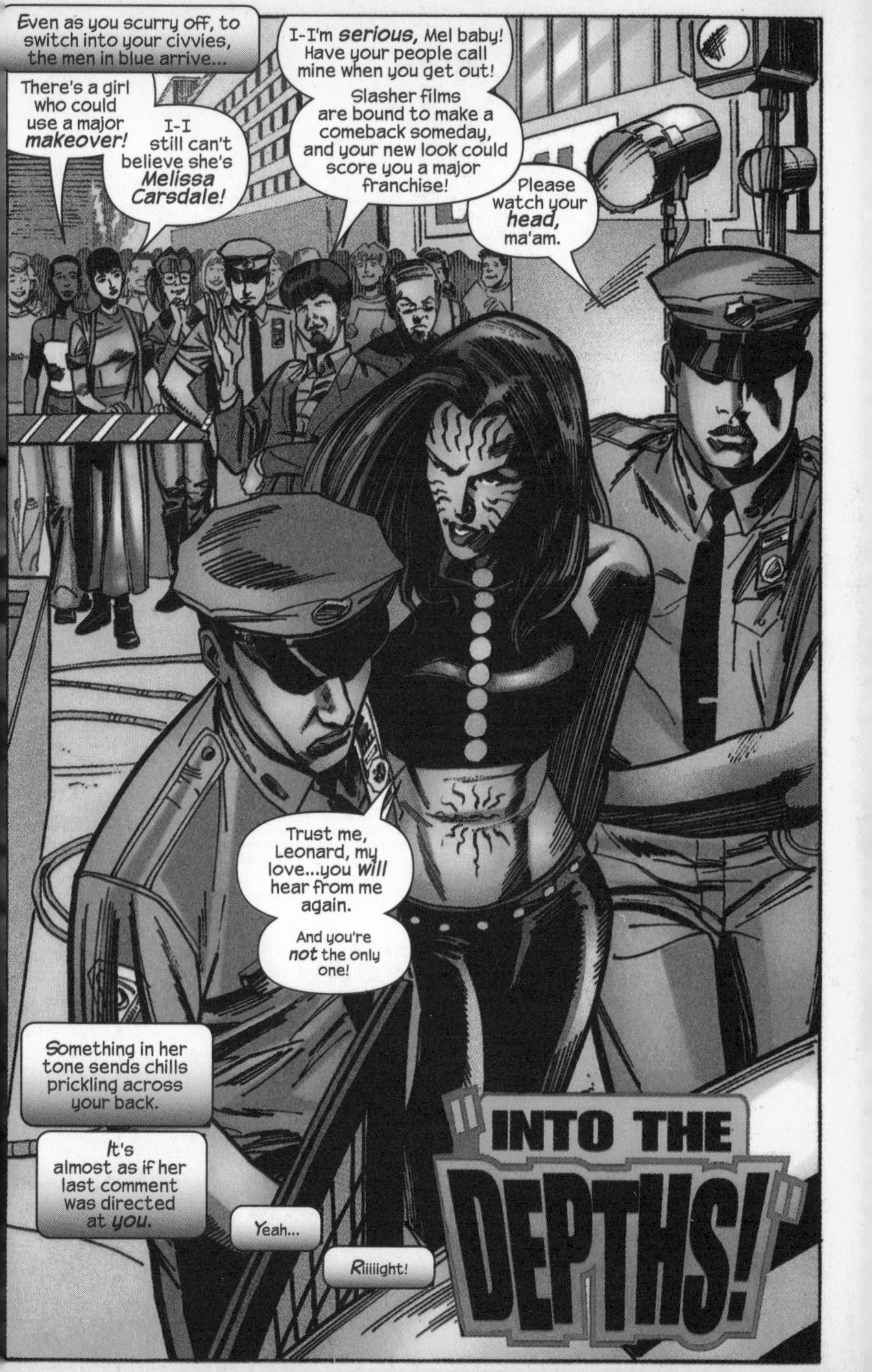

Even as you scurry off, to switch into your civvies, the men in blue arrive...
There's a girl who could use a major makeover!
I-I still can't believe she's Melissa Carsdale!
I-I'm serious, Mel baby! Have your people call mine when you get out!
Slasher films are bound to make a comeback someday, and your new look could score you a major franchise!
Please watch your head, ma'am.
Trust me, Leonard, my love...you will hear from me again.
And you're not the only one!
Something in her tone sends chills prickling across your back.
It's almost as if her last comment was directed at you.
Yeah...
Riiiiight!
"INTO THE DEPTHS!"

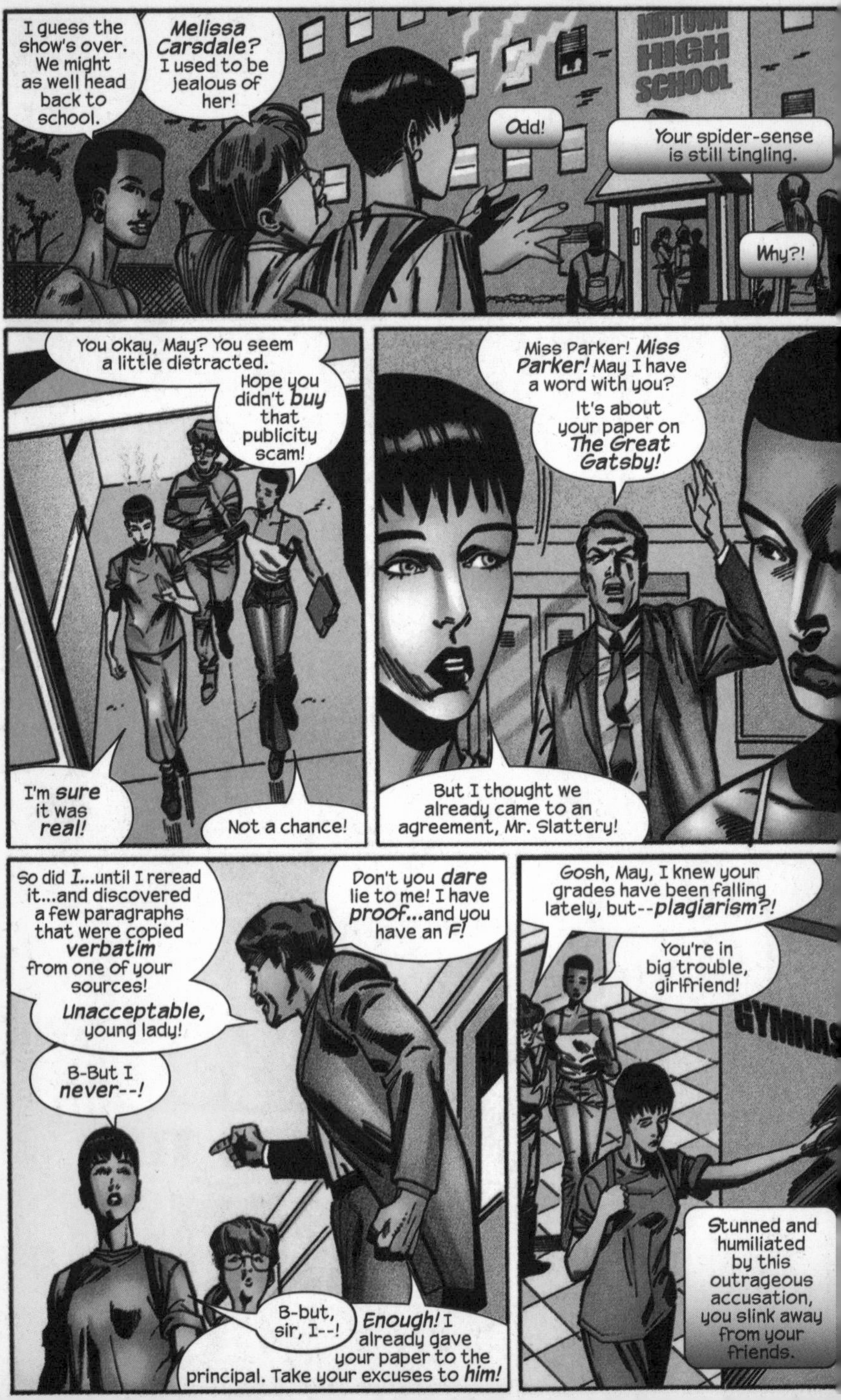
I guess the show's over. We might as well head back to school.
Melissa Carsdale? I used to be jealous of her!
MIDTOWN HIGH SCHOOL
Odd!
Your spider-sense is still tingling.
Why?!
You okay, May? You seem a little distracted.
Hope you didn't buy that publicity scam!
I'm sure it was real!
Not a chance!
Miss Parker! Miss Parker! May I have a word with you?
It's about your paper on The Great Gatsby!
But I thought we already came to an agreement, Mr. Slattery!
So did I...until I reread it...and discovered a few paragraphs that were copied verbatim from one of your sources!
Unacceptable, young lady!
Don't you dare lie to me! I have proof...and you have an F!
B-But I never--!
B-but, sir, I--!
Enough! I already gave your paper to the principal. Take your excuses to him!
Gosh, May, I knew your grades have been falling lately, but--plagiarism?!
You're in big trouble, girlfriend!
GYMNAS
Stunned and humiliated by this outrageous accusation, you slink away from your friends.

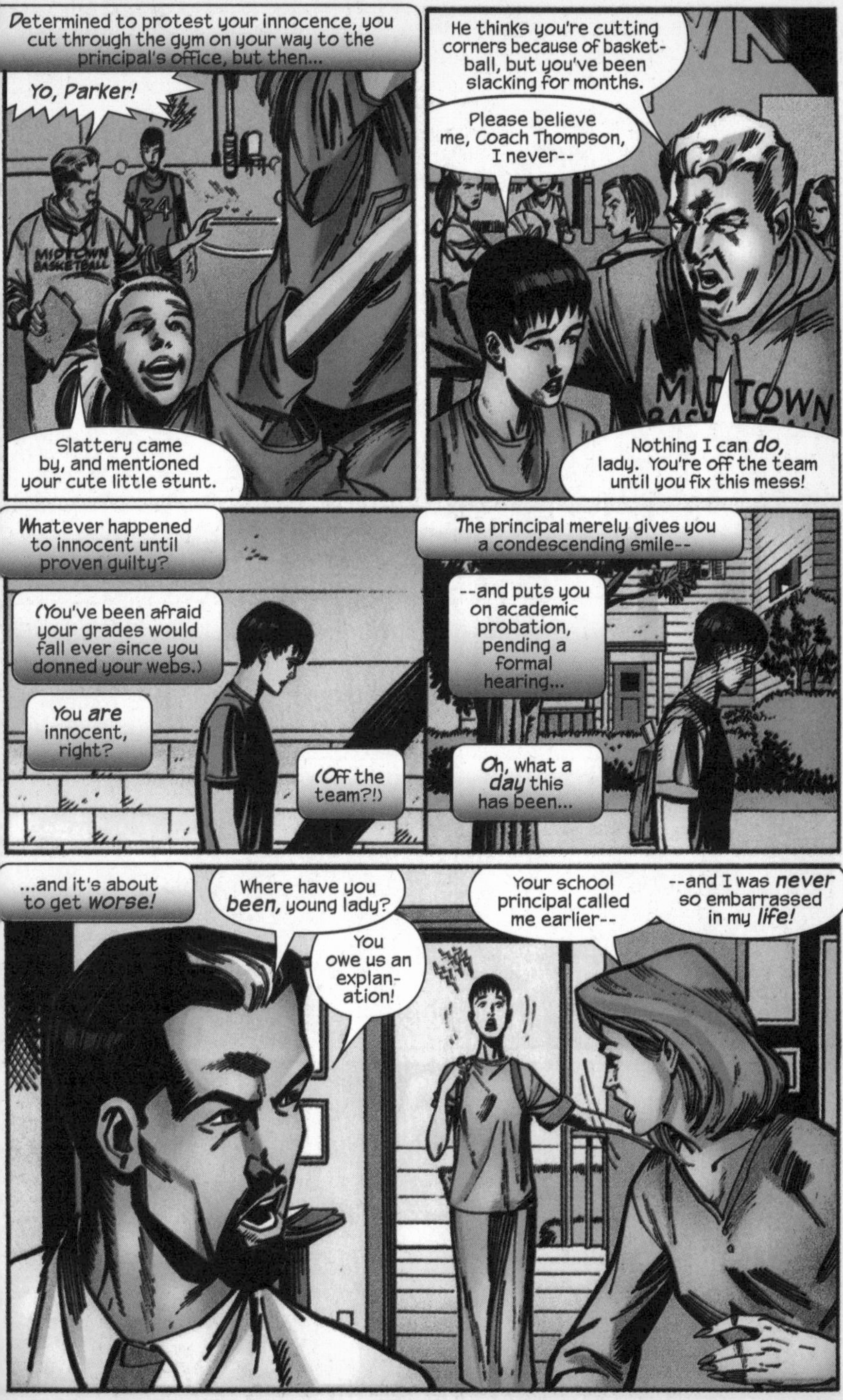
Determined to protest your innocence, you cut through the gym on your way to the principal's office, but then...
Yo, Parker!
Slattery came by, and mentioned your cute little stunt.
He thinks you're cutting corners because of basket-ball, but you've been slacking for months.
Please believe me, Coach Thompson, I never--
Nothing I can do, lady. You're off the team until you fix this mess!
Whatever happened to innocent until proven guilty?
(You've been afraid your grades would fall ever since you donned your webs.)
You are innocent, right?
(Off the team?!)
The principal merely gives you a condescending smile--
--and puts you on academic probation, pending a formal hearing...
Oh, what a day this has been...
...and it's about to get worse!
Where have you been, young lady?
You owe us an explan-ation!
Your school principal called me earlier--
--and I was never so embarrassed in my life!

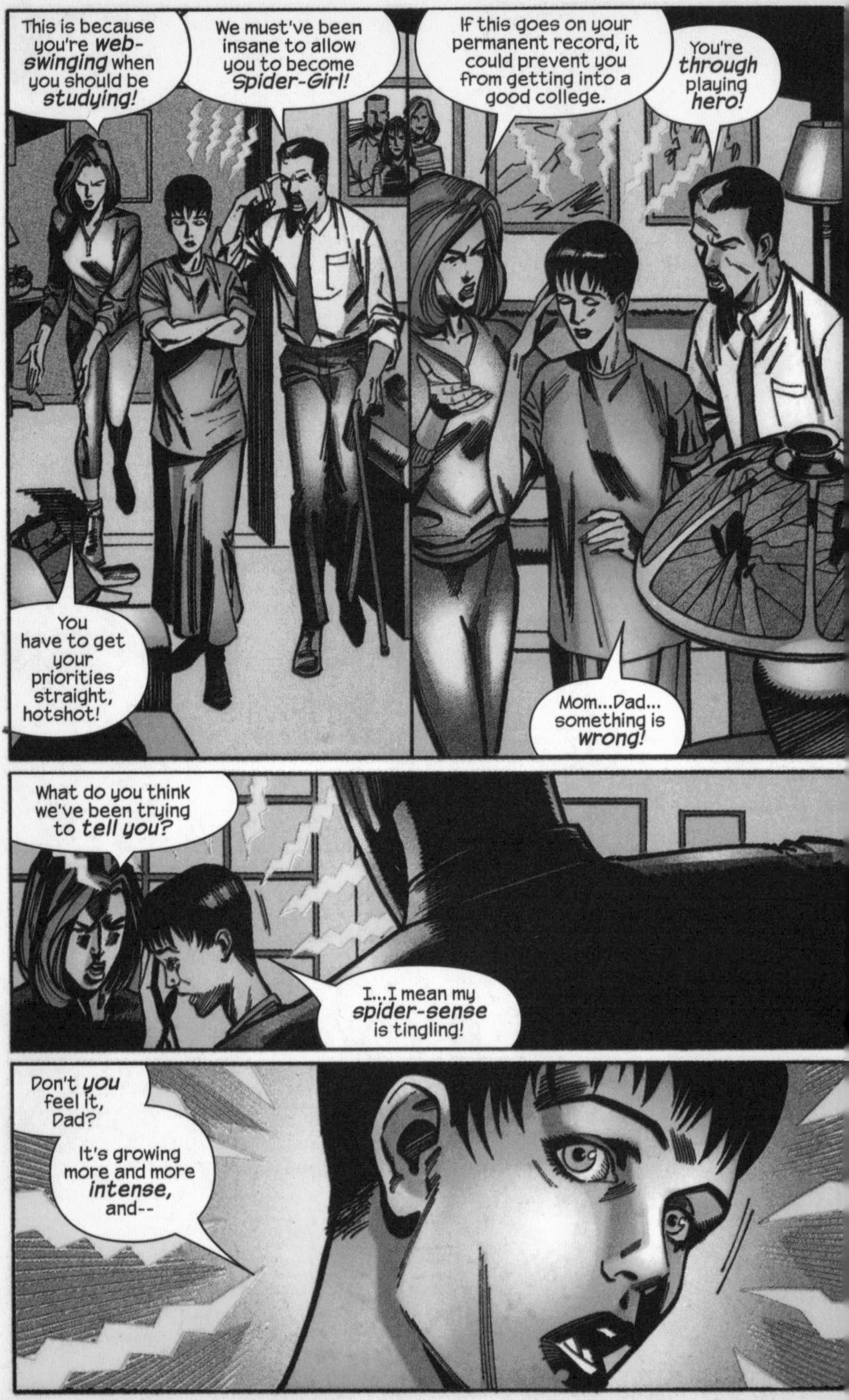
This is because you're web-swinging when you should be studying!
We must've been insane to allow you to become Spider-Girl!
If this goes on your permanent record, it could prevent you from getting into a good college.
You're through playing hero!
You have to get your priorities straight, hotshot!
Mom...Dad... something is wrong!
What do you think we've been trying to tell you?
I...I mean my spider-sense is tingling!
Don't you feel it, Dad?
It's growing more and more intense, and--

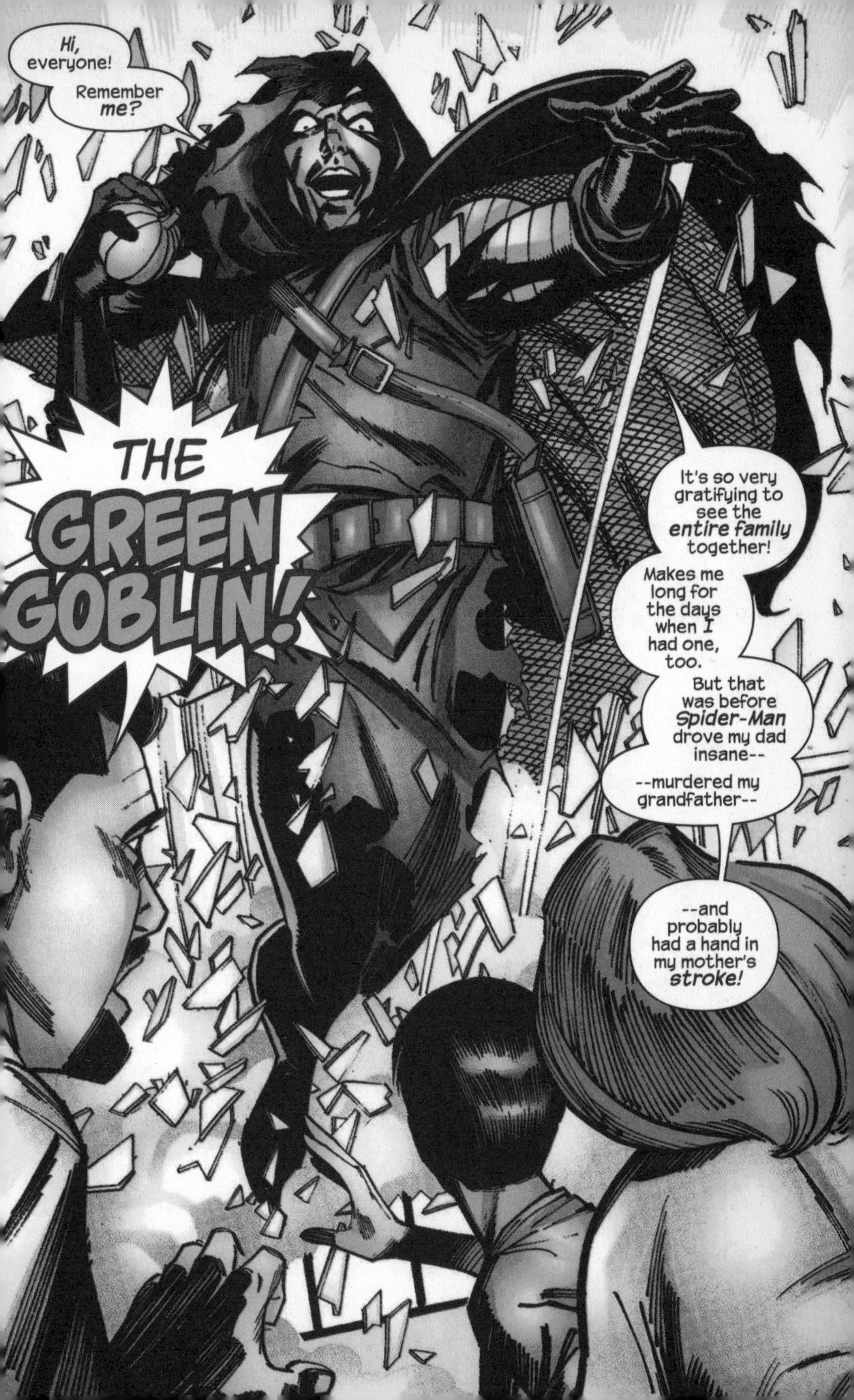
Hi, everyone! Remember *me?*
THE GREEN GOBLIN!
It's so very gratifying to see the *entire family* together!
Makes me long for the days when *I* had one, too.
But that was before *Spider-Man* drove my dad insane--
--murdered my grandfather--
--and probably had a hand in my mother's *stroke!*

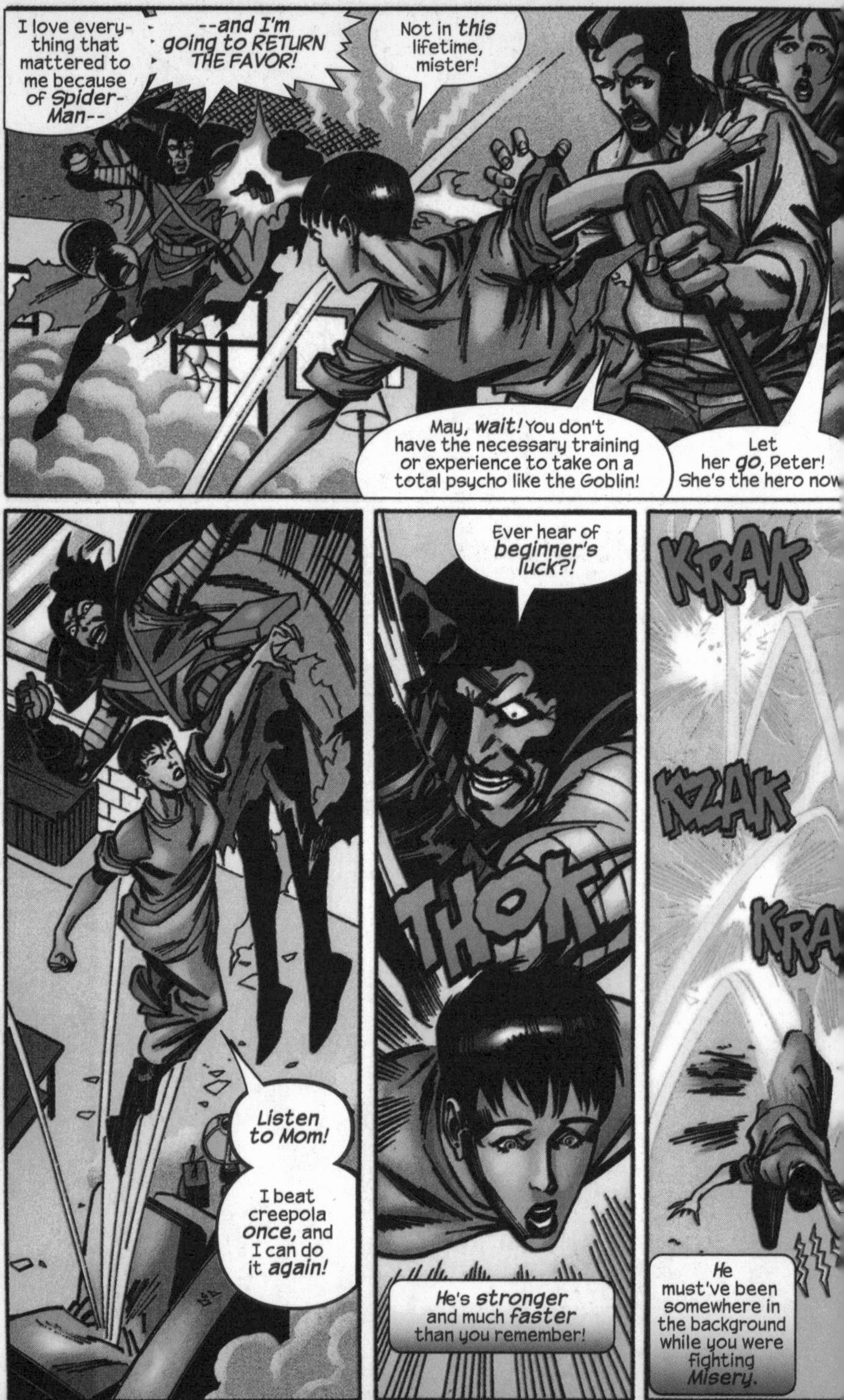
I love everything that mattered to me because of Spider-Man--
--and I'm going to RETURN THE FAVOR!
Not in this lifetime, mister!
May, wait! You don't have the necessary training or experience to take on a total psycho like the Goblin!
Let her go, Peter! She's the hero now
Listen to Mom!
I beat creepola once, and I can do it again!
Ever hear of beginner's luck?!
THOK
He's stronger and much faster than you remember!
KRAK
KZAK
He must've been somewhere in the background while you were fighting Misery.

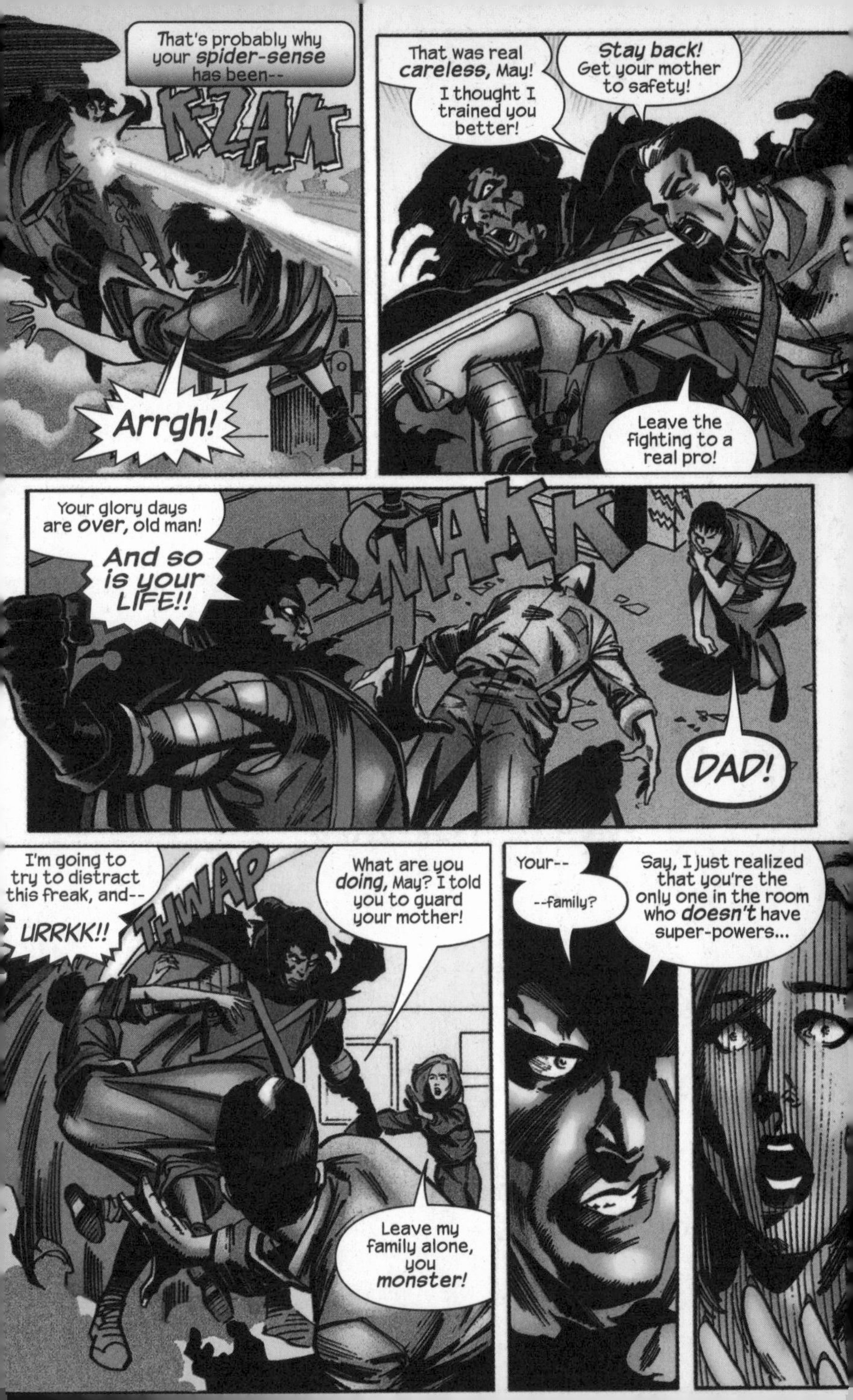
That's probably why your spider-sense has been--
K-ZAK
Arrgh!
That was real careless, May!
I thought I trained you better!
Stay back! Get your mother to safety!
Leave the fighting to a real pro!
Your glory days are over, old man!
And so is your LIFE!!
SMAKK
DAD!
I'm going to try to distract this freak, and--
URRKK!!
THWAP
What are you doing, May? I told you to guard your mother!
Leave my family alone, you monster!
Your--
--family?
Say, I just realized that you're the only one in the room who doesn't have super-powers...

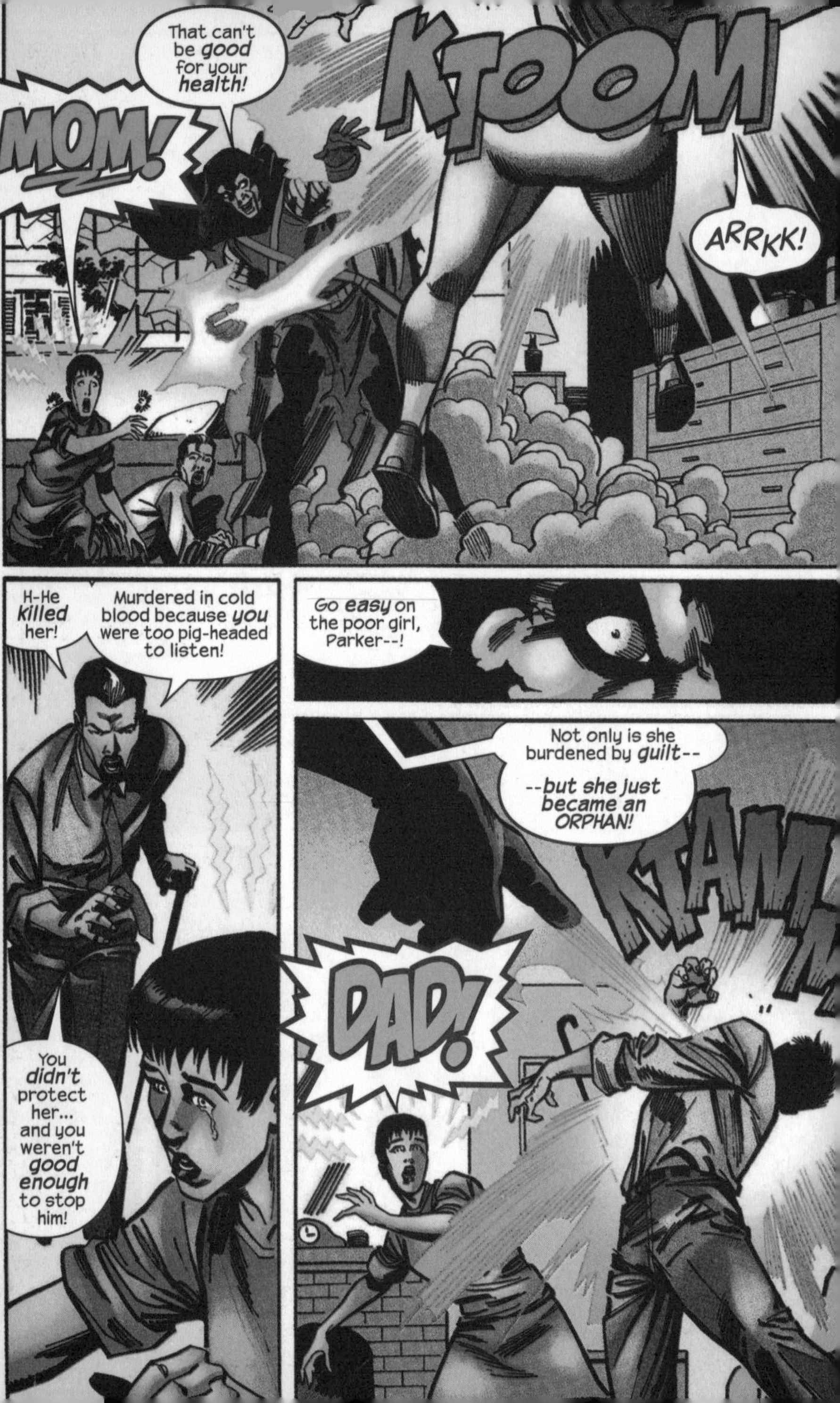
That can't be good for your health!
KTOOM
MOM!
ARRKK!
H-He killed her!
Murdered in cold blood because you were too pig-headed to listen!
Go easy on the poor girl, Parker--!
You didn't protect her... and you weren't good enough to stop him!
Not only is she burdened by guilt--
--but she just became an ORPHAN!
DAD!

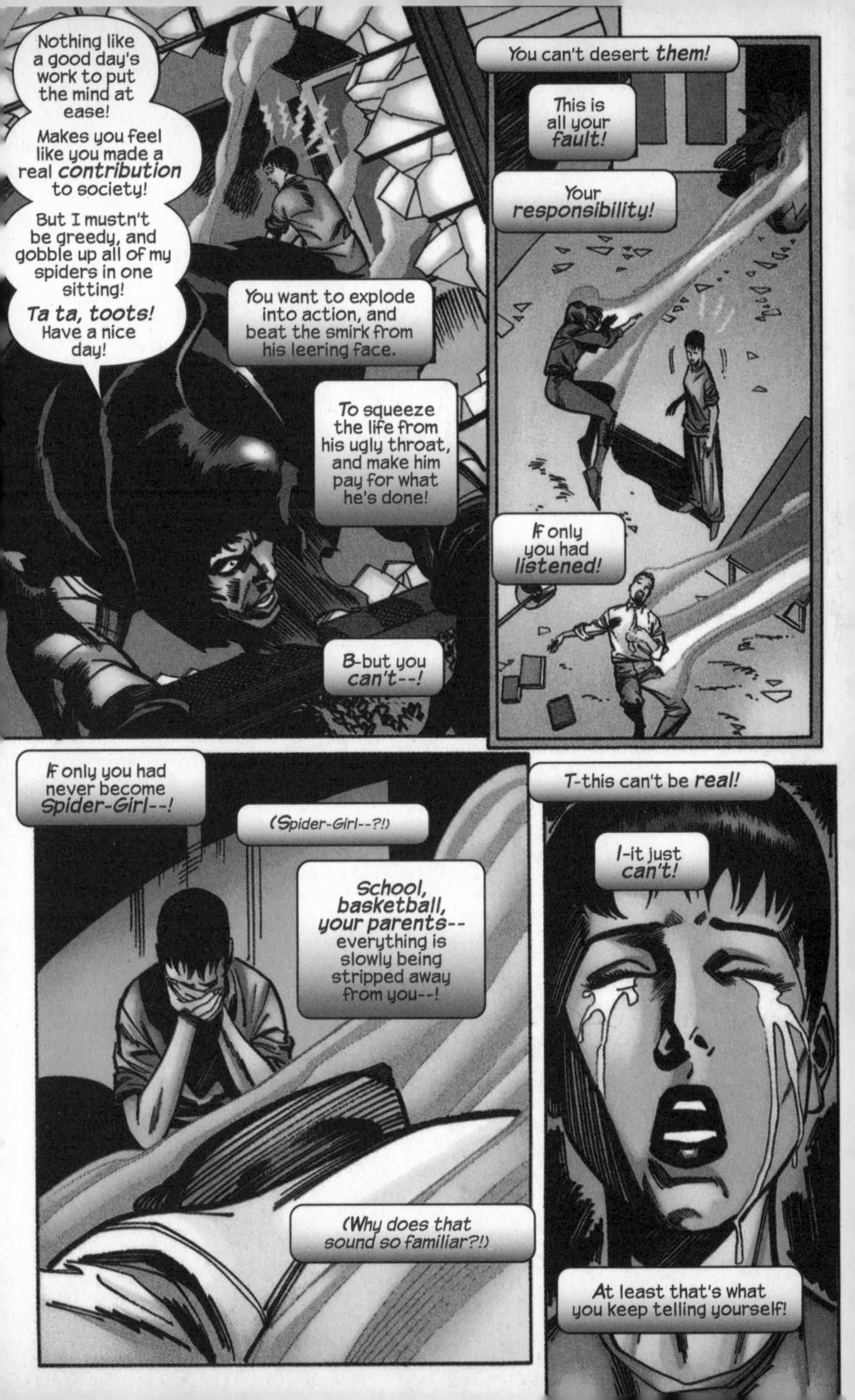
Nothing like a good day's work to put the mind at ease!
Makes you feel like you made a real contribution to society!
But I mustn't be greedy, and gobble up all of my spiders in one sitting!
Ta ta, toots! Have a nice day!
You want to explode into action, and beat the smirk from his leering face.
To squeeze the life from his ugly throat, and make him pay for what he's done!
B-but you can't--!
You can't desert them!
This is all your fault!
Your responsibility!
If only you had listened!
If only you had never become Spider-Girl--!
(Spider-Girl--?!)
School, basketball, your parents-- everything is slowly being stripped away from you--!
(Why does that sound so familiar?!)
T-this can't be real!
I-it just can't!
At least that's what you keep telling yourself!

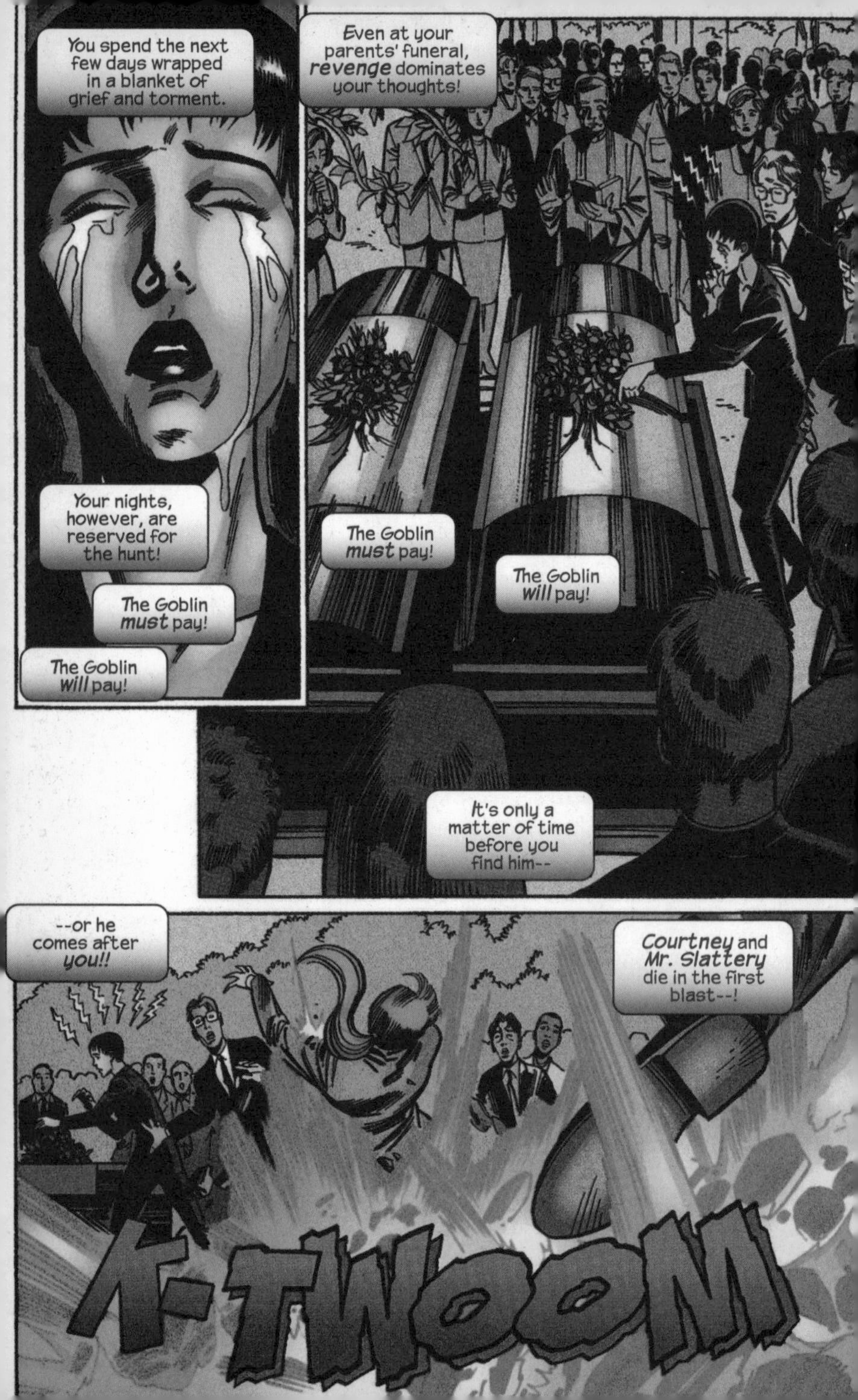
You spend the next few days wrapped in a blanket of grief and torment.
Your nights, however, are reserved for the hunt!
The Goblin must pay!
The Goblin will pay!
Even at your parents' funeral, revenge dominates your thoughts!
The Goblin must pay!
The Goblin will pay!
It's only a matter of time before you find him--
--or he comes after you!!
Courtney and Mr. Slattery die in the first blast--!
K-TWOOM

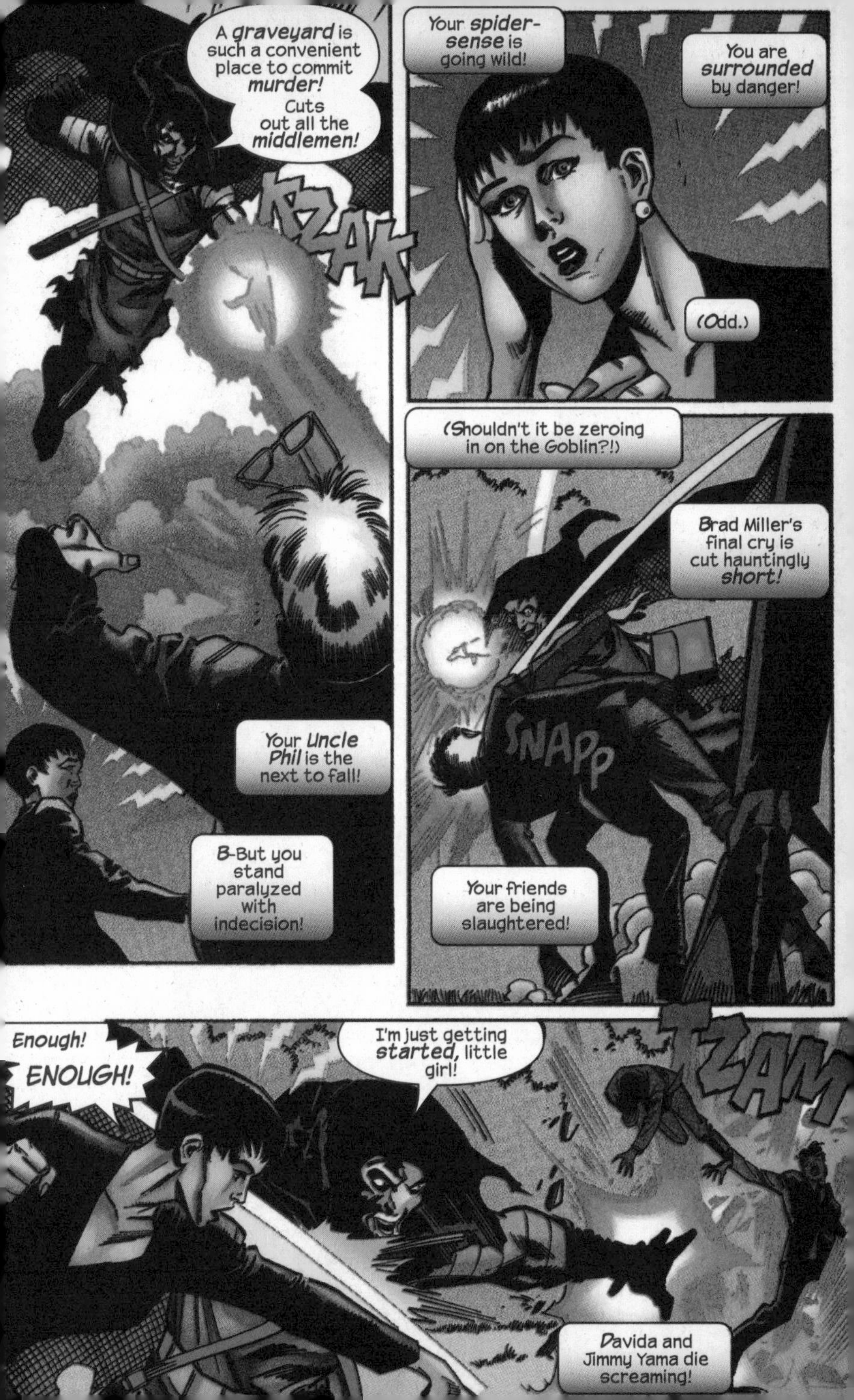
A graveyard is such a convenient place to commit murder!
Cuts out all the middlemen!
KRZAK
Your spider-sense is going wild!
You are surrounded by danger!
(Odd.)
Your Uncle Phil is the next to fall!
B-But you stand paralyzed with indecision!
(Shouldn't it be zeroing in on the Goblin?!)
Brad Miller's final cry is cut hauntingly short!
SNAPP
Your friends are being slaughtered!
Enough!
ENOUGH!
I'm just getting started, little girl!
TZAM
Davida and Jimmy Yama die screaming!

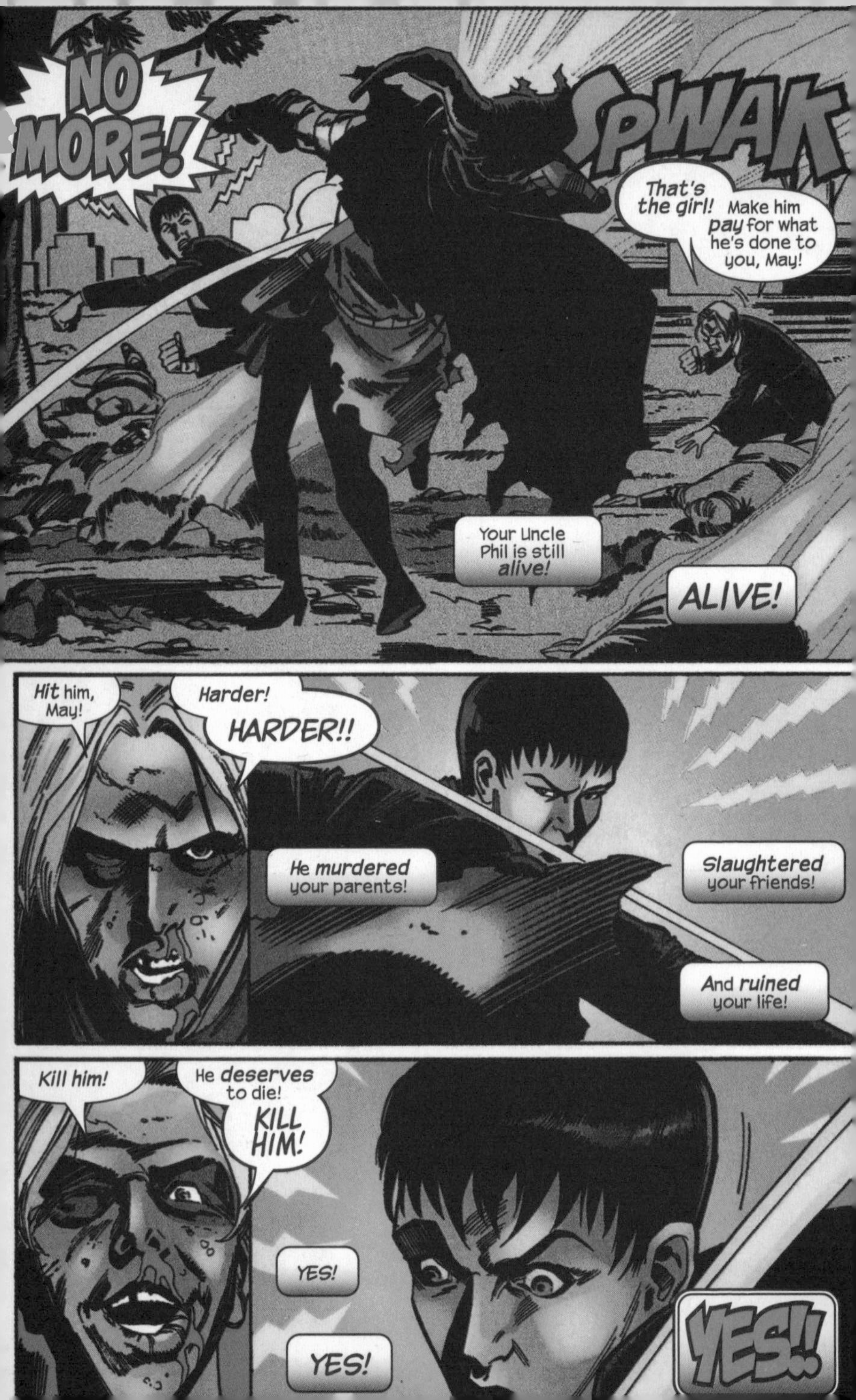
NO MORE!
SPWAK
That's the girl!
Make him pay for what he's done to you, May!
Your Uncle Phil is still alive!
ALIVE!
Hit him, May!
Harder!
HARDER!!
He murdered your parents!
Slaughtered your friends!
And ruined your life!
Kill him!
He deserves to die!
KILL HIM!
YES!
YES!
YES!!

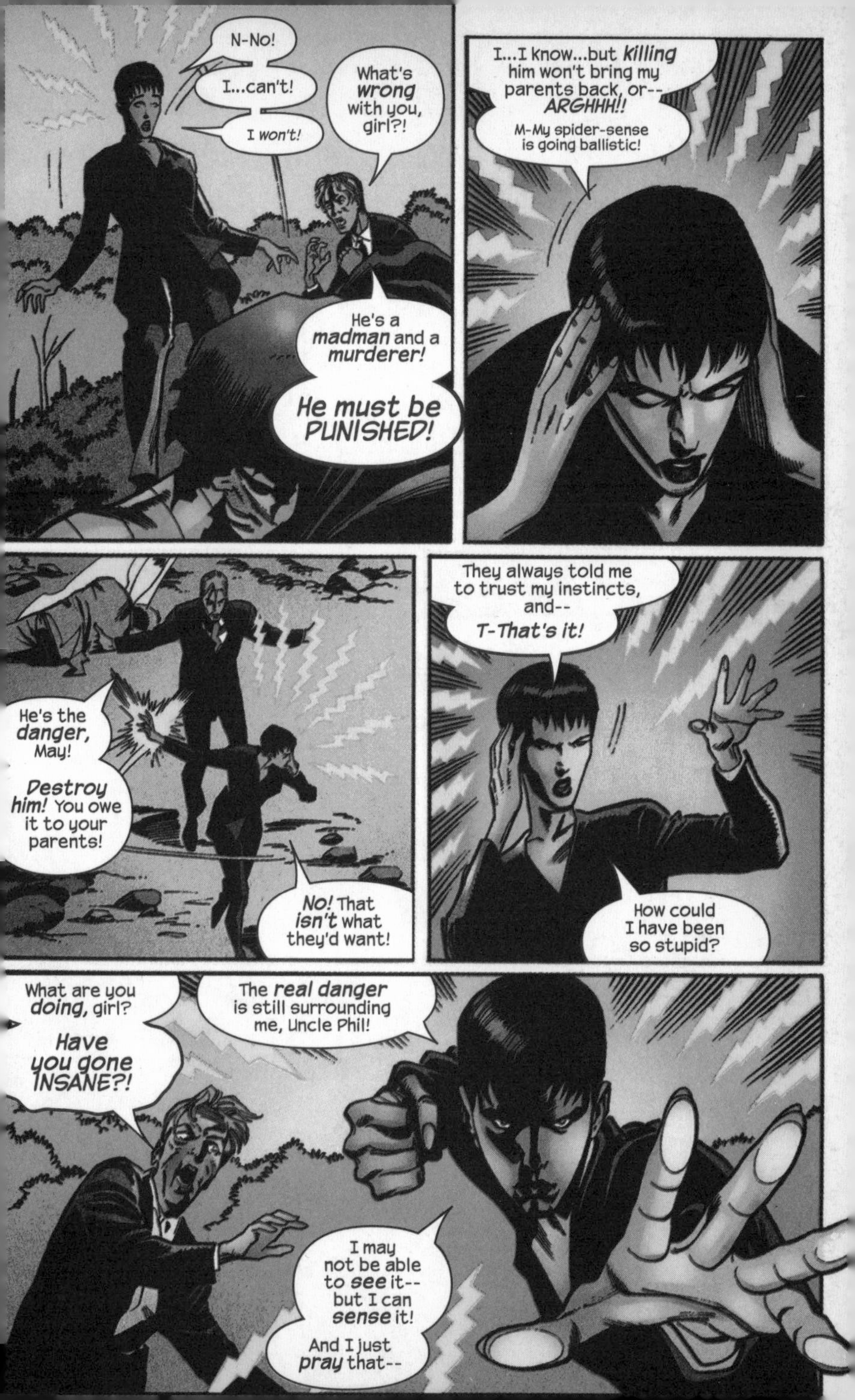

N-No!
I...can't!
I won't!
What's wrong with you, girl?!
He's a madman and a murderer!
He must be PUNISHED!
I...I know...but killing him won't bring my parents back, or-- ARGHHH!!
M-My spider-sense is going ballistic!
He's the danger, May!
Destroy him! You owe it to your parents!
No! That isn't what they'd want!
They always told me to trust my instincts, and--
T-That's it!
How could I have been so stupid?
What are you doing, girl?
Have you gone INSANE?!
The real danger is still surrounding me, Uncle Phil!
I may not be able to see it-- but I can sense it!
And I just pray that--

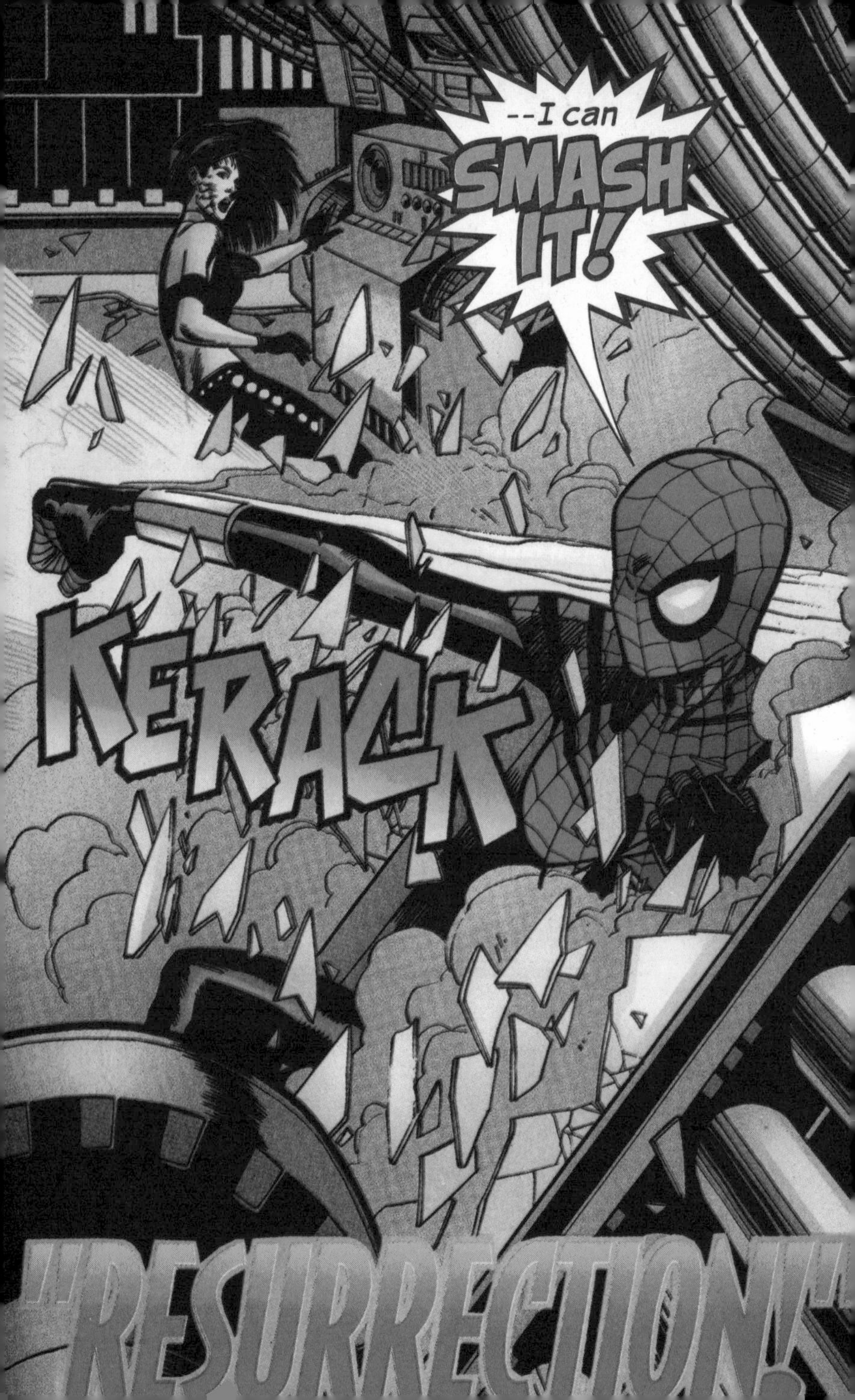
--I can SMASH IT!
KERACK
"RESURRECTION!"

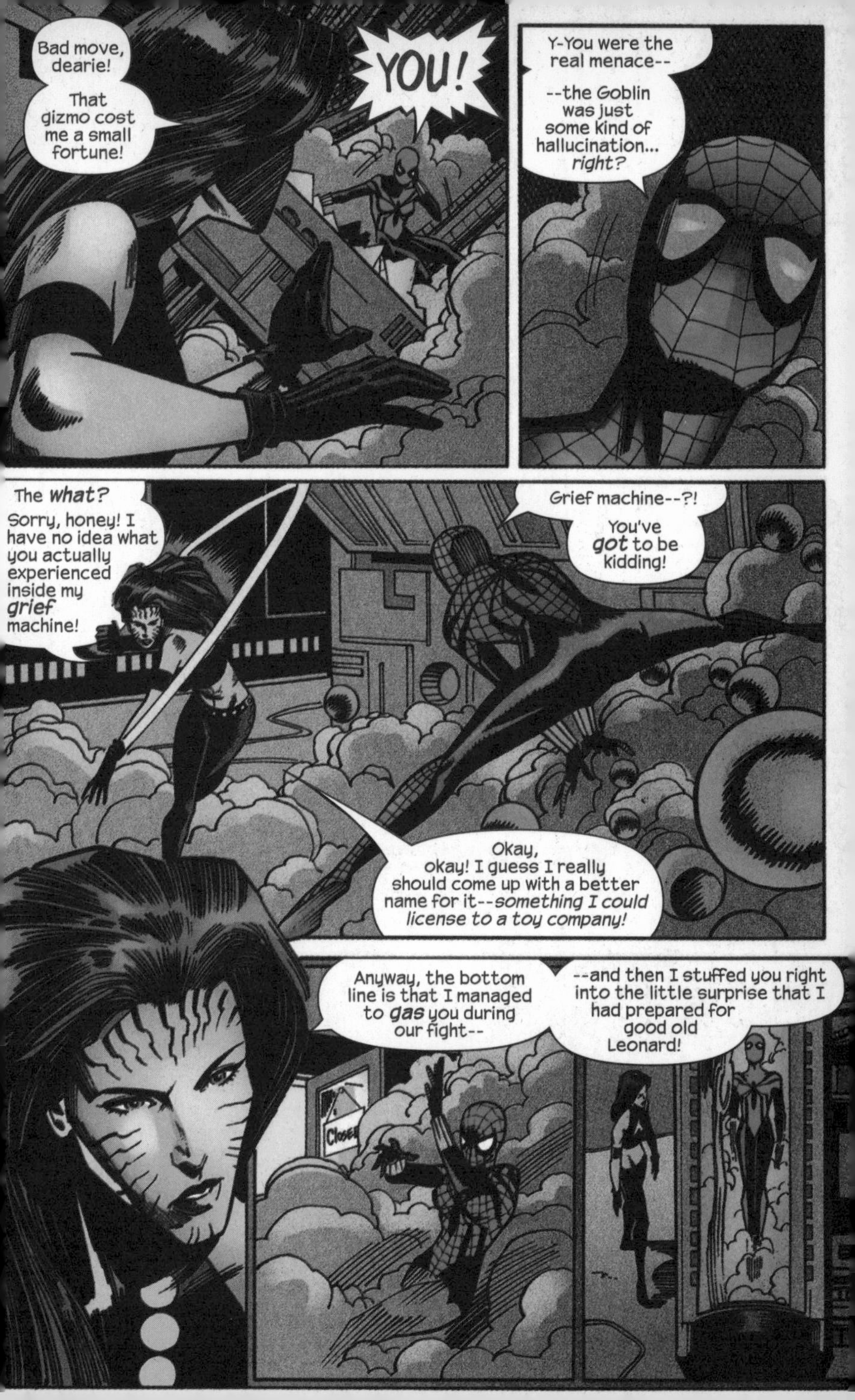
Bad move, dearie!
That gizmo cost me a small fortune!
YOU!
Y-You were the real menace--
--the Goblin was just some kind of hallucination... *right?*
The *what?*
Sorry, honey! I have no idea what you actually experienced inside my *grief* machine!
Grief machine--?!
You've *got* to be kidding!
Okay, okay! I guess I really should come up with a better name for it--*something I could license to a toy company!*
Anyway, the bottom line is that I managed to *gas* you during our fight--
--and then I stuffed you right into the little surprise that I had prepared for good old Leonard!
Closed

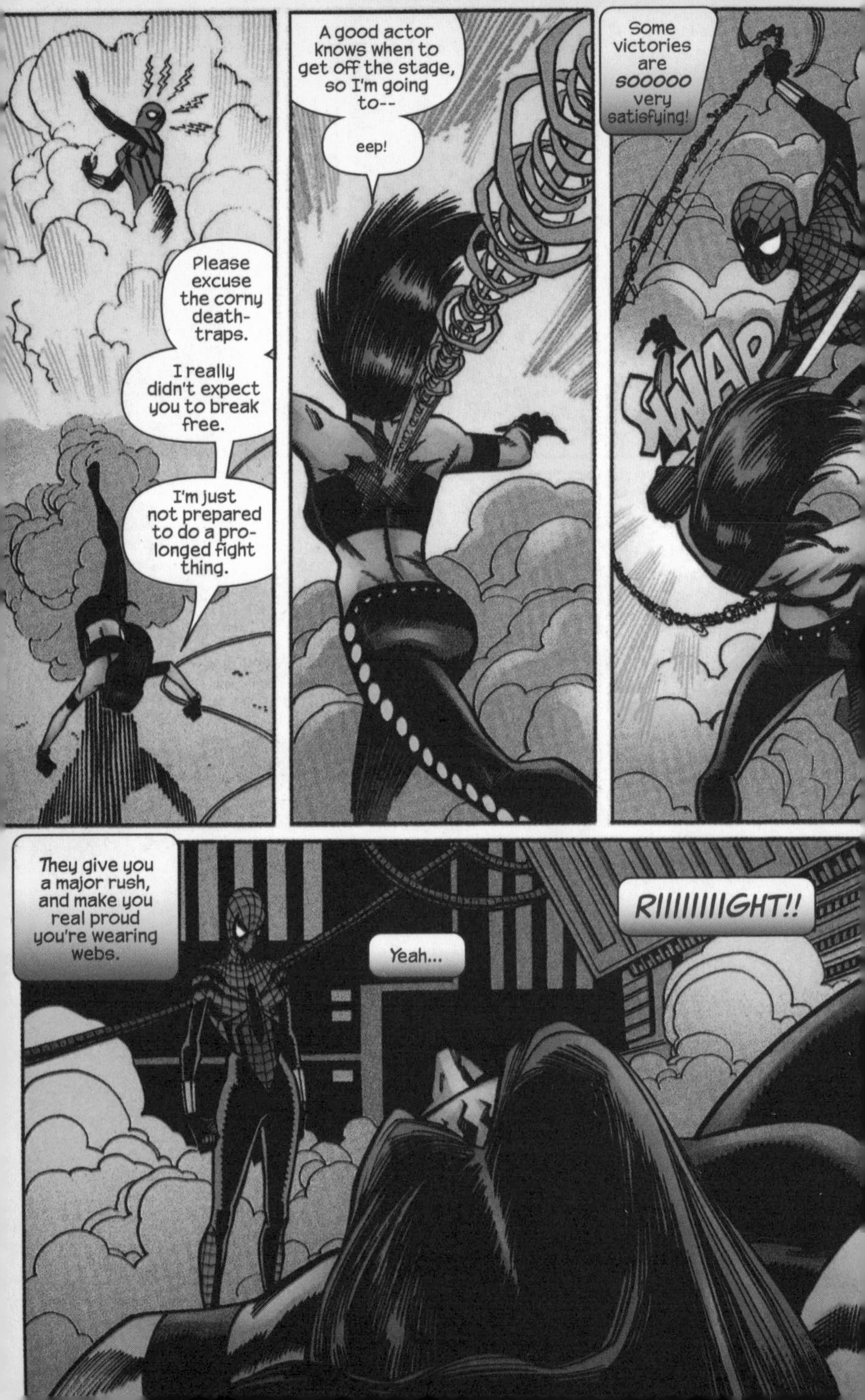
Please excuse the corny death-traps.
I really didn't expect you to break free.
I'm just not prepared to do a pro-longed fight thing.
A good actor knows when to get off the stage, so I'm going to--
eep!
Some victories are SOOOOO very satisfying!
SWAP
They give you a major rush, and make you real proud you're wearing webs.
Yeah...
RIIIIIIIIGHT!!

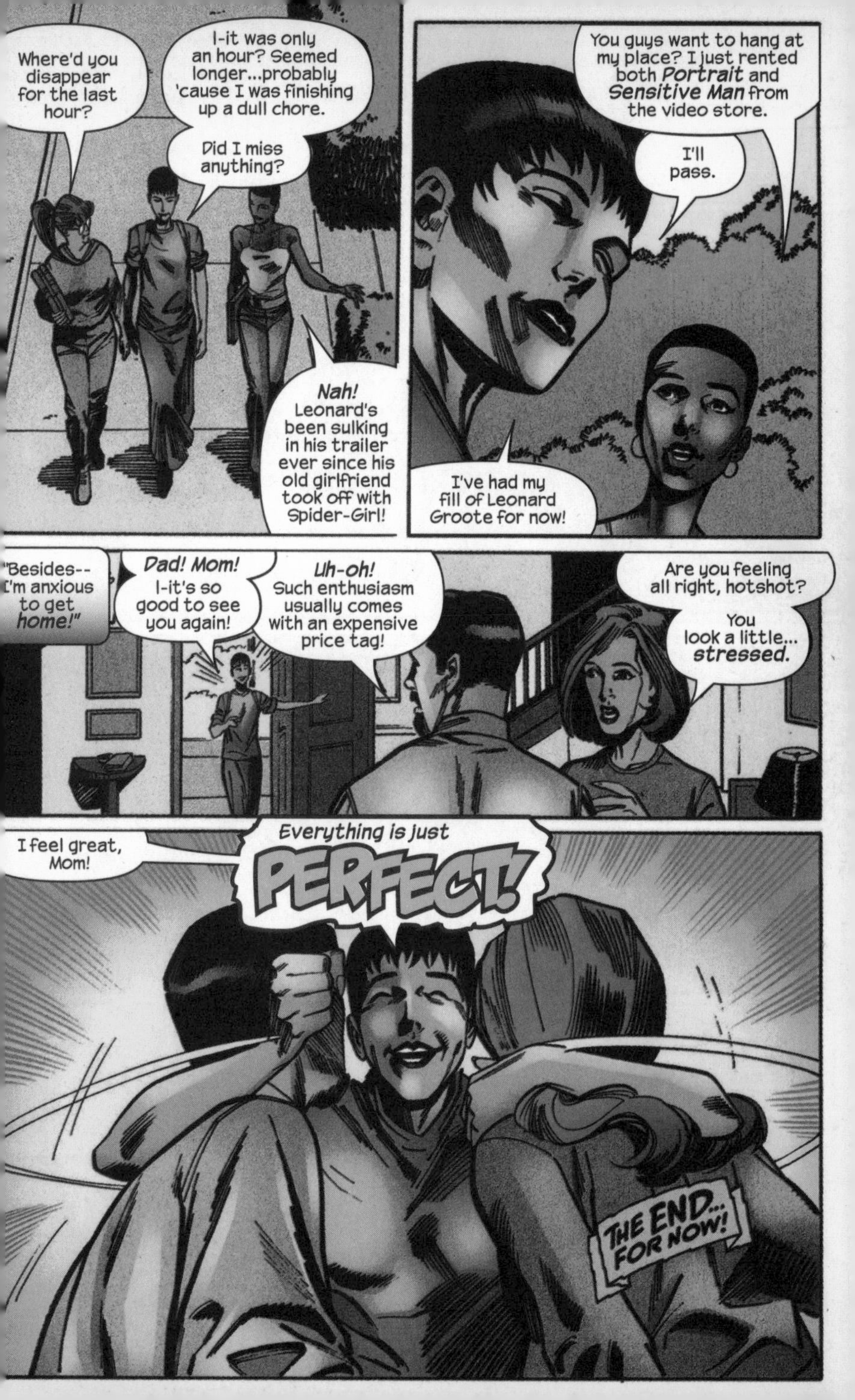
Where'd you disappear for the last hour?
I-it was only an hour? Seemed longer...probably 'cause I was finishing up a dull chore.
Did I miss anything?
Nah! Leonard's been sulking in his trailer ever since his old girlfriend took off with Spider-Girl!
You guys want to hang at my place? I just rented both Portrait and Sensitive Man from the video store.
I'll pass.
I've had my fill of Leonard Groote for now!
"Besides-- I'm anxious to get home!"
Dad! Mom! I-it's so good to see you again!
Uh-oh! Such enthusiasm usually comes with an expensive price tag!
Are you feeling all right, hotshot? You look a little... stressed.
I feel great, Mom!
Everything is just PERFECT!
THE END... FOR NOW!

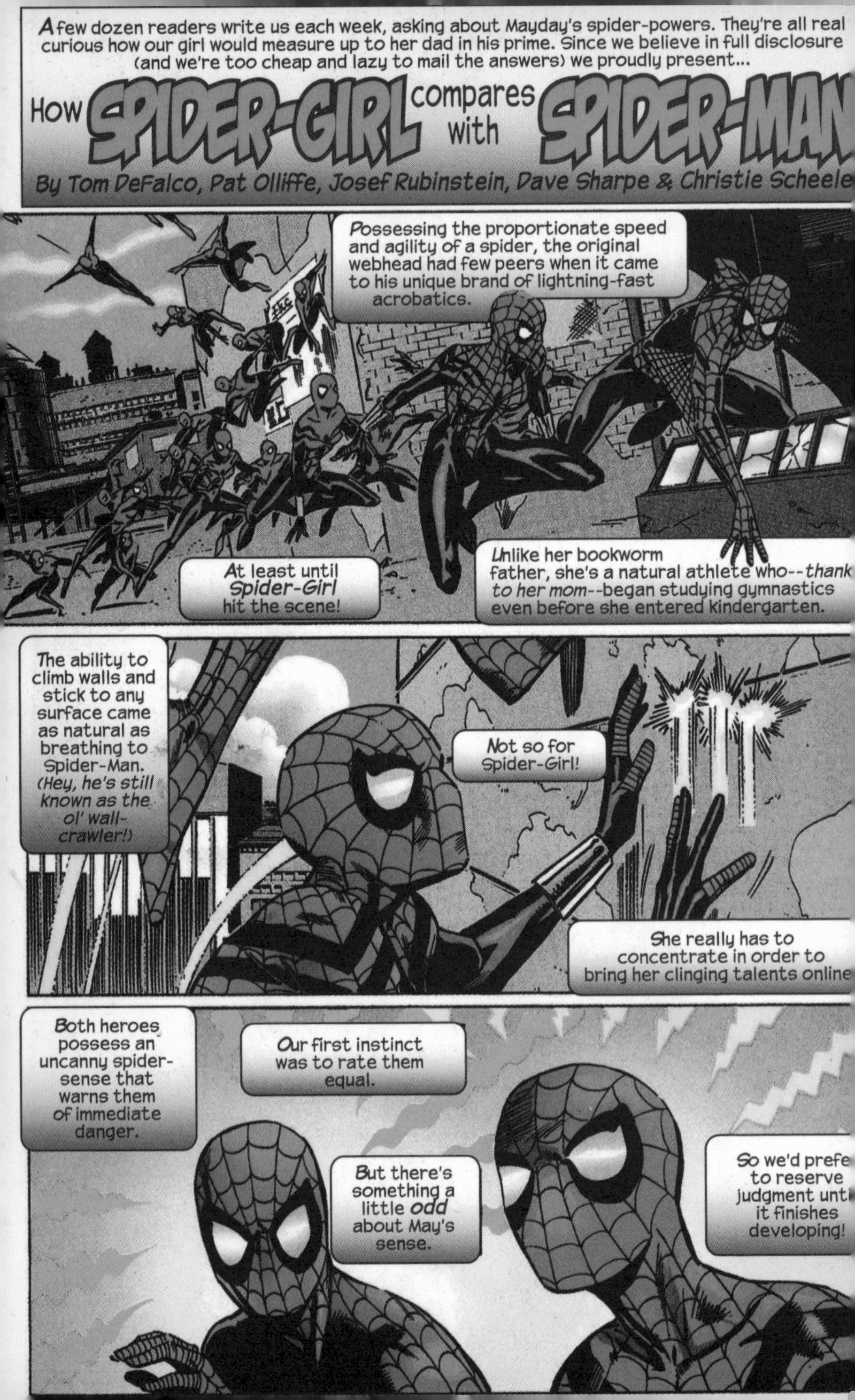
A few dozen readers write us each week, asking about Mayday's spider-powers. They're all real curious how our girl would measure up to her dad in his prime. Since we believe in full disclosure (and we're too cheap and lazy to mail the answers) we proudly present...
How SPIDER-GIRL compares with SPIDER-MAN
By Tom DeFalco, Pat Olliffe, Josef Rubinstein, Dave Sharpe & Christie Scheele
Possessing the proportionate speed and agility of a spider, the original webhead had few peers when it came to his unique brand of lightning-fast acrobatics.
At least until *Spider-Girl* hit the scene!
Unlike her bookworm father, she's a natural athlete who--*thank* *to her mom*--began studying gymnastics even before she entered kindergarten.
The ability to climb walls and stick to any surface came as natural as breathing to Spider-Man. *(Hey, he's still known as the ol' wall-crawler!)*
Not so for Spider-Girl!
She really has to concentrate in order to bring her clinging talents online
Both heroes possess an uncanny spider-sense that warns them of immediate danger.
Our first instinct was to rate them equal.
But there's something a little *odd* about May's sense.
So we'd prefe to reserve judgment unti it finishes developing!

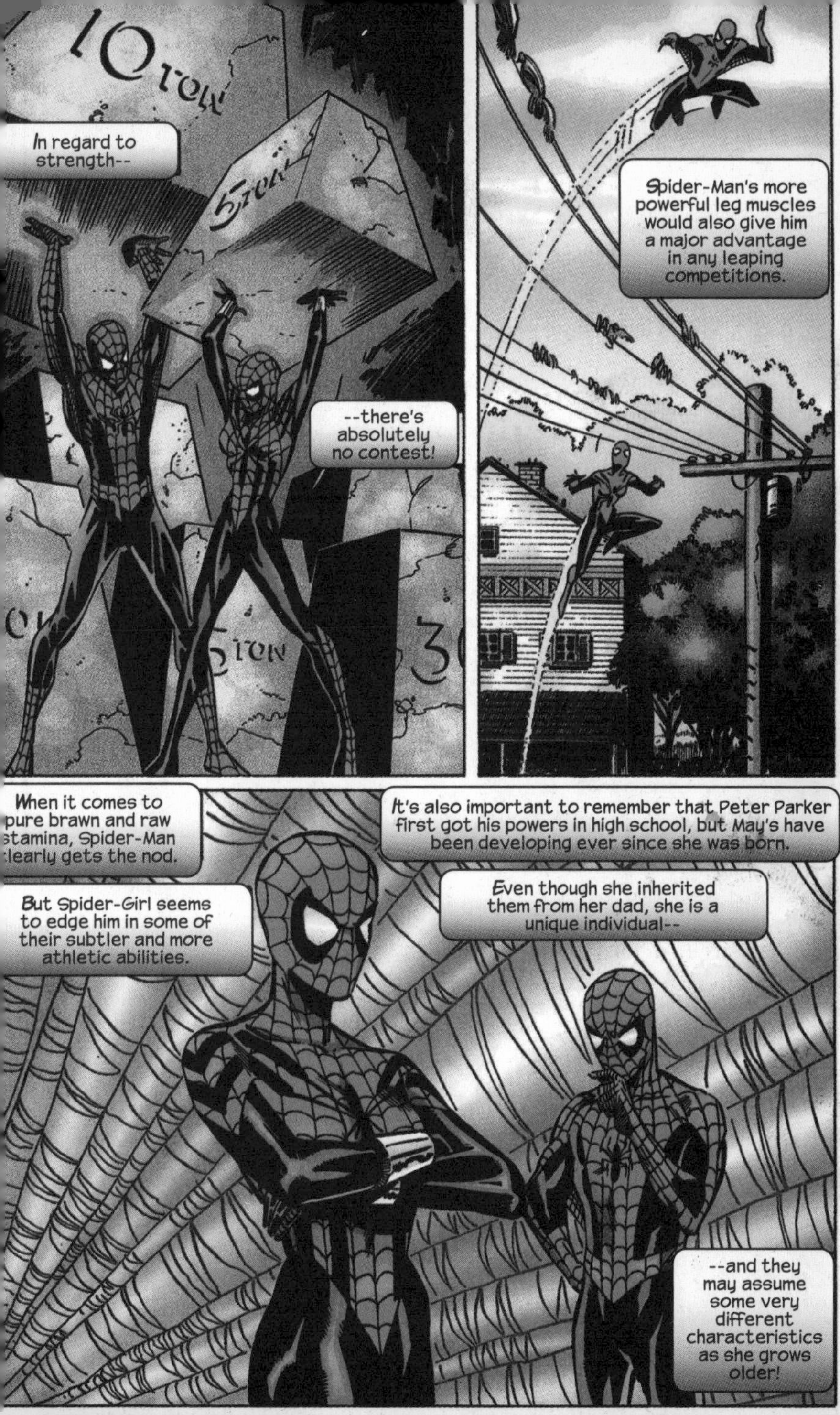

10 TON
In regard to strength--
5 TON
--there's absolutely no contest!
5 TON
Spider-Man's more powerful leg muscles would also give him a major advantage in any leaping competitions.
When it comes to pure brawn and raw stamina, Spider-Man clearly gets the nod.
But Spider-Girl seems to edge him in some of their subtler and more athletic abilities.
It's also important to remember that Peter Parker first got his powers in high school, but May's have been developing ever since she was born.
Even though she inherited them from her dad, she is a unique individual--
--and they may assume some very different characteristics as she grows older!

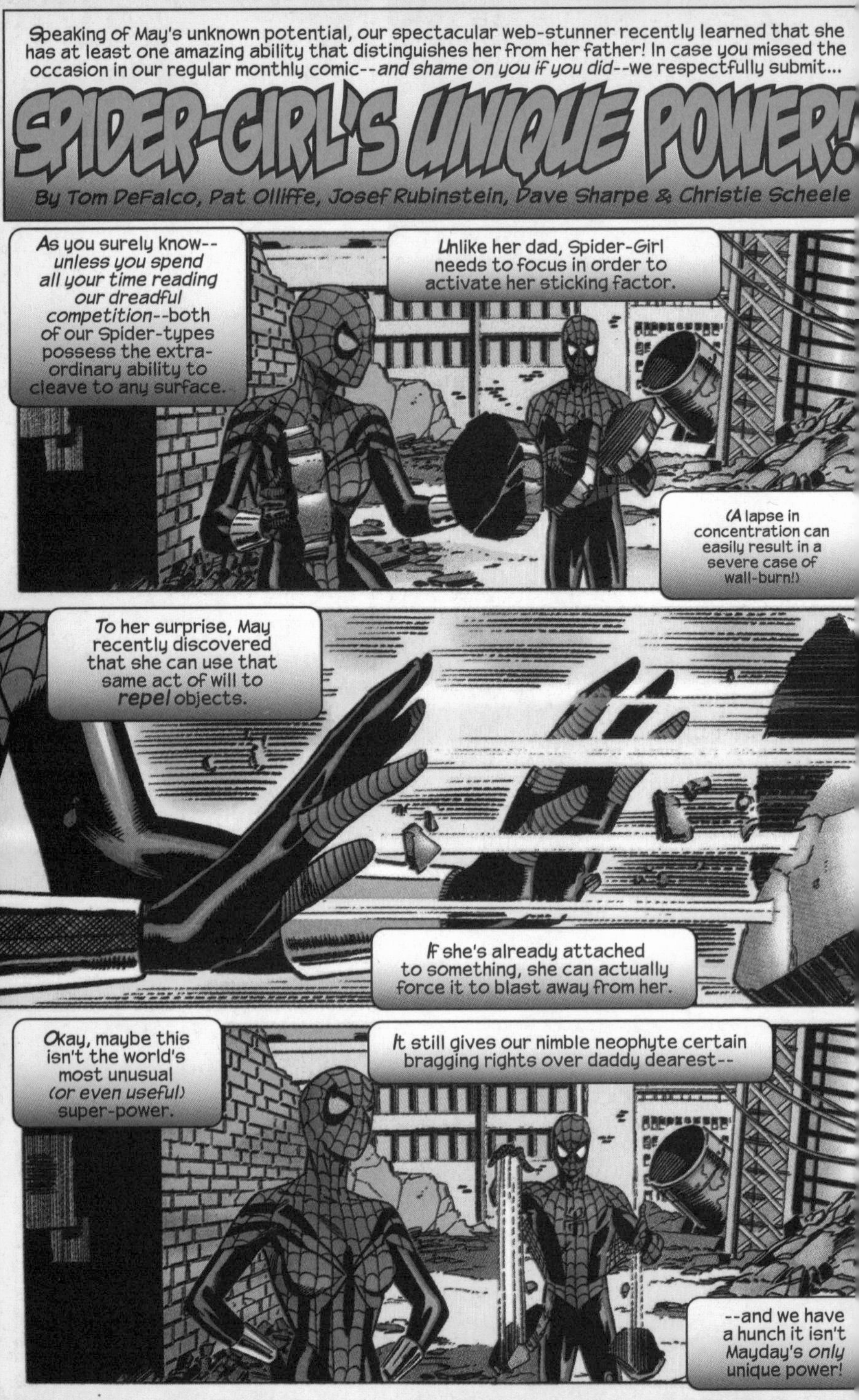
Speaking of May's unknown potential, our spectacular web-stunner recently learned that she has at least one amazing ability that distinguishes her from her father! In case you missed the occasion in our regular monthly comic--and shame on you if you did--we respectfully submit...
SPIDER-GIRL'S UNIQUE POWER!
By Tom DeFalco, Pat Olliffe, Josef Rubinstein, Dave Sharpe & Christie Scheele
As you surely know--unless you spend all your time reading our dreadful competition--both of our Spider-types possess the extra-ordinary ability to cleave to any surface.
Unlike her dad, Spider-Girl needs to focus in order to activate her sticking factor.
(A lapse in concentration can easily result in a severe case of wall-burn!)
To her surprise, May recently discovered that she can use that same act of will to repel objects.
If she's already attached to something, she can actually force it to blast away from her.
Okay, maybe this isn't the world's most unusual (or even useful) super-power.
It still gives our nimble neophyte certain bragging rights over daddy dearest--
--and we have a hunch it isn't Mayday's only unique power!

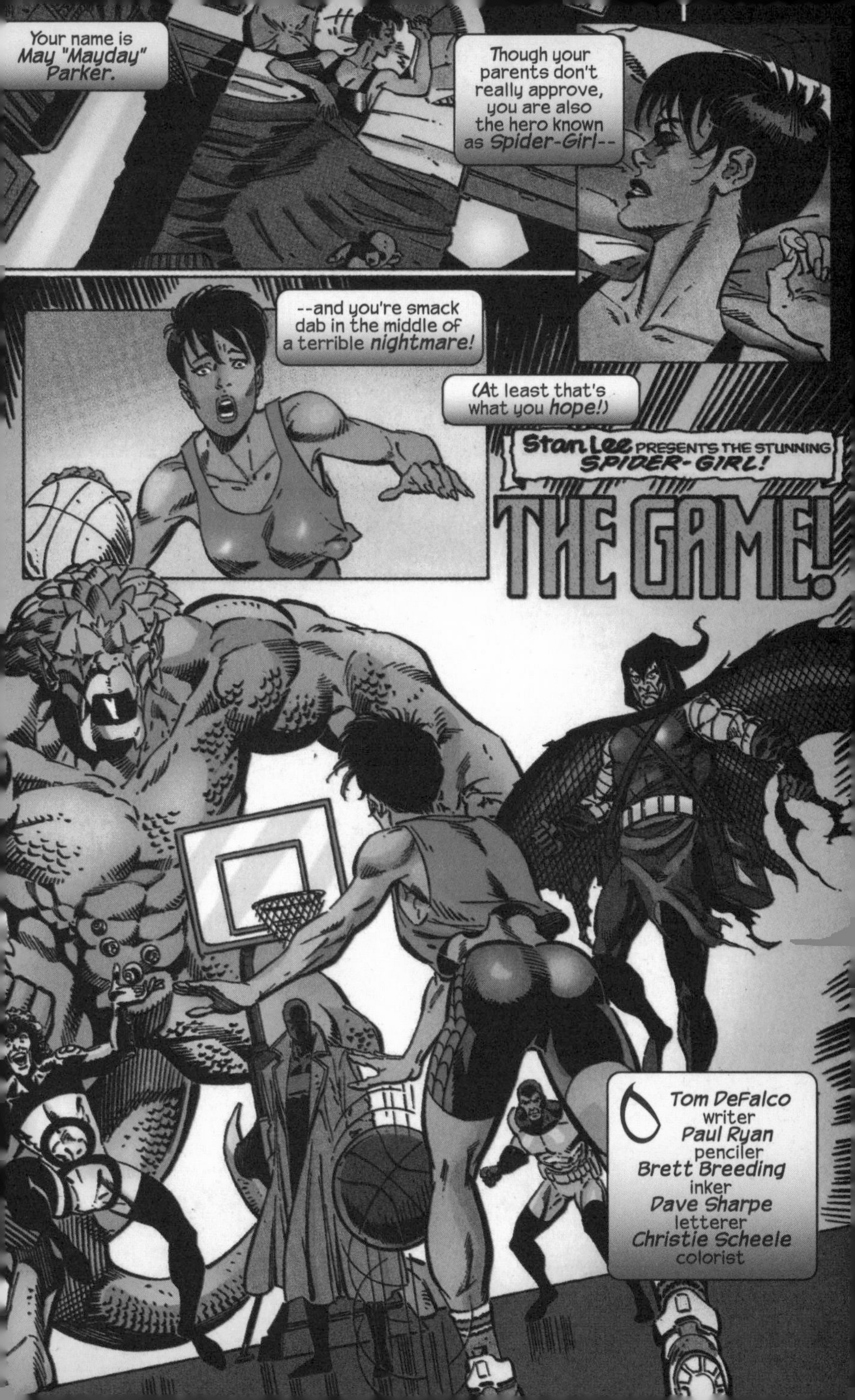
Your name is May "Mayday" Parker.
Though your parents don't really approve, you are also the hero known as Spider-Girl--
--and you're smack dab in the middle of a terrible nightmare!
(At least that's what you hope!)
Stan Lee PRESENTS THE STUNNING SPIDER-GIRL!
THE GAME!
Tom DeFalco writer
Paul Ryan penciler
Brett Breeding inker
Dave Sharpe letterer
Christie Scheele colorist

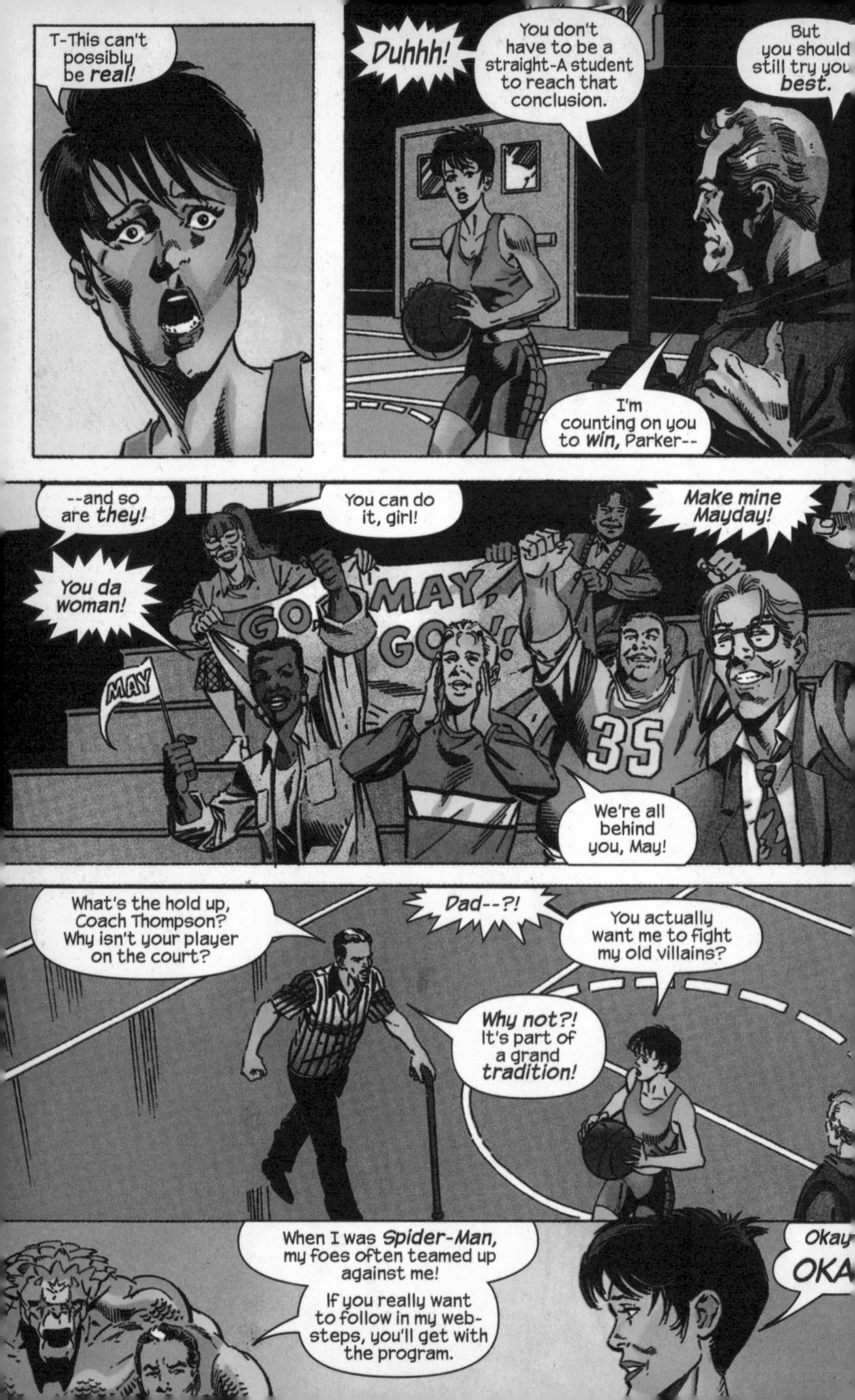
T-This can't possibly be real!
Duhhh!
You don't have to be a straight-A student to reach that conclusion.
But you should still try you best.
I'm counting on you to win, Parker--
--and so are they!
You can do it, girl!
Make mine Mayday!
You da woman!
GO MAY, GO!!
MAY
35
We're all behind you, May!
What's the hold up, Coach Thompson? Why isn't your player on the court?
Dad--?!
You actually want me to fight my old villains?
Why not?! It's part of a grand tradition!
When I was Spider-Man, my foes often teamed up against me!
If you really want to follow in my web-steps, you'll get with the program.

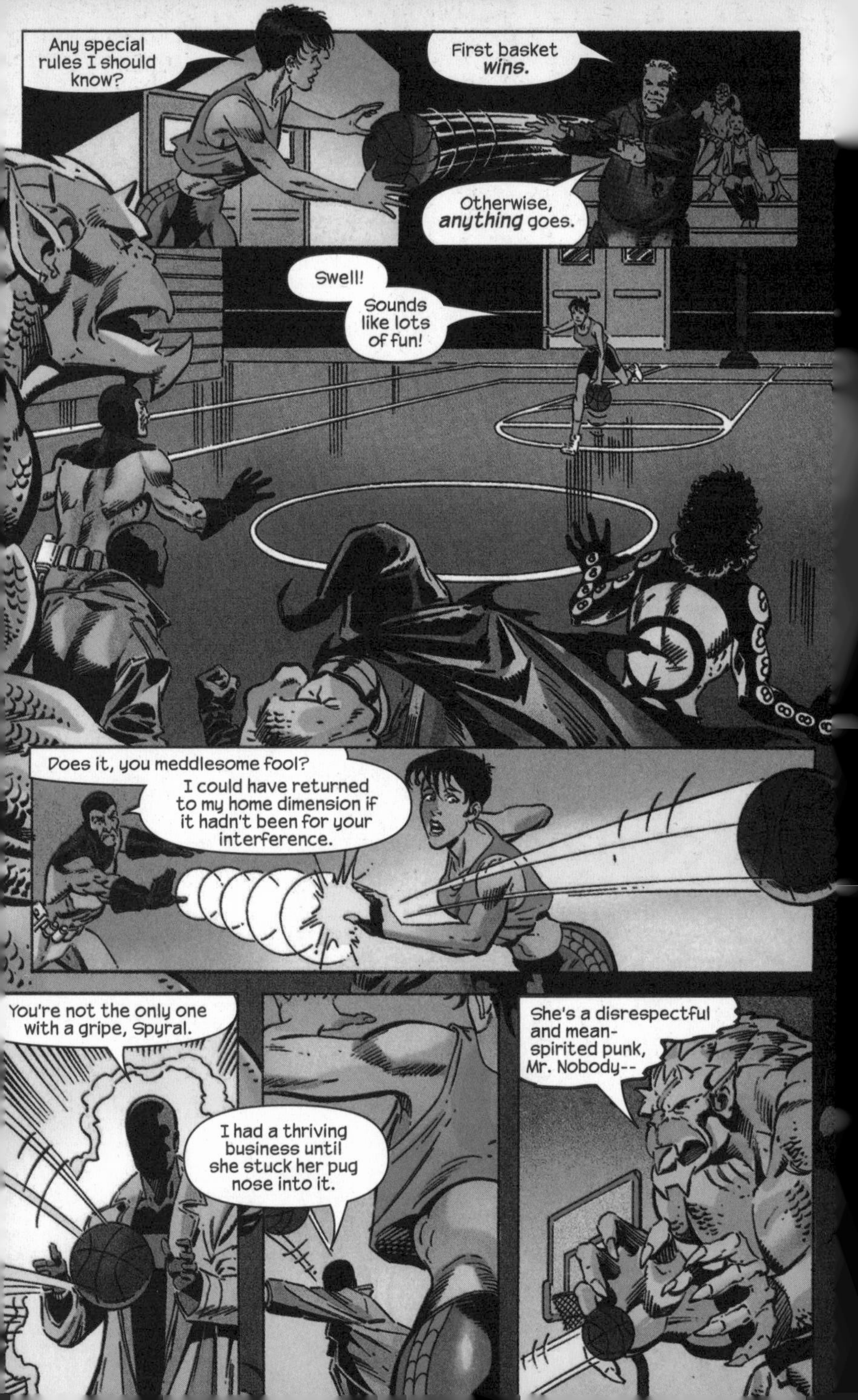
Any special rules I should know?
First basket *wins.*
Otherwise, *anything* goes.
Swell!
Sounds like lots of fun!
Does it, you meddlesome fool?
I could have returned to my home dimension if it hadn't been for your interference.
You're not the only one with a gripe, Spyral.
I had a thriving business until she stuck her pug nose into it.
She's a disrespectful and mean-spirited punk, Mr. Nobody--

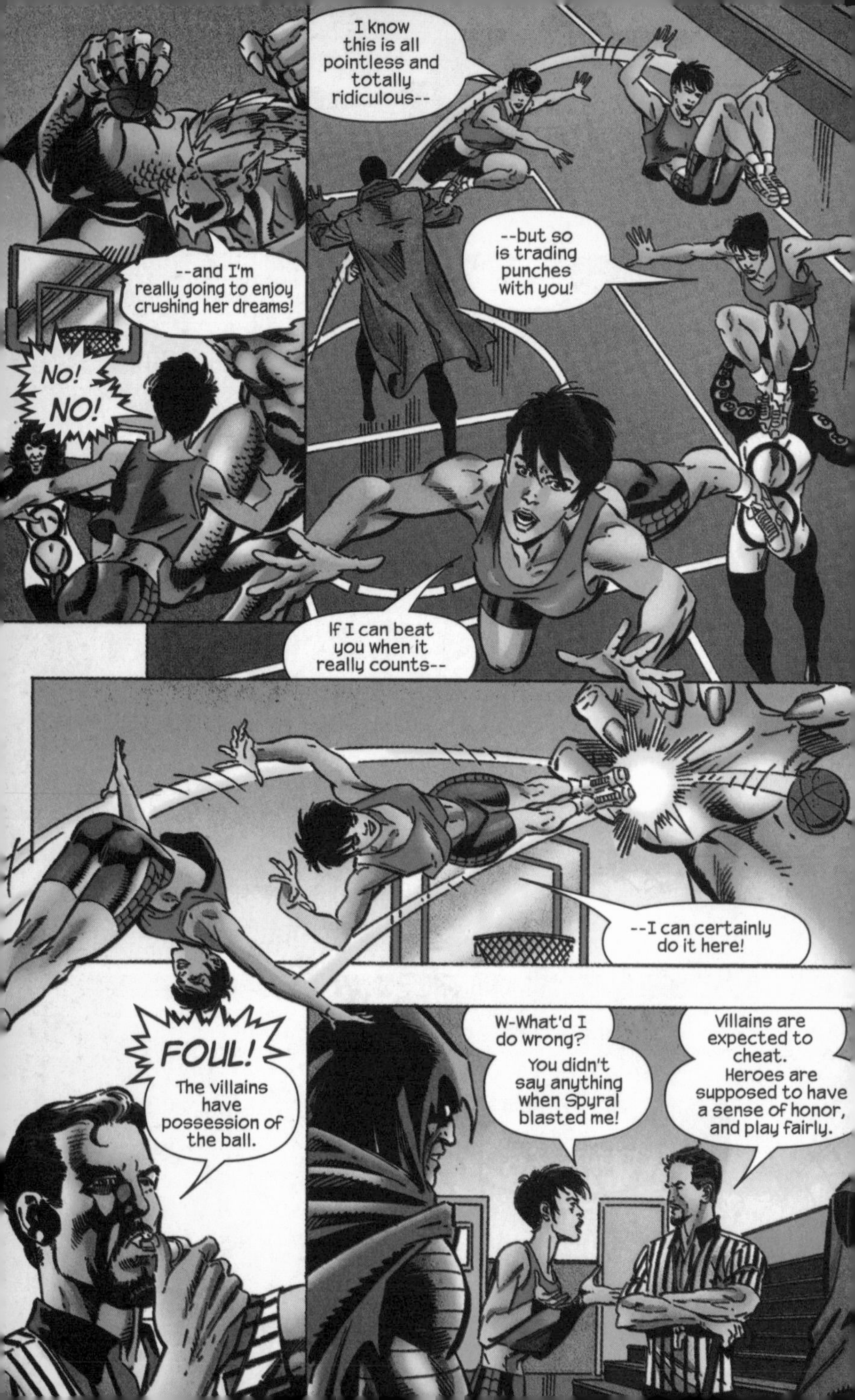
--and I'm really going to enjoy crushing her dreams!
NO! NO!
I know this is all pointless and totally ridiculous--
--but so is trading punches with you!
If I can beat you when it really counts--
--I can certainly do it here!
FOUL!
The villains have possession of the ball.
W-What'd I do wrong?
You didn't say anything when Spyral blasted me!
Villains are expected to cheat.
Heroes are supposed to have a sense of honor, and play fairly.

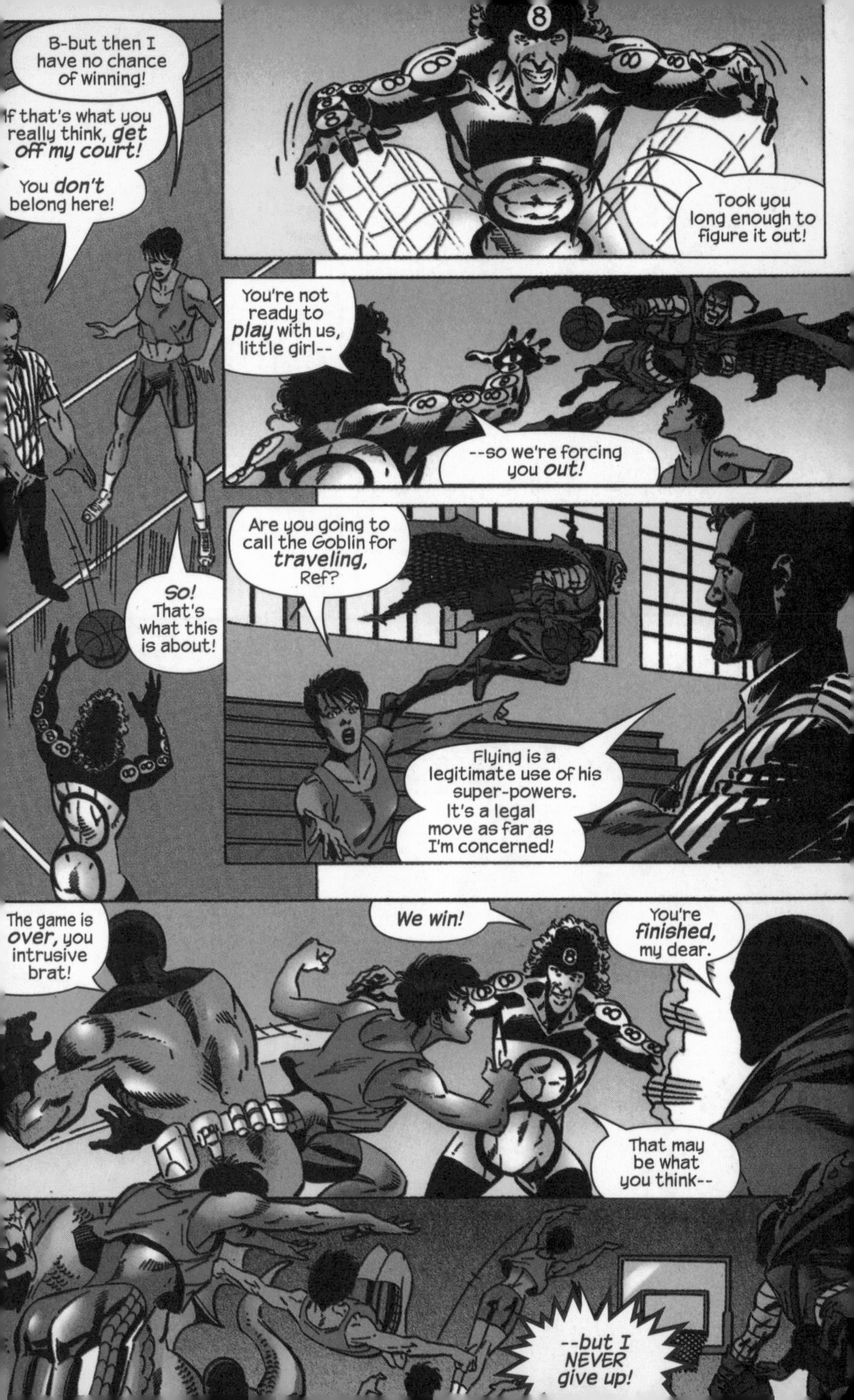
B-but then I have no chance of winning!
If that's what you really think, get off my court!
You don't belong here!
Took you long enough to figure it out!
You're not ready to play with us, little girl--
--so we're forcing you out!
So! That's what this is about!
Are you going to call the Goblin for traveling, Ref?
Flying is a legitimate use of his super-powers. It's a legal move as far as I'm concerned!
The game is over, you intrusive brat!
We win!
You're finished, my dear.
That may be what you think--
--but I NEVER give up!

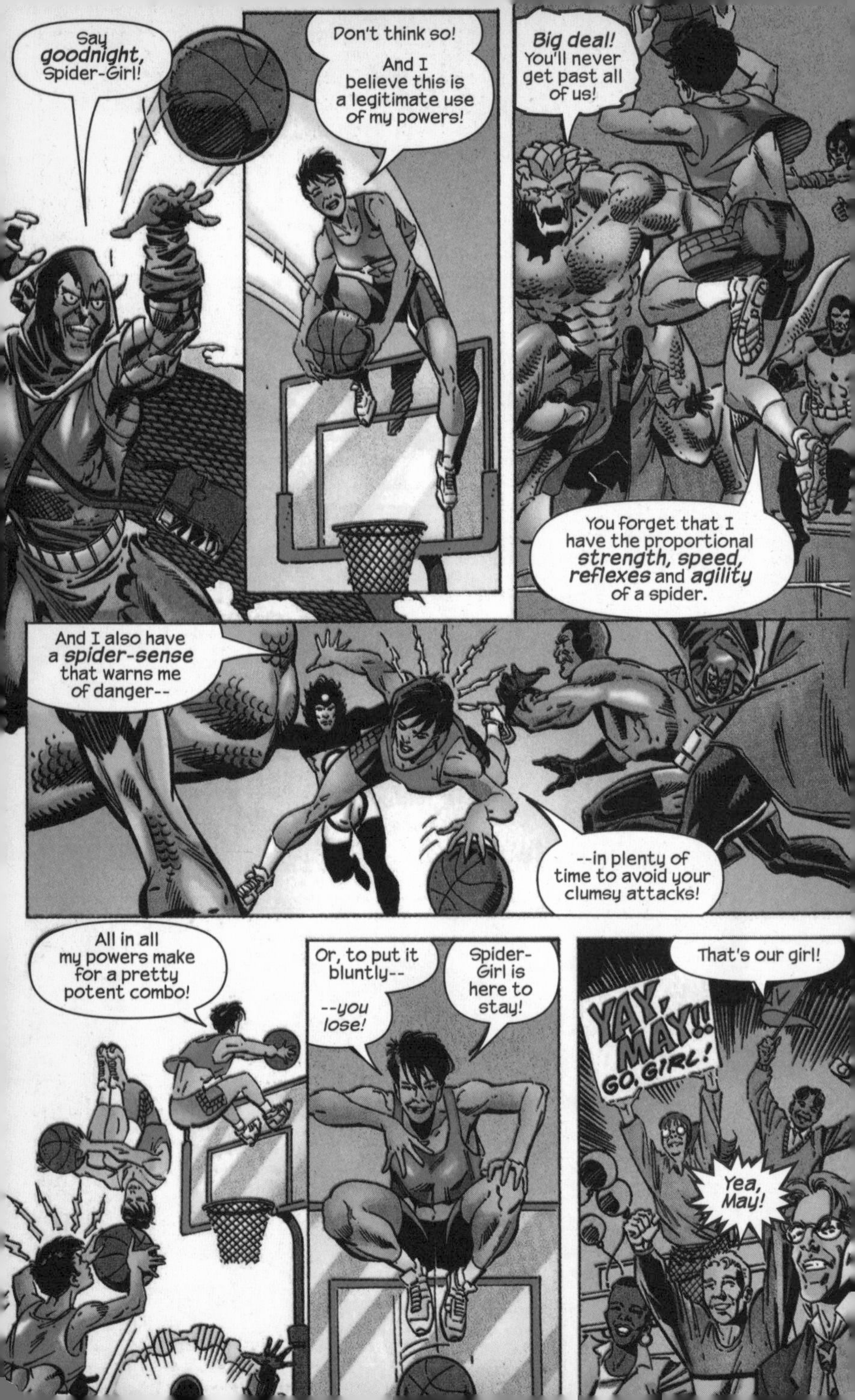
Say *goodnight,* Spider-Girl!
Don't think so!
And I believe this is a legitimate use of my powers!
Big deal! You'll never get past all of us!
You forget that I have the proportional *strength, speed, reflexes* and *agility* of a spider.
And I also have a *spider-sense* that warns me of danger--
--in plenty of time to avoid your clumsy attacks!
All in all my powers make for a pretty potent combo!
Or, to put it bluntly--
--you lose!
Spider-Girl is here to stay!
That's our girl!
YAY, MAY!! GO, GIRL!
Yea, May!

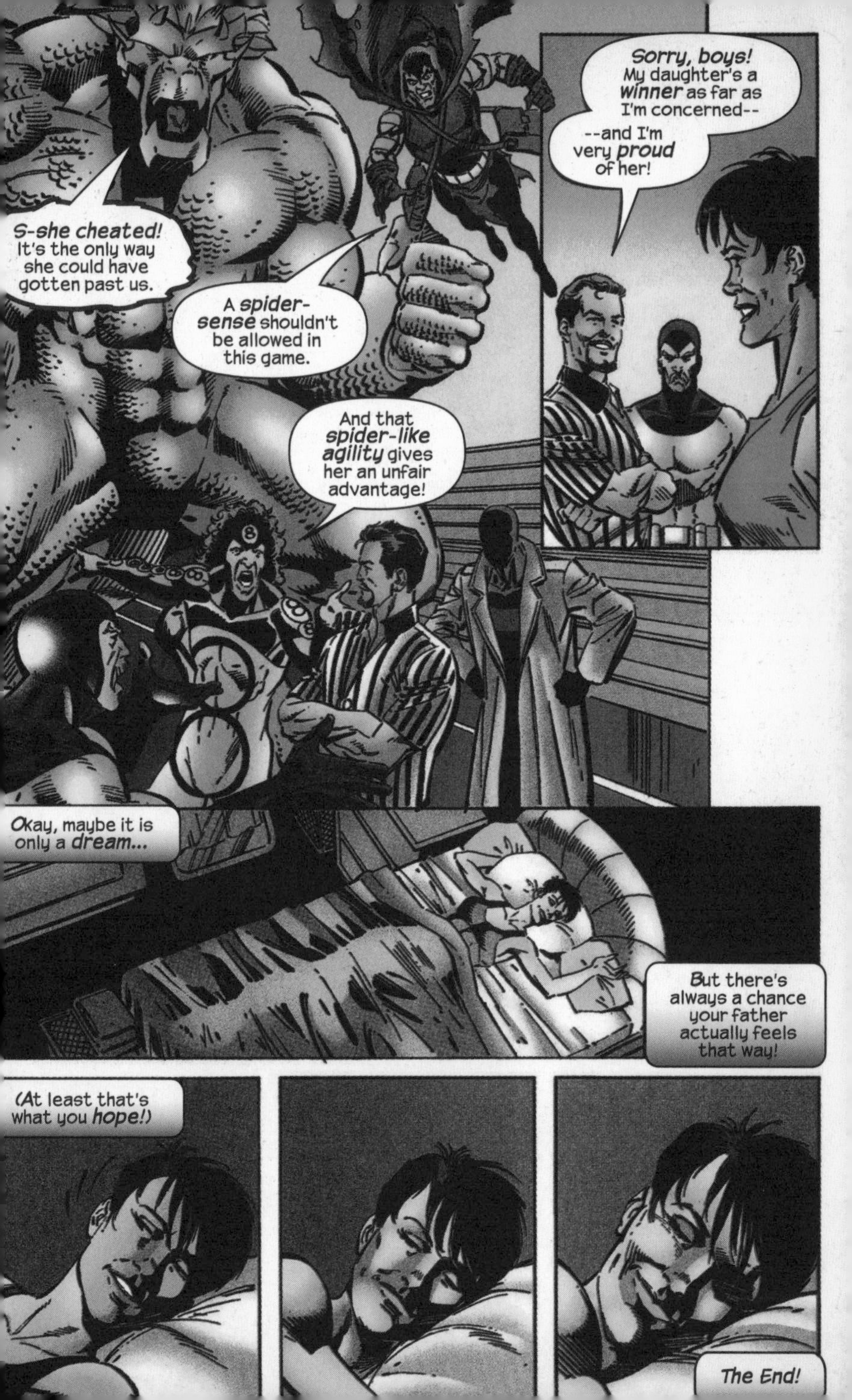
S-she cheated! It's the only way she could have gotten past us.
A spider-sense shouldn't be allowed in this game.
And that spider-like agility gives her an unfair advantage!
Sorry, boys! My daughter's a winner as far as I'm concerned--
--and I'm very proud of her!
Okay, maybe it is only a dream...
But there's always a chance your father actually feels that way!
(At least that's what you hope!)
The End!

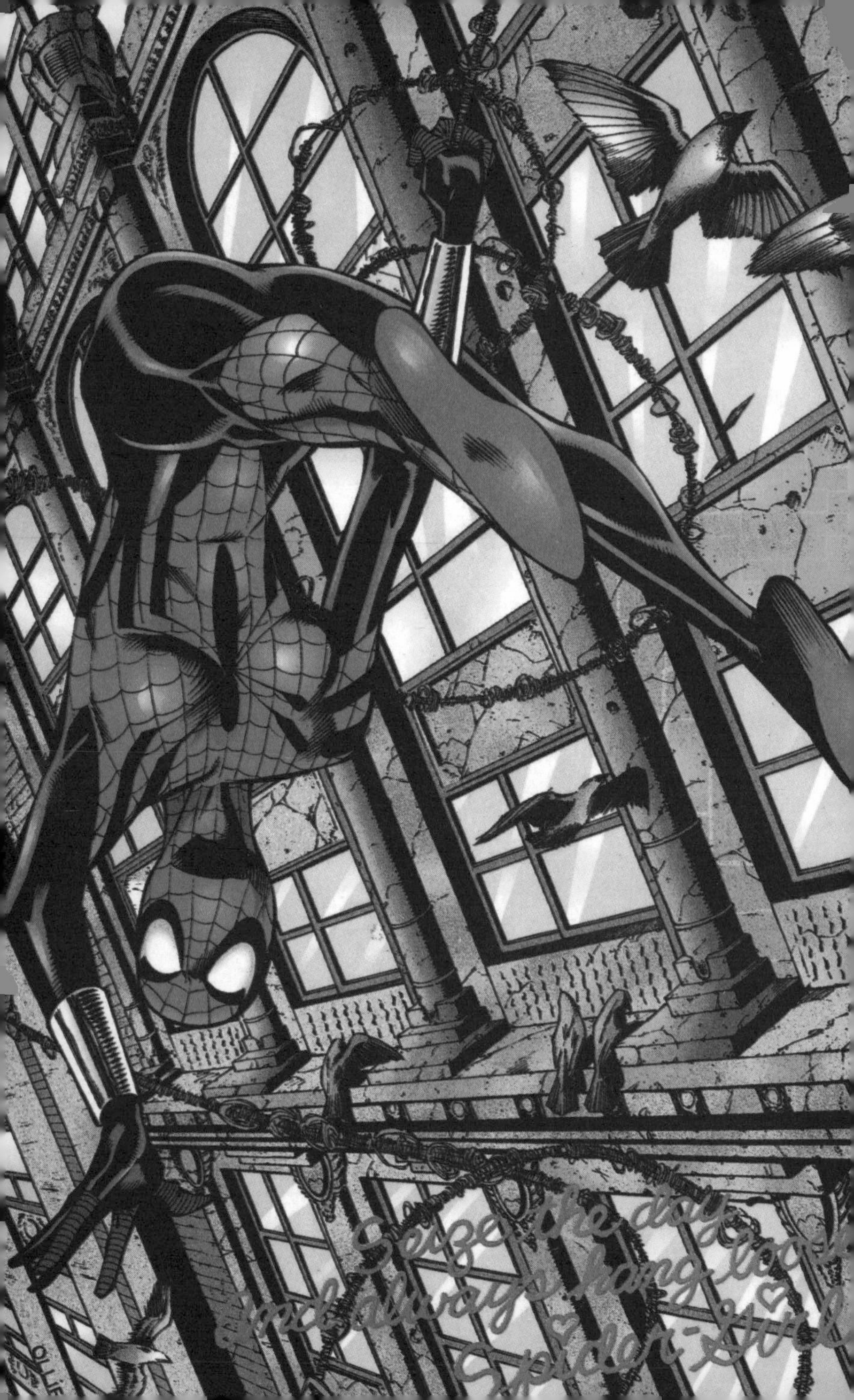
Seize the day
always hang
Spider-Girl

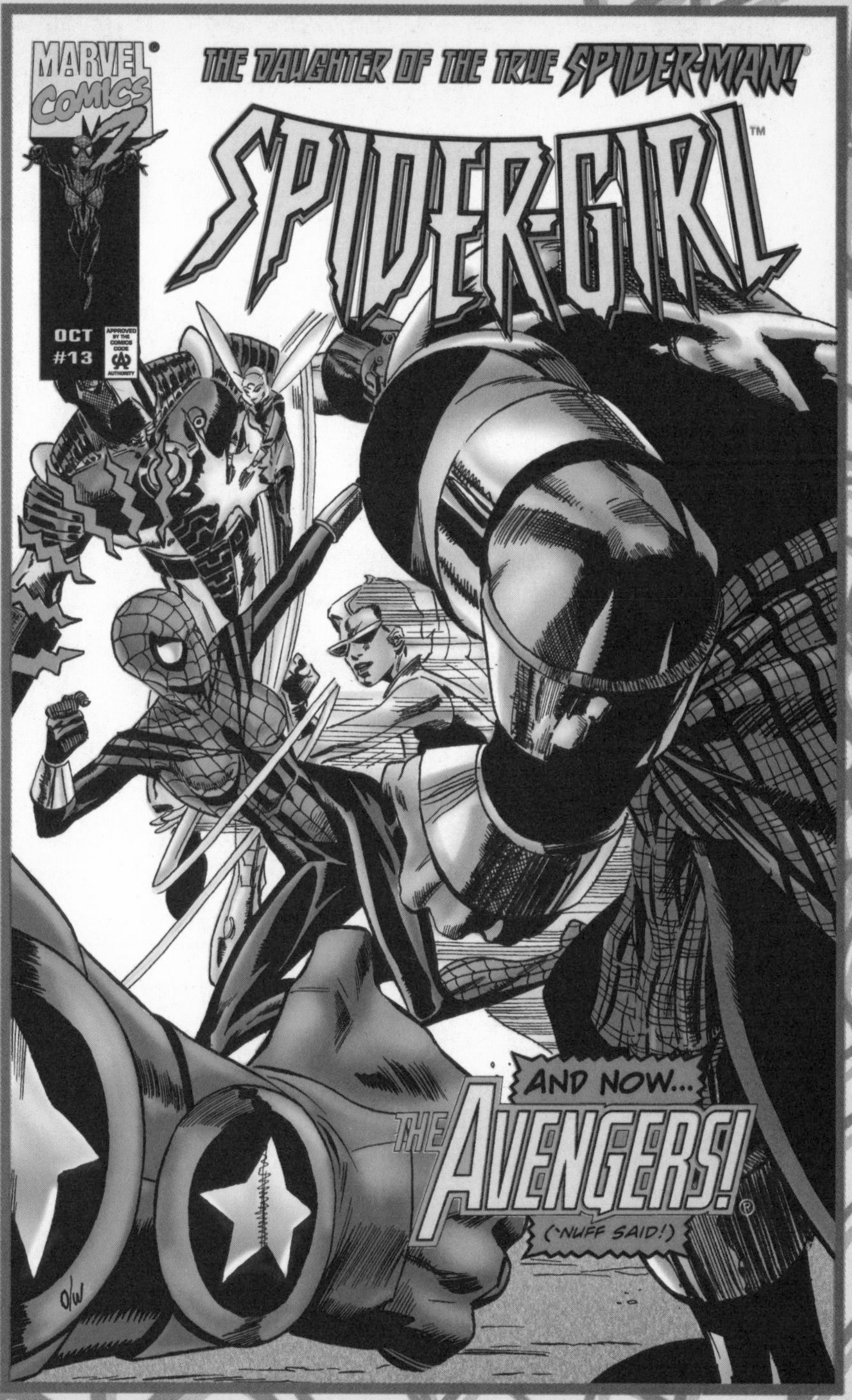
MARVEL COMICS
THE DAUGHTER OF THE TRUE SPIDER-MAN!
SPIDER-GIRL
OCT
#13
APPROVED BY THE COMICS CODE AUTHORITY
AND NOW...
THE AVENGERS!
('NUFF SAID!)

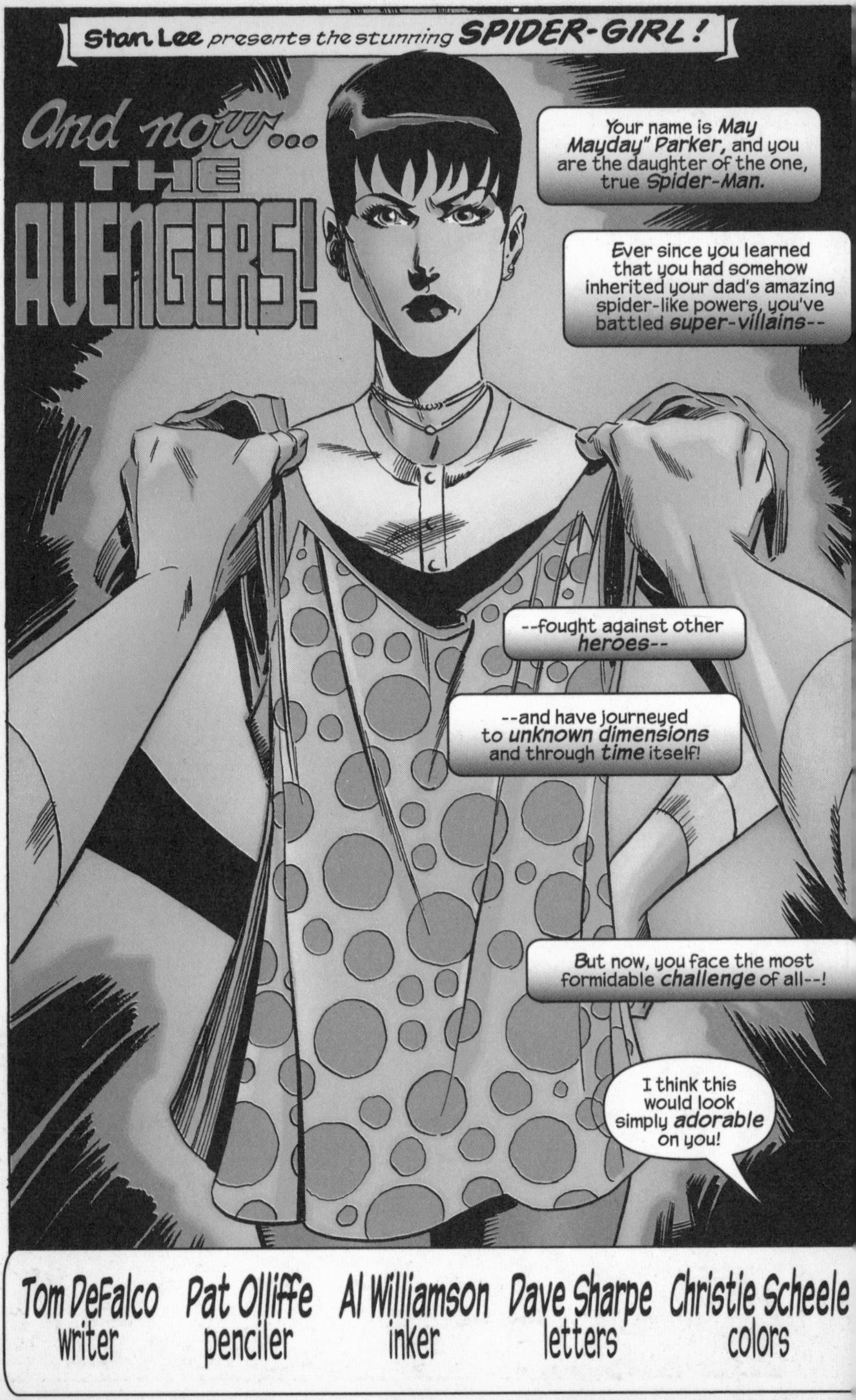
Stan Lee presents the stunning SPIDER-GIRL!
And now... THE AVENGERS!
Your name is May Mayday" Parker, and you are the daughter of the one, true Spider-Man.
Ever since you learned that you had somehow inherited your dad's amazing spider-like powers, you've battled super-villains--
--fought against other heroes--
--and have journeyed to unknown dimensions and through time itself!
But now, you face the most formidable challenge of all--!
I think this would look simply adorable on you!
Tom DeFalco writer
Pat Olliffe penciler
Al Williamson inker
Dave Sharpe letters
Christie Scheele colors

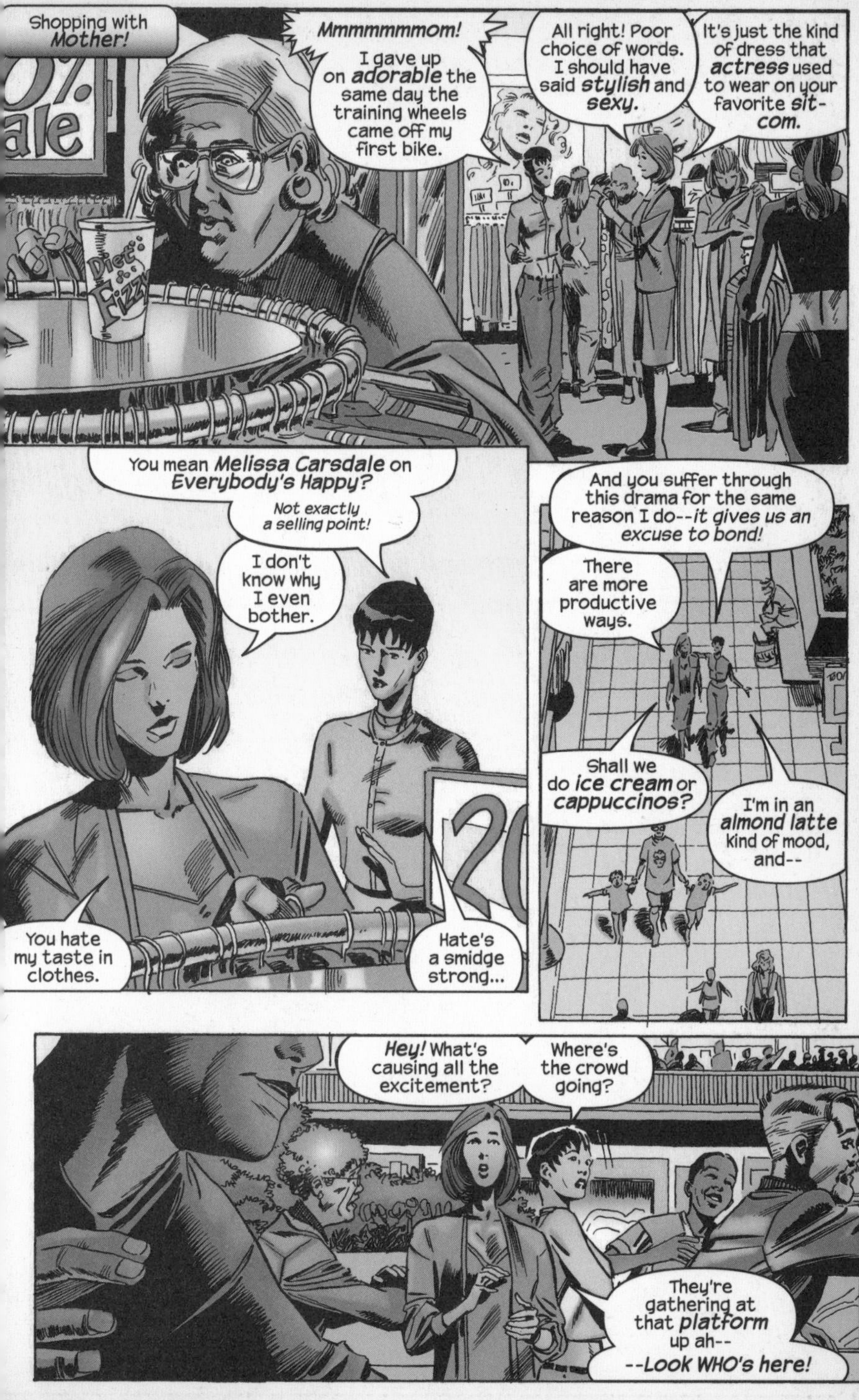
Shopping with Mother!
Mmmmmmmom! I gave up on adorable the same day the training wheels came off my first bike.
All right! Poor choice of words. I should have said stylish and sexy.
It's just the kind of dress that actress used to wear on your favorite sit-com.
You mean Melissa Carsdale on Everybody's Happy?
Not exactly a selling point!
I don't know why I even bother.
You hate my taste in clothes.
Hate's a smidge strong...
And you suffer through this drama for the same reason I do--it gives us an excuse to bond!
There are more productive ways.
Shall we do ice cream or cappuccinos?
I'm in an almond latte kind of mood, and--
Hey! What's causing all the excitement?
Where's the crowd going?
They're gathering at that platform up ah--
--Look WHO's here!

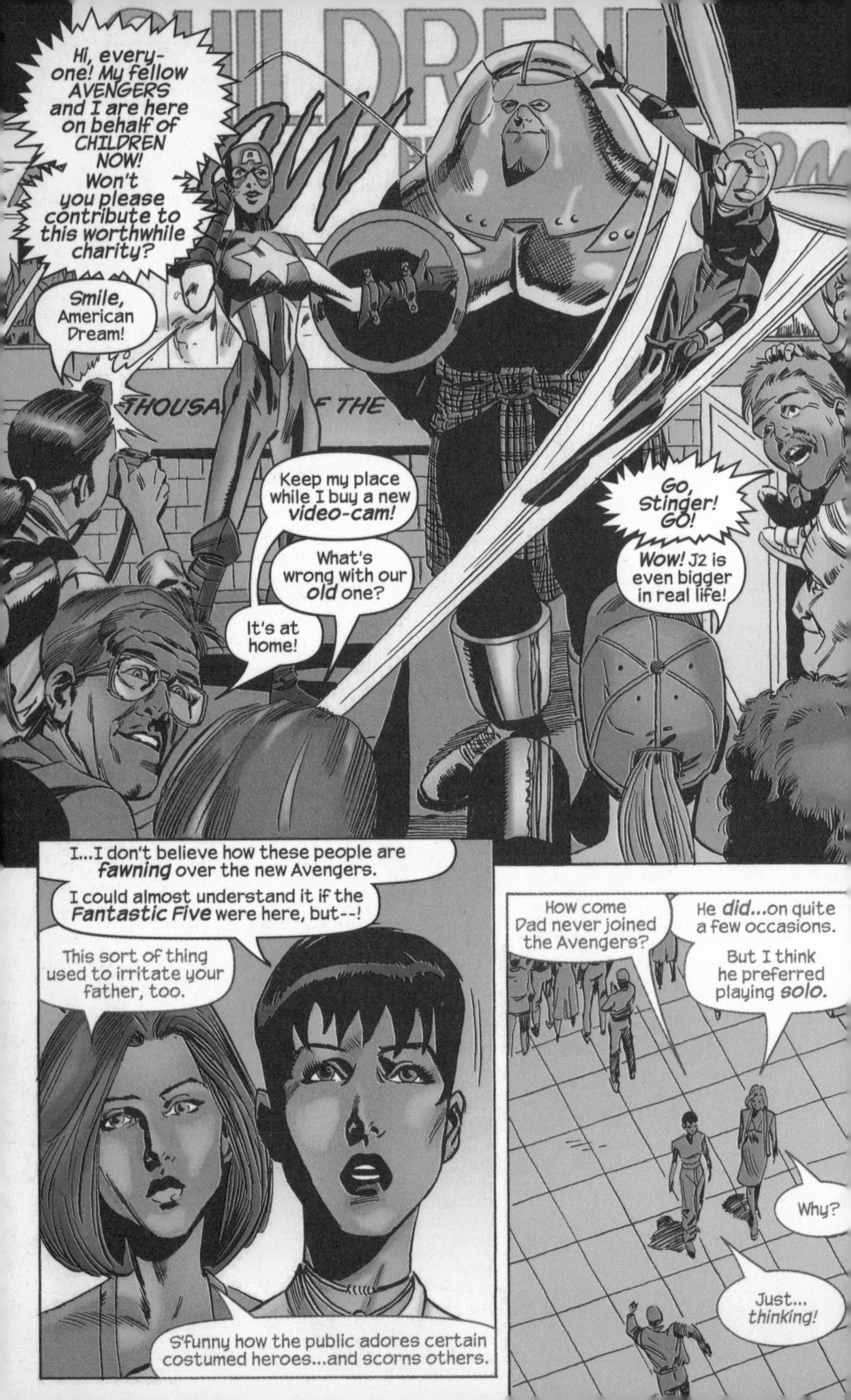

Hi, every-one! My fellow AVENGERS and I are here on behalf of CHILDREN NOW! Won't you please contribute to this worthwhile charity?
Smile, American Dream!
THOUSA F THE
Keep my place while I buy a new video-cam!
What's wrong with our old one?
It's at home!
Go, Stinger! GO!
Wow! J2 is even bigger in real life!
I...I don't believe how these people are fawning over the new Avengers.
I could almost understand it if the Fantastic Five were here, but--!
This sort of thing used to irritate your father, too.
S'funny how the public adores certain costumed heroes...and scorns others.
How come Dad never joined the Avengers?
He did...on quite a few occasions.
But I think he preferred playing solo.
Why?
Just... thinking!

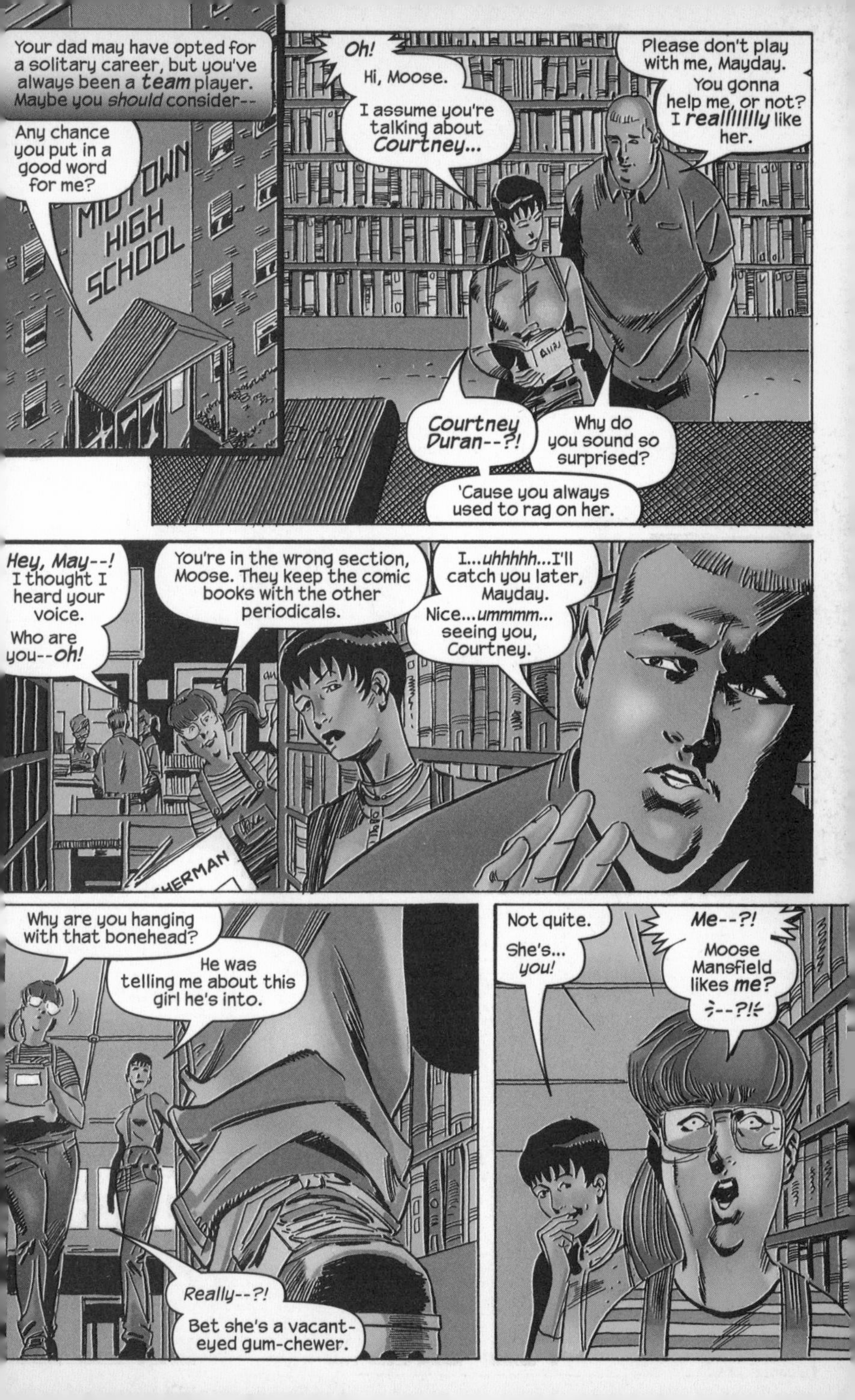
Your dad may have opted for a solitary career, but you've always been a *team* player. Maybe you *should* consider--
Any chance you put in a good word for me?
MIDTOWN HIGH SCHOOL
Oh!
Hi, Moose.
I assume you're talking about *Courtney...*
Please don't play with me, Mayday.
You gonna help me, or not? I *reallllllly* like her.
Courtney Duran--?!
Why do you sound so surprised?
'Cause you always used to rag on her.
Hey, May--! I thought I heard your voice.
Who are you--*oh!*
You're in the wrong section, Moose. They keep the comic books with the other periodicals.
I...*uhhhhh*...I'll catch you later, Mayday.
Nice...*ummmm*... seeing you, Courtney.
Why are you hanging with that bonehead?
He was telling me about this girl he's into.
Really--?!
Bet she's a vacant-eyed gum-chewer.
Not quite.
She's... *you!*
Me--?!
Moose Mansfield likes *me?*
--?!

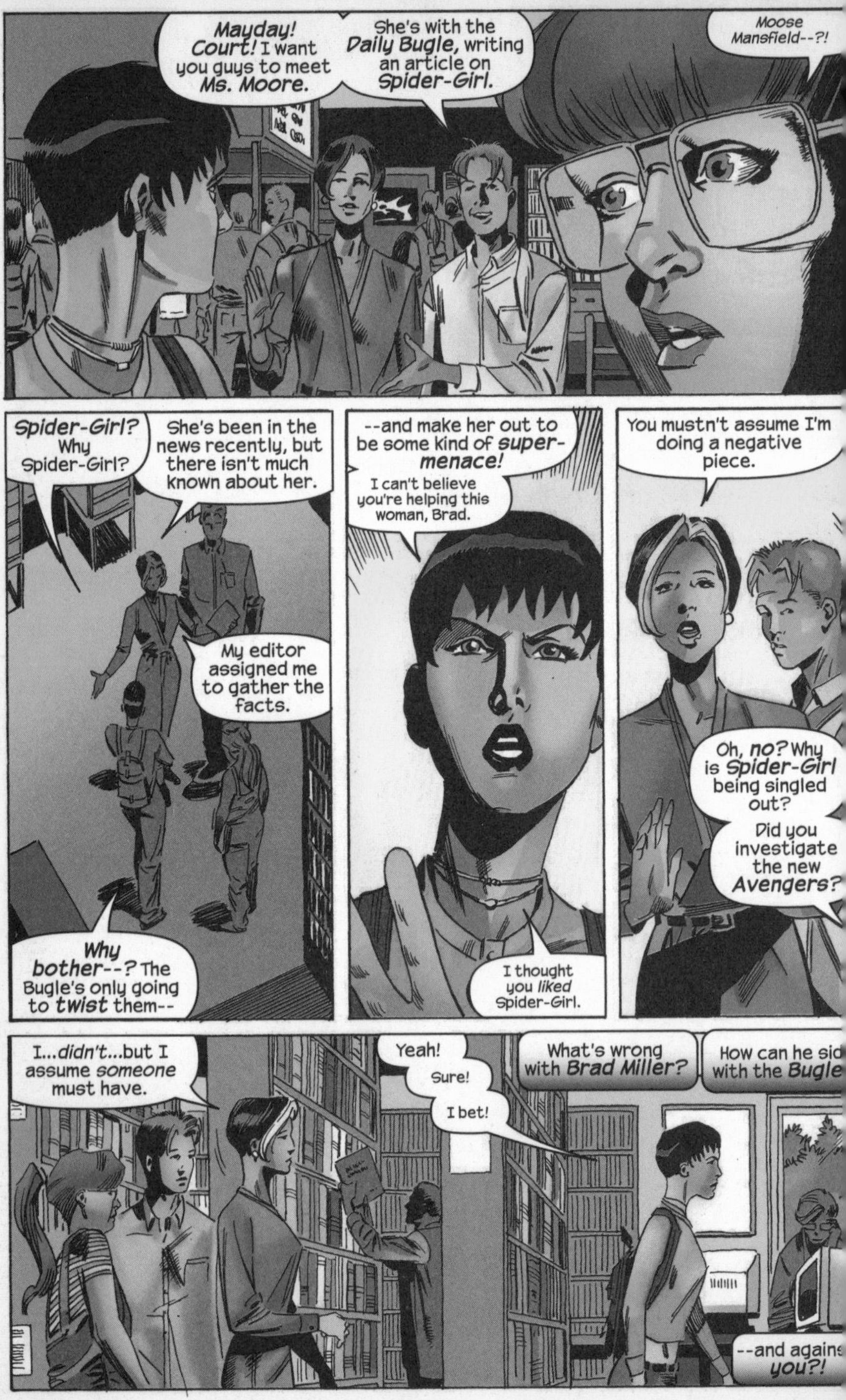
Mayday! Court! I want you guys to meet Ms. Moore.
She's with the Daily Bugle, writing an article on Spider-Girl.
Moose Mansfield--?!
Spider-Girl? Why Spider-Girl?
She's been in the news recently, but there isn't much known about her.
My editor assigned me to gather the facts.
Why bother--? The Bugle's only going to twist them--
--and make her out to be some kind of super-menace!
I can't believe you're helping this woman, Brad.
I thought you liked Spider-Girl.
You mustn't assume I'm doing a negative piece.
Oh, no? Why is Spider-Girl being singled out?
Did you investigate the new Avengers?
I...didn't...but I assume someone must have.
Yeah!
Sure!
I bet!
What's wrong with Brad Miller?
How can he sid with the Bugle
--and agains you?!

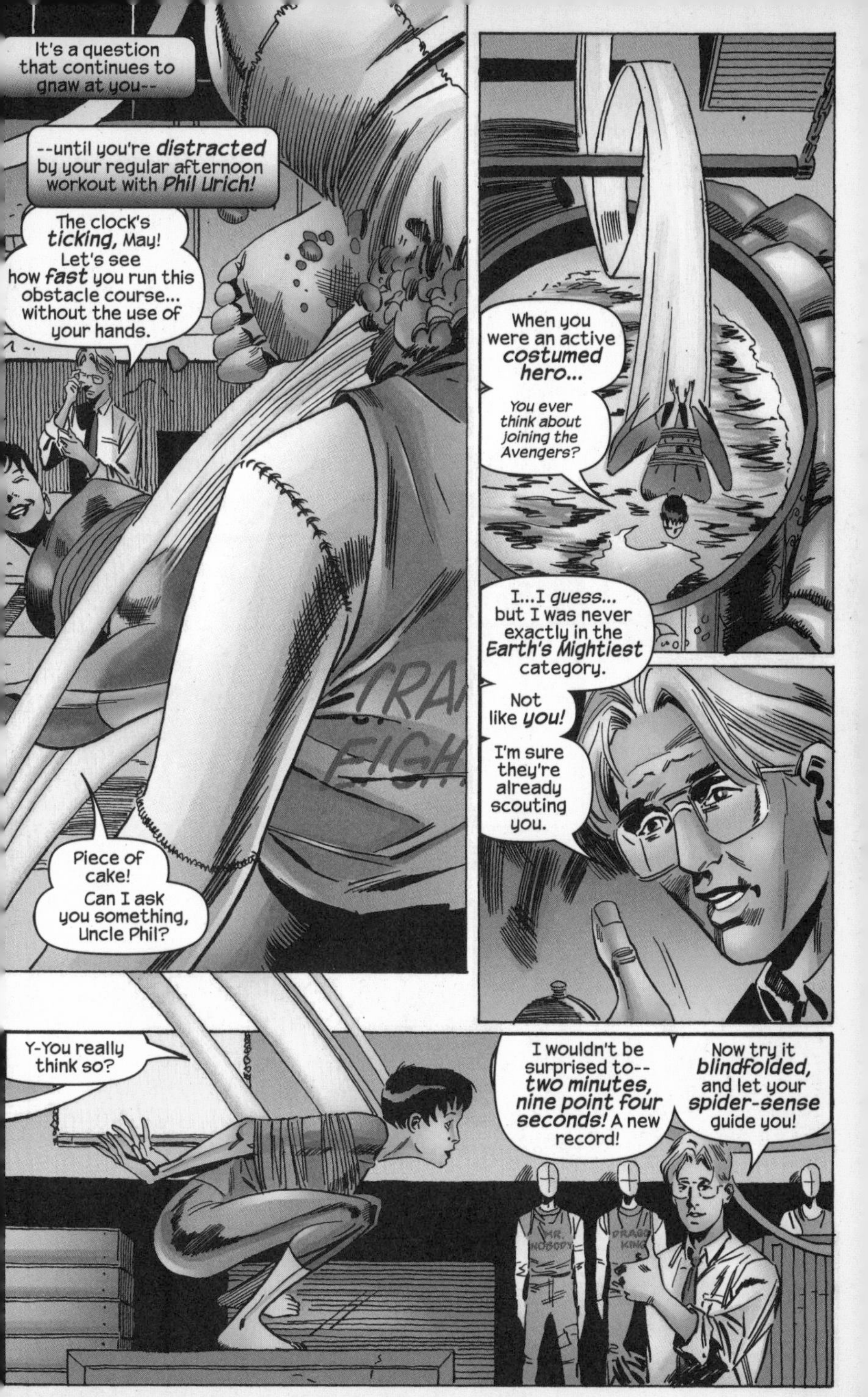
It's a question that continues to gnaw at you--
--until you're *distracted* by your regular afternoon workout with *Phil Urich!*
The clock's *ticking,* May! Let's see how *fast* you run this obstacle course... without the use of your hands.
Piece of cake!
Can I ask you something, Uncle Phil?
When you were an active *costumed hero...*
You ever think about joining the Avengers?
I...I *guess...* but I was never exactly in the *Earth's Mightiest* category.
Not like *you!*
I'm sure they're already scouting you.
Y-You really think so?
I wouldn't be surprised to-- *two minutes, nine point four seconds!* A new record!
Now try it *blindfolded,* and let your *spider-sense* guide you!

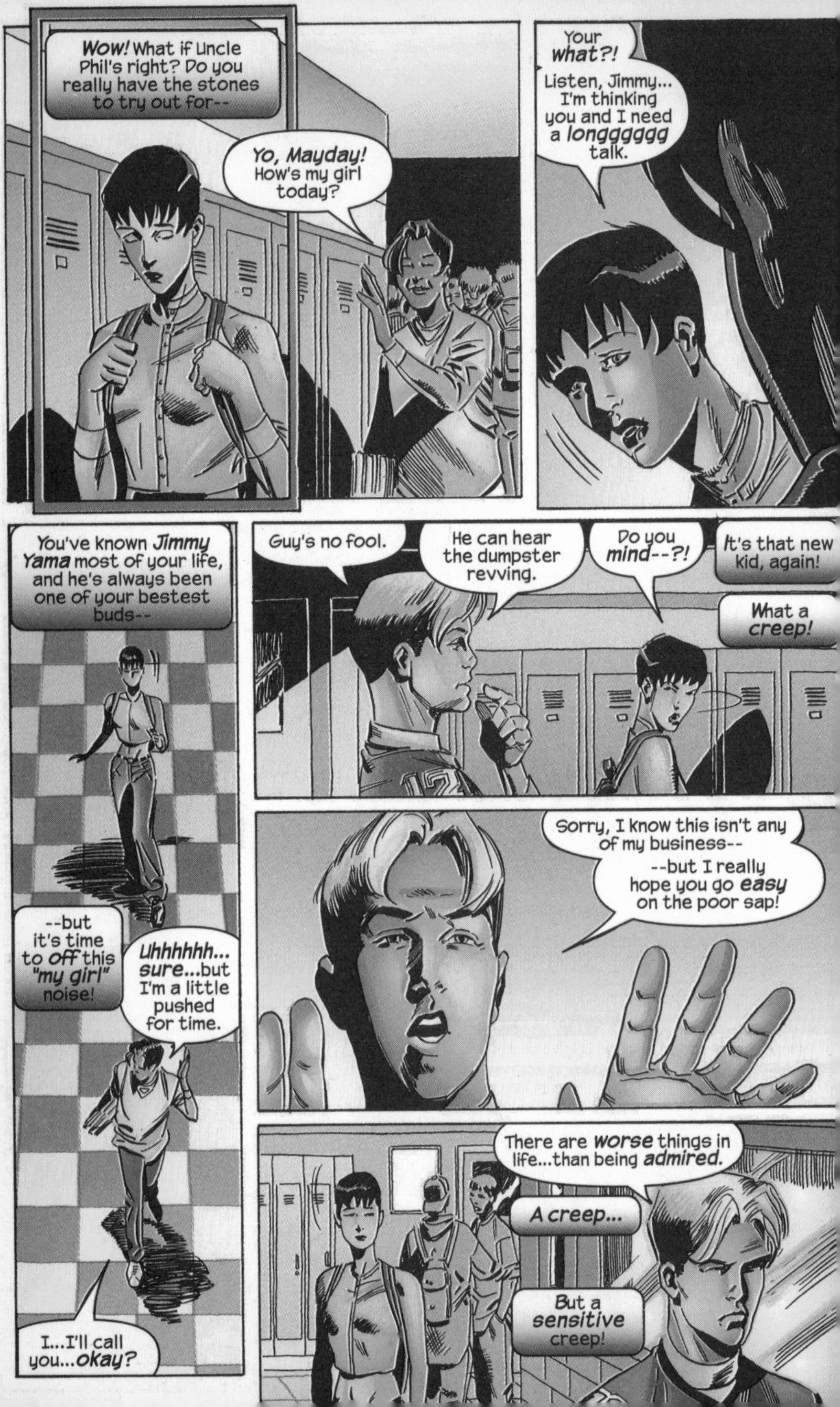
Wow! What if Uncle Phil's right? Do you really have the stones to try out for--
Yo, Mayday! How's my girl today?
Your what?!
Listen, Jimmy... I'm thinking you and I need a longgggggg talk.
You've known Jimmy Yama most of your life, and he's always been one of your bestest buds--
--but it's time to off this "my girl" noise!
Uhhhhhh... sure...but I'm a little pushed for time.
I...I'll call you...okay?
Guy's no fool.
He can hear the dumpster revving.
Do you mind--?!
It's that new kid, again!
What a creep!
Sorry, I know this isn't any of my business--
--but I really hope you go easy on the poor sap!
There are worse things in life...than being admired.
A creep...
But a sensitive creep!

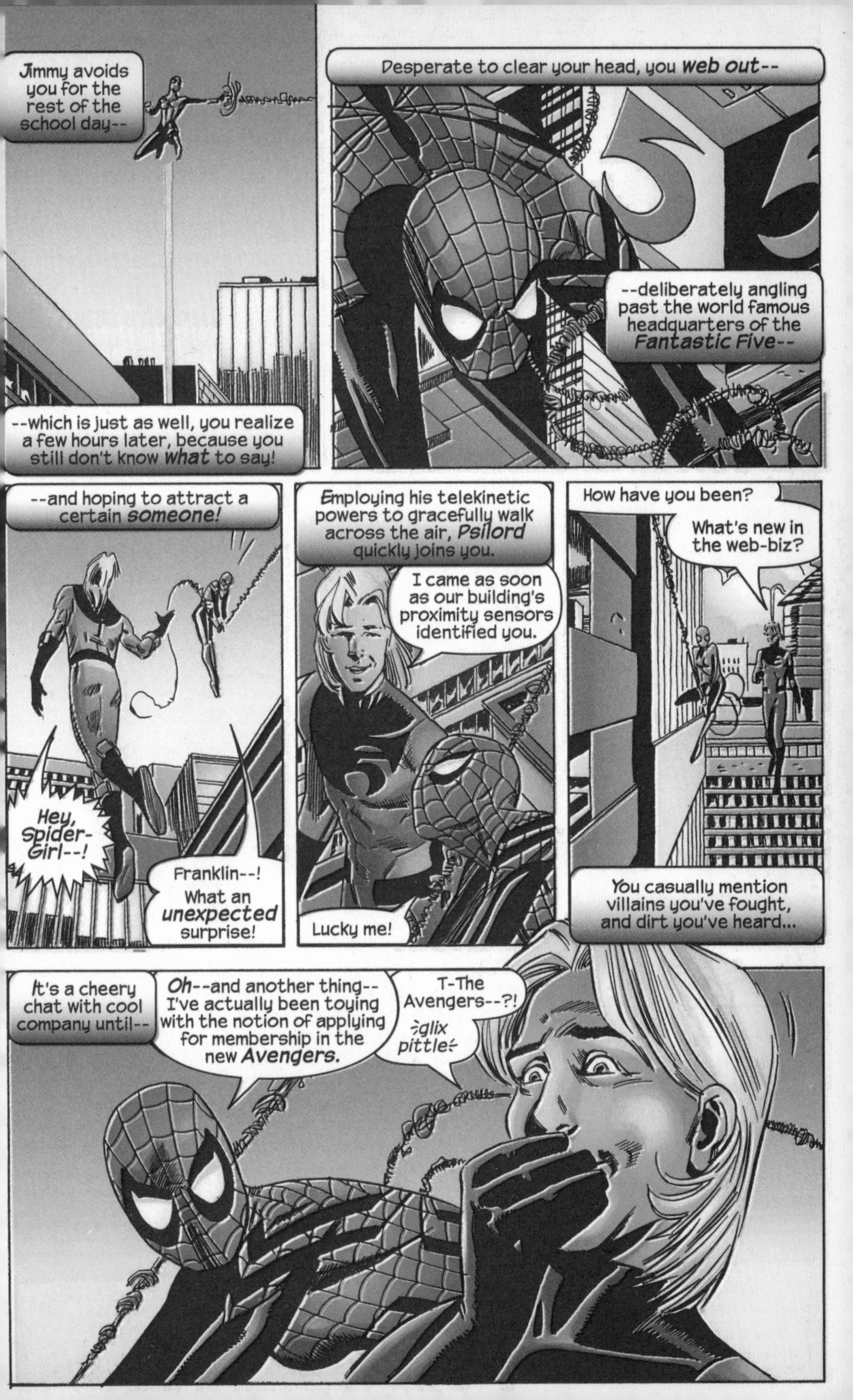

Jimmy avoids you for the rest of the school day--
--which is just as well, you realize a few hours later, because you still don't know *what* to say!
Desperate to clear your head, you *web out*--
--deliberately angling past the world famous headquarters of the *Fantastic Five*--
--and hoping to attract a certain *someone!*
Hey, Spider-Girl--!
Franklin--! What an *unexpected* surprise!
Employing his telekinetic powers to gracefully walk across the air, *Psilord* quickly joins you.
I came as soon as our building's proximity sensors identified you.
Lucky me!
How have you been?
What's new in the web-biz?
You casually mention villains you've fought, and dirt you've heard...
It's a cheery chat with cool company until--
Oh--and another thing-- I've actually been toying with the notion of applying for membership in the new *Avengers.*
T-The Avengers--?!
glix pittle

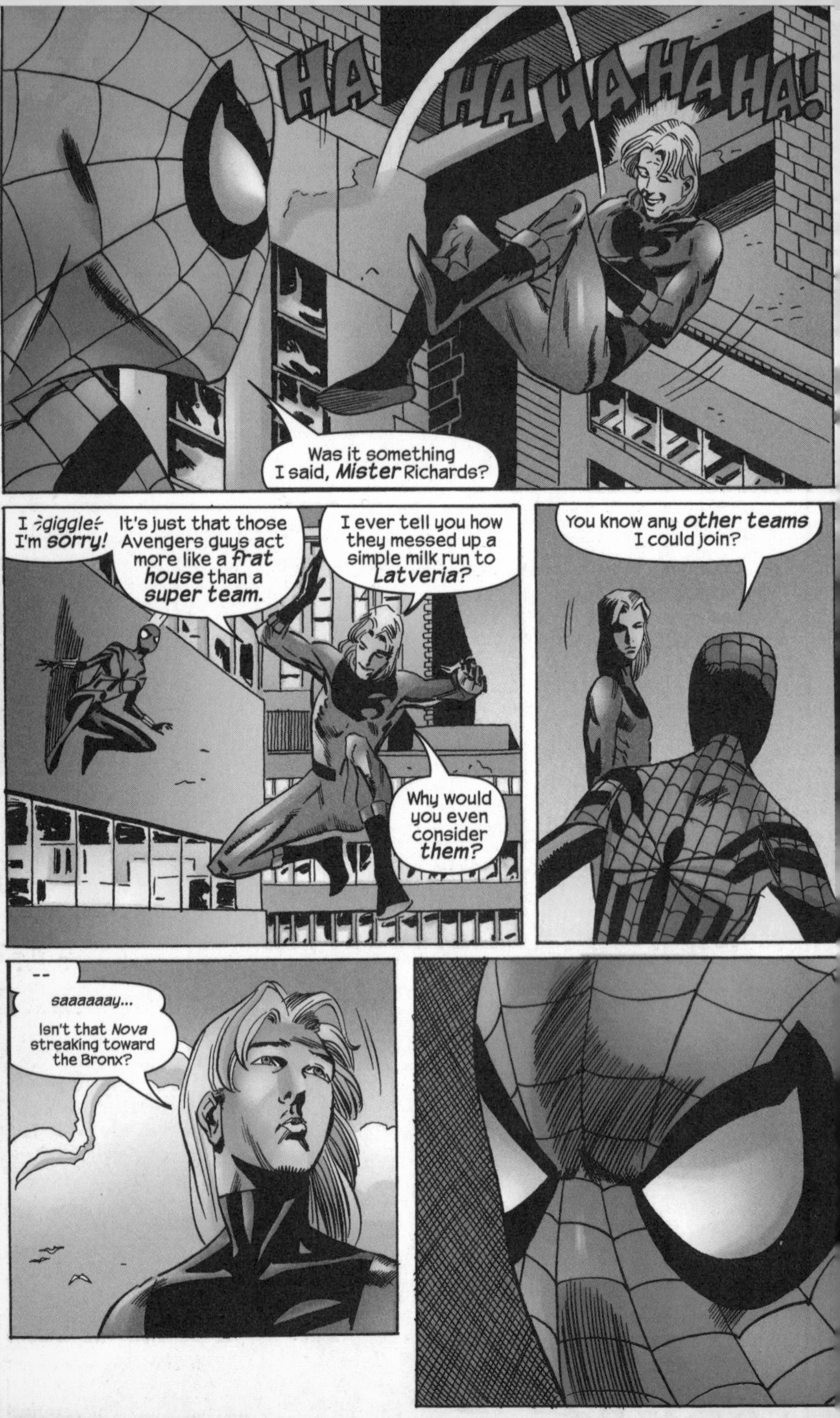
HA HA HA HA HA HA!
Was it something I said, *Mister* Richards?
I *giggle* I'm *sorry!*
It's just that those Avengers guys act more like a *frat house* than a *super team.*
I ever tell you how they messed up a simple milk run to *Latveria?*
Why would you even consider *them?*
You know any *other teams* I could join?
--
saaaaaay...
Isn't that *Nova* streaking toward the Bronx?

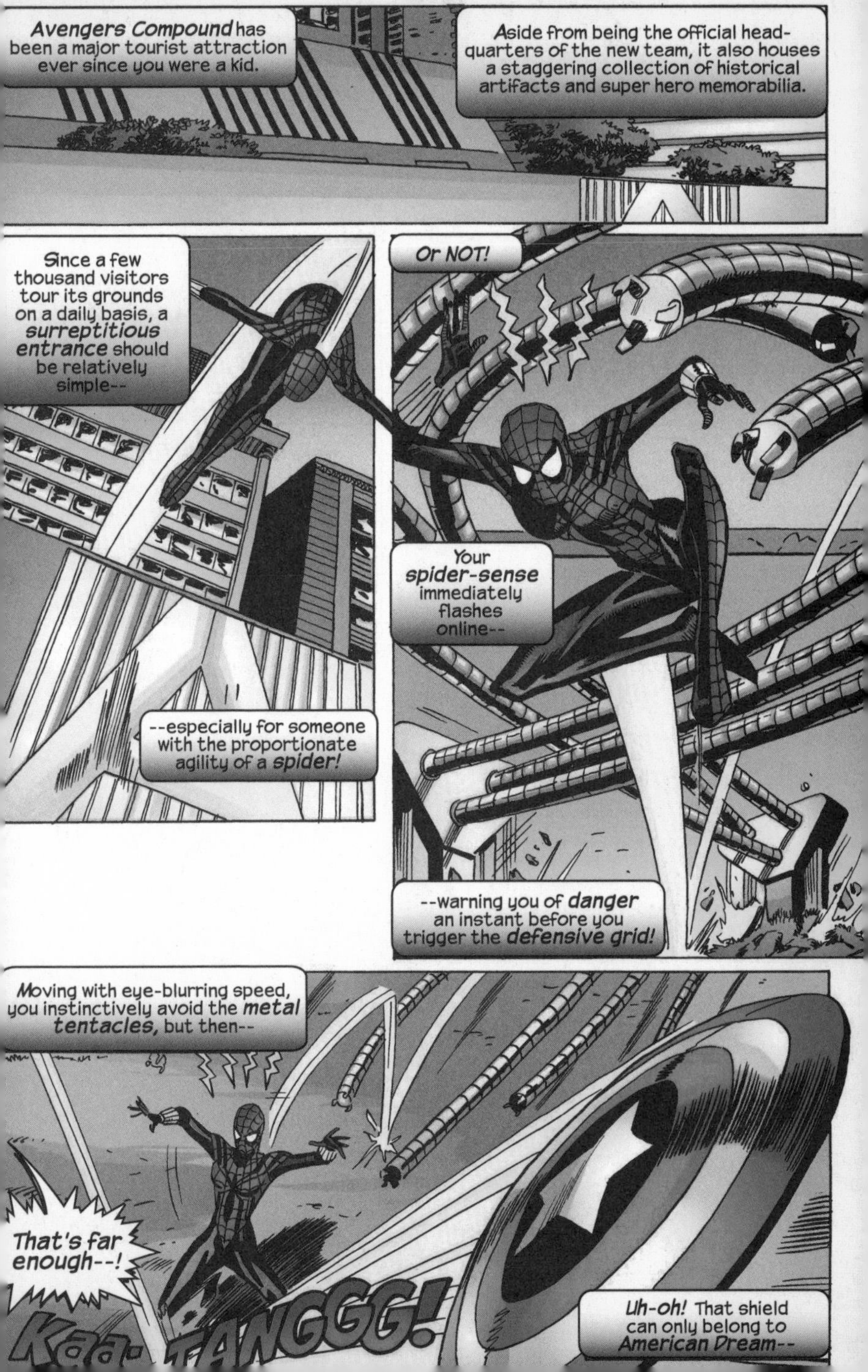
Avengers Compound has been a major tourist attraction ever since you were a kid.
Aside from being the official head-quarters of the new team, it also houses a staggering collection of historical artifacts and super hero memorabilia.
Since a few thousand visitors tour its grounds on a daily basis, a surreptitious entrance should be relatively simple--
--especially for someone with the proportionate agility of a spider!
Or NOT!
Your spider-sense immediately flashes online--
--warning you of danger an instant before you trigger the defensive grid!
Moving with eye-blurring speed, you instinctively avoid the metal tentacles, but then--
That's far enough--!
KAA-TANGGG!
Uh-oh! That shield can only belong to American Dream--

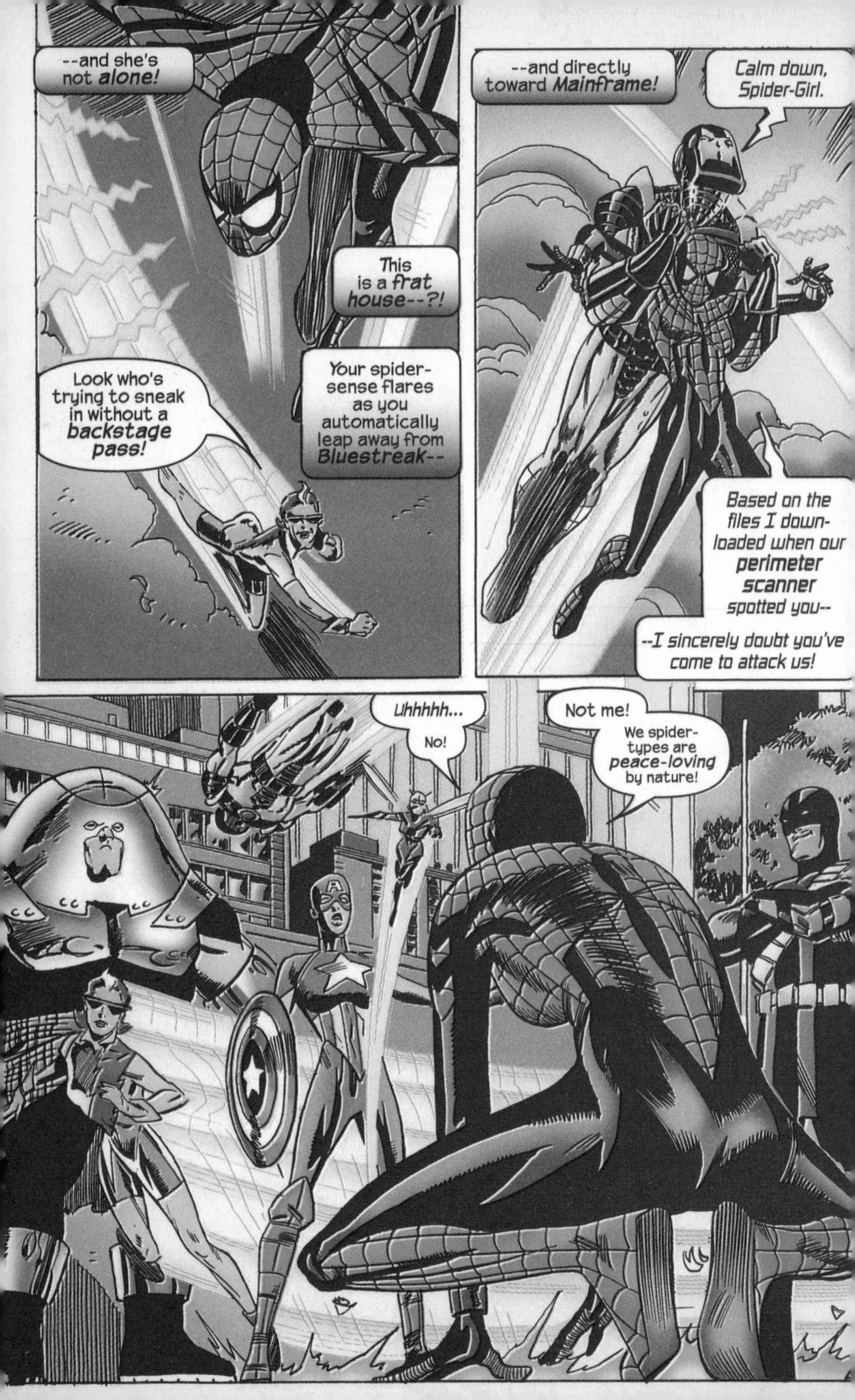
--and she's not alone!
This is a frat house--?!
Your spider-sense flares as you automatically leap away from Bluestreak--
Look who's trying to sneak in without a backstage pass!
--and directly toward Mainframe!
Calm down, Spider-Girl.
Based on the files I down-loaded when our perimeter scanner spotted you--
--I sincerely doubt you've come to attack us!
Uhhhhh...
No!
Not me!
We spider-types are peace-loving by nature!

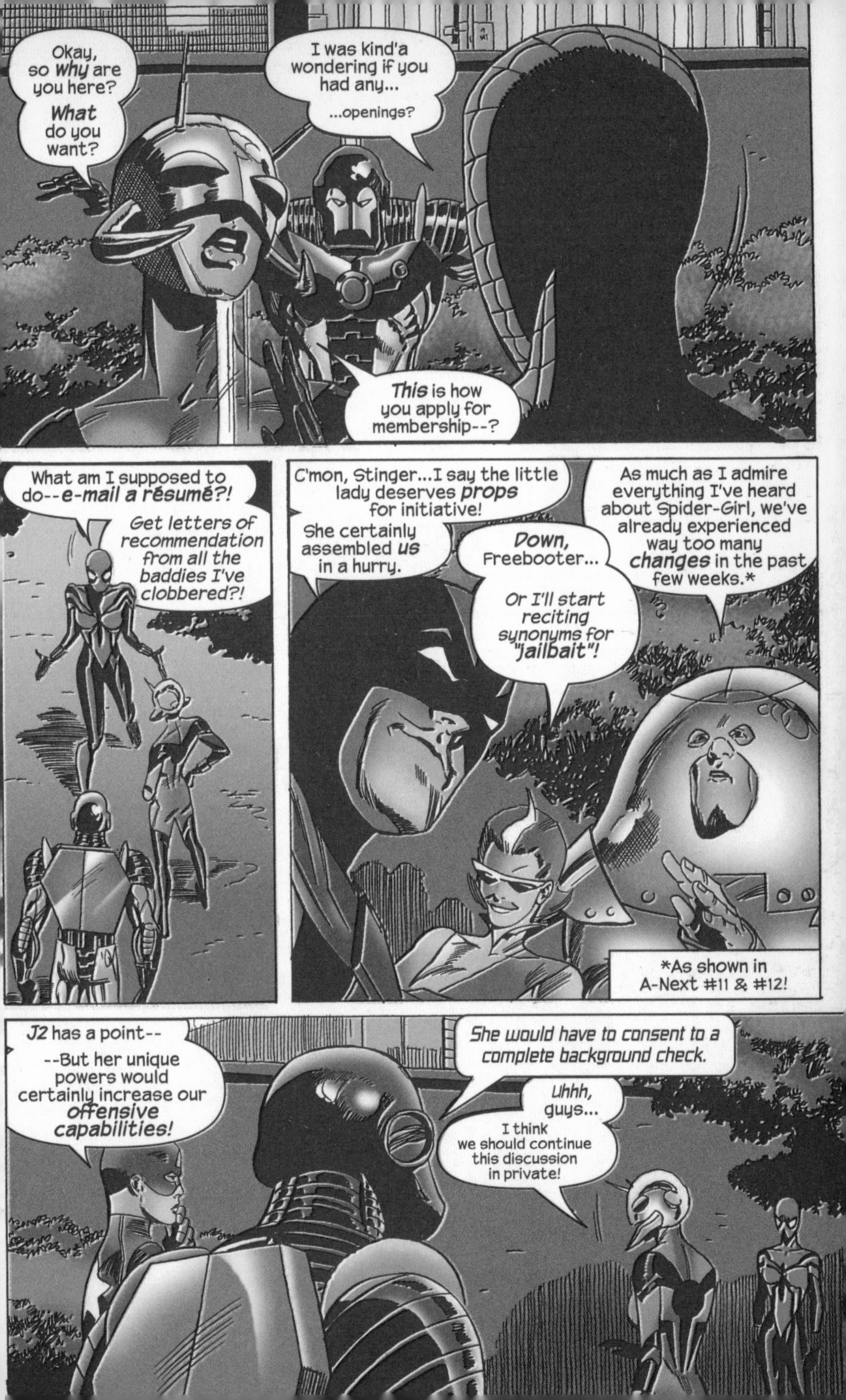

Okay, so why are you here? What do you want?
I was kind'a wondering if you had any... ...openings?
This is how you apply for membership--?
What am I supposed to do--e-mail a résumé?!
Get letters of recommendation from all the baddies I've clobbered?!
C'mon, Stinger...I say the little lady deserves props for initiative!
She certainly assembled us in a hurry.
Down, Freebooter...
Or I'll start reciting synonyms for "jailbait"!
As much as I admire everything I've heard about Spider-Girl, we've already experienced way too many changes in the past few weeks.*
*As shown in A-Next #11 & #12!
J2 has a point--
--But her unique powers would certainly increase our offensive capabilities!
She would have to consent to a complete background check.
Uhhh, guys...
I think we should continue this discussion in private!

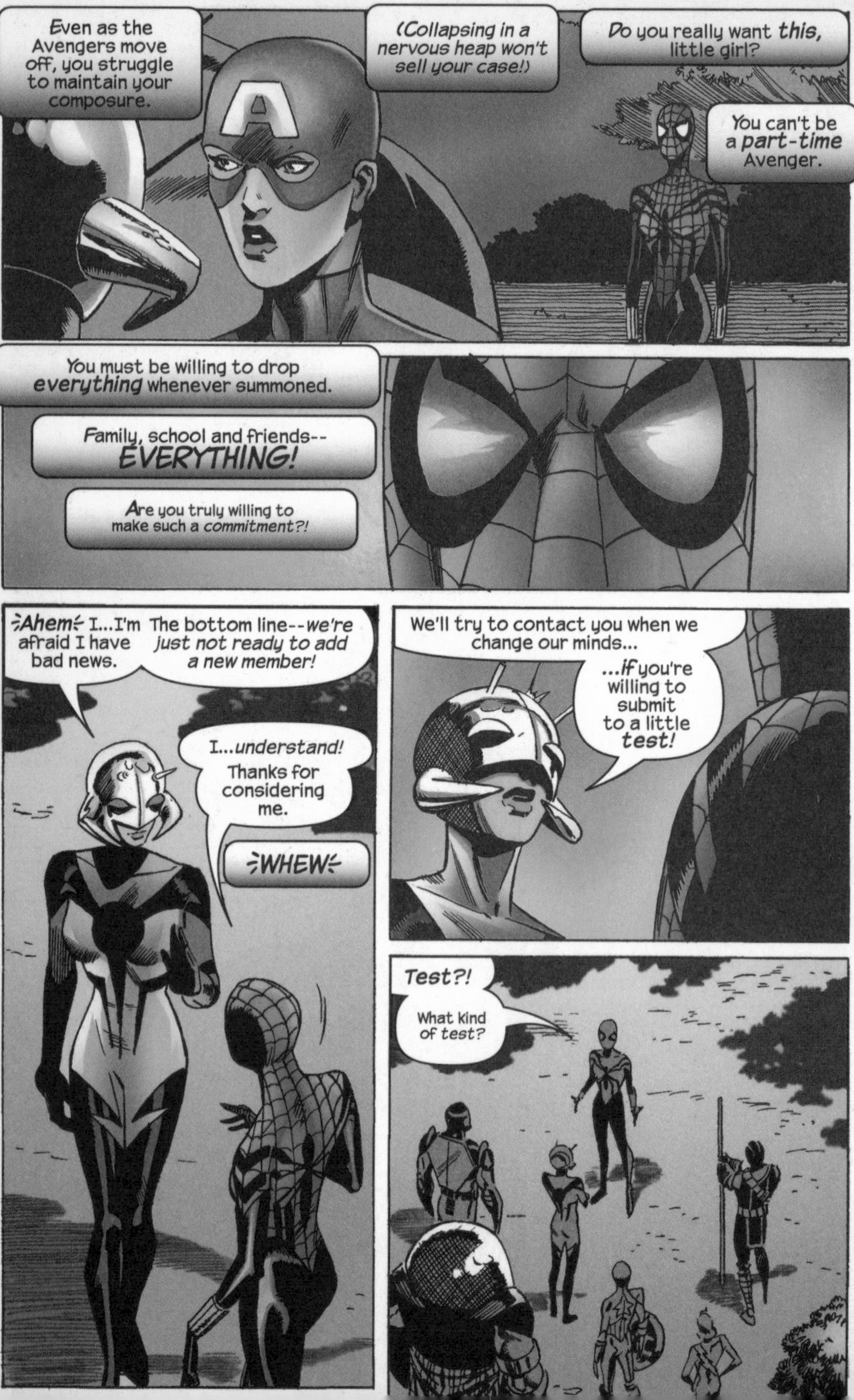

Even as the Avengers move off, you struggle to maintain your composure.
(Collapsing in a nervous heap won't sell your case!)
Do you really want this, little girl?
You can't be a part-time Avenger.
You must be willing to drop everything whenever summoned.
Family, school and friends-- EVERYTHING!
Are you truly willing to make such a commitment?!
Ahem I...I'm afraid I have bad news.
The bottom line--we're just not ready to add a new member!
I...understand! Thanks for considering me.
WHEW
We'll try to contact you when we change our minds...
...if you're willing to submit to a little test!
Test?!
What kind of test?

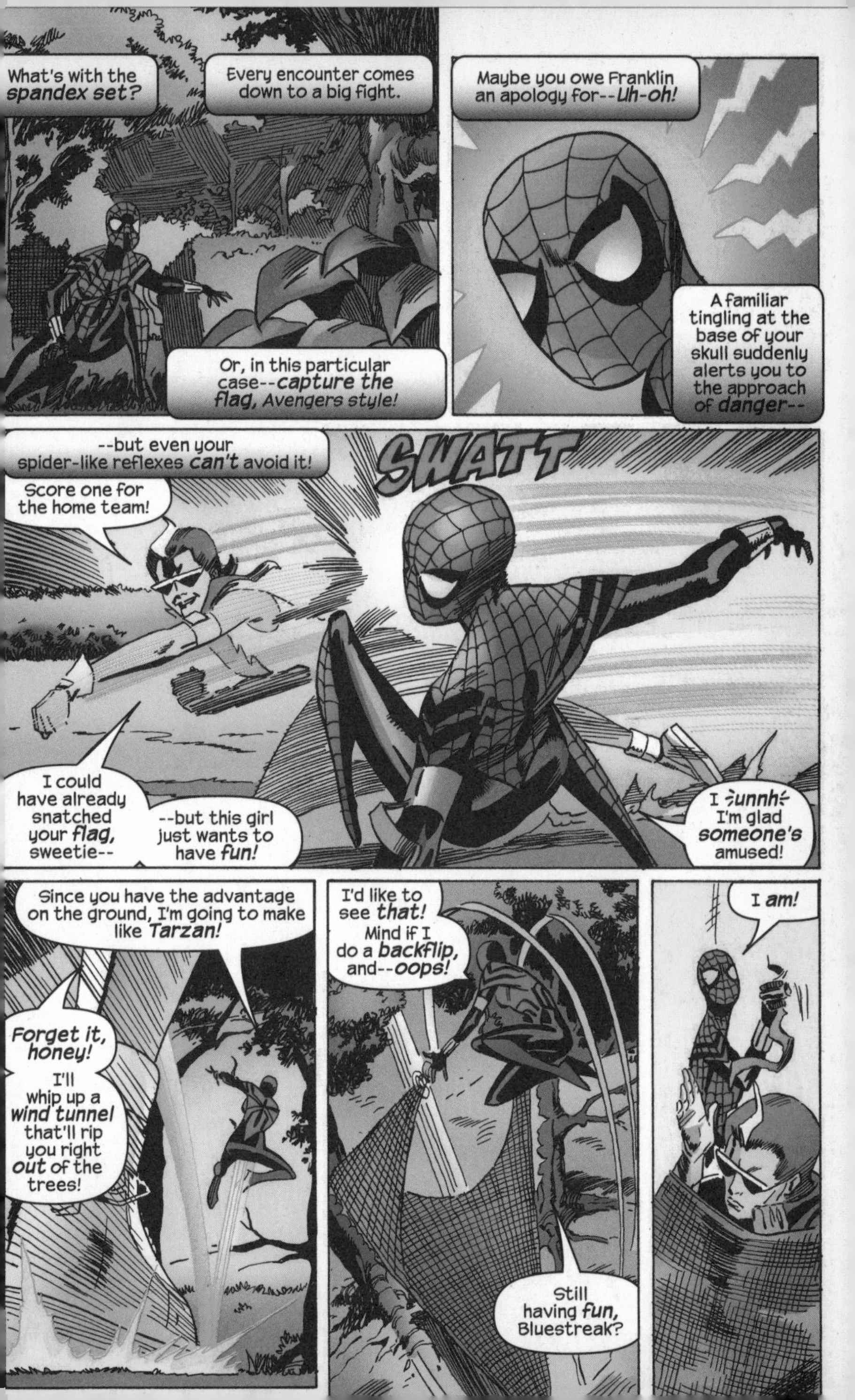
What's with the spandex set?
Every encounter comes down to a big fight.
Or, in this particular case--capture the flag, Avengers style!
Maybe you owe Franklin an apology for--Uh-oh!
A familiar tingling at the base of your skull suddenly alerts you to the approach of danger--
--but even your spider-like reflexes can't avoid it!
SWATT
Score one for the home team!
I could have already snatched your flag, sweetie--
--but this girl just wants to have fun!
I unnh I'm glad someone's amused!
Since you have the advantage on the ground, I'm going to make like Tarzan!
Forget it, honey!
I'll whip up a wind tunnel that'll rip you right out of the trees!
I'd like to see that!
Mind if I do a backflip, and--oops!
Still having fun, Bluestreak?
I am!

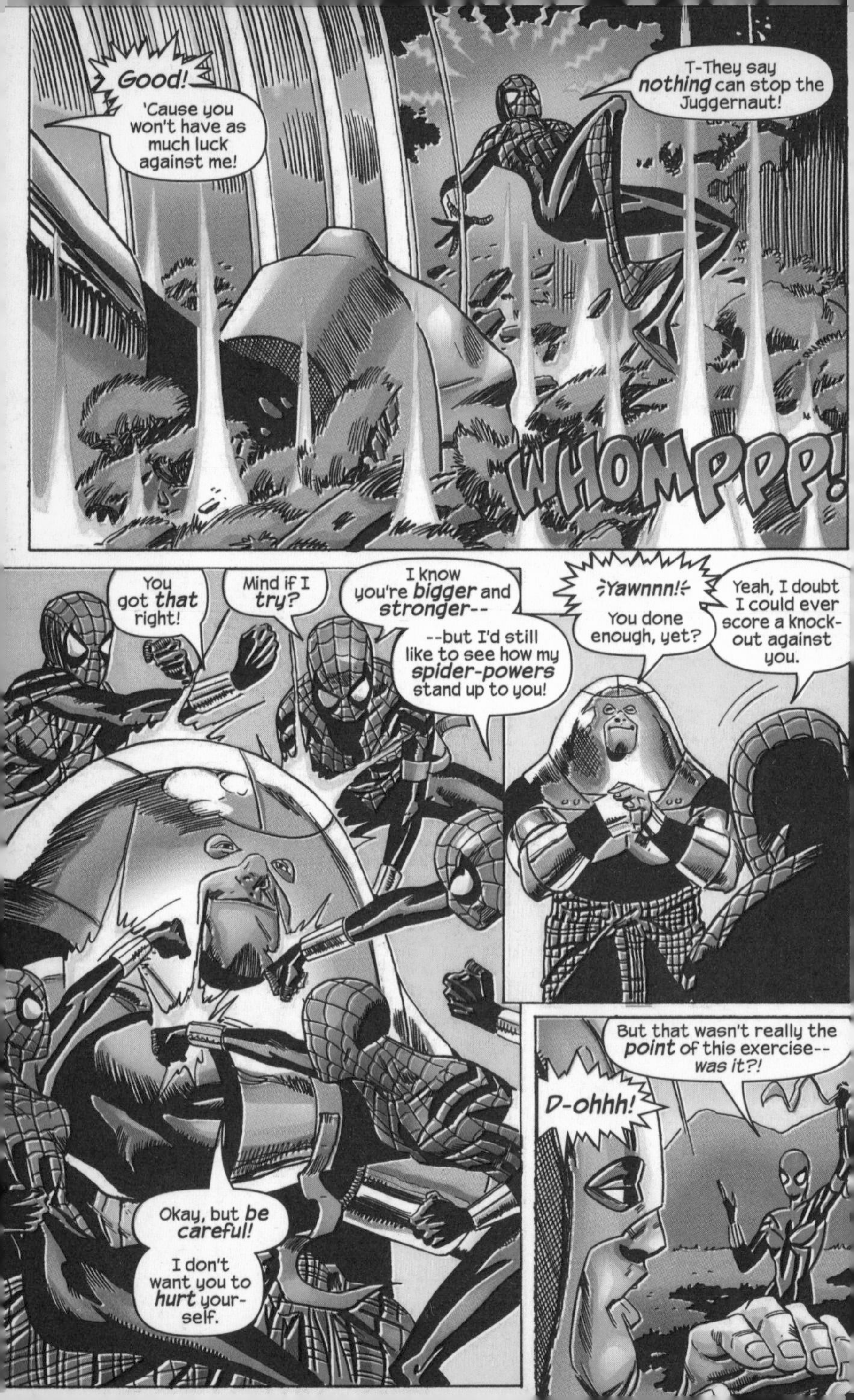

T-They say nothing can stop the Juggernaut!
Good!
'Cause you won't have as much luck against me!
WHOMPPP!
Mind if I try?
You got that right!
Okay, but be careful!
I don't want you to hurt your-self.
I know you're bigger and stronger--
--but I'd still like to see how my spider-powers stand up to you!
Yawnnn!
You done enough, yet?
Yeah, I doubt I could ever score a knock-out against you.
But that wasn't really the point of this exercise-- was it?!
D-ohhh!

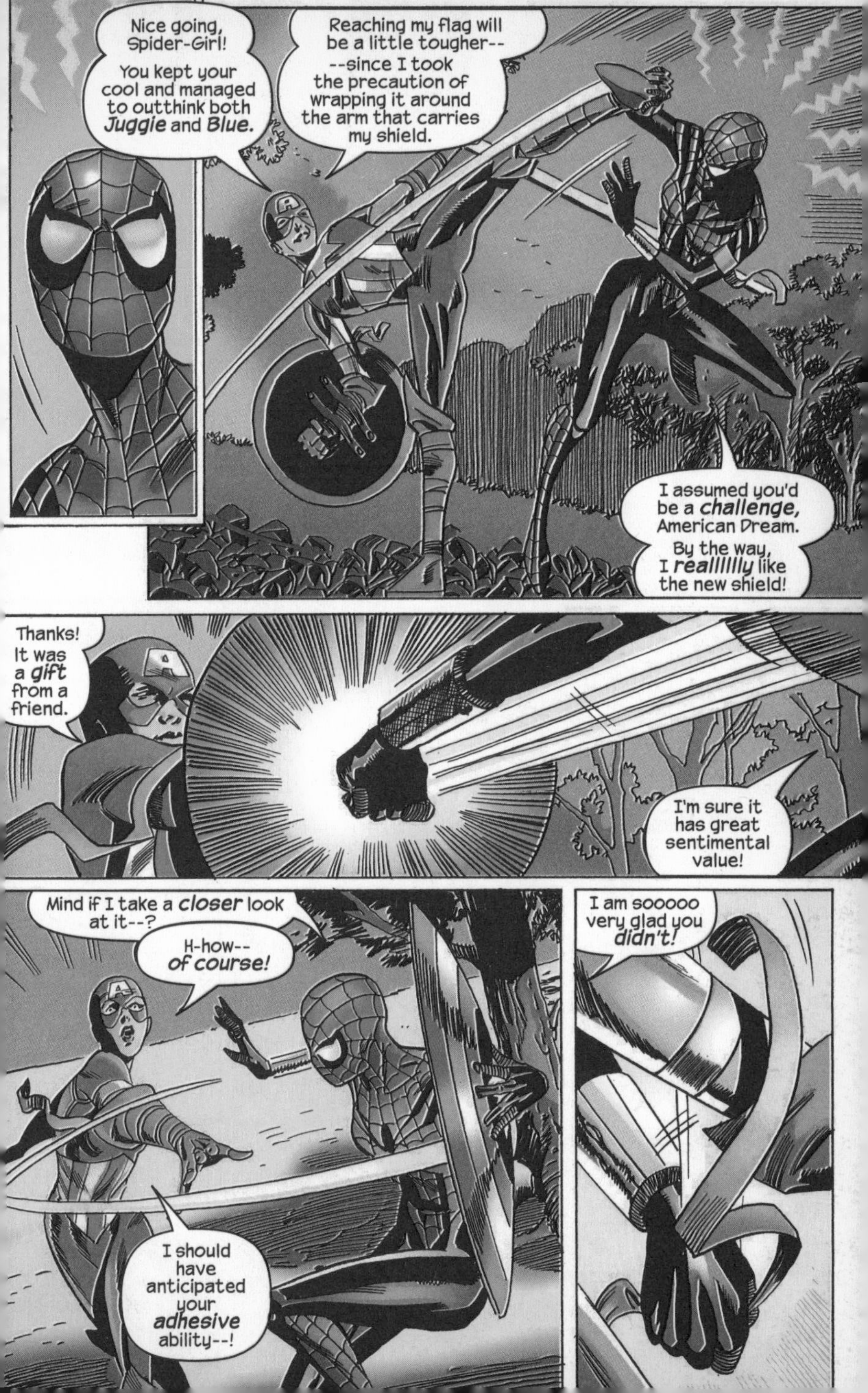

Nice going, Spider-Girl!
You kept your cool and managed to outthink both Juggie and Blue.
Reaching my flag will be a little tougher--
--since I took the precaution of wrapping it around the arm that carries my shield.
I assumed you'd be a challenge, American Dream.
By the way, I reallllly like the new shield!
Thanks! It was a gift from a friend.
I'm sure it has great sentimental value!
Mind if I take a closer look at it--?
H-how-- of course!
I should have anticipated your adhesive ability--!
I am sooooo very glad you didn't!

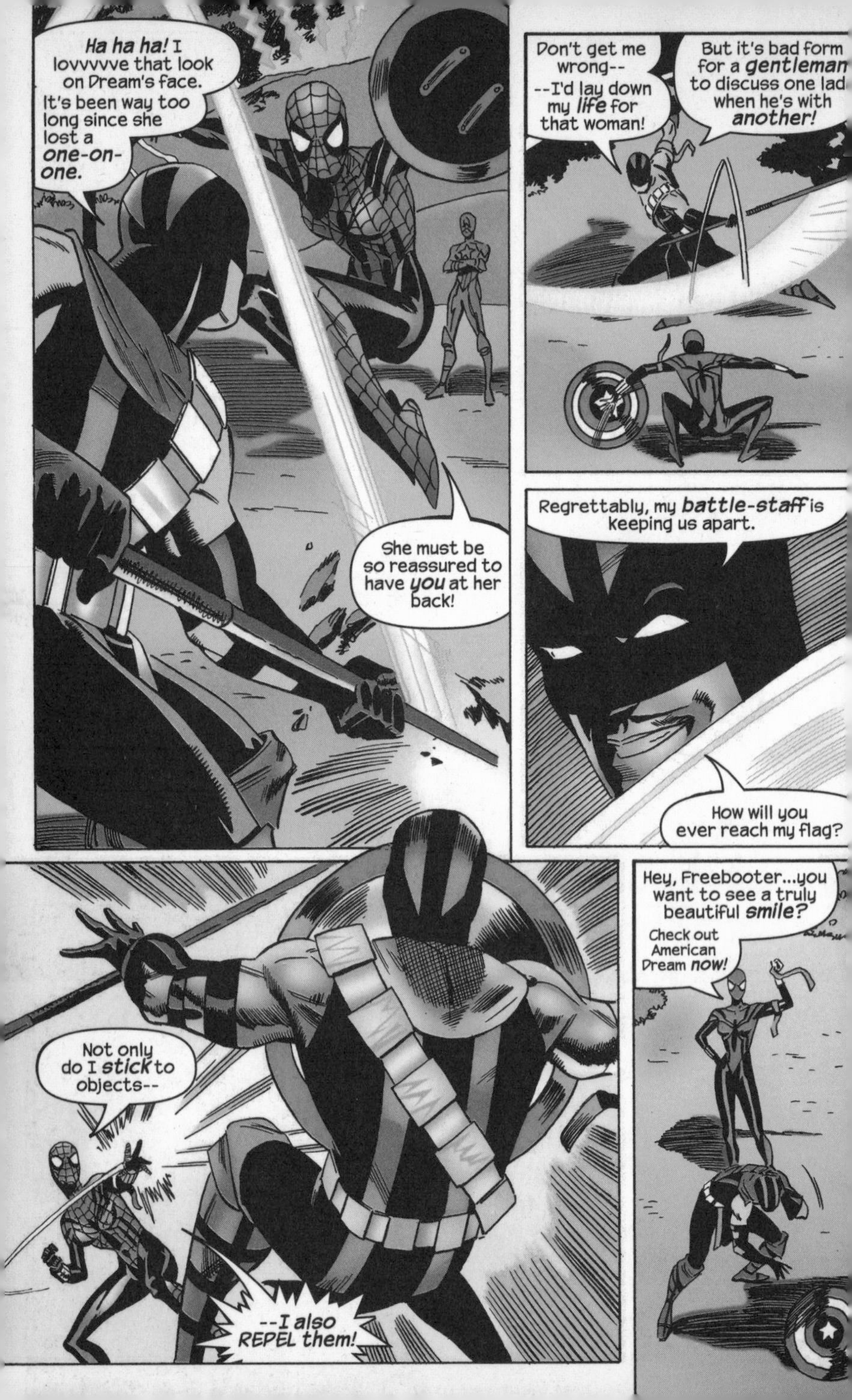
Ha ha ha! I lovvvvve that look on Dream's face.
It's been way too long since she lost a one-on-one.
She must be so reassured to have you at her back!
Don't get me wrong--
--I'd lay down my life for that woman!
But it's bad form for a gentleman to discuss one lad when he's with another!
Regrettably, my battle-staff is keeping us apart.
How will you ever reach my flag?
Not only do I stick to objects--
--I also REPEL them!
Hey, Freebooter...you want to see a truly beautiful smile?
Check out American Dream now!

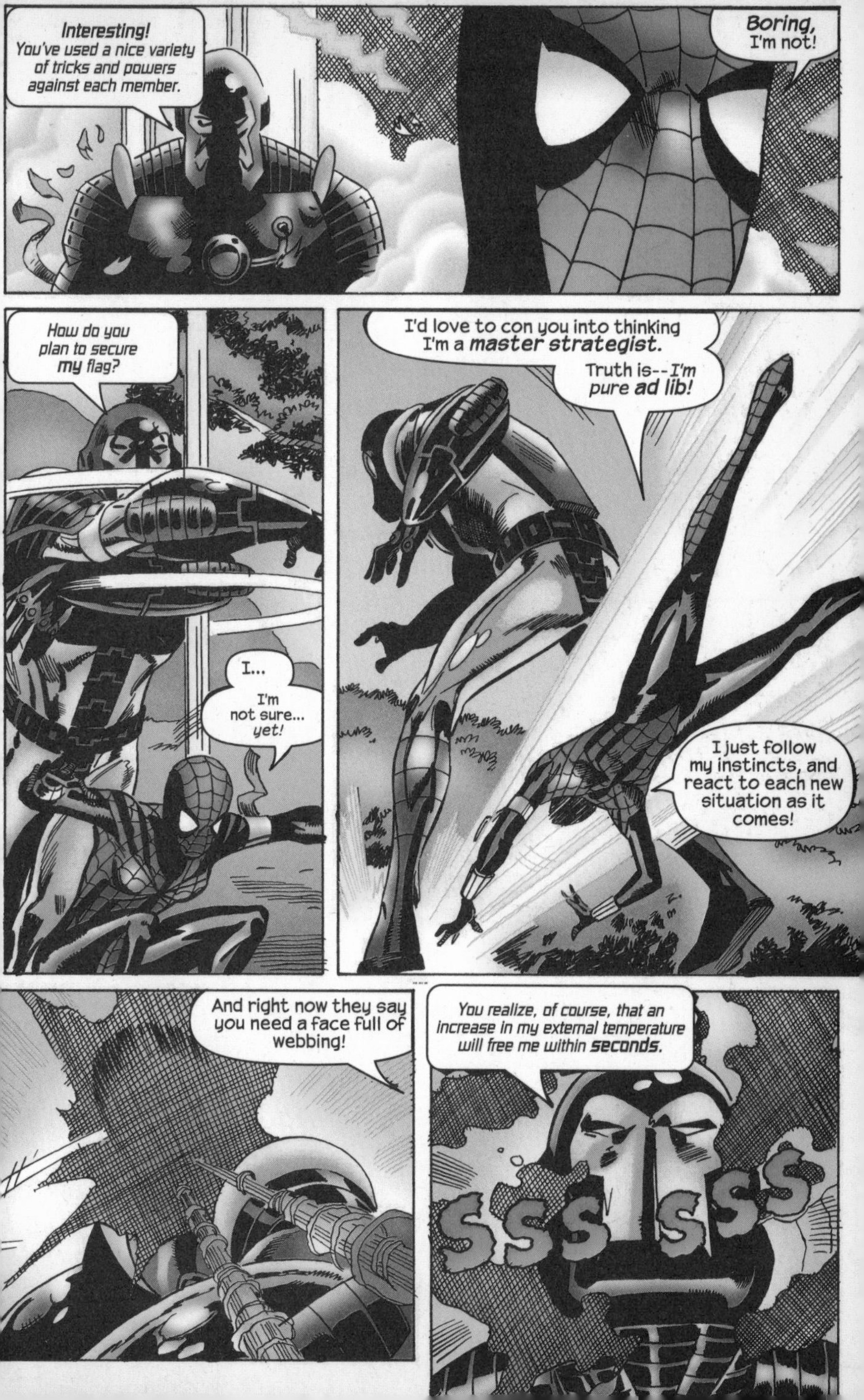

Interesting! You've used a nice variety of tricks and powers against each member.
Boring, I'm not!
How do you plan to secure my flag?
I...
I'm not sure... yet!
I'd love to con you into thinking I'm a master strategist.
Truth is--I'm pure ad lib!
I just follow my instincts, and react to each new situation as it comes!
And right now they say you need a face full of webbing!
You realize, of course, that an increase in my external temperature will free me within seconds.
SSSSSS

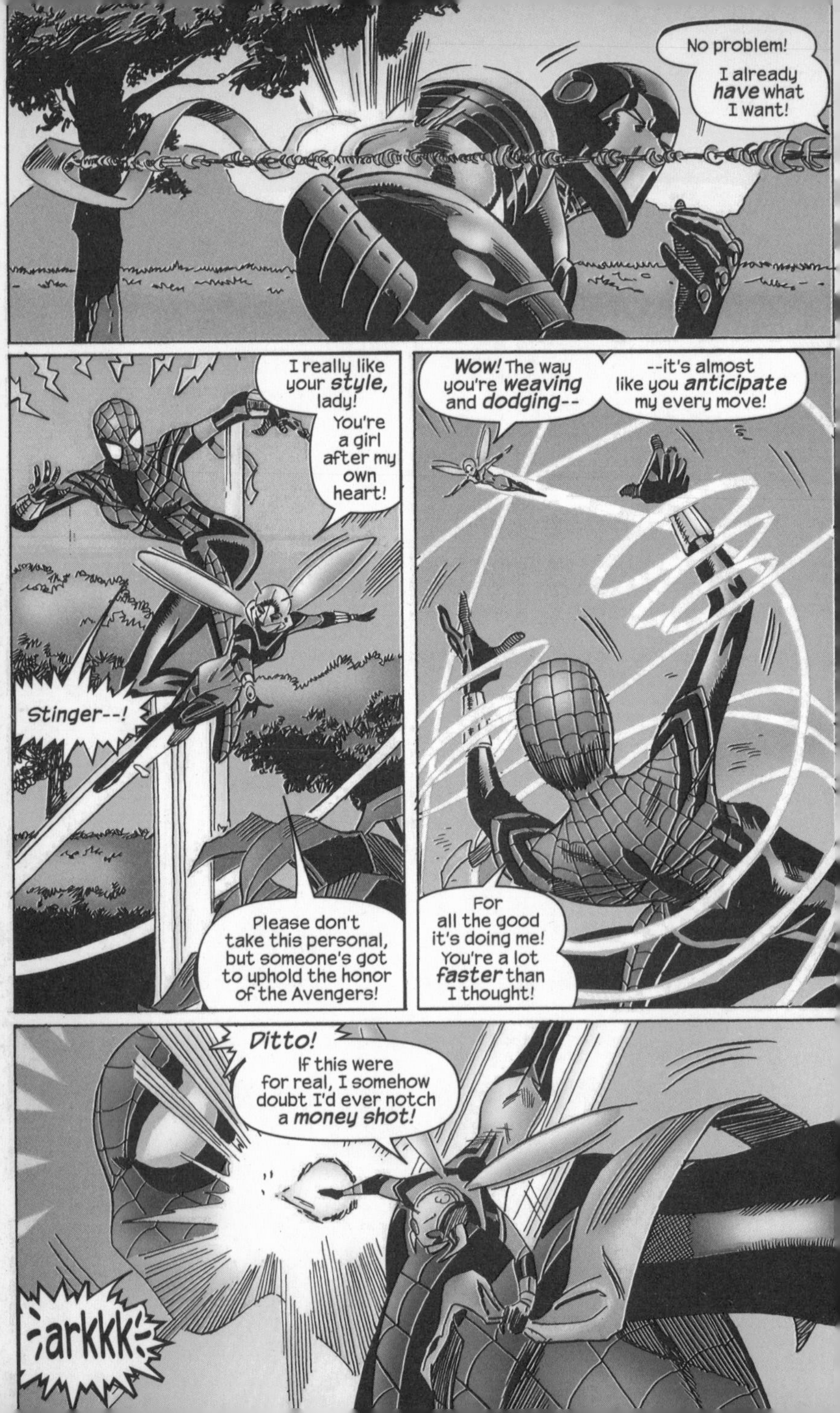
No problem! I already *have* what I want!
I really like your *style,* lady! You're a girl after my own heart!
Stinger--!
Please don't take this personal, but someone's got to uphold the honor of the Avengers!
Wow! The way you're *weaving* and *dodging*--
--it's almost like you *anticipate* my every move!
For all the good it's doing me! You're a lot *faster* than I thought!
Ditto! If this were for real, I somehow doubt I'd ever notch a *money shot!*
arkkk

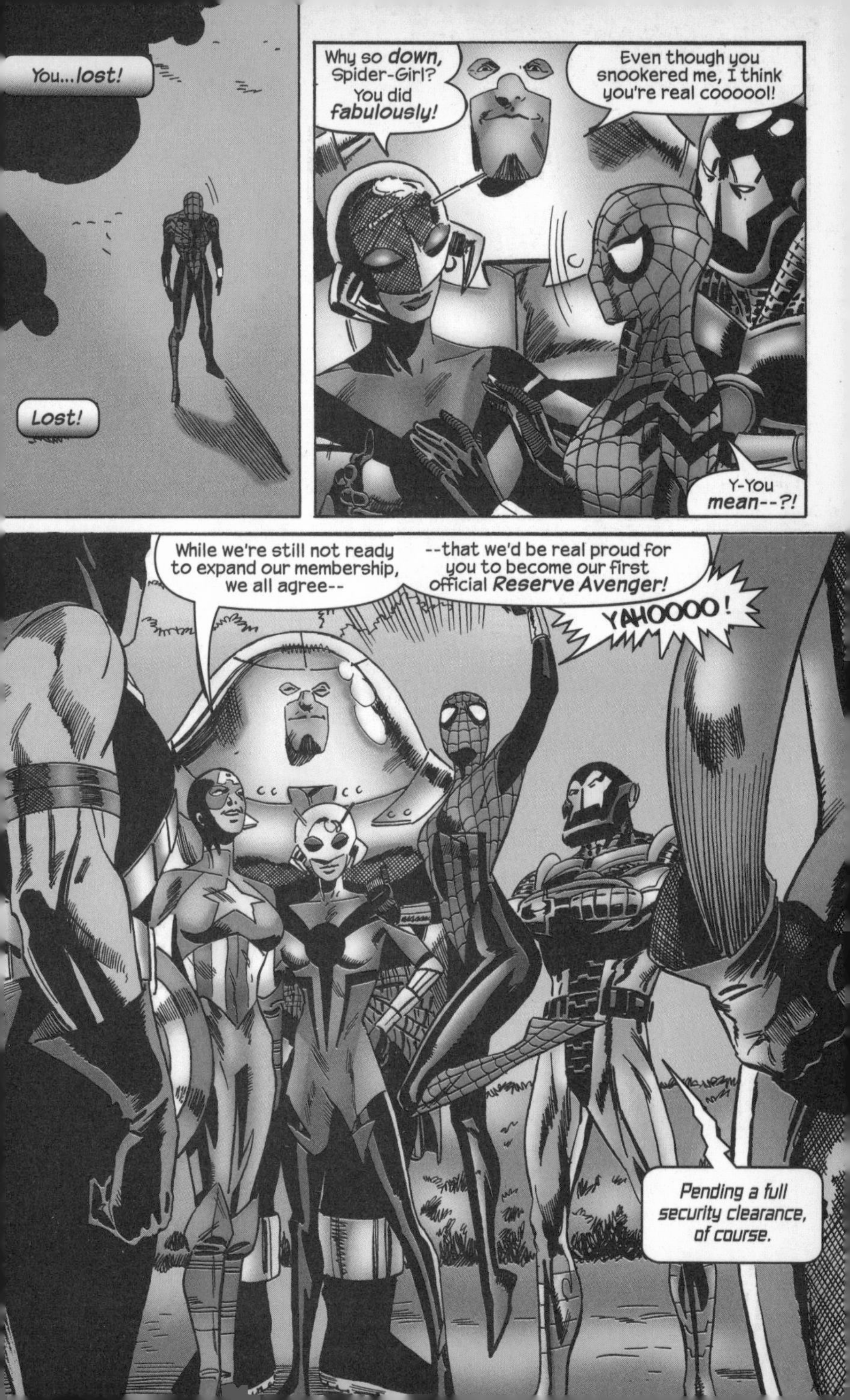
You...lost!
Lost!
Why so down, Spider-Girl? You did fabulously!
Even though you snookered me, I think you're real coooool!
Y-You mean--?!
While we're still not ready to expand our membership, we all agree--
--that we'd be real proud for you to become our first official Reserve Avenger!
YAHOOOO!
Pending a full security clearance, of course.

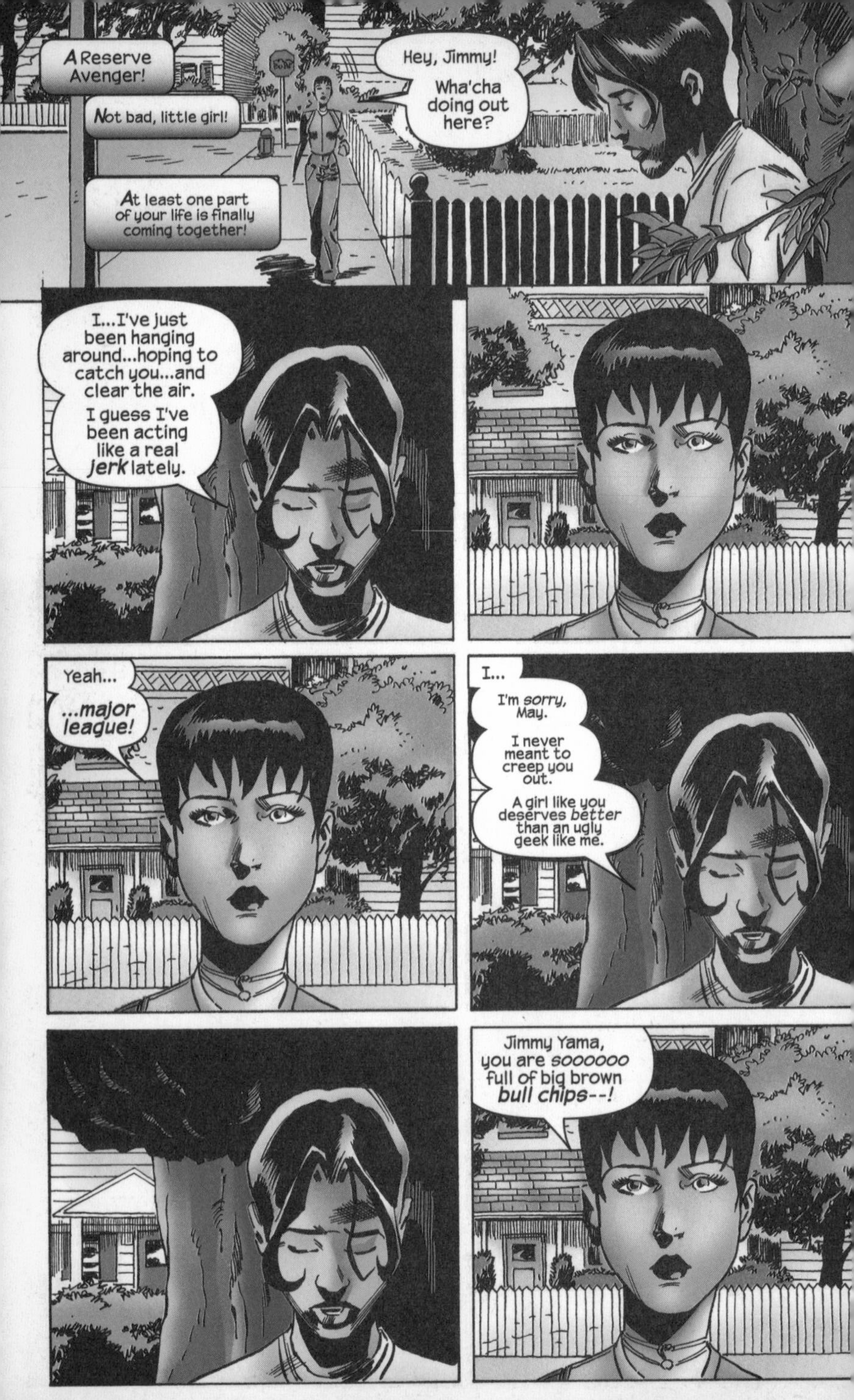
A Reserve Avenger!
Not bad, little girl!
At least one part of your life is finally coming together!
Hey, Jimmy!
Wha'cha doing out here?
I...I've just been hanging around...hoping to catch you...and clear the air.
I guess I've been acting like a real *jerk* lately.
Yeah...
...*major league!*
I...
I'm *sorry*, May.
I never meant to creep you out.
A girl like you deserves *better* than an ugly geek like me.
Jimmy Yama, you are *soooooo* full of big brown *bull chips--!*

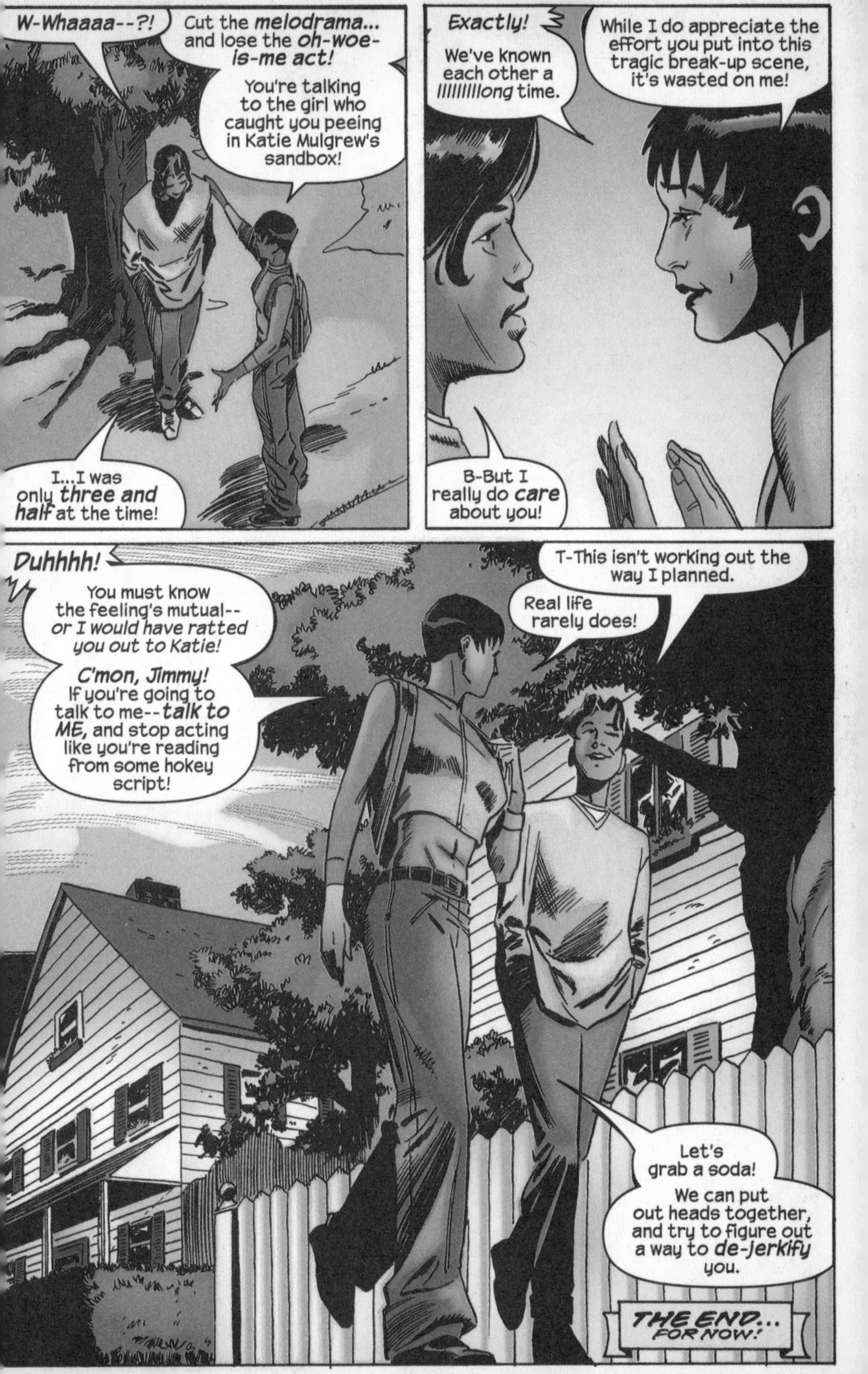

W-Whaaaa--?!
Cut the *melodrama...* and lose the *oh-woe-is-me act!*
You're talking to the girl who caught you peeing in Katie Mulgrew's sandbox!
I...I was only *three and half* at the time!
Exactly!
We've known each other a *llllllllong* time.
While I do appreciate the effort you put into this tragic break-up scene, it's wasted on me!
B-But I really do *care* about you!
Duhhhh!
You must know the feeling's mutual-- *or I would have ratted you out to Katie!*
C'mon, Jimmy! If you're going to talk to me--*talk to ME,* and stop acting like you're reading from some hokey script!
T-This isn't working out the way I planned.
Real life rarely does!
Let's grab a soda!
We can put out heads together, and try to figure out a way to *de-jerkify* you.
THE END... FOR NOW!

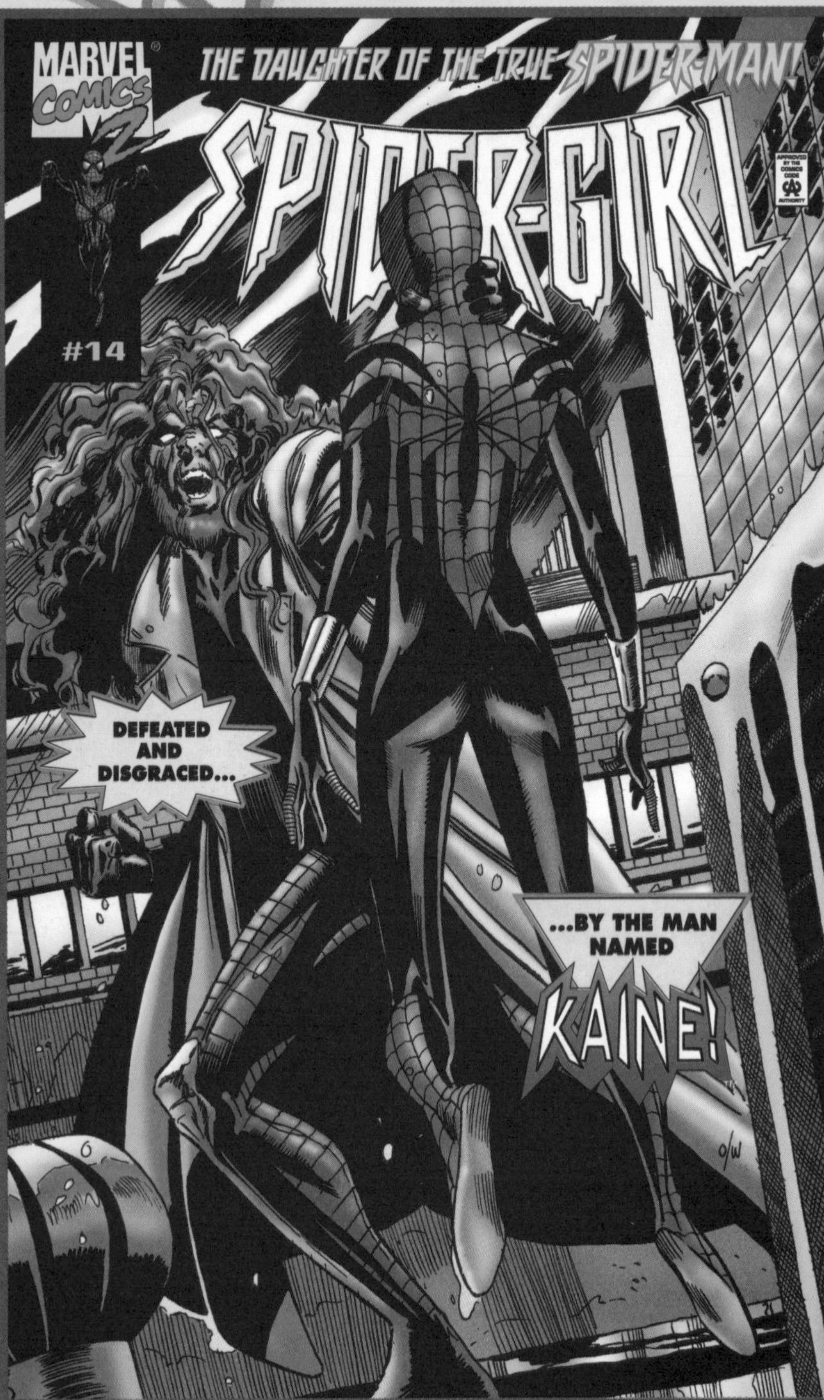
MARVEL COMICS
THE DAUGHTER OF THE TRUE SPIDER-MAN!
SPIDER-GIRL
#14
DEFEATED AND DISGRACED...
...BY THE MAN NAMED
KAINE!

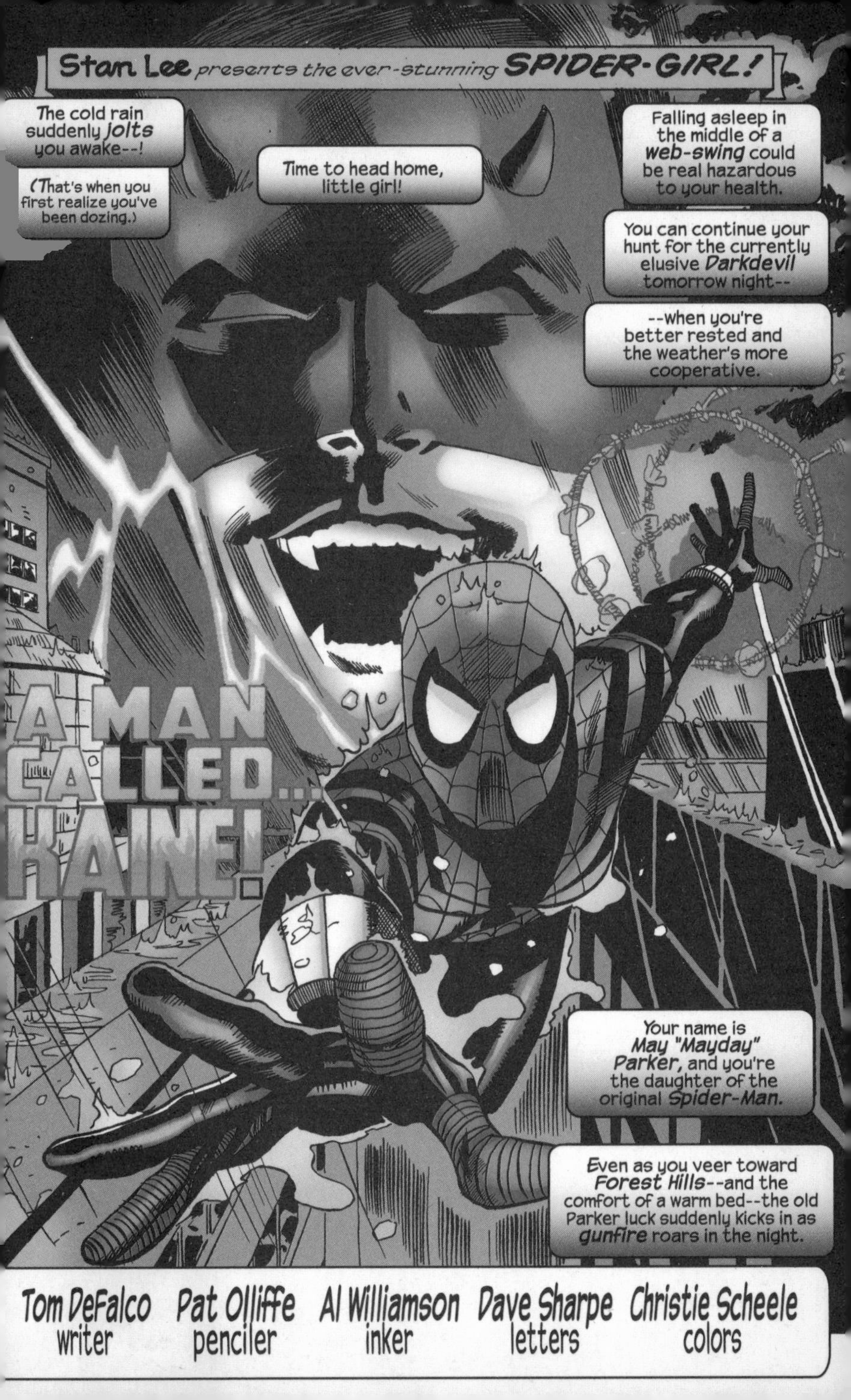
Stan Lee presents the ever-stunning SPIDER-GIRL!
The cold rain suddenly jolts you awake--!
(That's when you first realize you've been dozing.)
Time to head home, little girl!
Falling asleep in the middle of a web-swing could be real hazardous to your health.
You can continue your hunt for the currently elusive Darkdevil tomorrow night--
--when you're better rested and the weather's more cooperative.
A MAN CALLED... KAINE!
Your name is May "Mayday" Parker, and you're the daughter of the original Spider-Man.
Even as you veer toward Forest Hills--and the comfort of a warm bed--the old Parker luck suddenly kicks in as gunfire roars in the night.
Tom DeFalco writer
Pat Olliffe penciler
Al Williamson inker
Dave Sharpe letters
Christie Scheele colors

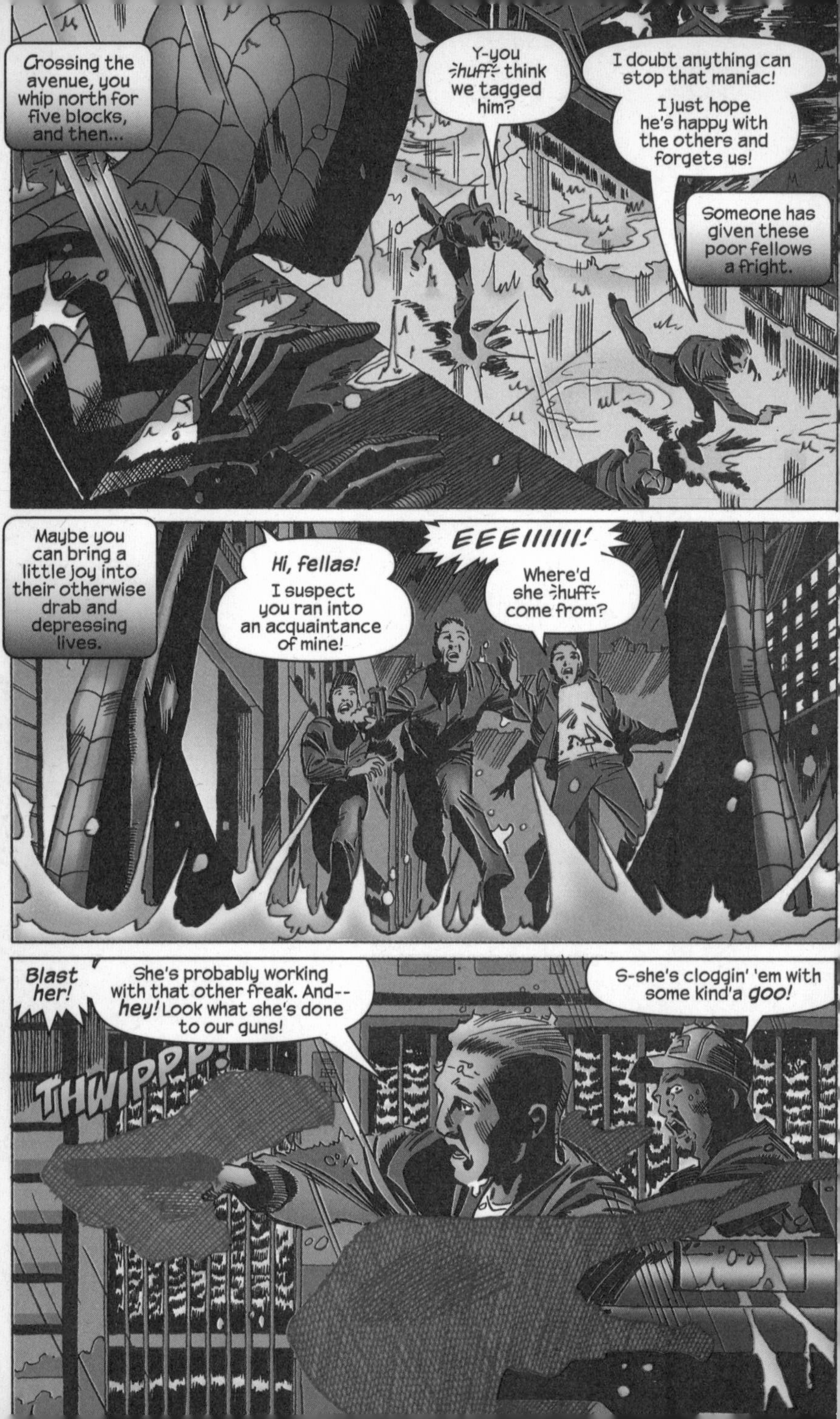

Crossing the avenue, you whip north for five blocks, and then...
Y-you -huff- think we tagged him?
I doubt anything can stop that maniac!
I just hope he's happy with the others and forgets us!
Someone has given these poor fellows a fright.
Maybe you can bring a little joy into their otherwise drab and depressing lives.
Hi, fellas! I suspect you ran into an acquaintance of mine!
EEEIIIIII!
Where'd she -huff- come from?
Blast her!
She's probably working with that other freak. And-- hey! Look what she's done to our guns!
S-she's cloggin' 'em with some kind'a goo!
THWIPPP!

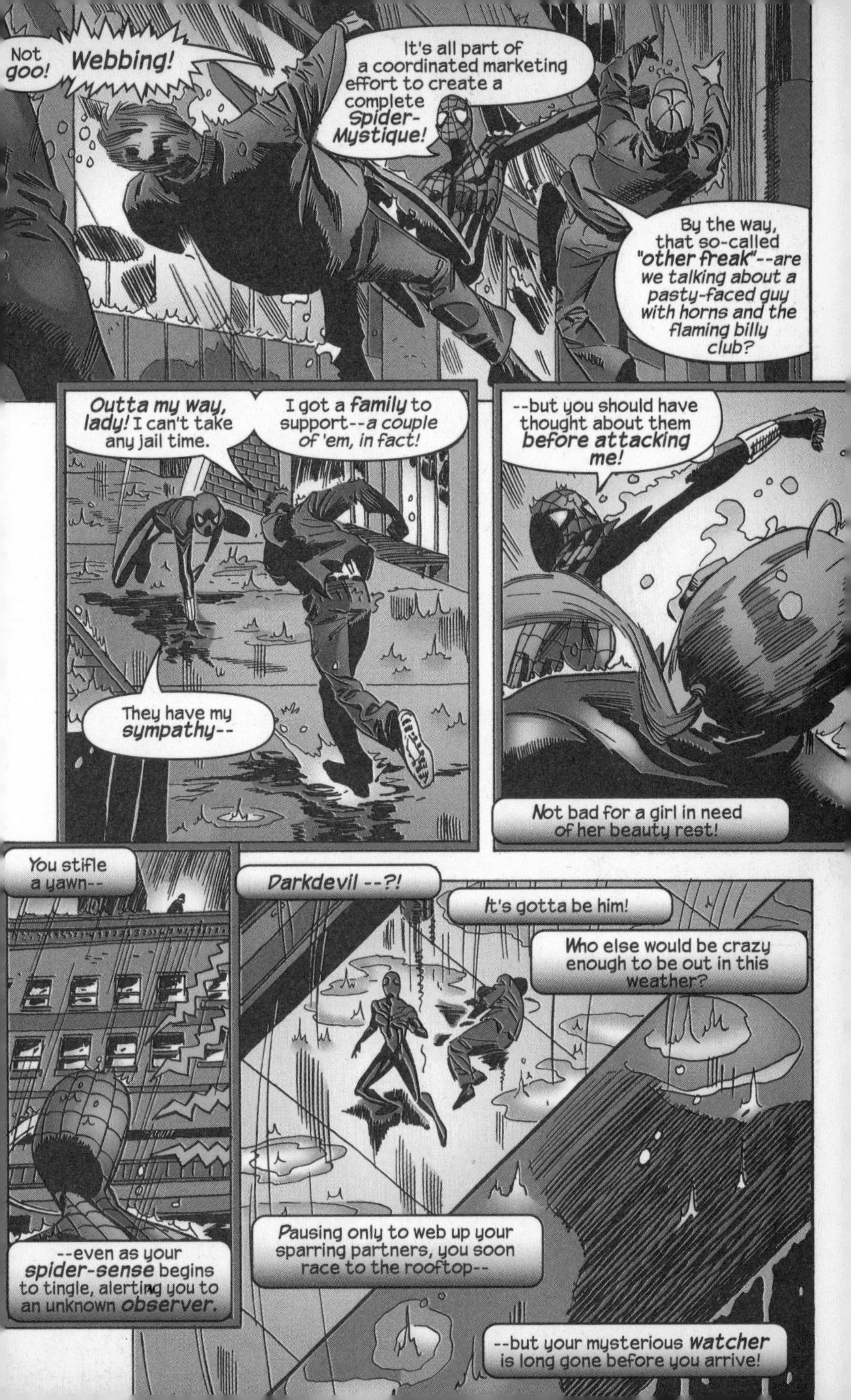
Not goo!
Webbing!
It's all part of a coordinated marketing effort to create a complete Spider-Mystique!
By the way, that so-called "other freak"--are we talking about a pasty-faced guy with horns and the flaming billy club?
Outta my way, lady! I can't take any jail time.
I got a family to support--a couple of 'em, in fact!
They have my sympathy--
--but you should have thought about them before attacking me!
Not bad for a girl in need of her beauty rest!
You stifle a yawn--
--even as your spider-sense begins to tingle, alerting you to an unknown observer.
Darkdevil --?!
It's gotta be him!
Who else would be crazy enough to be out in this weather?
Pausing only to web up your sparring partners, you soon race to the rooftop--
--but your mysterious watcher is long gone before you arrive!

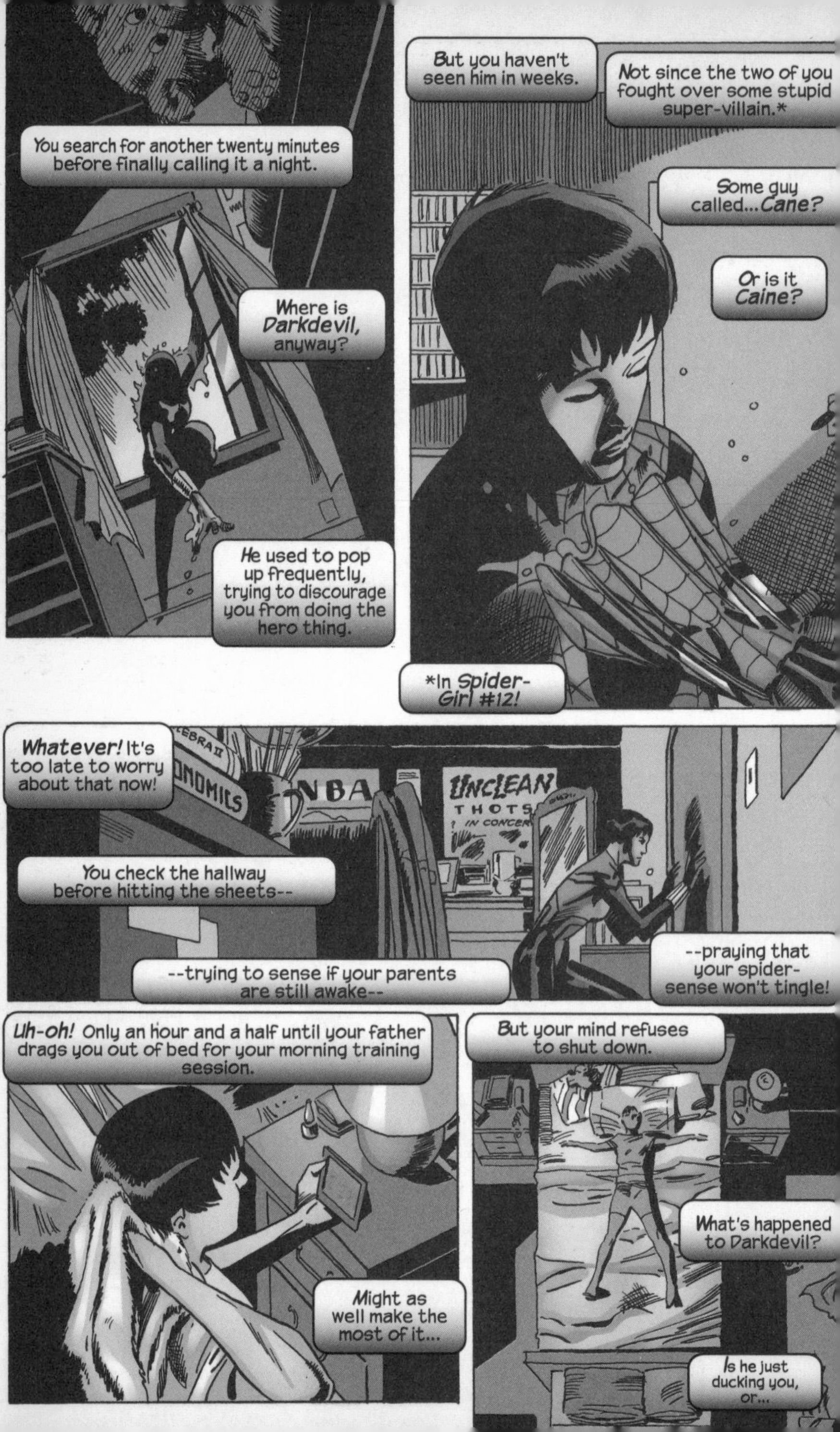
You search for another twenty minutes before finally calling it a night.
Where is Darkdevil, anyway?
He used to pop up frequently, trying to discourage you from doing the hero thing.
But you haven't seen him in weeks.
Not since the two of you fought over some stupid super-villain.*
Some guy called...Cane?
Or is it Caine?
*In Spider-Girl #12!
Whatever! It's too late to worry about that now!
You check the hallway before hitting the sheets--
--trying to sense if your parents are still awake--
--praying that your spider-sense won't tingle!
UNCLEAN THOTS IN CONCERT
NBA
Uh-oh! Only an hour and a half until your father drags you out of bed for your morning training session.
Might as well make the most of it...
But your mind refuses to shut down.
What's happened to Darkdevil?
Is he just ducking you, or...

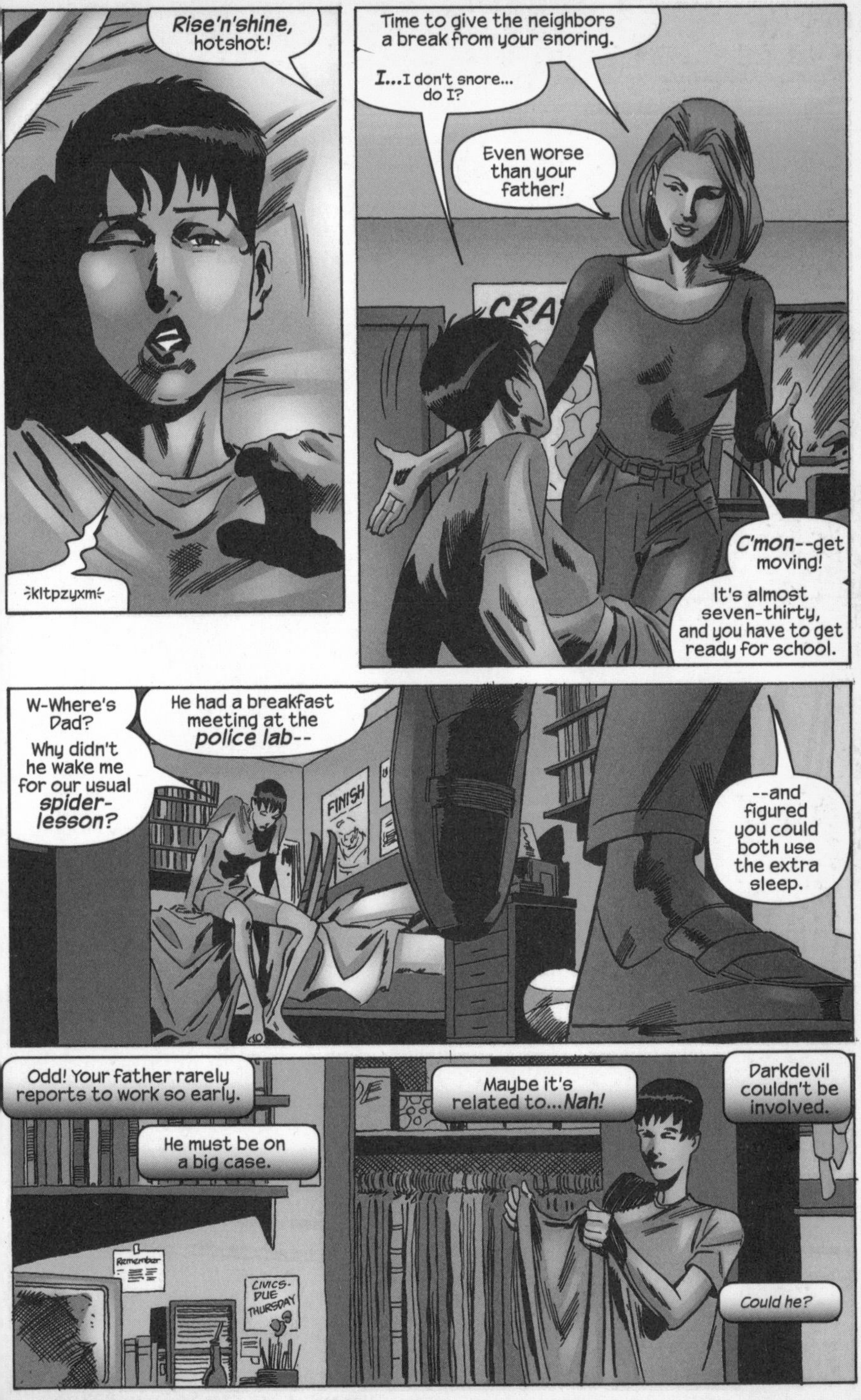
Rise'n'shine, hotshot!
⚡kltpzyxm⚡
Time to give the neighbors a break from your snoring.
I...I don't snore... do I?
Even worse than your father!
C'mon--get moving!
It's almost seven-thirty, and you have to get ready for school.
CRA
W-Where's Dad?
Why didn't he wake me for our usual spider-lesson?
He had a breakfast meeting at the police lab--
--and figured you could both use the extra sleep.
FINISH
Odd! Your father rarely reports to work so early.
He must be on a big case.
Maybe it's related to...Nah!
Darkdevil couldn't be involved.
Remember
CIVICS-DUE THURSDAY
Could he?

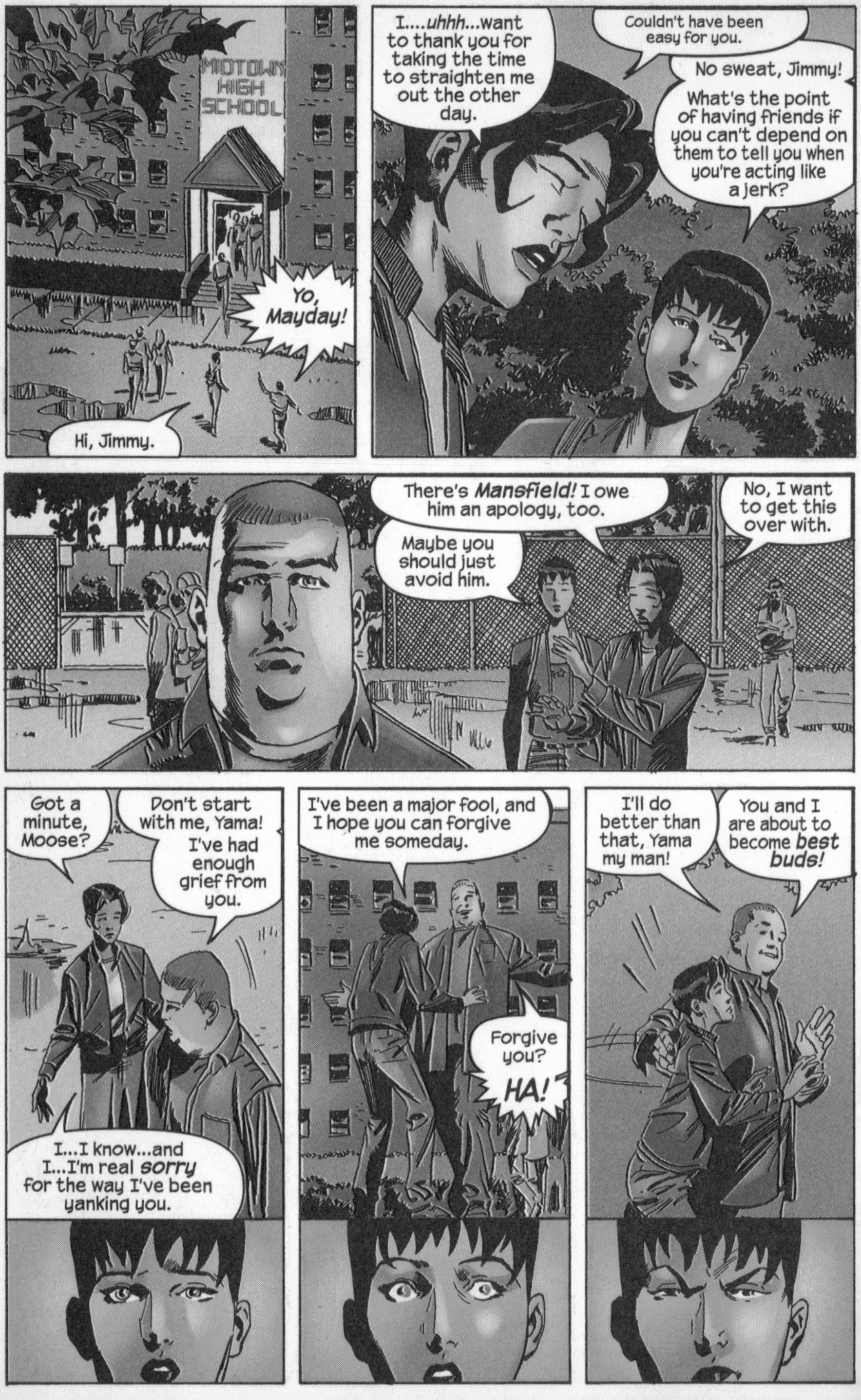
MIDTOWN HIGH SCHOOL
Yo, Mayday!
Hi, Jimmy.
I....uhhh...want to thank you for taking the time to straighten me out the other day.
Couldn't have been easy for you.
No sweat, Jimmy!
What's the point of having friends if you can't depend on them to tell you when you're acting like a jerk?
There's Mansfield! I owe him an apology, too.
Maybe you should just avoid him.
No, I want to get this over with.
Got a minute, Moose?
Don't start with me, Yama!
I've had enough grief from you.
I...I know...and I...I'm real sorry for the way I've been yanking you.
I've been a major fool, and I hope you can forgive me someday.
Forgive you? HA!
I'll do better than that, Yama my man!
You and I are about to become best buds!

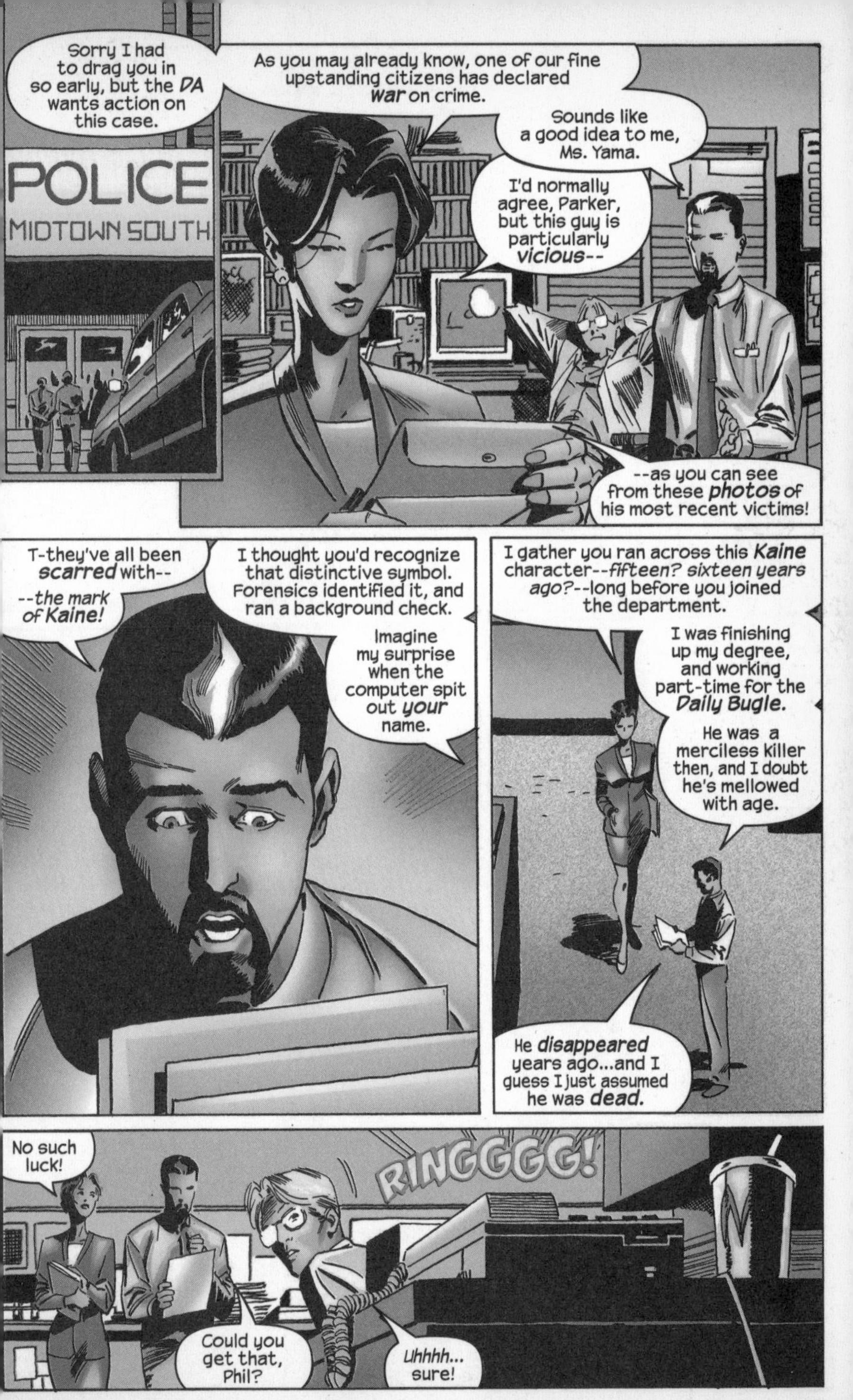

Sorry I had to drag you in so early, but the DA wants action on this case.
POLICE
MIDTOWN SOUTH
As you may already know, one of our fine upstanding citizens has declared war on crime.
Sounds like a good idea to me, Ms. Yama.
I'd normally agree, Parker, but this guy is particularly vicious--
--as you can see from these photos of his most recent victims!
T-they've all been scarred with--
--the mark of Kaine!
I thought you'd recognize that distinctive symbol. Forensics identified it, and ran a background check.
Imagine my surprise when the computer spit out your name.
I gather you ran across this Kaine character--fifteen? sixteen years ago?--long before you joined the department.
I was finishing up my degree, and working part-time for the Daily Bugle.
He was a merciless killer then, and I doubt he's mellowed with age.
He disappeared years ago...and I guess I just assumed he was dead.
No such luck!
RINGGGG!
Could you get that, Phil?
Uhhhh... sure!

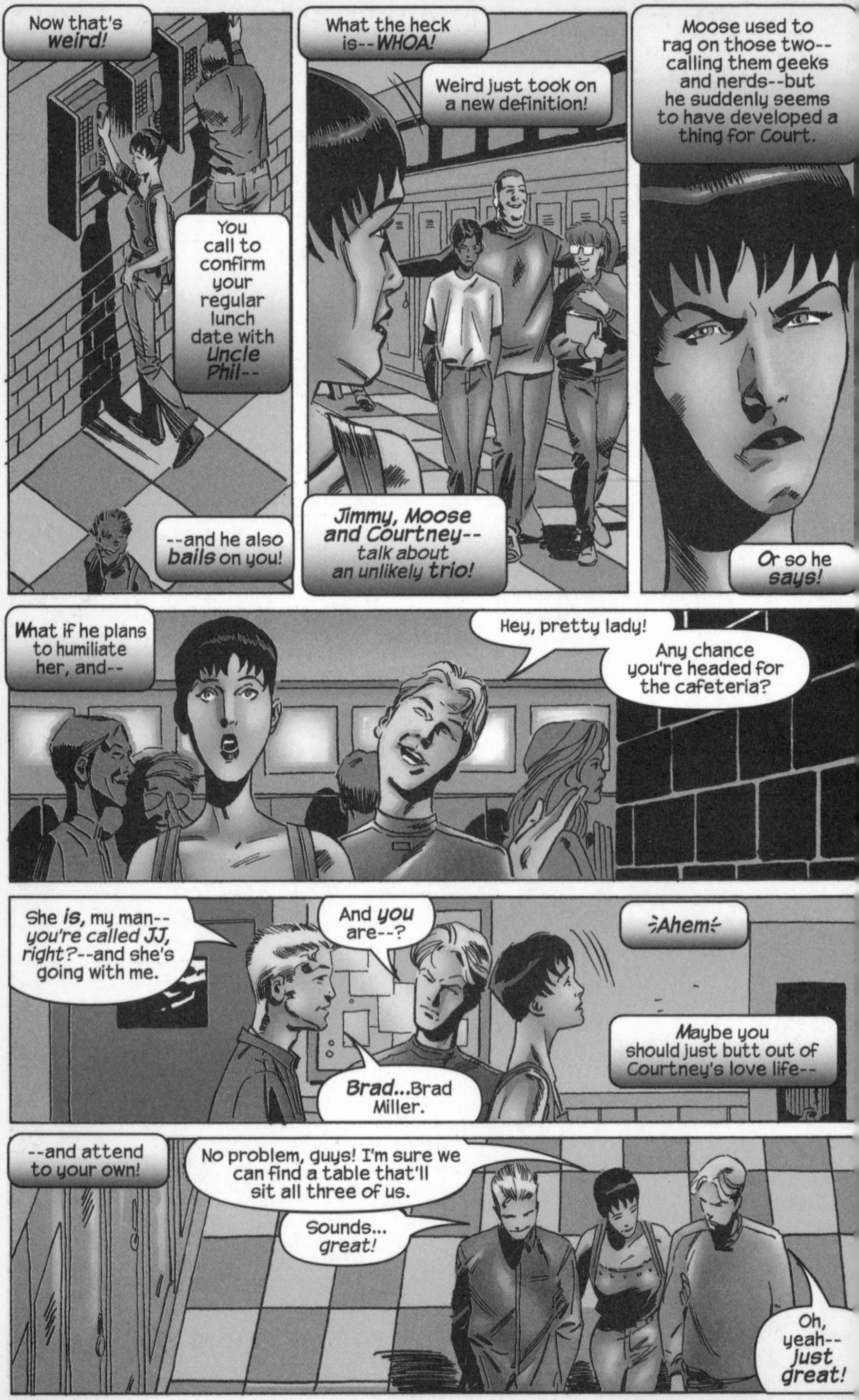

Now that's *weird!*
You call to confirm your regular lunch date with *Uncle Phil--*
--and he also *bails* on you!
What the heck is--*WHOA!*
Weird just took on a new definition!
Jimmy, Moose and Courtney-- talk about an unlikely *trio!*
Moose used to rag on those two--calling them geeks and nerds--but he suddenly seems to have developed a thing for Court.
Or so he *says!*
What if he plans to humiliate her, and--
Hey, pretty lady!
Any chance you're headed for the cafeteria?
She *is,* my man--*you're called JJ, right?*--and she's going with me.
And *you* are--?
*Brad...*Brad Miller.
Ahem
Maybe you should just butt out of Courtney's love life--
--and attend to your own!
No problem, guys! I'm sure we can find a table that'll sit all three of us.
Sounds... *great!*
Oh, yeah--*just great!*

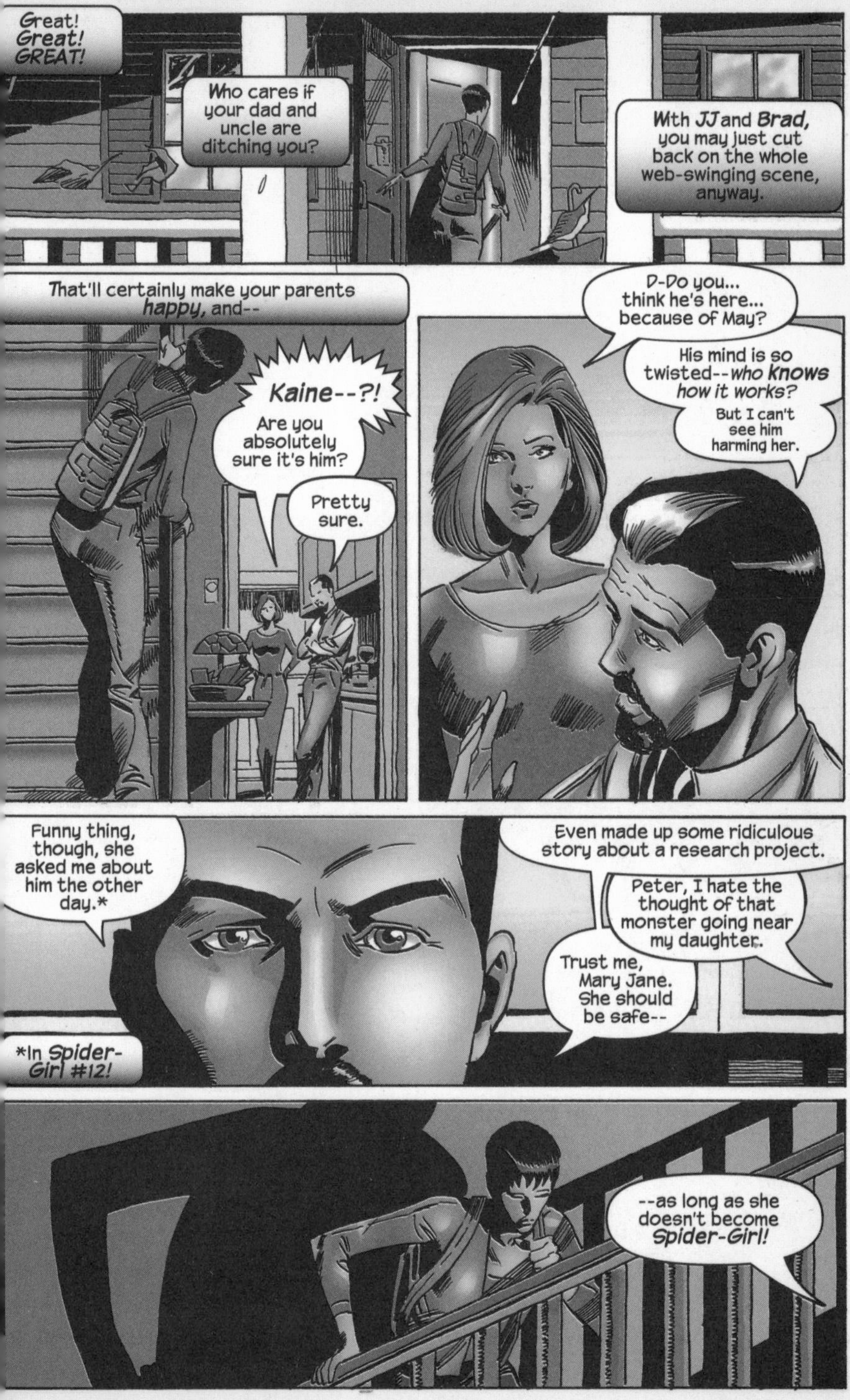
Great! Great! GREAT!
Who cares if your dad and uncle are ditching you?
With JJ and Brad, you may just cut back on the whole web-swinging scene, anyway.
That'll certainly make your parents happy, and--
Kaine--?!
Are you absolutely sure it's him?
Pretty sure.
D-Do you... think he's here... because of May?
His mind is so twisted--who knows how it works?
But I can't see him harming her.
Funny thing, though, she asked me about him the other day.*
Even made up some ridiculous story about a research project.
Peter, I hate the thought of that monster going near my daughter.
Trust me, Mary Jane. She should be safe--
*In Spider-Girl #12!
--as long as she doesn't become Spider-Girl!

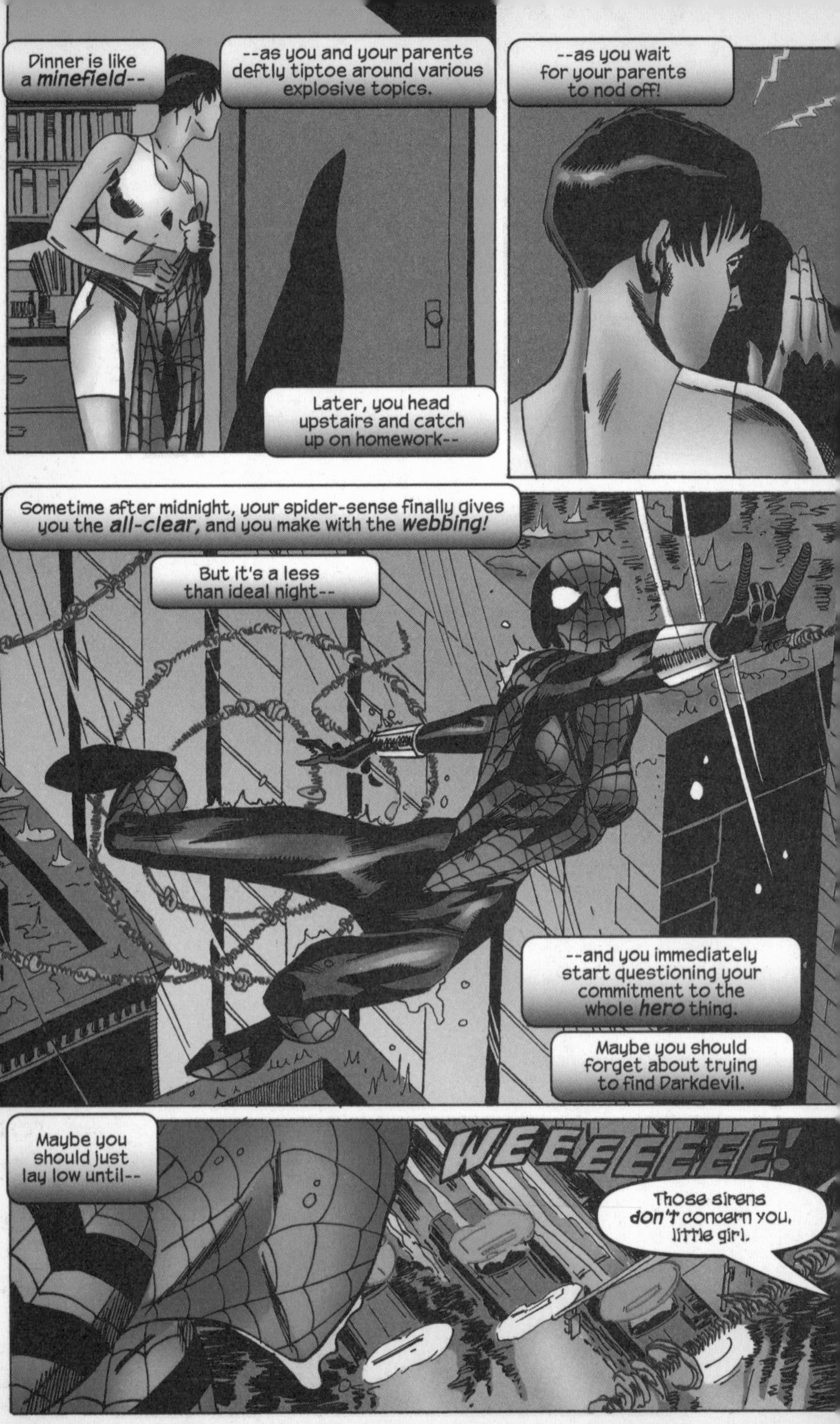
Dinner is like a minefield--
--as you and your parents deftly tiptoe around various explosive topics.
Later, you head upstairs and catch up on homework--
--as you wait for your parents to nod off!
Sometime after midnight, your spider-sense finally gives you the all-clear, and you make with the webbing!
But it's a less than ideal night--
--and you immediately start questioning your commitment to the whole hero thing.
Maybe you should forget about trying to find Darkdevil.
Maybe you should just lay low until--
WEEEEEEE!
Those sirens don't concern you, little girl.

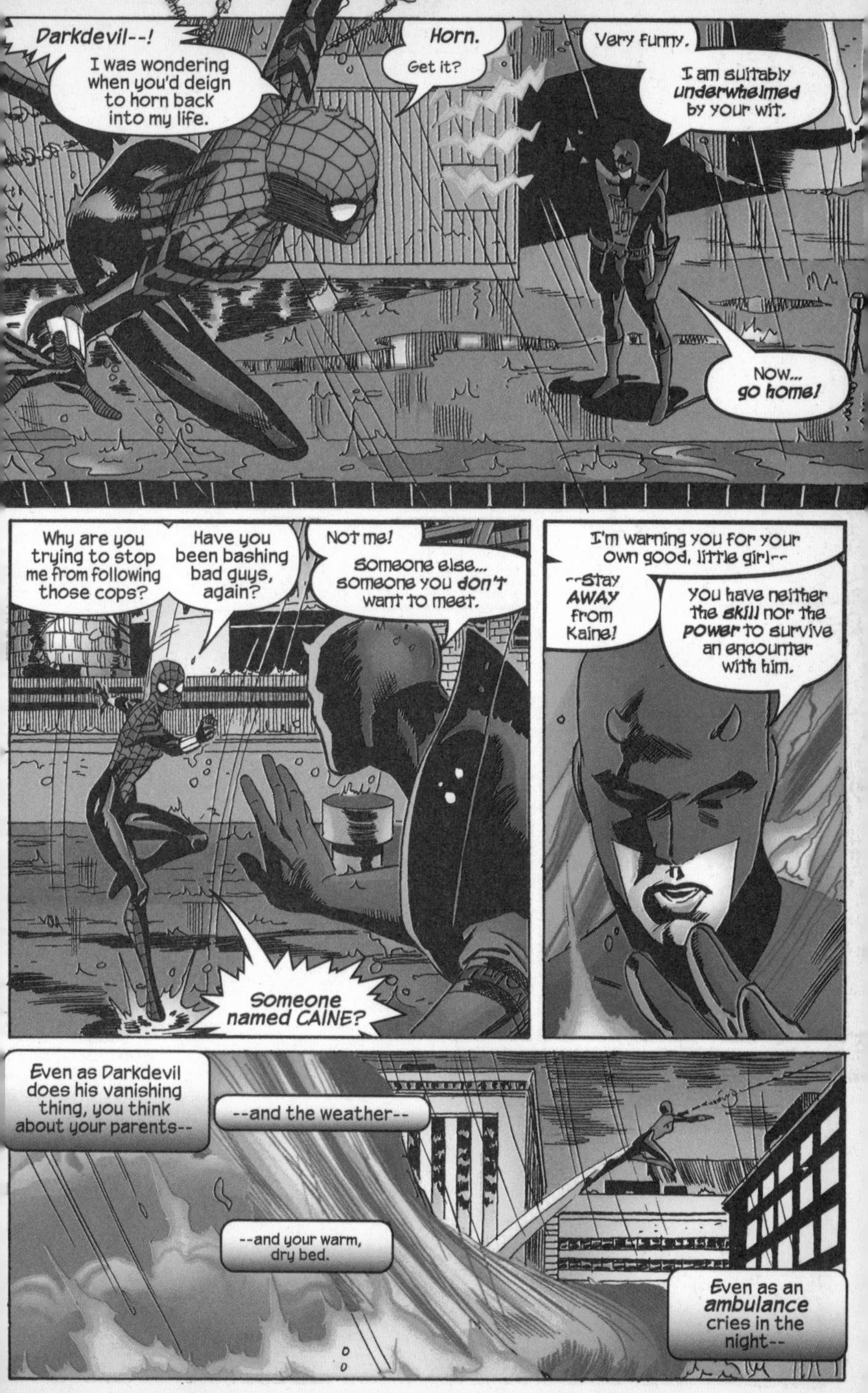
Darkdevil--!
I was wondering when you'd deign to horn back into my life.
Horn.
Get it?
Very funny.
I am suitably *underwhelmed* by your wit.
Now... *go home!*
Why are you trying to stop me from following those cops?
Have you been bashing bad guys, again?
Not me!
Someone else... someone you *don't* want to meet.
Someone named CAINE?
I'm warning you for your own good, little girl--
--Stay *AWAY* from Kaine!
You have neither the *skill* nor the *power* to survive an encounter with him.
Even as Darkdevil does his vanishing thing, you think about your parents--
--and the weather--
--and your warm, dry bed.
Even as an *ambulance* cries in the night--

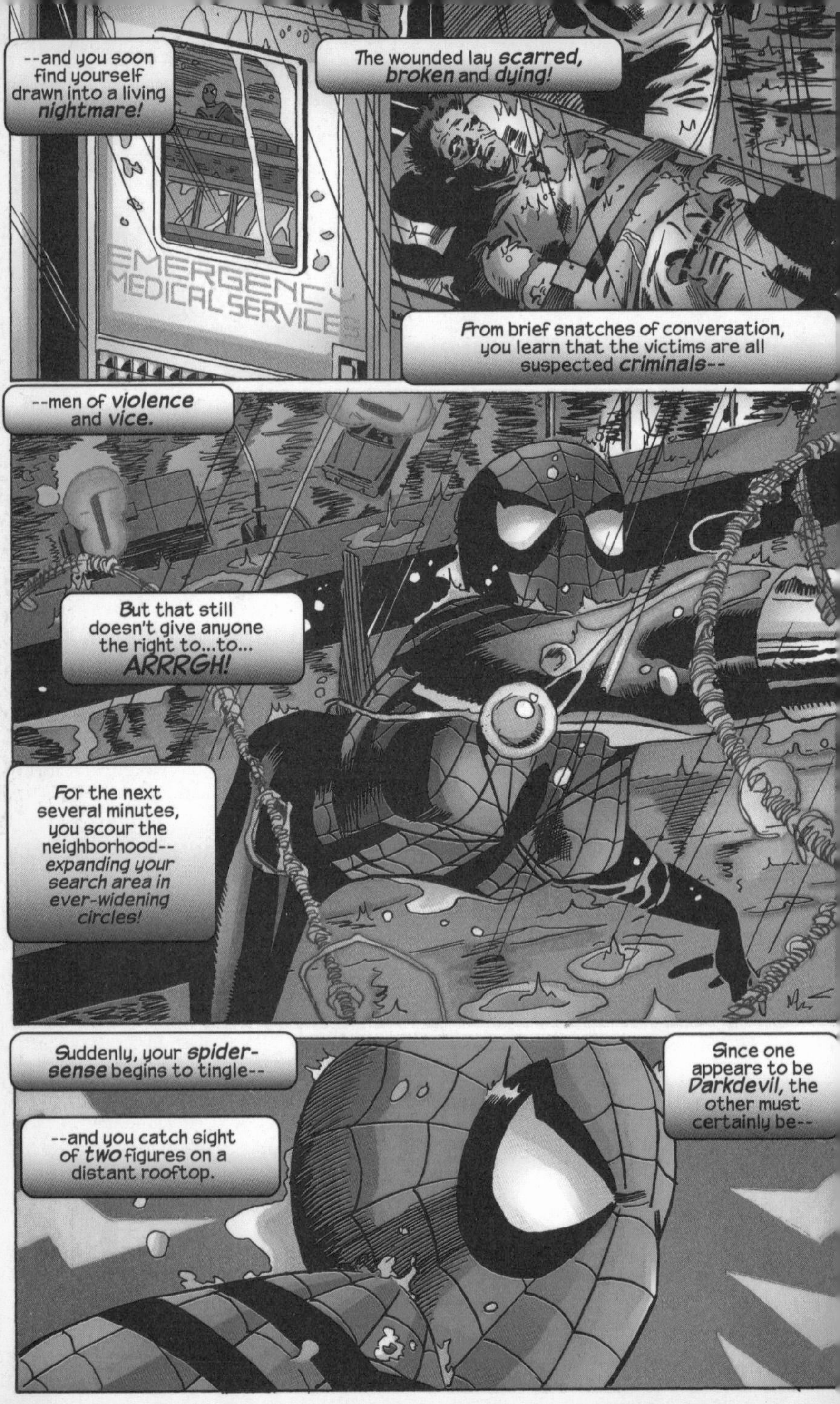
--and you soon find yourself drawn into a living nightmare!
EMERGENCY MEDICAL SERVICES
The wounded lay scarred, broken and dying!
From brief snatches of conversation, you learn that the victims are all suspected criminals--
--men of violence and vice.
But that still doesn't give anyone the right to...to... ARRRGH!
For the next several minutes, you scour the neighborhood--expanding your search area in ever-widening circles!
Suddenly, your spider-sense begins to tingle--
--and you catch sight of two figures on a distant rooftop.
Since one appears to be Darkdevil, the other must certainly be--

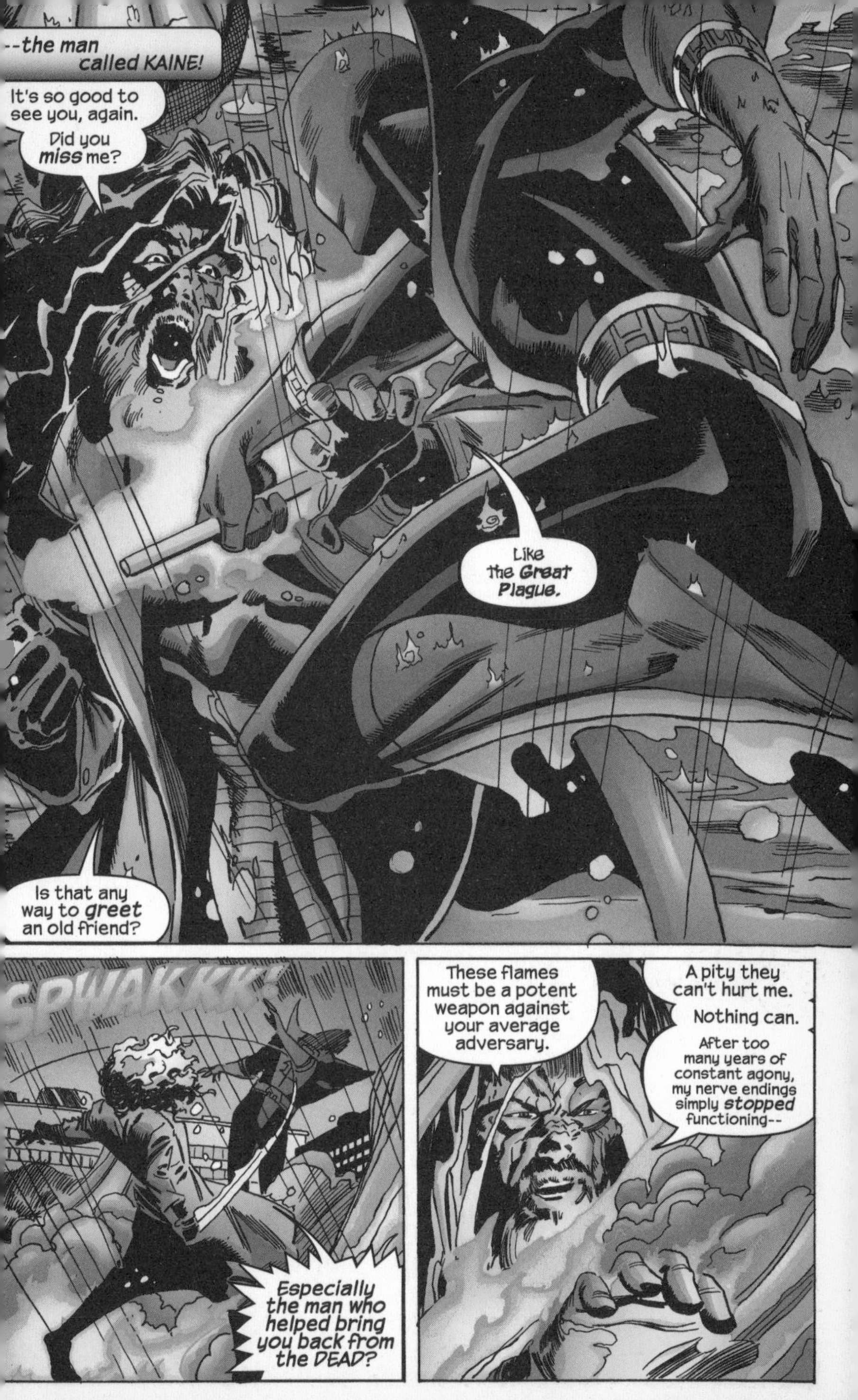
--the man called KAINE!
It's so good to see you, again.
Did you miss me?
Like the Great Plague.
Is that any way to greet an old friend?
SPWAKKK!
Especially the man who helped bring you back from the DEAD?
These flames must be a potent weapon against your average adversary.
A pity they can't hurt me.
Nothing can.
After too many years of constant agony, my nerve endings simply stopped functioning--

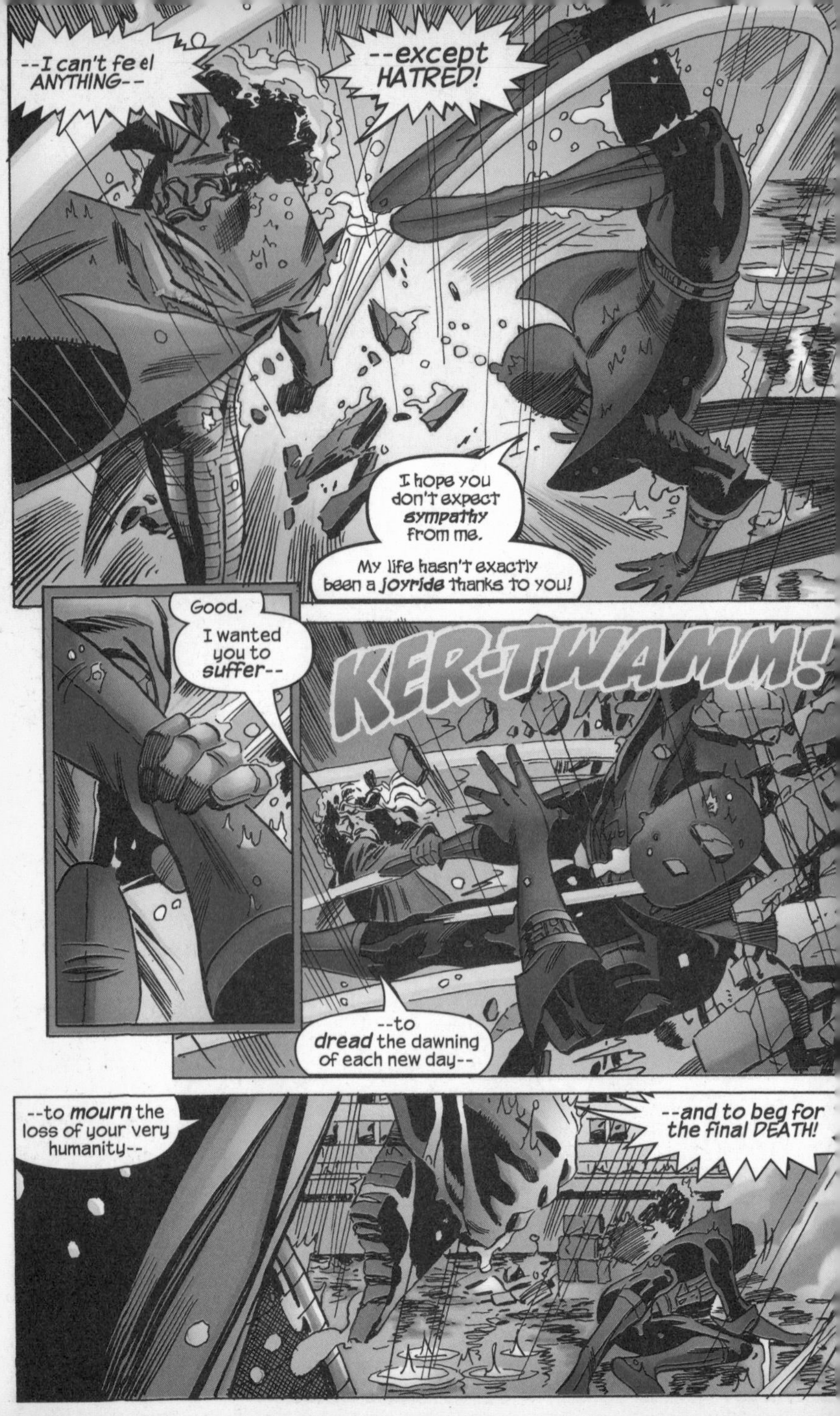
--I can't feel ANYTHING--
--except HATRED!
I hope you don't expect sympathy from me.
My life hasn't exactly been a joyride thanks to you!
Good.
I wanted you to suffer--
KER-TWAMM!
--to dread the dawning of each new day--
--to mourn the loss of your very humanity--
--and to beg for the final DEATH!

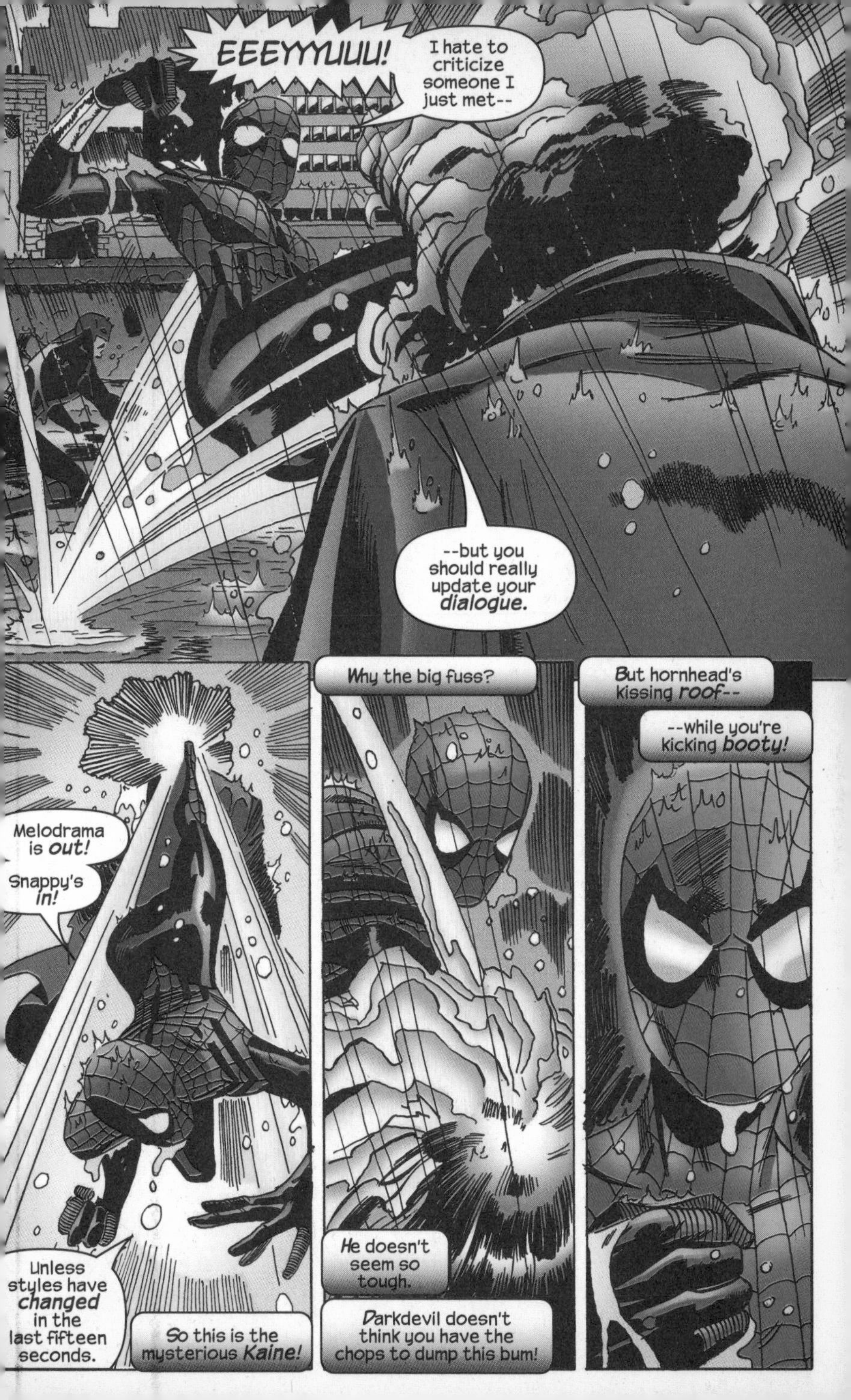
EEEYYYUUUU!
I hate to criticize someone I just met--
--but you should really update your dialogue.
Melodrama is out!
Snappy's in!
Unless styles have changed in the last fifteen seconds.
So this is the mysterious Kaine!
Why the big fuss?
He doesn't seem so tough.
Darkdevil doesn't think you have the chops to dump this bum!
But hornhead's kissing roof--
--while you're kicking booty!

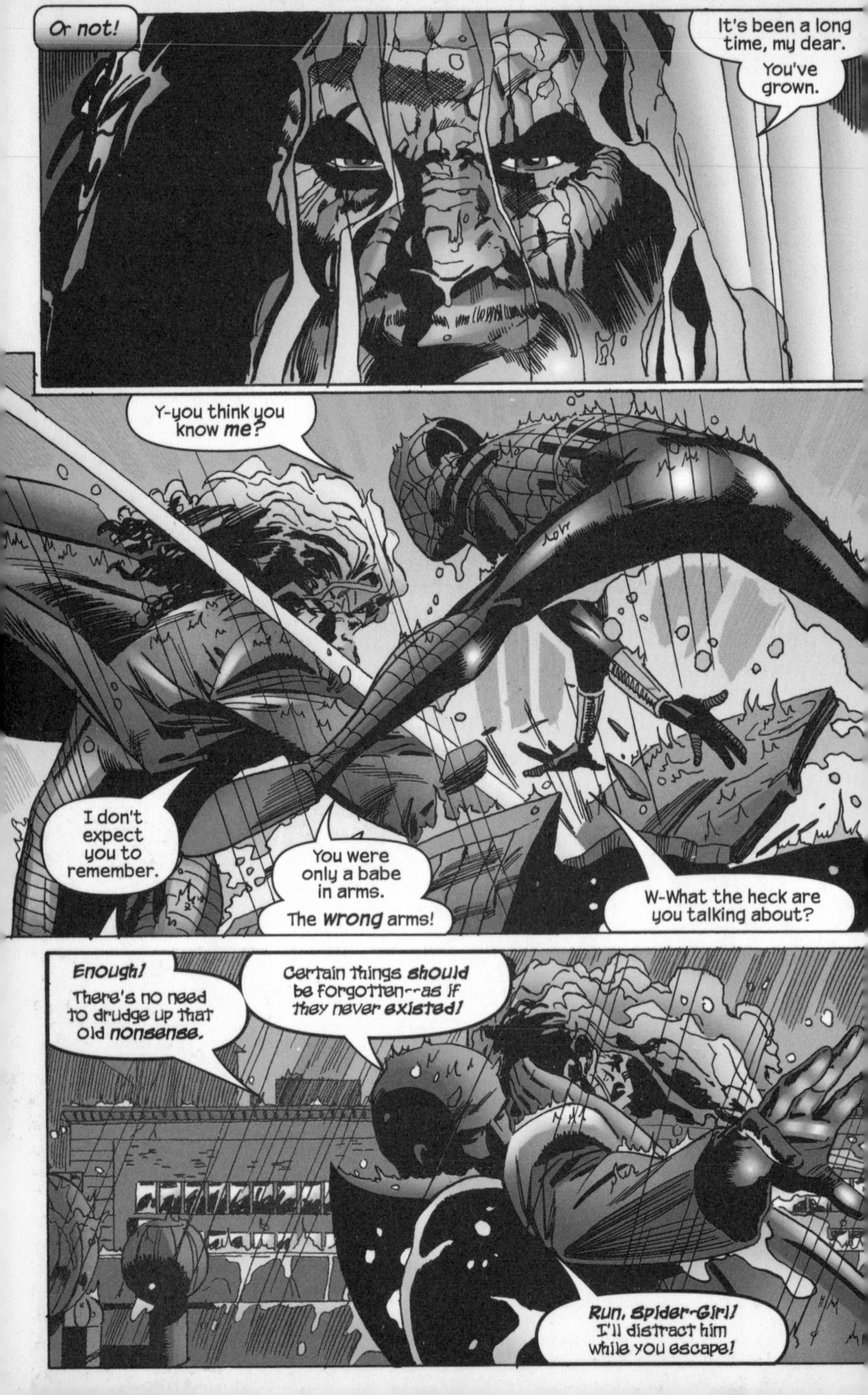
Or not!
It's been a long time, my dear.
You've grown.
Y-you think you know *me*?
I don't expect you to remember.
You were only a babe in arms.
The *wrong* arms!
W-What the heck are you talking about?
Enough!
There's no need to drudge up that old *nonsense.*
Certain things *should* be forgotten--as if *they never existed!*
Run, Spider-Girl!
I'll distract him while you escape!

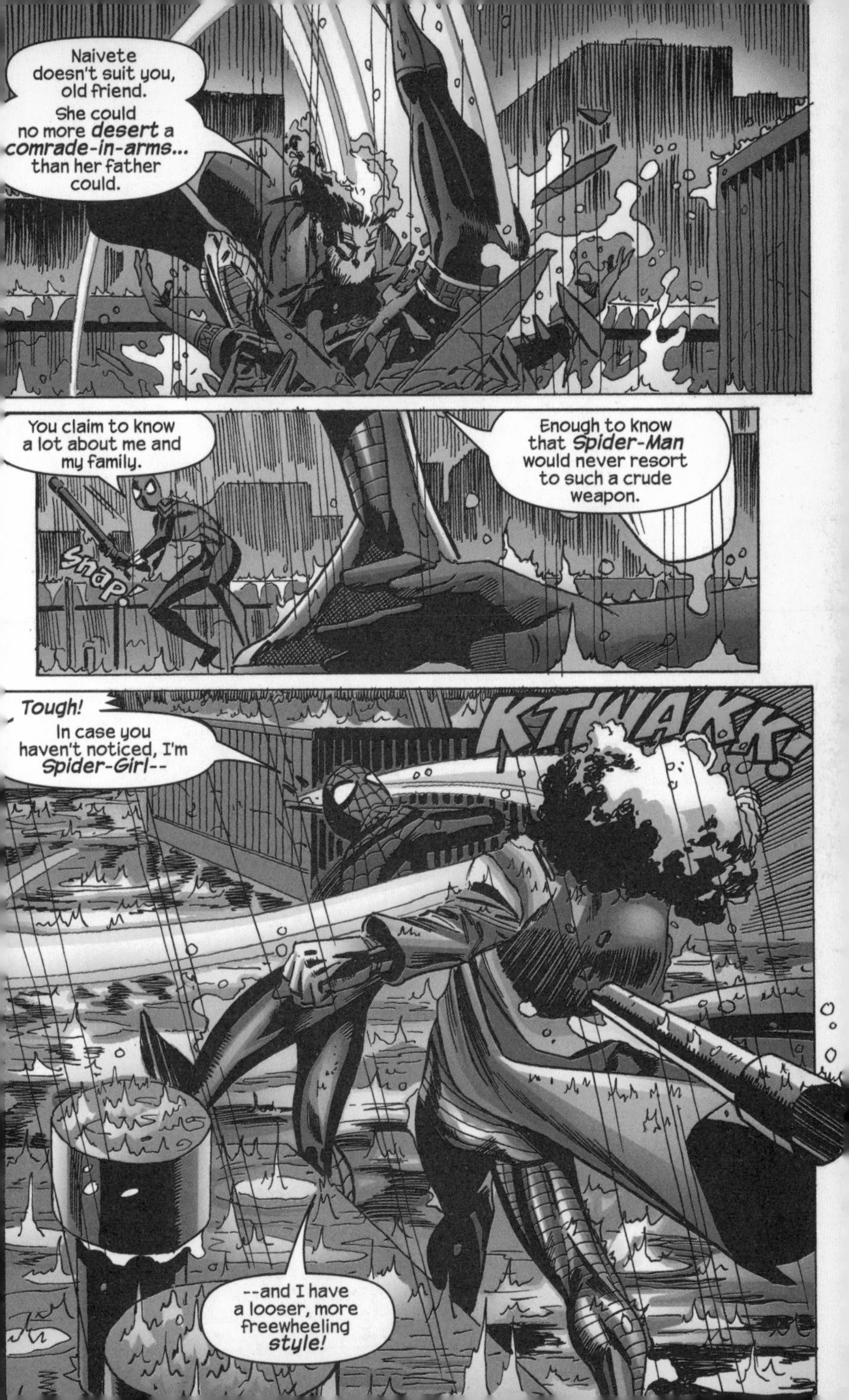
Naivete doesn't suit you, old friend.
She could no more *desert* a *comrade-in-arms...* than her father could.
You claim to know a lot about me and my family.
Enough to know that *Spider-Man* would never resort to such a crude weapon.
Snap!
Tough!
In case you haven't noticed, I'm *Spider-Girl*--
KTWAKK!
--and I have a looser, more freewheeling *style!*

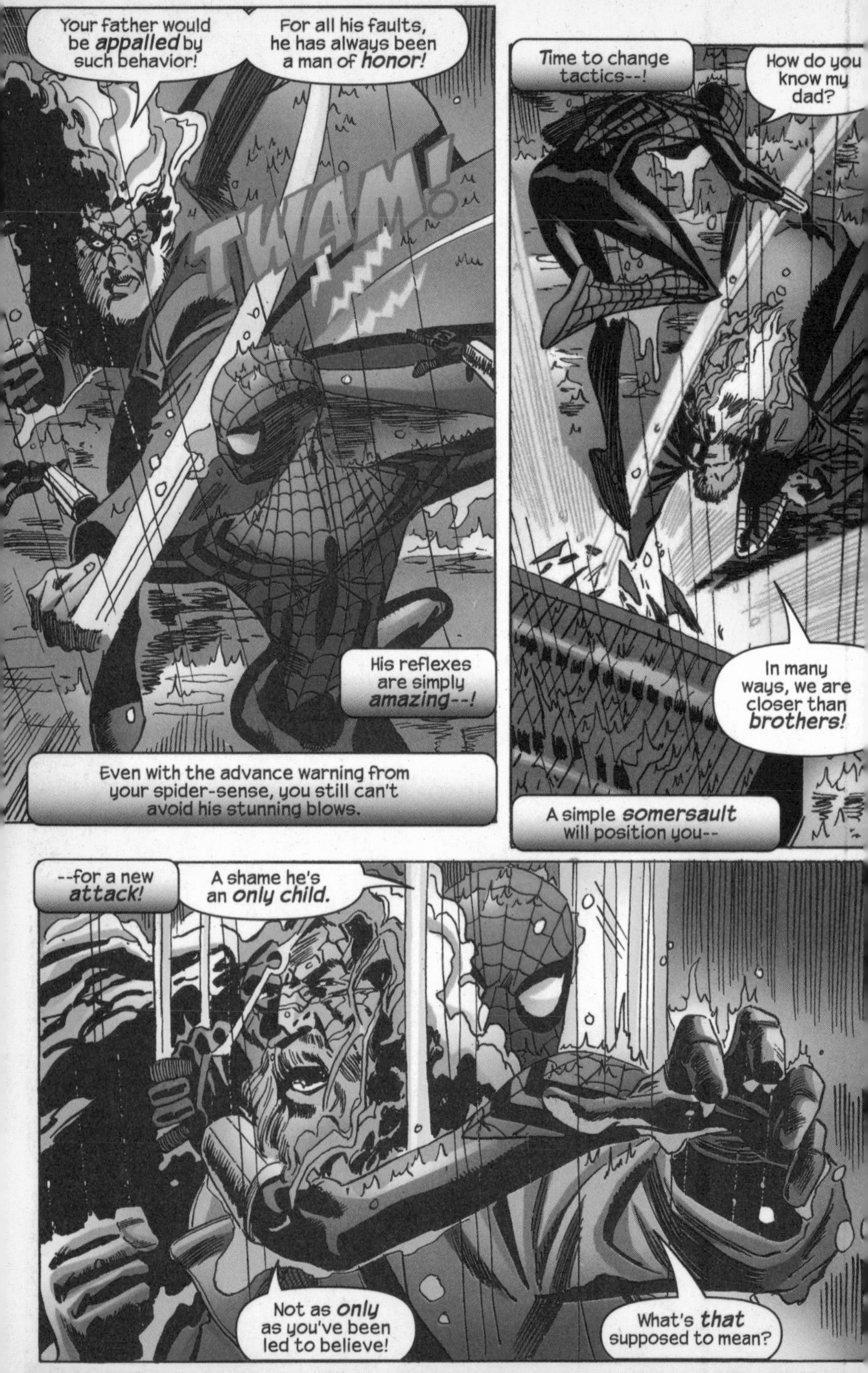
Your father would be appalled by such behavior!
For all his faults, he has always been a man of honor!
TWAM!
His reflexes are simply amazing--!
Even with the advance warning from your spider-sense, you still can't avoid his stunning blows.
Time to change tactics--!
How do you know my dad?
In many ways, we are closer than brothers!
A simple somersault will position you--
--for a new attack!
A shame he's an only child.
Not as only as you've been led to believe!
What's that supposed to mean?

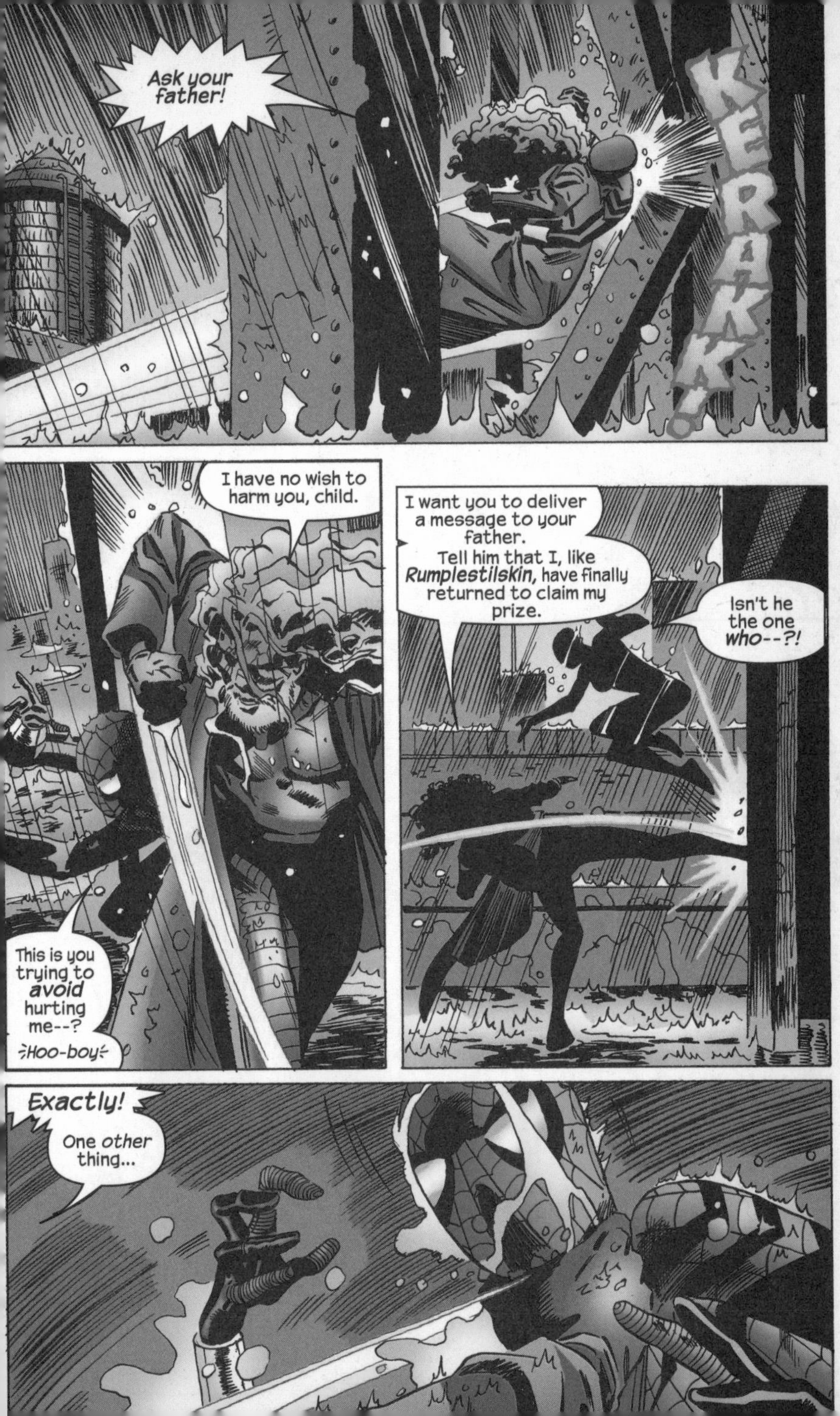
Ask your father!
KERAKK!
I have no wish to harm you, child.
This is you trying to avoid hurting me--? ≷Hoo-boy≶
I want you to deliver a message to your father. Tell him that I, like Rumplestilskin, have finally returned to claim my prize.
Isn't he the one who--?!
Exactly!
One other thing...

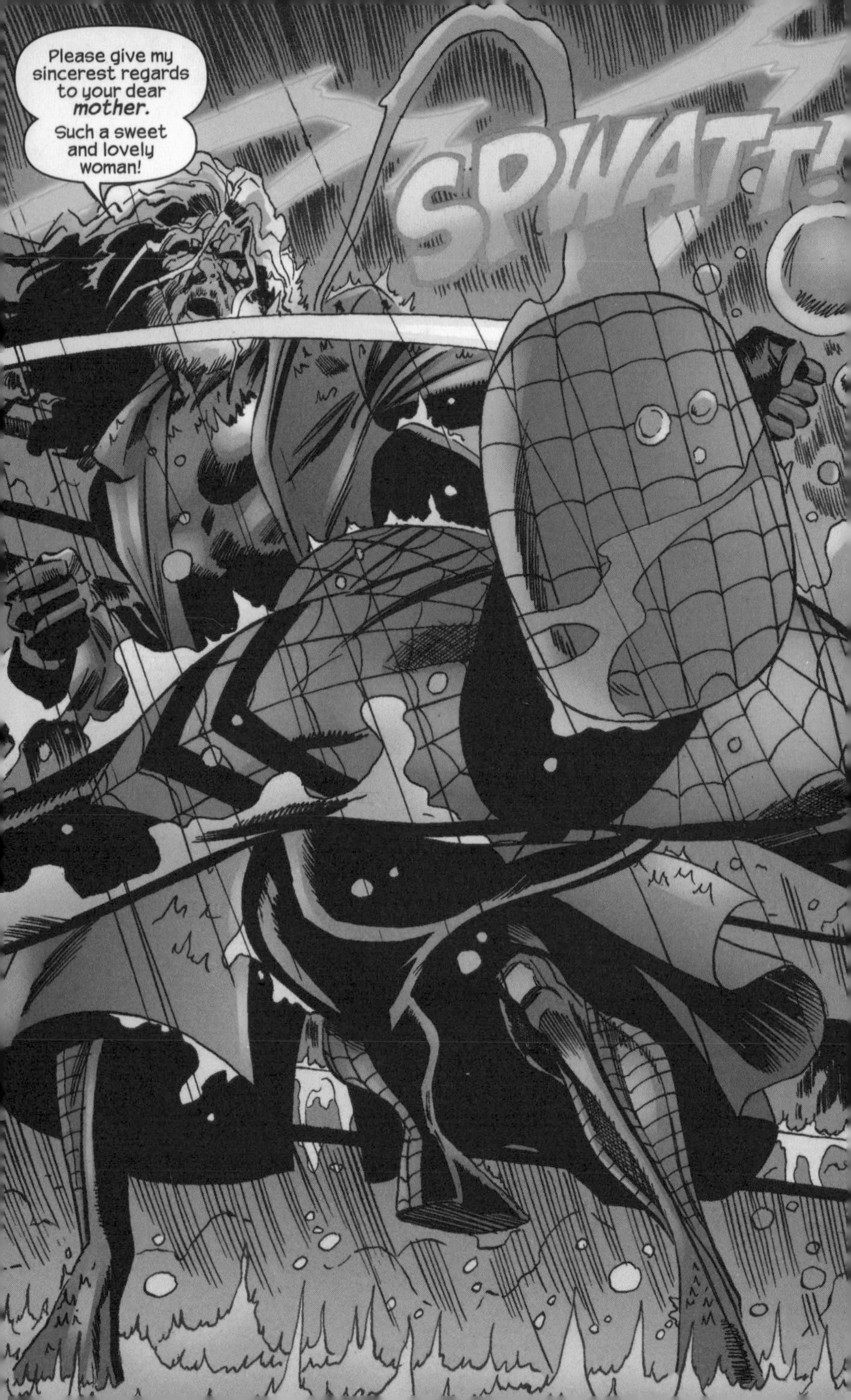
Please give my sincerest regards to your dear *mother.*
Such a sweet and lovely woman!
SPWATT!

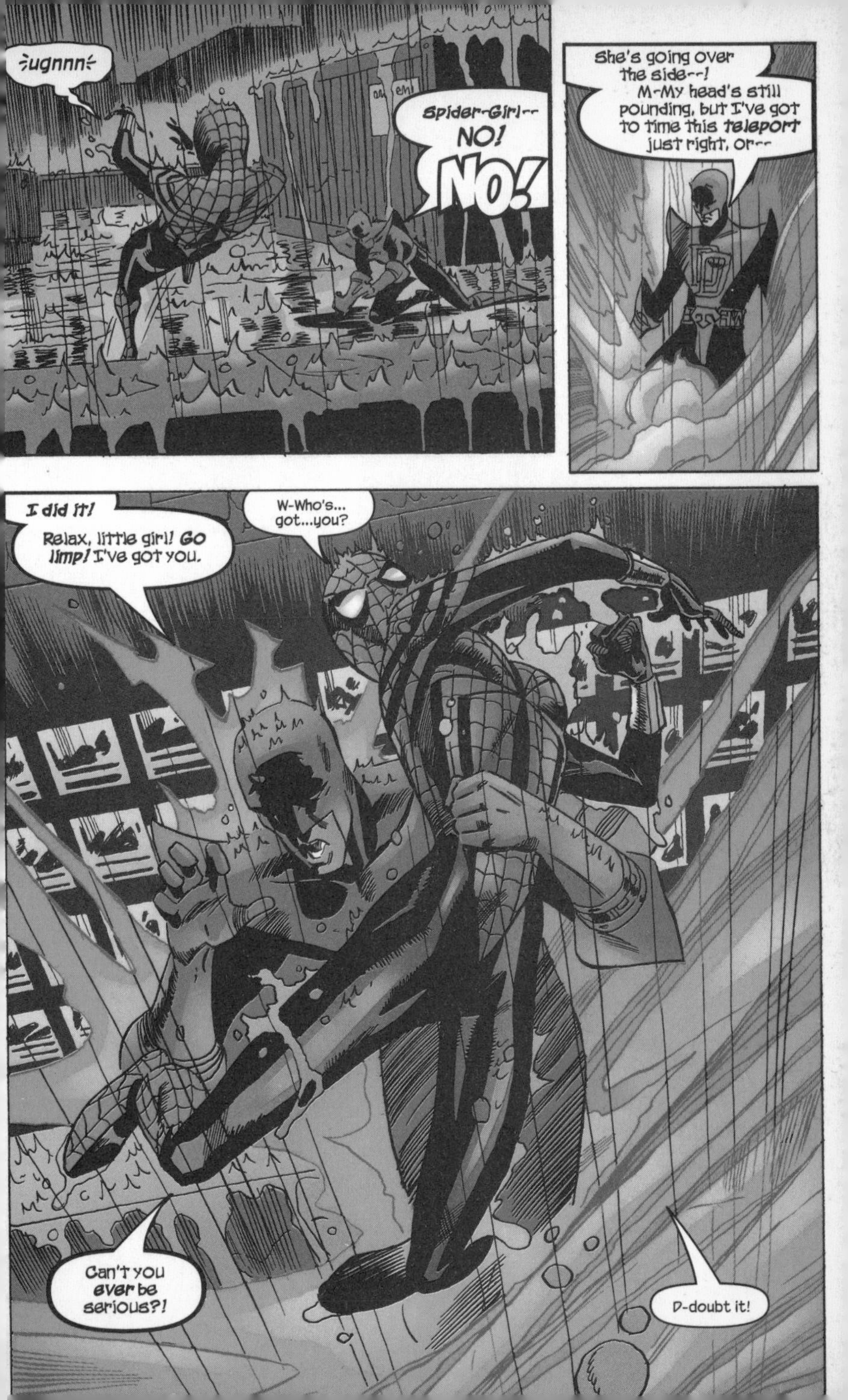

ugnnn
Spider-Girl-- NO! NO!
She's going over the side--! M-My head's still pounding, but I've got to time this teleport just right, or--
I did it!
Relax, little girl! GO limp! I've got you.
W-Who's... got...you?
Can't you ever be serious?!
D-doubt it!

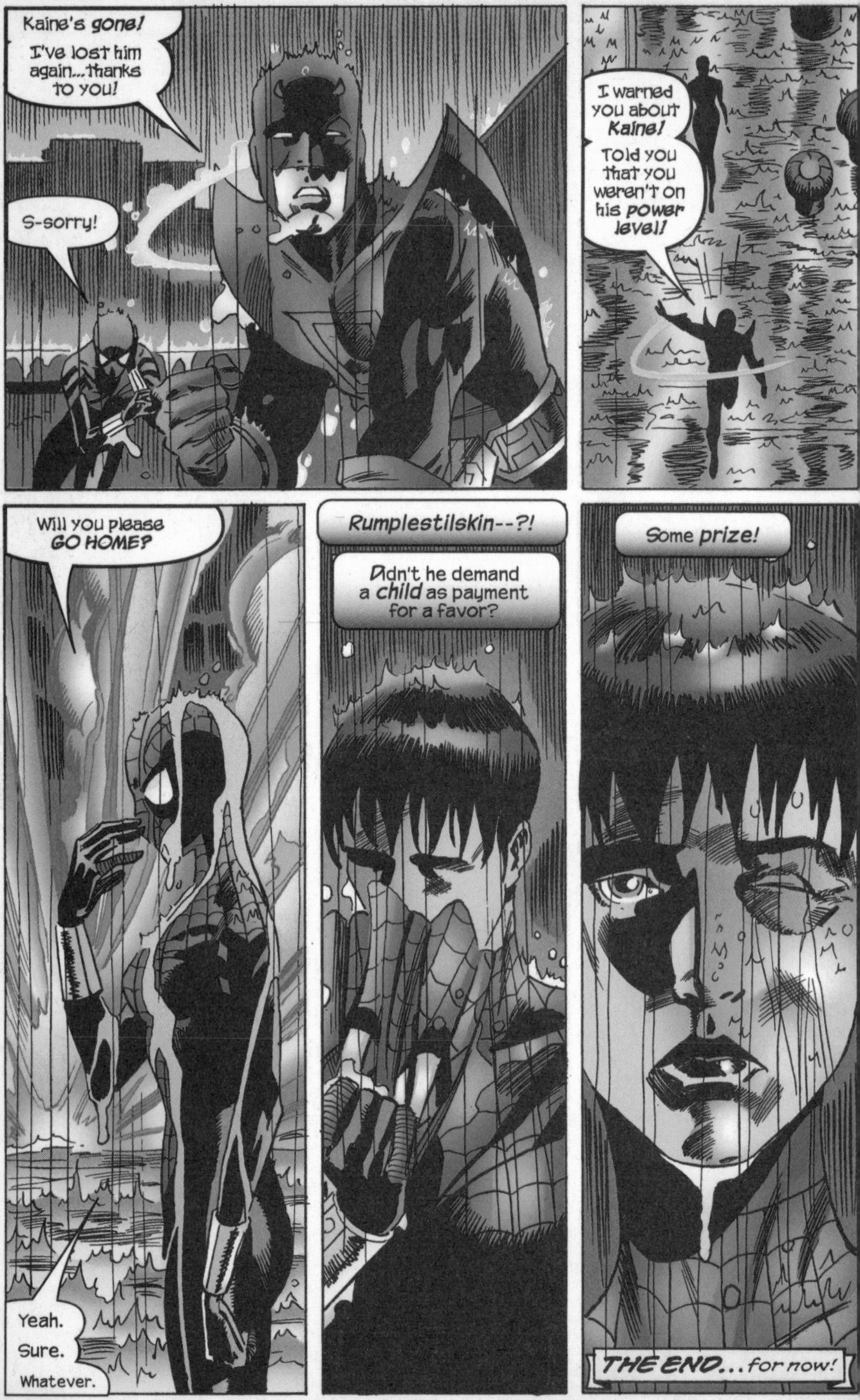
Kaine's gone!
I've lost him again...thanks to you!
S-sorry!
I warned you about Kaine!
Told you that you weren't on his power level!
Will you please GO HOME?
Yeah.
Sure.
Whatever.
Rumplestilskin--?!
Didn't he demand a child as payment for a favor?
Some prize!
THE END...for now!

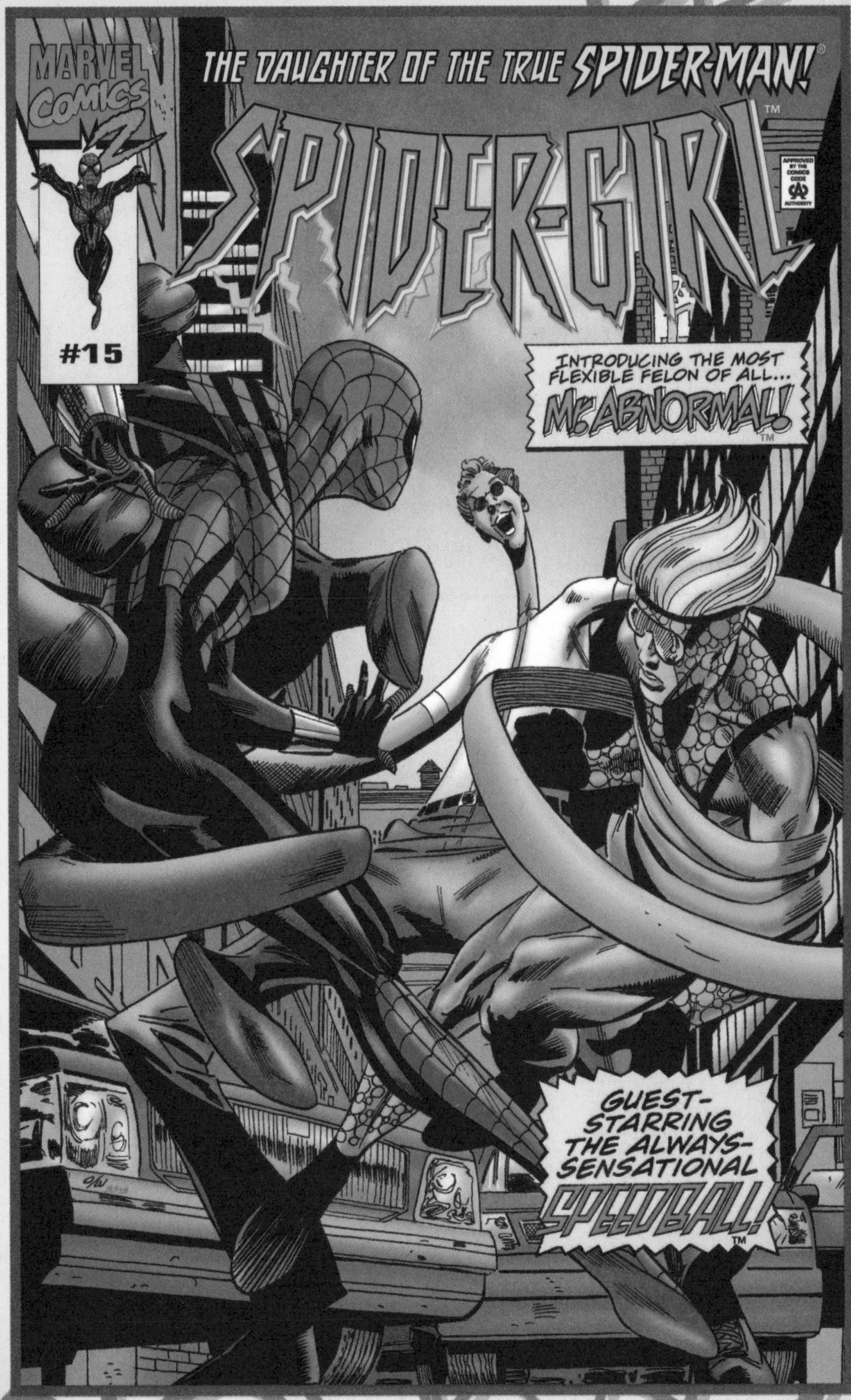
MARVEL COMICS
THE DAUGHTER OF THE TRUE SPIDER-MAN!
SPIDER-GIRL
#15
INTRODUCING THE MOST FLEXIBLE FELON OF ALL... Mr. ABNORMAL!
GUEST-STARRING THE ALWAYS-SENSATIONAL SPEEDBALL!

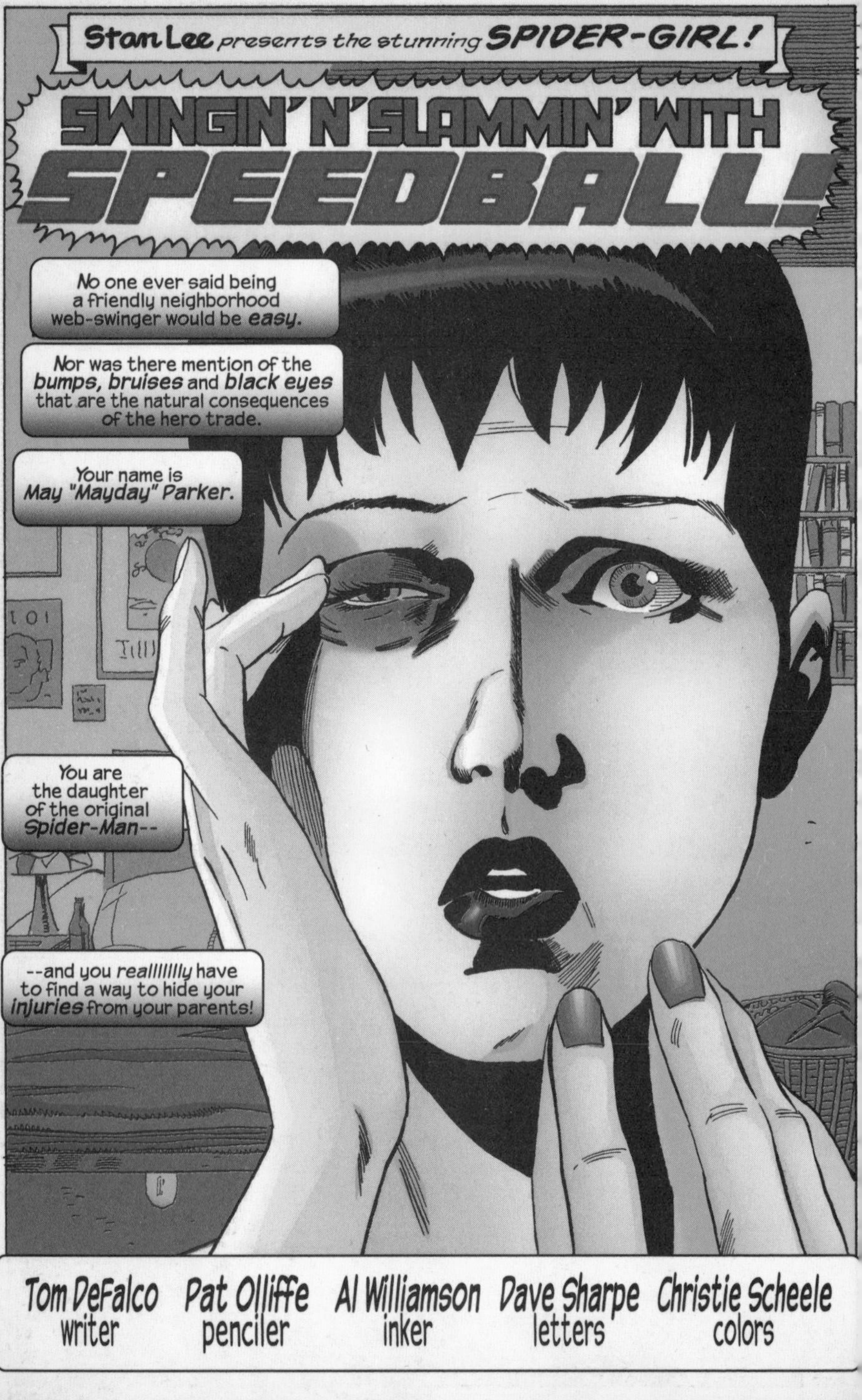
Stan Lee presents the stunning SPIDER-GIRL!
SWINGIN' 'N' SLAMMIN' WITH SPEEDBALL!
No one ever said being a friendly neighborhood web-swinger would be easy.
Nor was there mention of the bumps, bruises and black eyes that are the natural consequences of the hero trade.
Your name is May "Mayday" Parker.
You are the daughter of the original Spider-Man--
--and you reallllllly have to find a way to hide your injuries from your parents!
Tom DeFalco writer
Pat Olliffe penciler
Al Williamson inker
Dave Sharpe letters
Christie Scheele colors

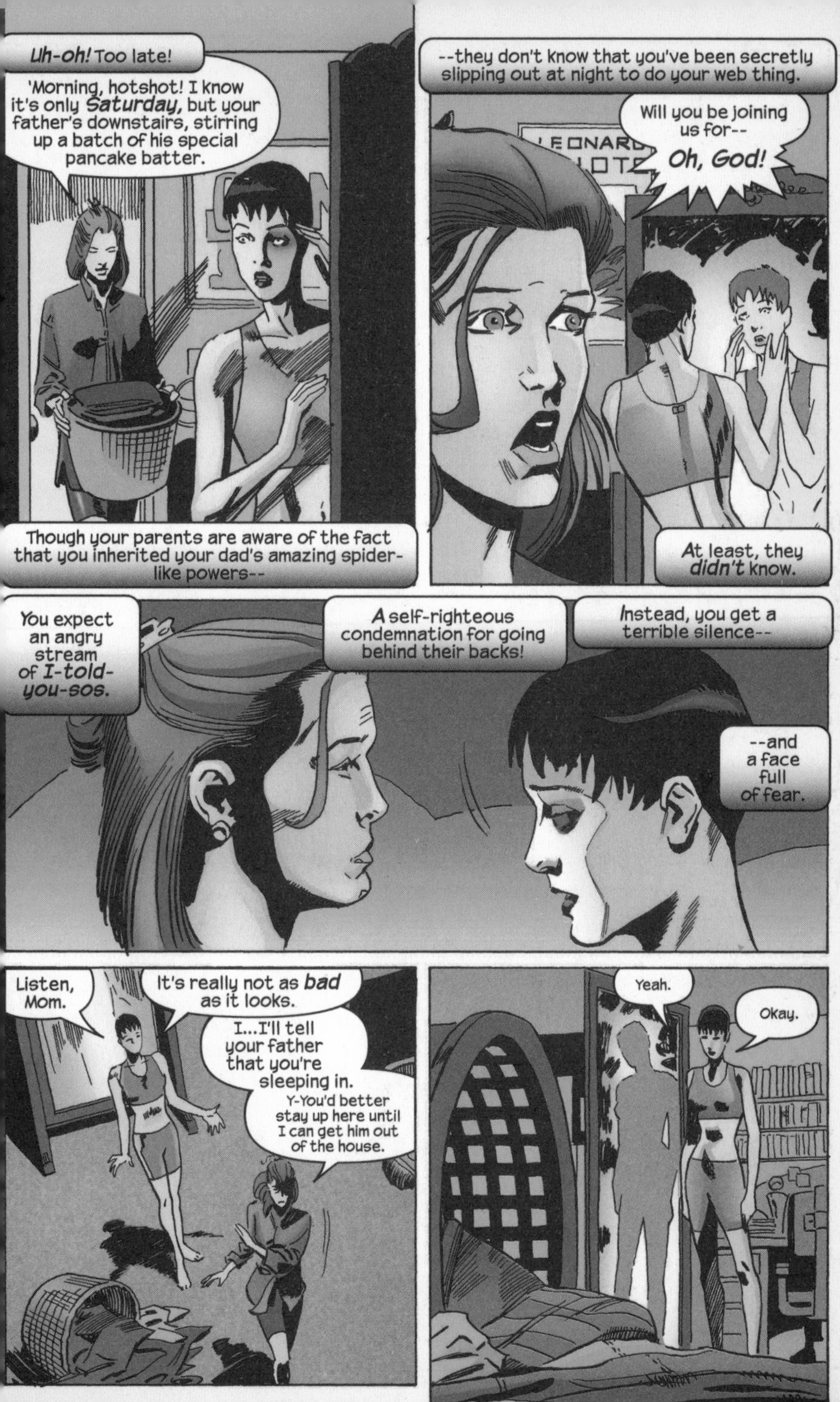
Uh-oh! Too late!
'Morning, hotshot! I know it's only Saturday, but your father's downstairs, stirring up a batch of his special pancake batter.
Though your parents are aware of the fact that you inherited your dad's amazing spider-like powers--
--they don't know that you've been secretly slipping out at night to do your web thing.
Will you be joining us for--
Oh, God!
At least, they didn't know.
You expect an angry stream of I-told-you-sos.
A self-righteous condemnation for going behind their backs!
Instead, you get a terrible silence--
--and a face full of fear.
Listen, Mom.
It's really not as bad as it looks.
I...I'll tell your father that you're sleeping in.
Y-You'd better stay up here until I can get him out of the house.
Yeah.
Okay.

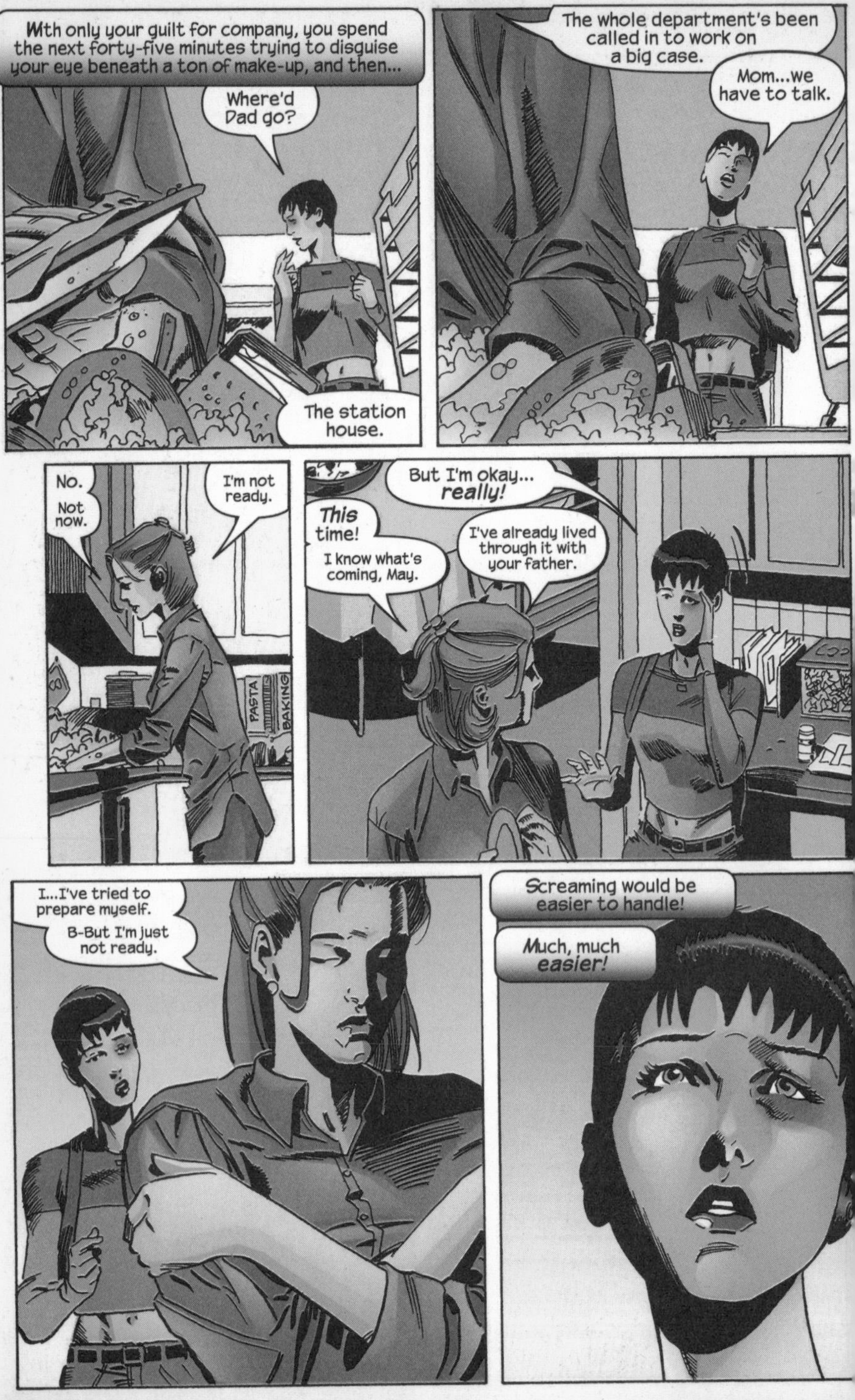
With only your guilt for company, you spend the next forty-five minutes trying to disguise your eye beneath a ton of make-up, and then...
Where'd Dad go?
The station house.
The whole department's been called in to work on a big case.
Mom...we have to talk.
No.
Not now.
I'm not ready.
But I'm okay... really!
This time!
I know what's coming, May.
I've already lived through it with your father.
PASTA
BAKING
I...I've tried to prepare myself.
B-But I'm just not ready.
Screaming would be easier to handle!
Much, much easier!

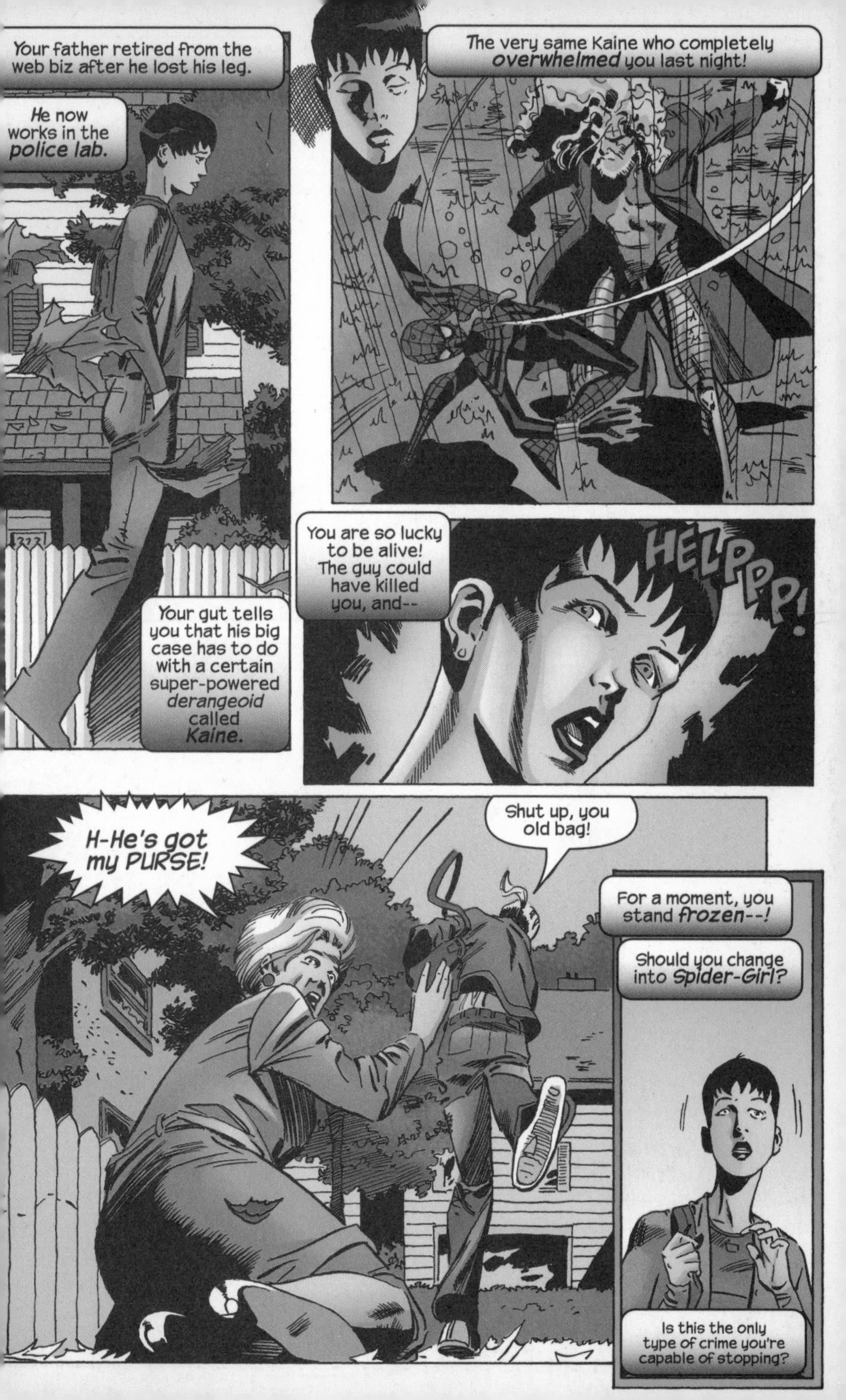
Your father retired from the web biz after he lost his leg.
He now works in the police lab.
Your gut tells you that his big case has to do with a certain super-powered derangeoid called Kaine.
The very same Kaine who completely overwhelmed you last night!
You are so lucky to be alive! The guy could have killed you, and--
HELPPP!
H-He's got my PURSE!
Shut up, you old bag!
For a moment, you stand frozen--!
Should you change into Spider-Girl?
Is this the only type of crime you're capable of stopping?

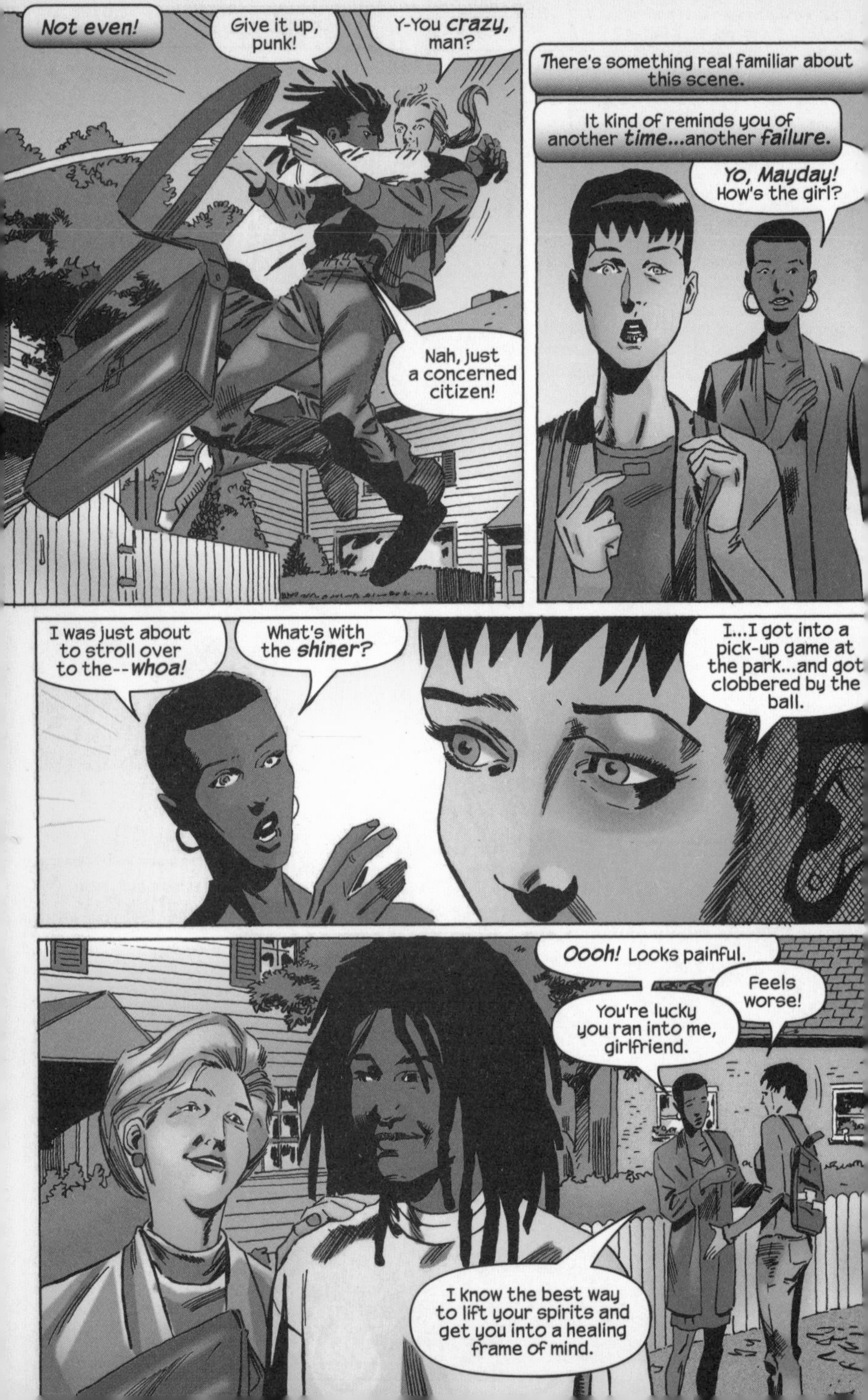
Not even!
Give it up, punk!
Y-You crazy, man?
Nah, just a concerned citizen!
There's something real familiar about this scene.
It kind of reminds you of another time...another failure.
Yo, Mayday! How's the girl?
I was just about to stroll over to the--whoa!
What's with the shiner?
I...I got into a pick-up game at the park...and got clobbered by the ball.
Oooh! Looks painful.
Feels worse!
You're lucky you ran into me, girlfriend.
I know the best way to lift your spirits and get you into a healing frame of mind.

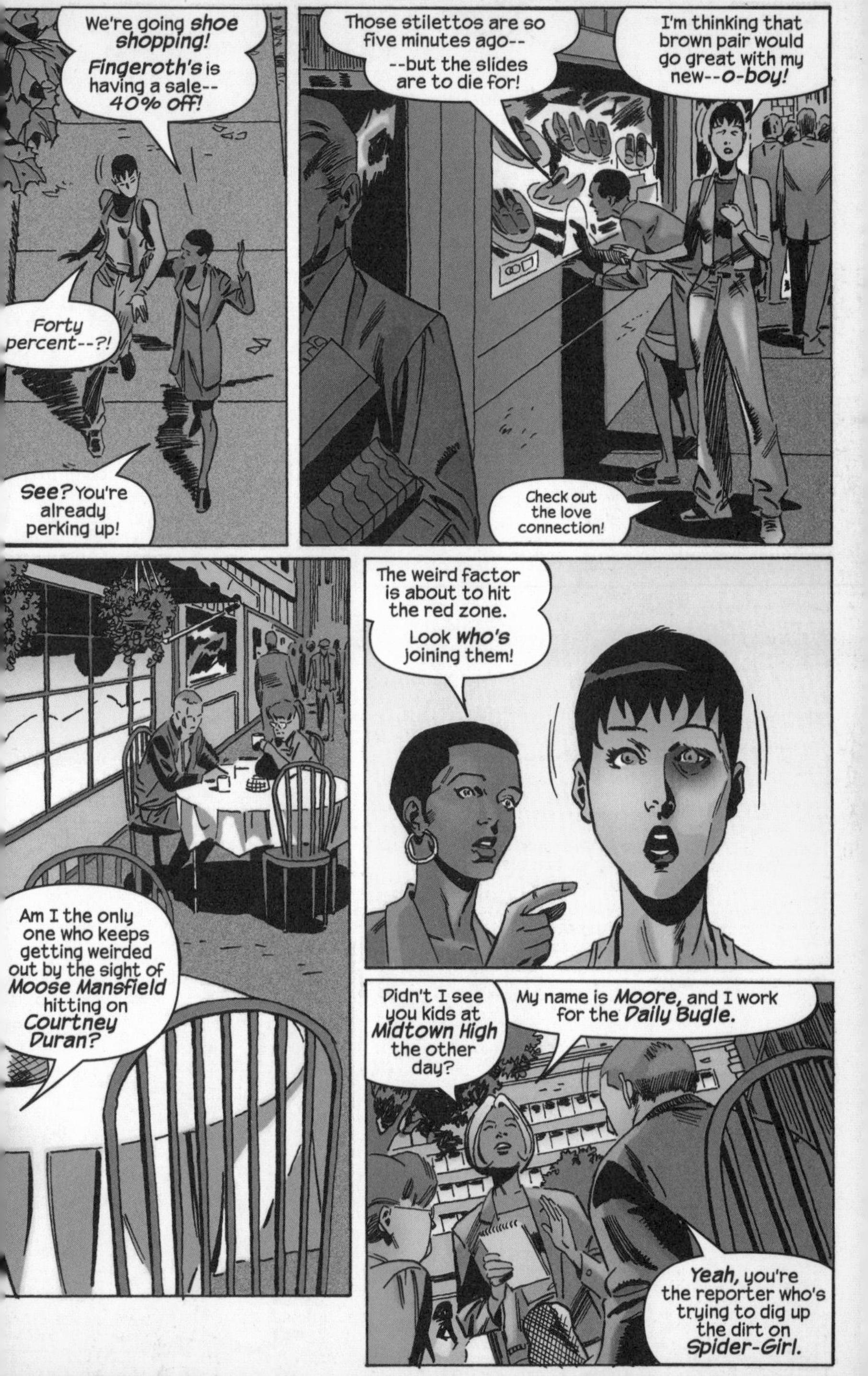
We're going shoe shopping!
Fingeroth's is having a sale-- 40% off!
Forty percent--?!
See? You're already perking up!
Those stilettos are so five minutes ago--
--but the slides are to die for!
I'm thinking that brown pair would go great with my new--o-boy!
Check out the love connection!
Am I the only one who keeps getting weirded out by the sight of Moose Mansfield hitting on Courtney Duran?
The weird factor is about to hit the red zone.
Look who's joining them!
Didn't I see you kids at Midtown High the other day?
My name is Moore, and I work for the Daily Bugle.
Yeah, you're the reporter who's trying to dig up the dirt on Spider-Girl.

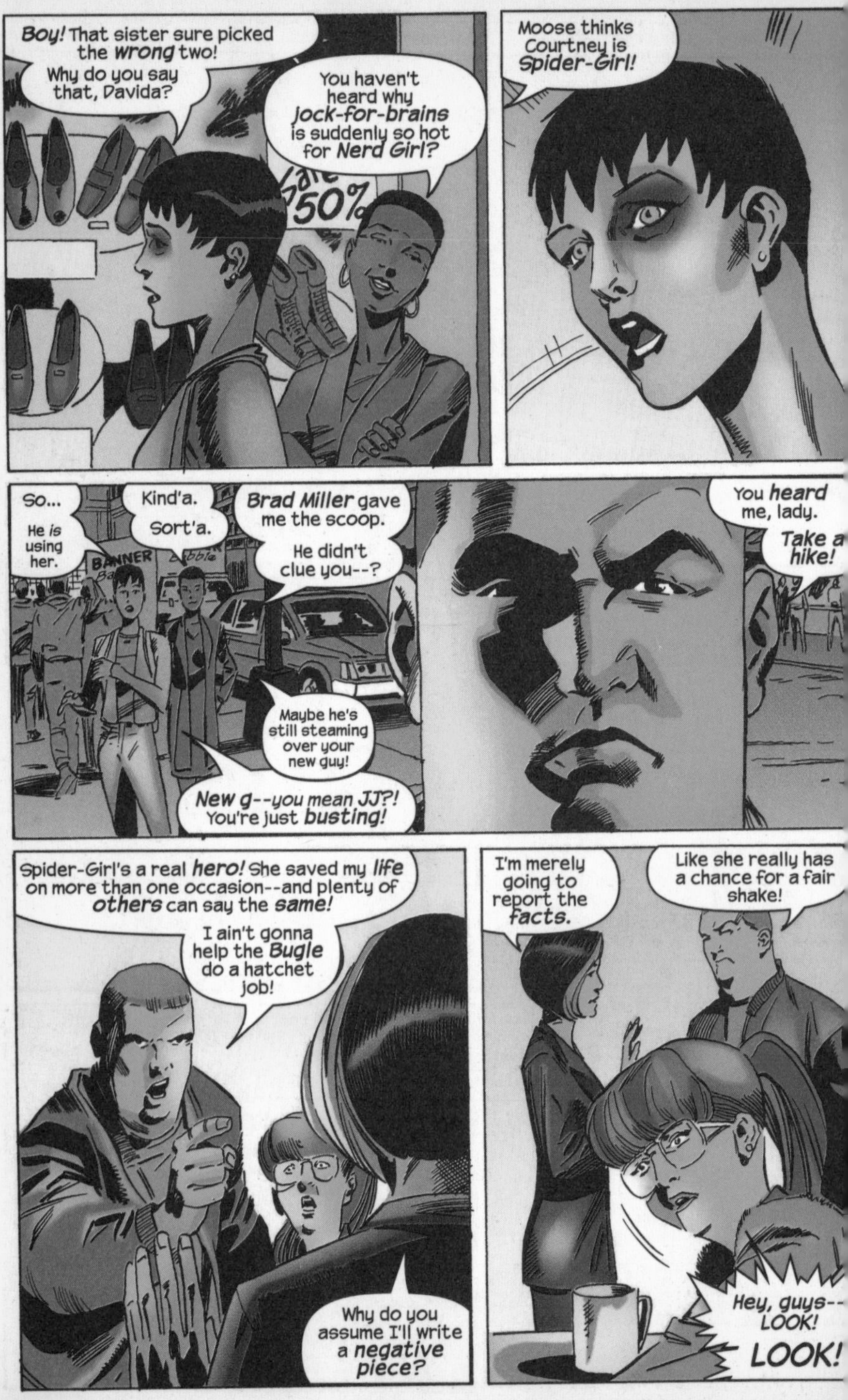
Boy! That sister sure picked the wrong two!
Why do you say that, Davida?
You haven't heard why jock-for-brains is suddenly so hot for Nerd Girl?
50%
Moose thinks Courtney is Spider-Girl!
So...
He is using her.
Kind'a.
Sort'a.
Brad Miller gave me the scoop.
He didn't clue you--?
BANNER
Maybe he's still steaming over your new guy!
New g--you mean JJ?! You're just busting!
You heard me, lady.
Take a hike!
Spider-Girl's a real hero! She saved my life on more than one occasion--and plenty of others can say the same!
I ain't gonna help the Bugle do a hatchet job!
Why do you assume I'll write a negative piece?
I'm merely going to report the facts.
Like she really has a chance for a fair shake!
Hey, guys-- LOOK!
LOOK!

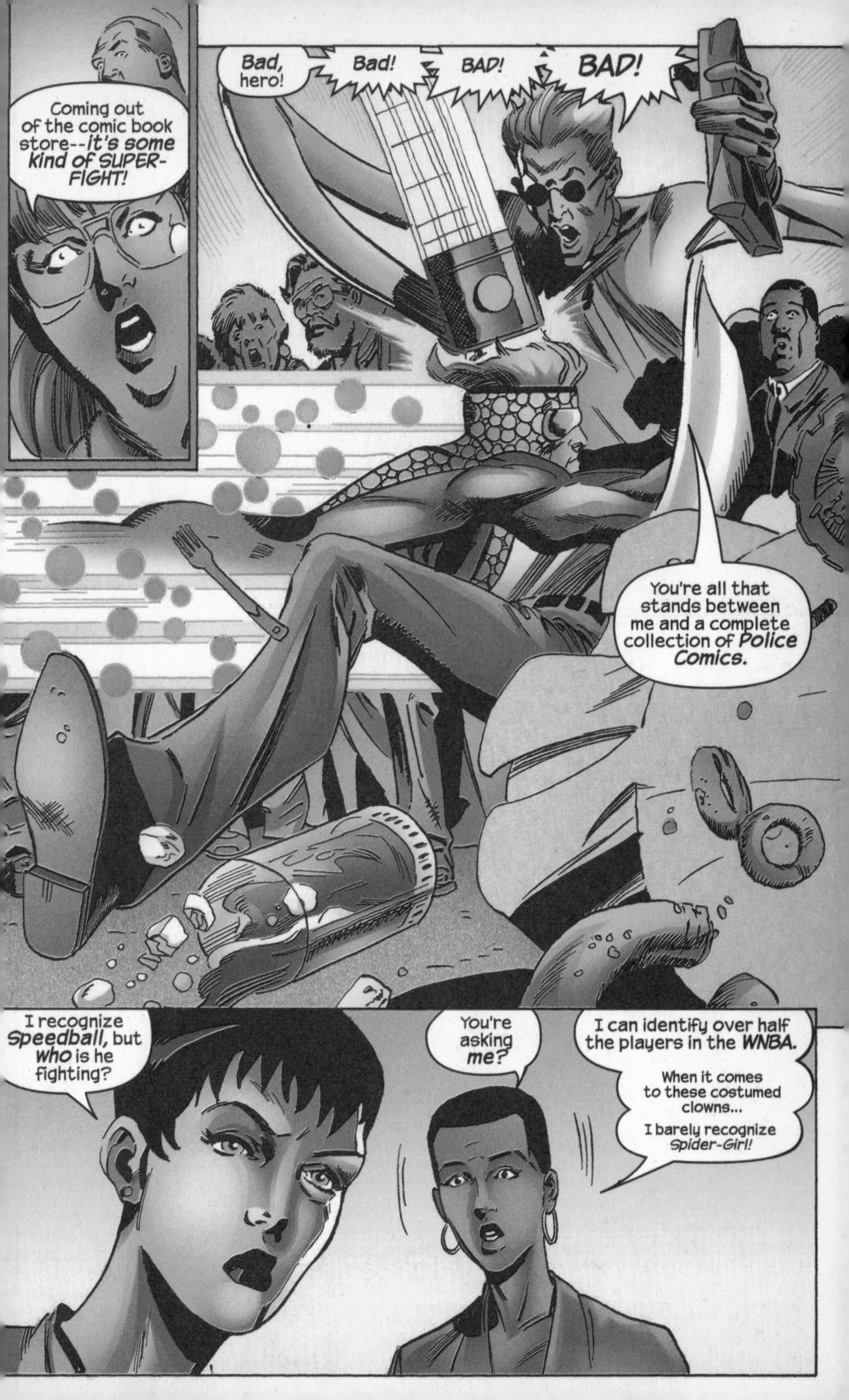
Coming out of the comic book store--it's some kind of SUPER-FIGHT!
Bad, hero!
Bad!
BAD!
BAD!
You're all that stands between me and a complete collection of Police Comics.
I recognize Speedball, but who is he fighting?
You're asking me?
I can identify over half the players in the WNBA.
When it comes to these costumed clowns...
I barely recognize Spider-Girl!

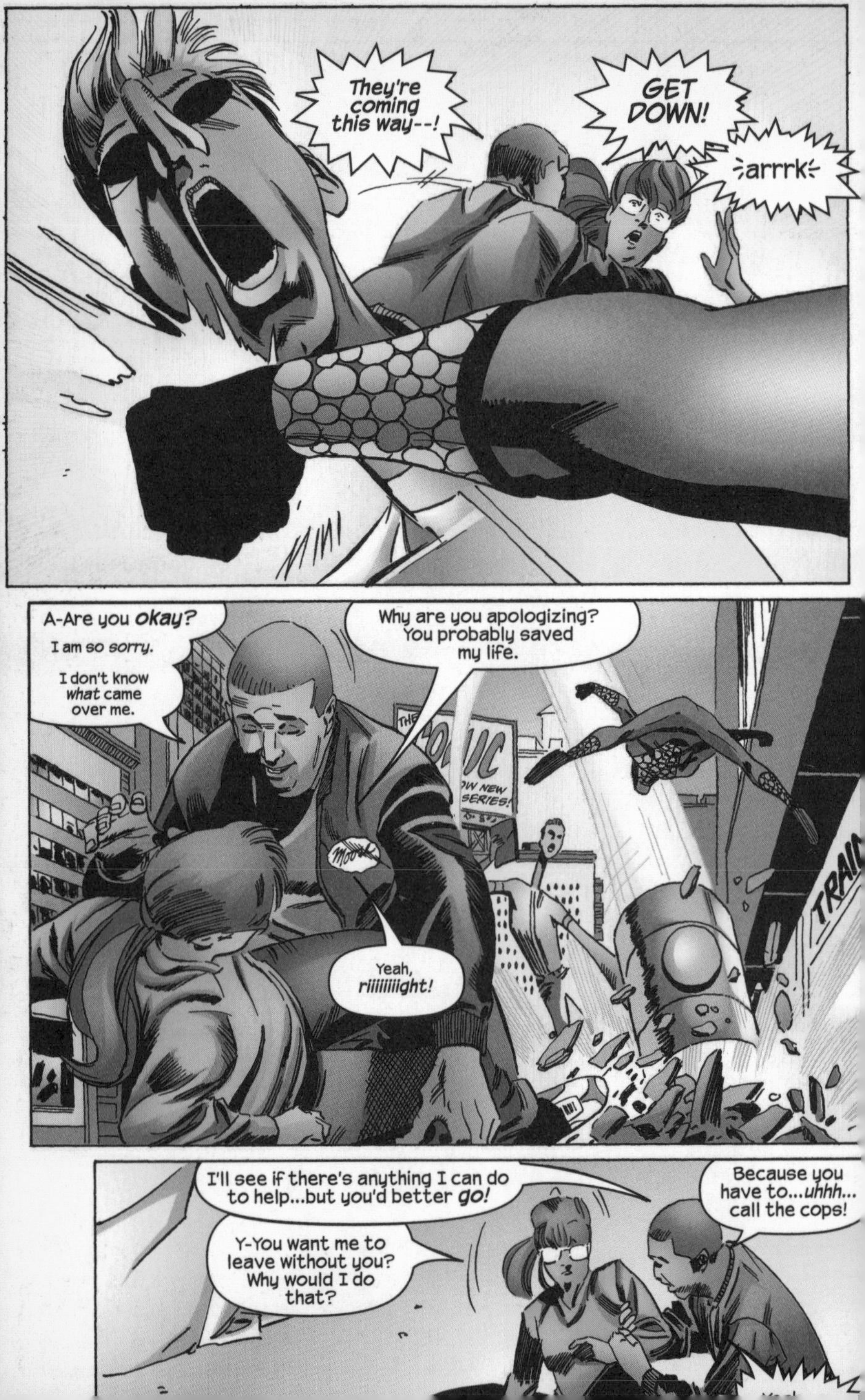
They're coming this way--!
GET DOWN!
arrrk
A-Are you okay?
I am so sorry.
I don't know what came over me.
Why are you apologizing? You probably saved my life.
Yeah, riiiiiiight!
I'll see if there's anything I can do to help...but you'd better go!
Y-You want me to leave without you? Why would I do that?
Because you have to...uhhh... call the cops!

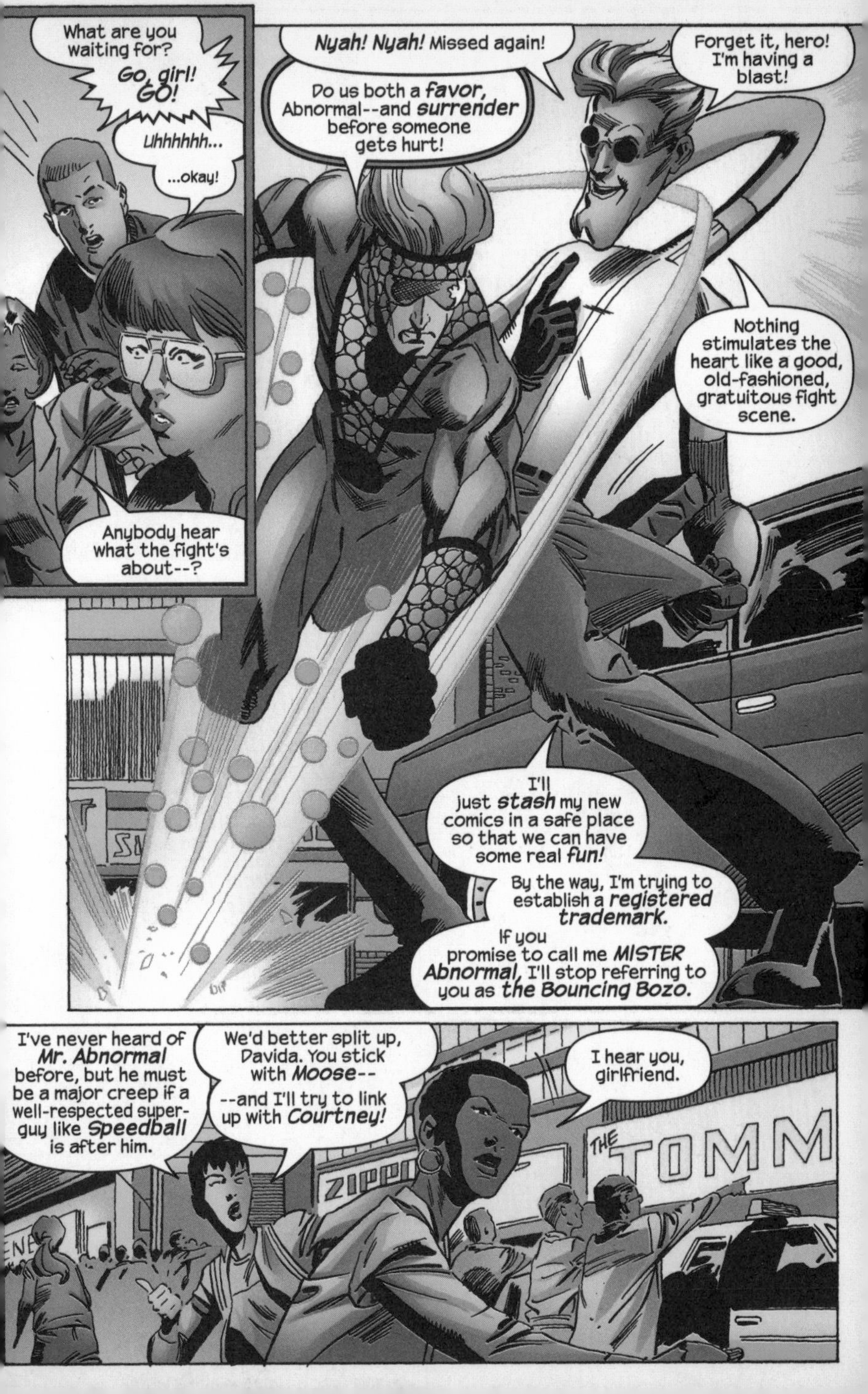
What are you waiting for? Go, girl! GO!
Uhhhhhh...
...okay!
Anybody hear what the fight's about--?
Nyah! Nyah! Missed again!
Do us both a favor, Abnormal--and surrender before someone gets hurt!
Forget it, hero! I'm having a blast!
Nothing stimulates the heart like a good, old-fashioned, gratuitous fight scene.
I'll just stash my new comics in a safe place so that we can have some real fun!
By the way, I'm trying to establish a registered trademark.
If you promise to call me MISTER Abnormal, I'll stop referring to you as the Bouncing Bozo.
I've never heard of Mr. Abnormal before, but he must be a major creep if a well-respected super-guy like Speedball is after him.
We'd better split up, Davida. You stick with Moose--
--and I'll try to link up with Courtney!
I hear you, girlfriend.
THE TOMM
ZIPP

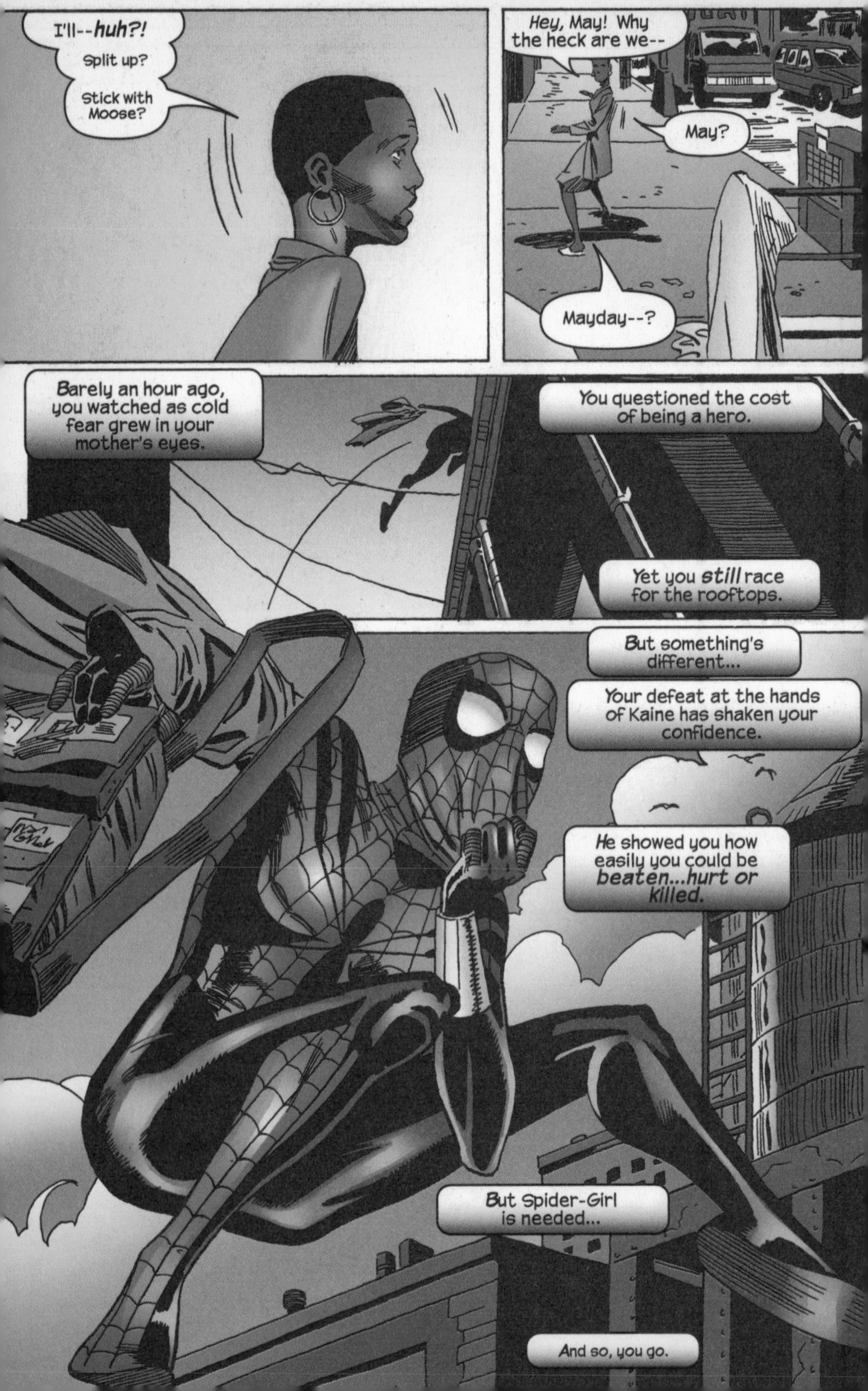

I'll--*huh?!*
Split up?
Stick with Moose?
Hey, May! Why the heck are we--
May?
Mayday--?
Barely an hour ago, you watched as cold fear grew in your mother's eyes.
You questioned the cost of being a hero.
Yet you *still* race for the rooftops.
But something's different...
Your defeat at the hands of Kaine has shaken your confidence.
He showed you how easily you could be *beaten...hurt or killed.*
But Spider-Girl is needed...
And so, you go.

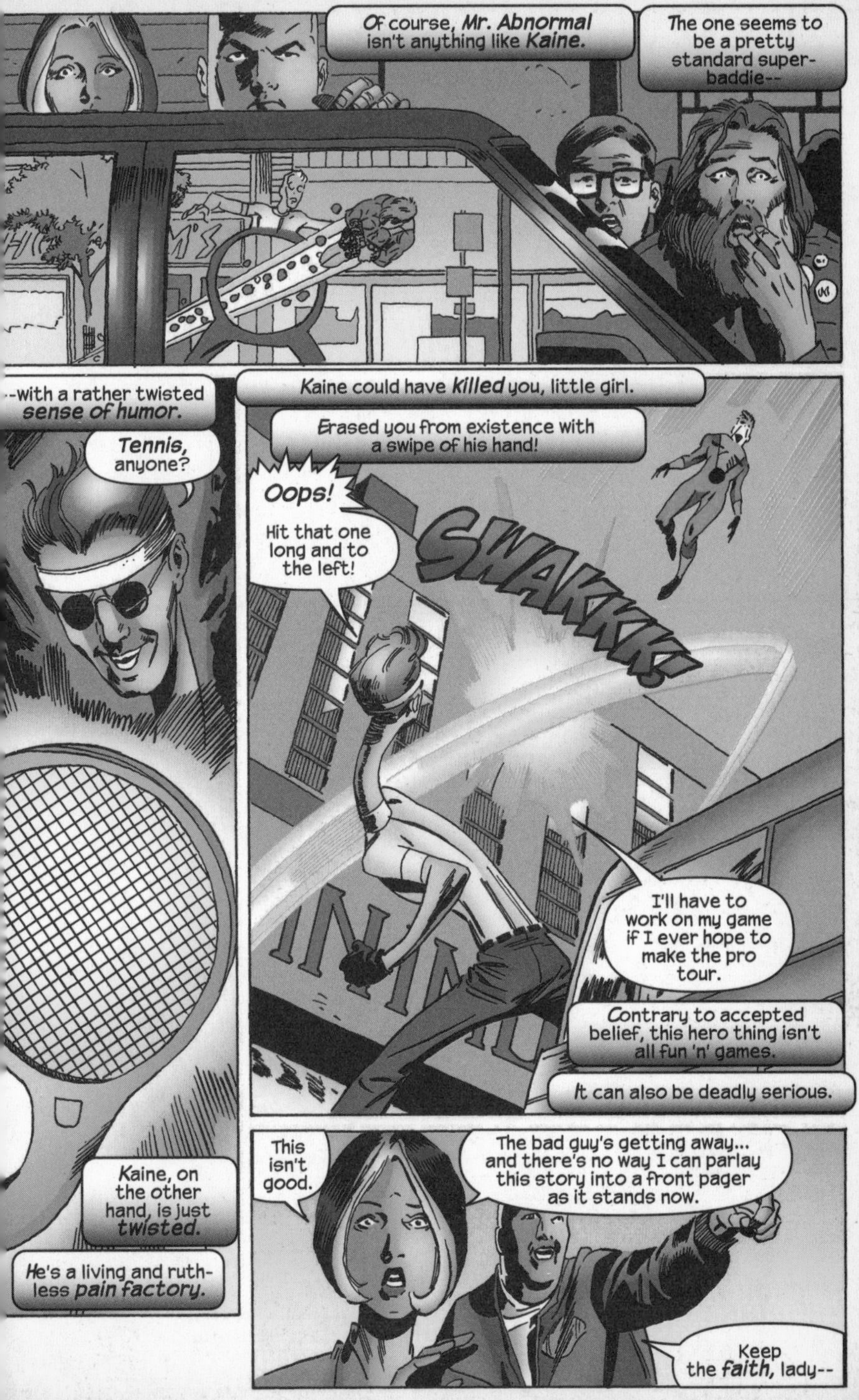

Of course, Mr. Abnormal isn't anything like Kaine.
The one seems to be a pretty standard super-baddie--
--with a rather twisted sense of humor.
Tennis, anyone?
Kaine, on the other hand, is just twisted.
He's a living and ruthless pain factory.
Kaine could have killed you, little girl.
Erased you from existence with a swipe of his hand!
Oops!
Hit that one long and to the left!
SWAKKK!
I'll have to work on my game if I ever hope to make the pro tour.
Contrary to accepted belief, this hero thing isn't all fun 'n' games.
It can also be deadly serious.
This isn't good.
The bad guy's getting away... and there's no way I can parlay this story into a front pager as it stands now.
Keep the faith, lady--

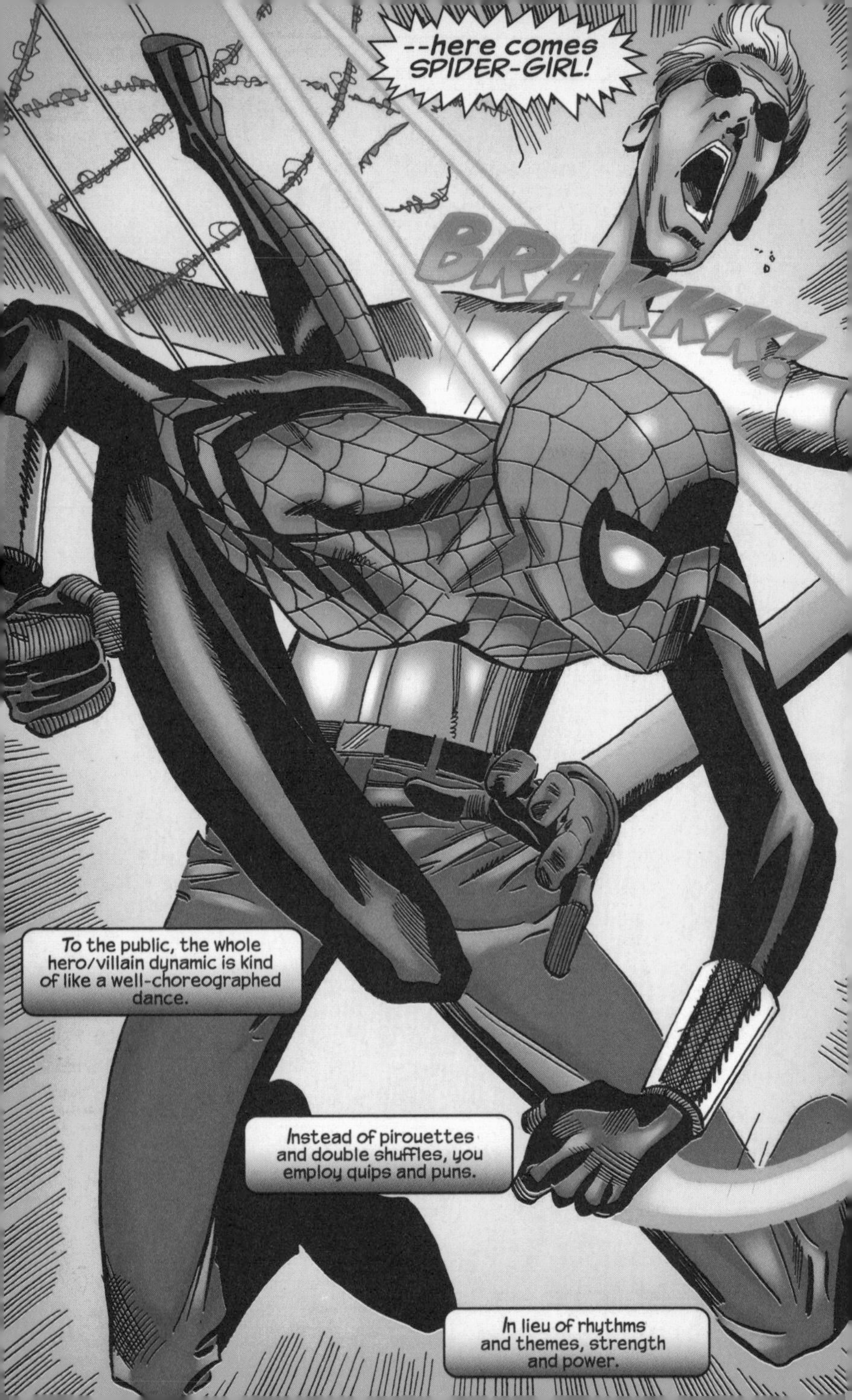
--here comes SPIDER-GIRL!
BRAKKK!
To the public, the whole hero/villain dynamic is kind of like a well-choreographed dance.
Instead of pirouettes and double shuffles, you employ quips and puns.
In lieu of rhythms and themes, strength and power.

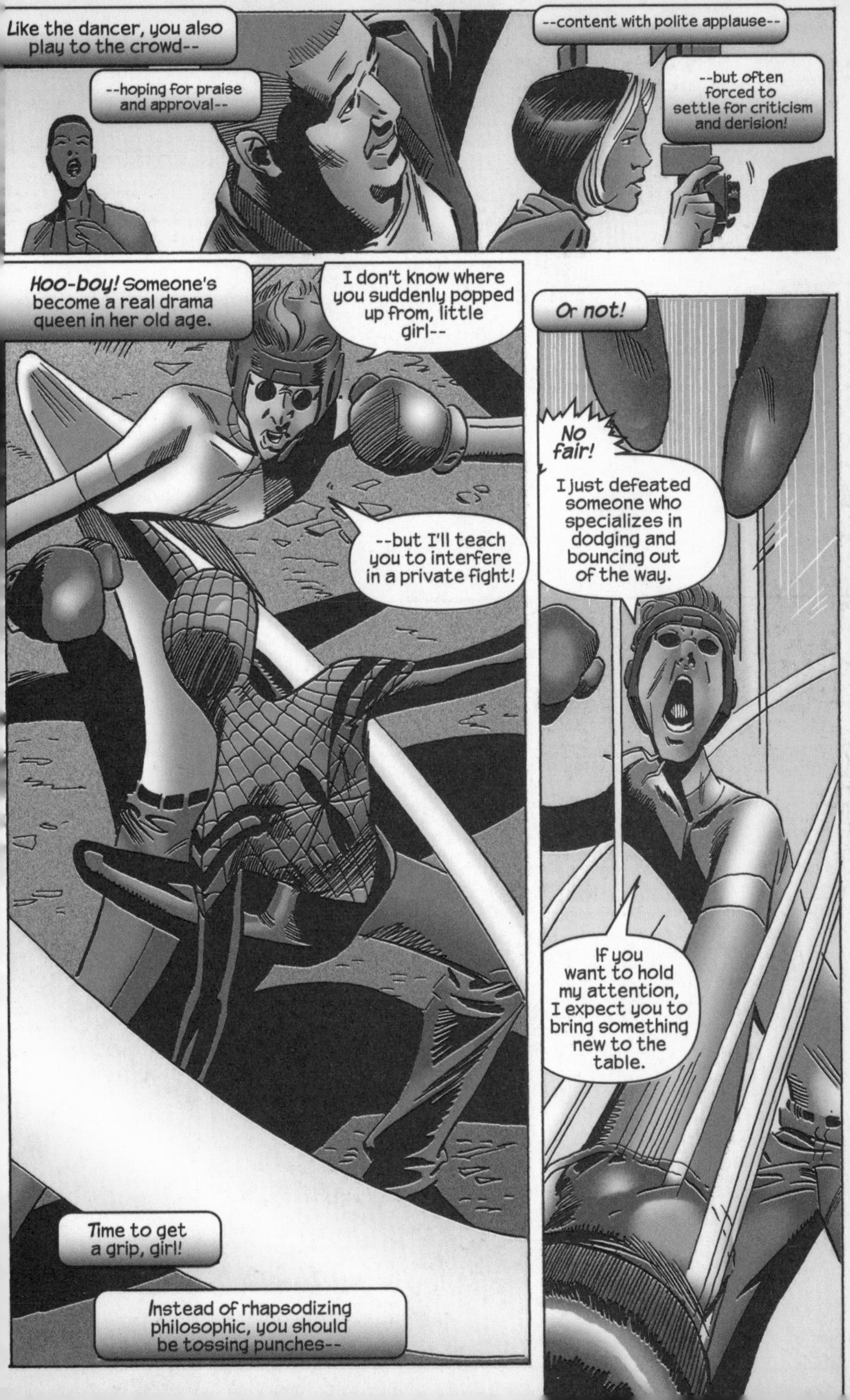

Like the dancer, you also play to the crowd--
--hoping for praise and approval--
--content with polite applause--
--but often forced to settle for criticism and derision!
Hoo-boy! Someone's become a real drama queen in her old age.
I don't know where you suddenly popped up from, little girl--
--but I'll teach you to interfere in a private fight!
Time to get a grip, girl!
Instead of rhapsodizing philosophic, you should be tossing punches--
Or not!
No fair!
I just defeated someone who specializes in dodging and bouncing out of the way.
If you want to hold my attention, I expect you to bring something new to the table.

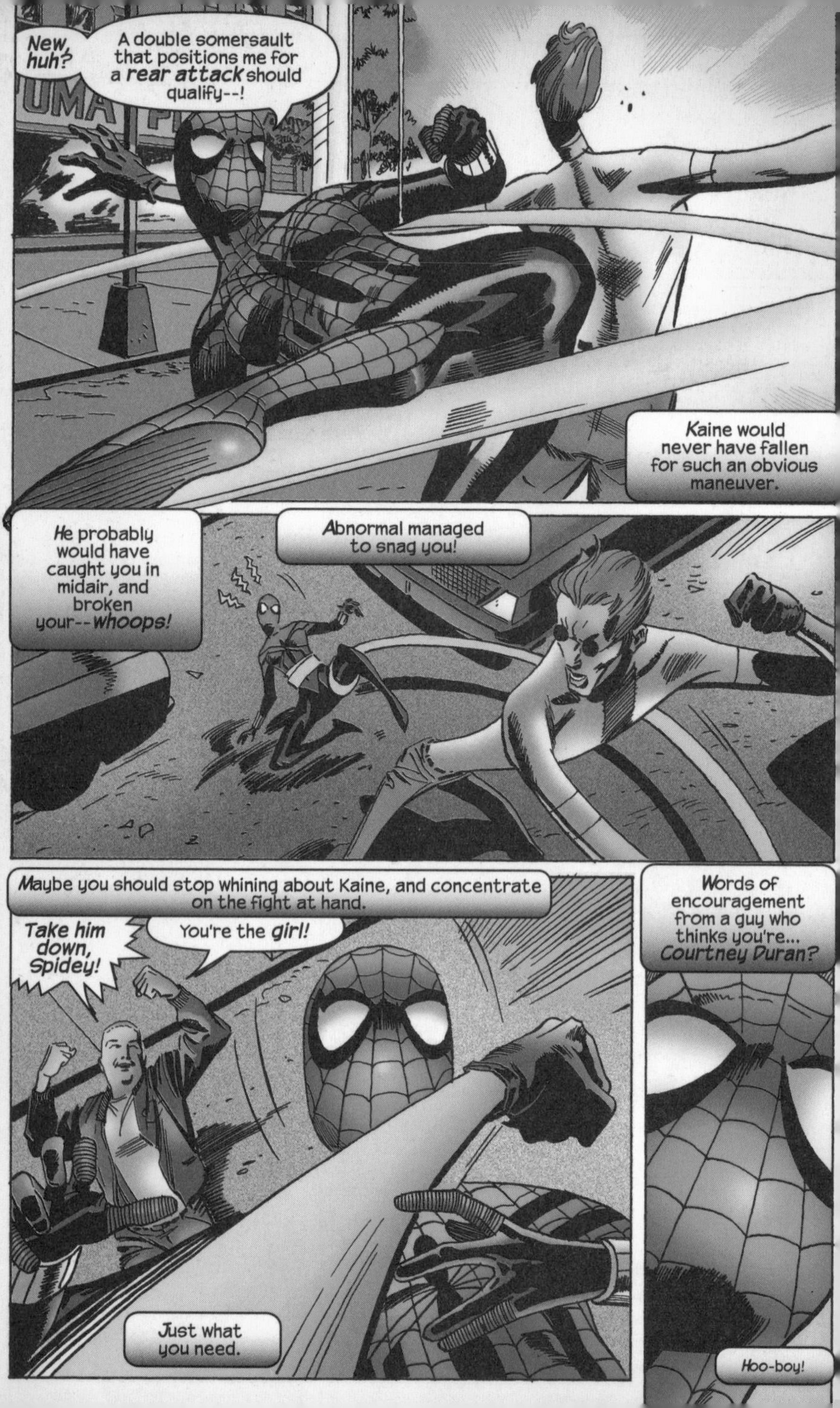
New, huh?
A double somersault that positions me for a rear attack should qualify--!
Kaine would never have fallen for such an obvious maneuver.
He probably would have caught you in midair, and broken your--whoops!
Abnormal managed to snag you!
Maybe you should stop whining about Kaine, and concentrate on the fight at hand.
Take him down, Spidey!
You're the girl!
Words of encouragement from a guy who thinks you're... Courtney Duran?
Just what you need.
Hoo-boy!

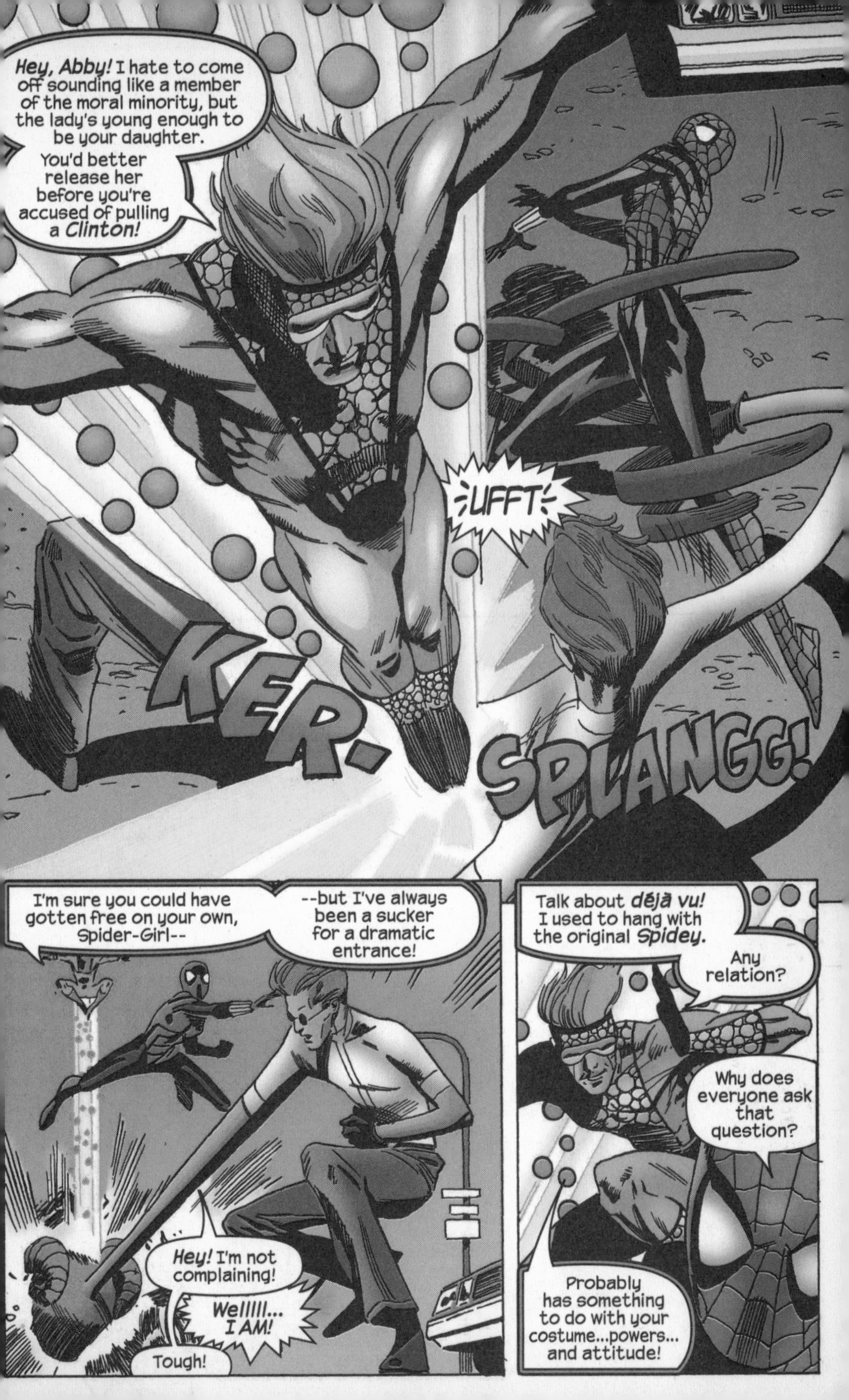
Hey, Abby! I hate to come off sounding like a member of the moral minority, but the lady's young enough to be your daughter.
You'd better release her before you're accused of pulling a Clinton!
UFFT!
KER-SPLANGG!
I'm sure you could have gotten free on your own, Spider-Girl--
--but I've always been a sucker for a dramatic entrance!
Hey! I'm not complaining!
Wellllll... I AM!
Tough!
Talk about déjà vu! I used to hang with the original Spidey.
Any relation?
Why does everyone ask that question?
Probably has something to do with your costume...powers... and attitude!

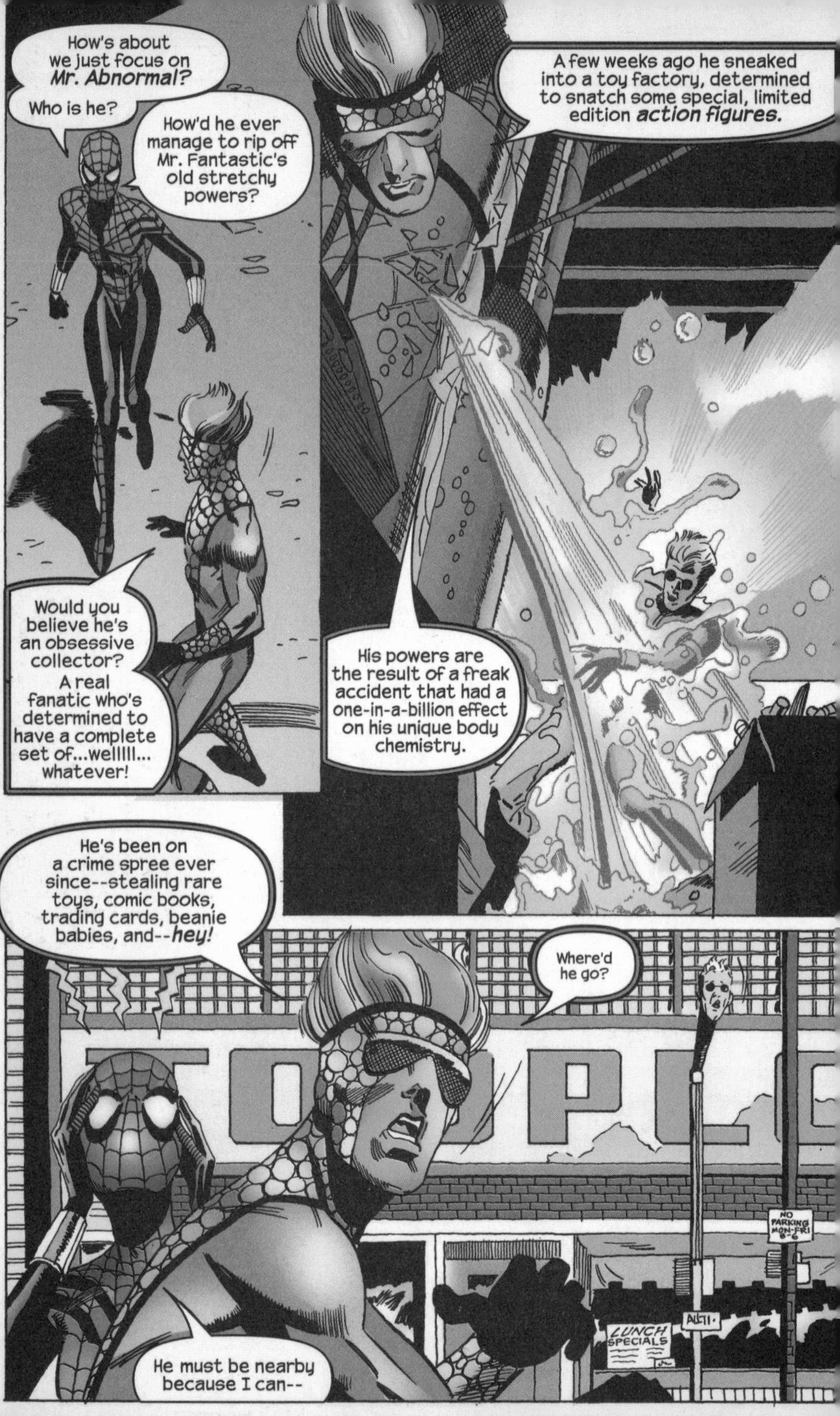
How's about we just focus on *Mr. Abnormal?*
Who is he?
How'd he ever manage to rip off Mr. Fantastic's old stretchy powers?
A few weeks ago he sneaked into a toy factory, determined to snatch some special, limited edition *action figures.*
Would you believe he's an obsessive collector?
A real fanatic who's determined to have a complete set of...welllll... whatever!
His powers are the result of a freak accident that had a one-in-a-billion effect on his unique body chemistry.
He's been on a crime spree ever since--stealing rare toys, comic books, trading cards, beanie babies, and--*hey!*
Where'd he go?
NO PARKING MON-FRI 8-6
LUNCH SPECIALS
He must be nearby because I can--

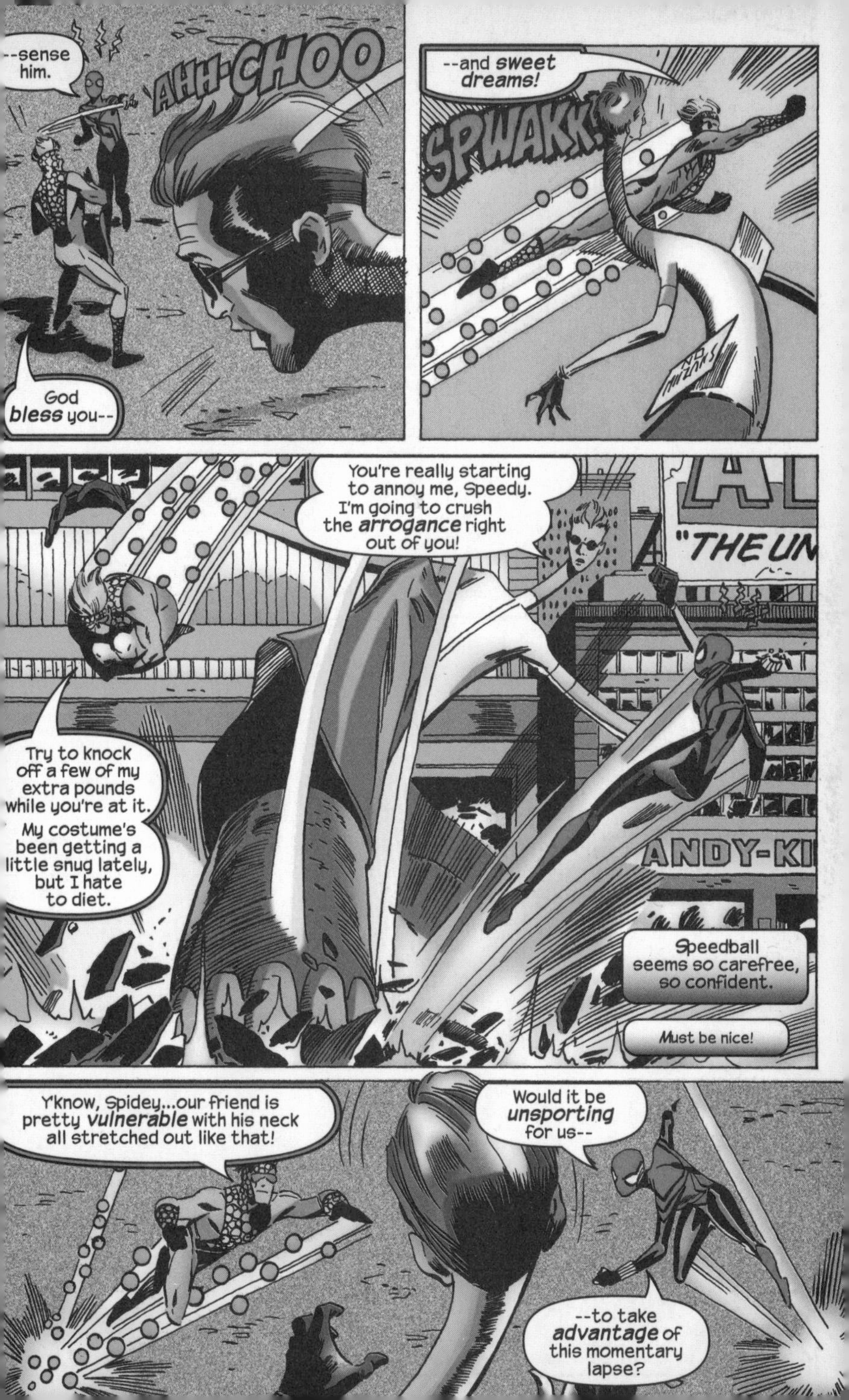
--sense him.
AHH-CHOO
God bless you--
--and sweet dreams!
SPWAKK!
You're really starting to annoy me, Speedy. I'm going to crush the arrogance right out of you!
"THE UN
ANDY-KI
Try to knock off a few of my extra pounds while you're at it.
My costume's been getting a little snug lately, but I hate to diet.
Speedball seems so carefree, so confident.
Must be nice!
Y'know, Spidey...our friend is pretty vulnerable with his neck all stretched out like that!
Would it be unsporting for us--
--to take advantage of this momentary lapse?

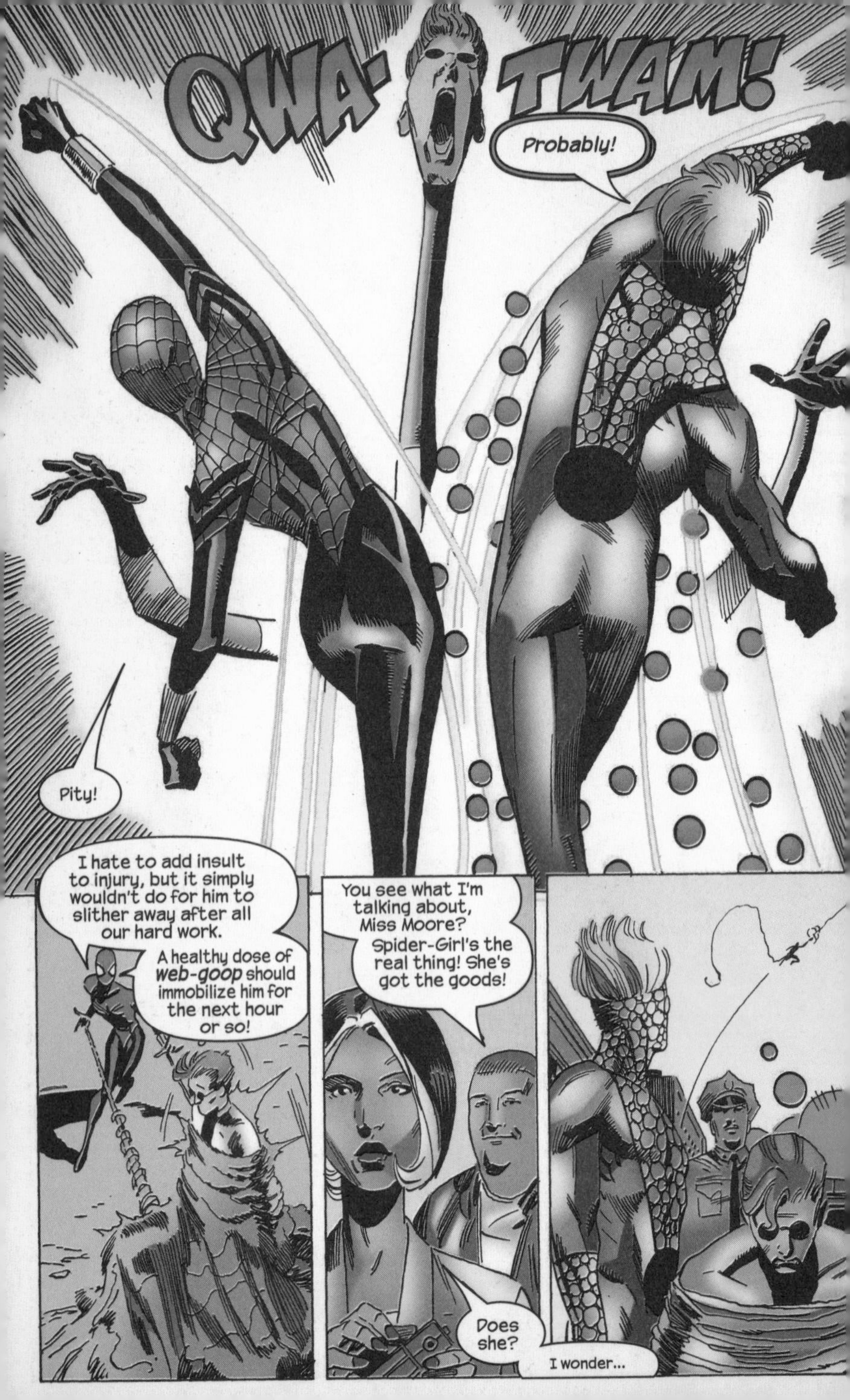
QWA-TWAM!
Probably!
Pity!
I hate to add insult to injury, but it simply wouldn't do for him to slither away after all our hard work.
A healthy dose of *web-goop* should immobilize him for the next hour or so!
You see what I'm talking about, Miss Moore?
Spider-Girl's the real thing! She's got the goods!
Does she?
I wonder...

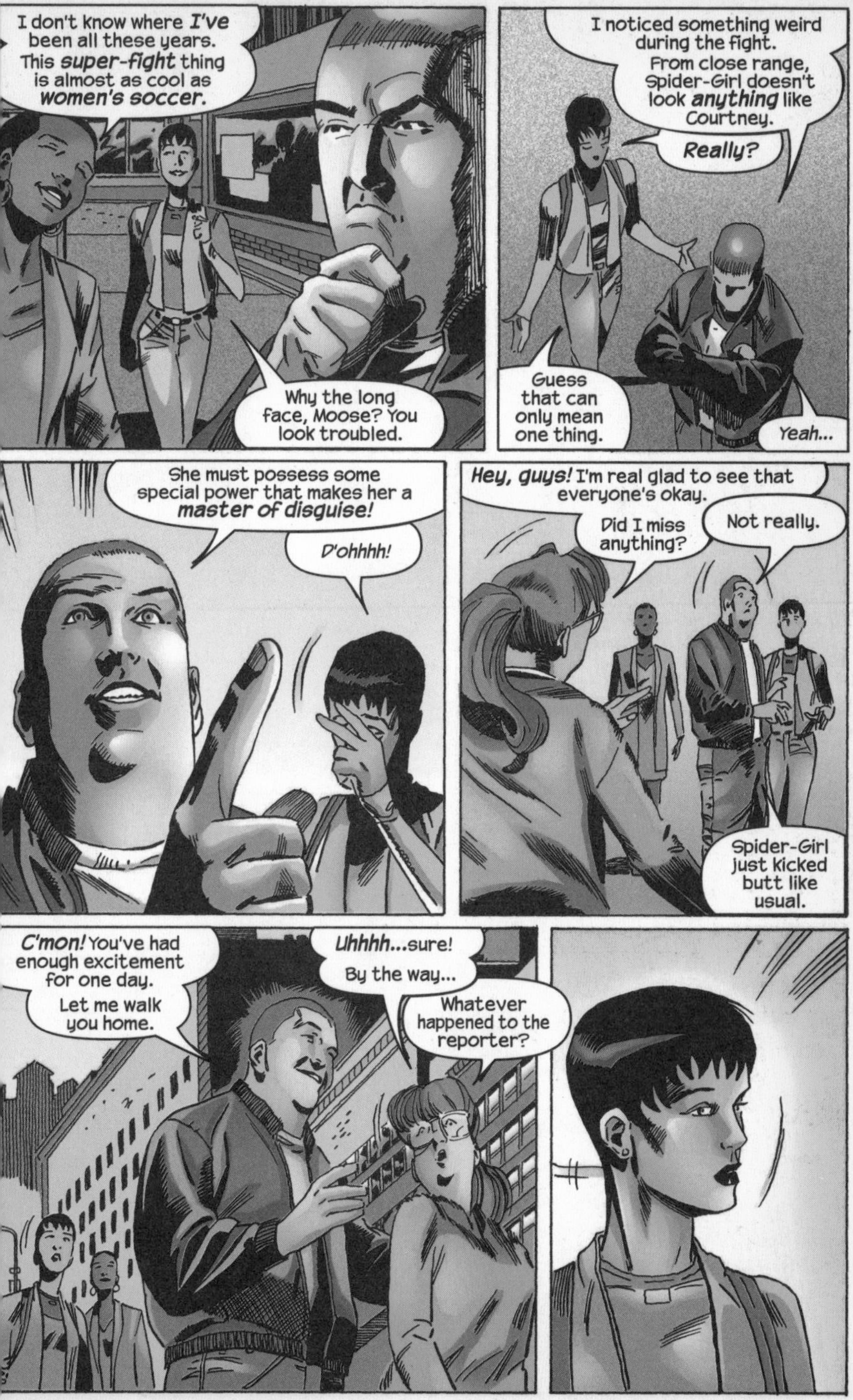
I don't know where *I've* been all these years. This *super-fight* thing is almost as cool as *women's soccer.*
Why the long face, Moose? You look troubled.
I noticed something weird during the fight.
From close range, Spider-Girl doesn't look *anything* like Courtney.
Really?
Guess that can only mean one thing.
Yeah...
She must possess some special power that makes her a *master of disguise!*
D'ohhhh!
Hey, guys! I'm real glad to see that everyone's okay.
Did I miss anything?
Not really.
Spider-Girl just kicked butt like usual.
C'mon! You've had enough excitement for one day.
Let me walk you home.
*Uhhhh...*sure!
By the way...
Whatever happened to the reporter?

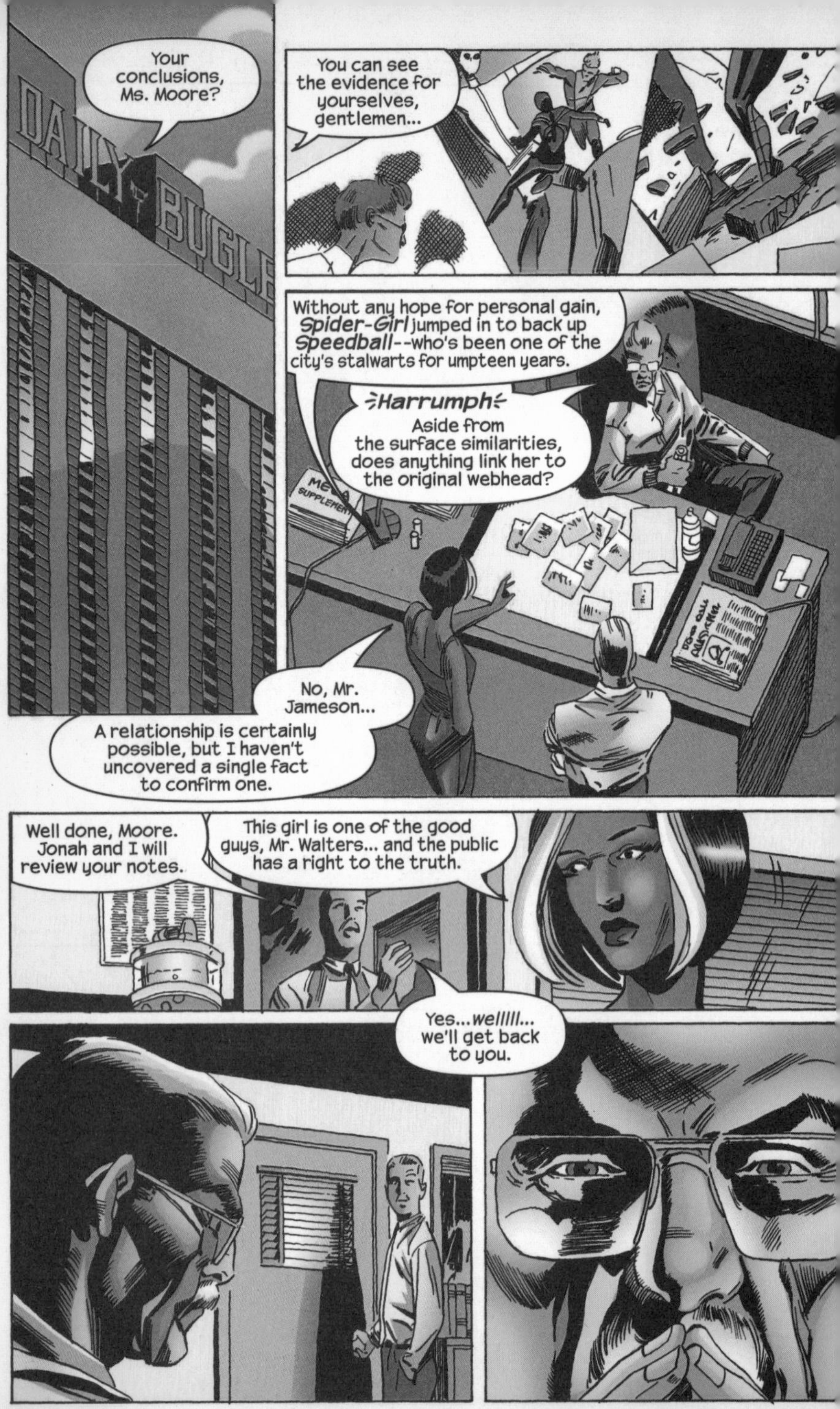
Your conclusions, Ms. Moore?
You can see the evidence for yourselves, gentlemen...
Without any hope for personal gain, Spider-Girl jumped in to back up Speedball--who's been one of the city's stalwarts for umpteen years.
Harrumph
Aside from the surface similarities, does anything link her to the original webhead?
No, Mr. Jameson...
A relationship is certainly possible, but I haven't uncovered a single fact to confirm one.
Well done, Moore. Jonah and I will review your notes.
This girl is one of the good guys, Mr. Walters... and the public has a right to the truth.
Yes...wellll... we'll get back to you.

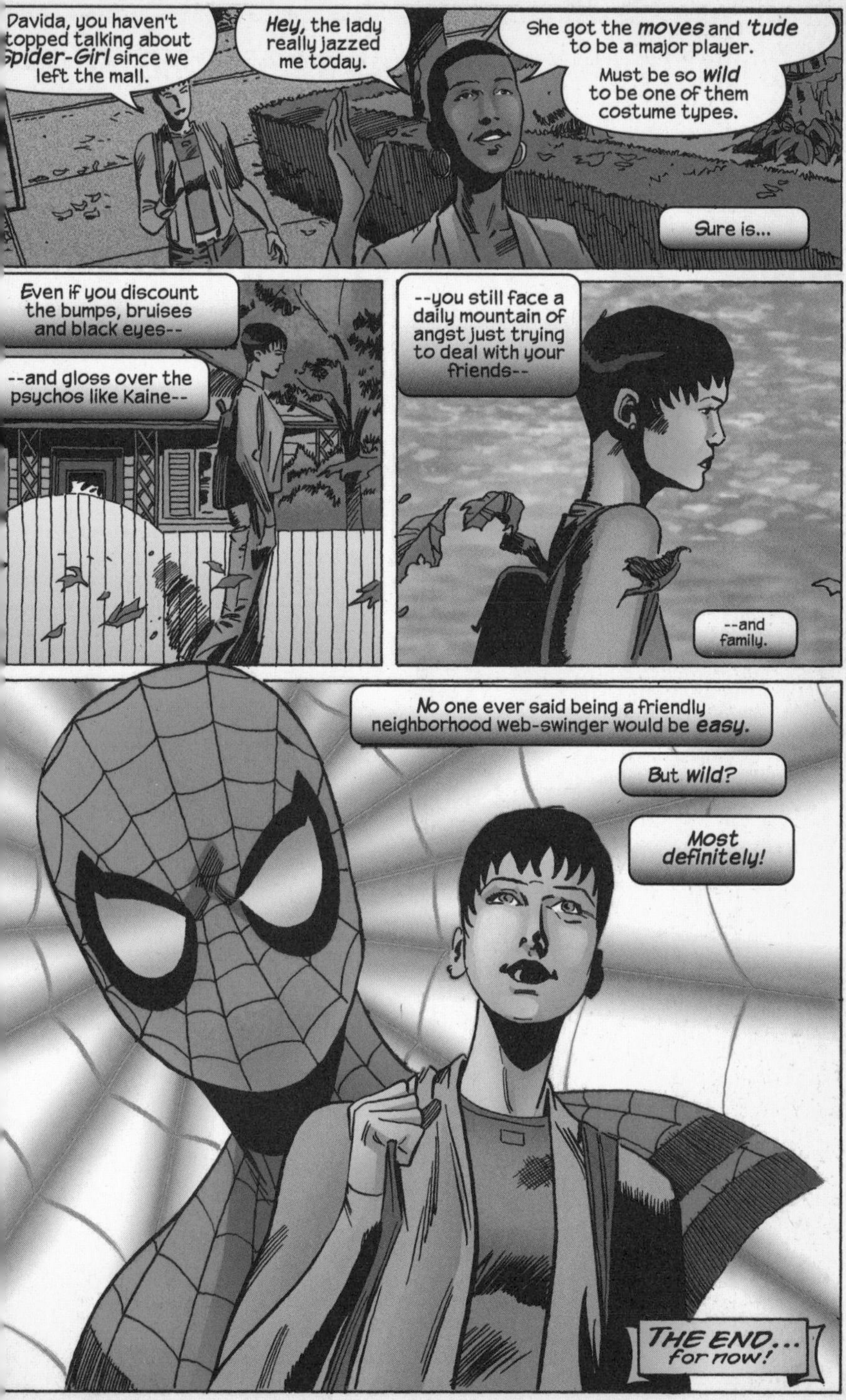
Davida, you haven't stopped talking about Spider-Girl since we left the mall.
Hey, the lady really jazzed me today.
She got the moves and 'tude to be a major player.
Must be so wild to be one of them costume types.
Sure is...
Even if you discount the bumps, bruises and black eyes--
--and gloss over the psychos like Kaine--
--you still face a daily mountain of angst just trying to deal with your friends--
--and family.
No one ever said being a friendly neighborhood web-swinger would be easy.
But wild?
Most definitely!
THE END... for now!

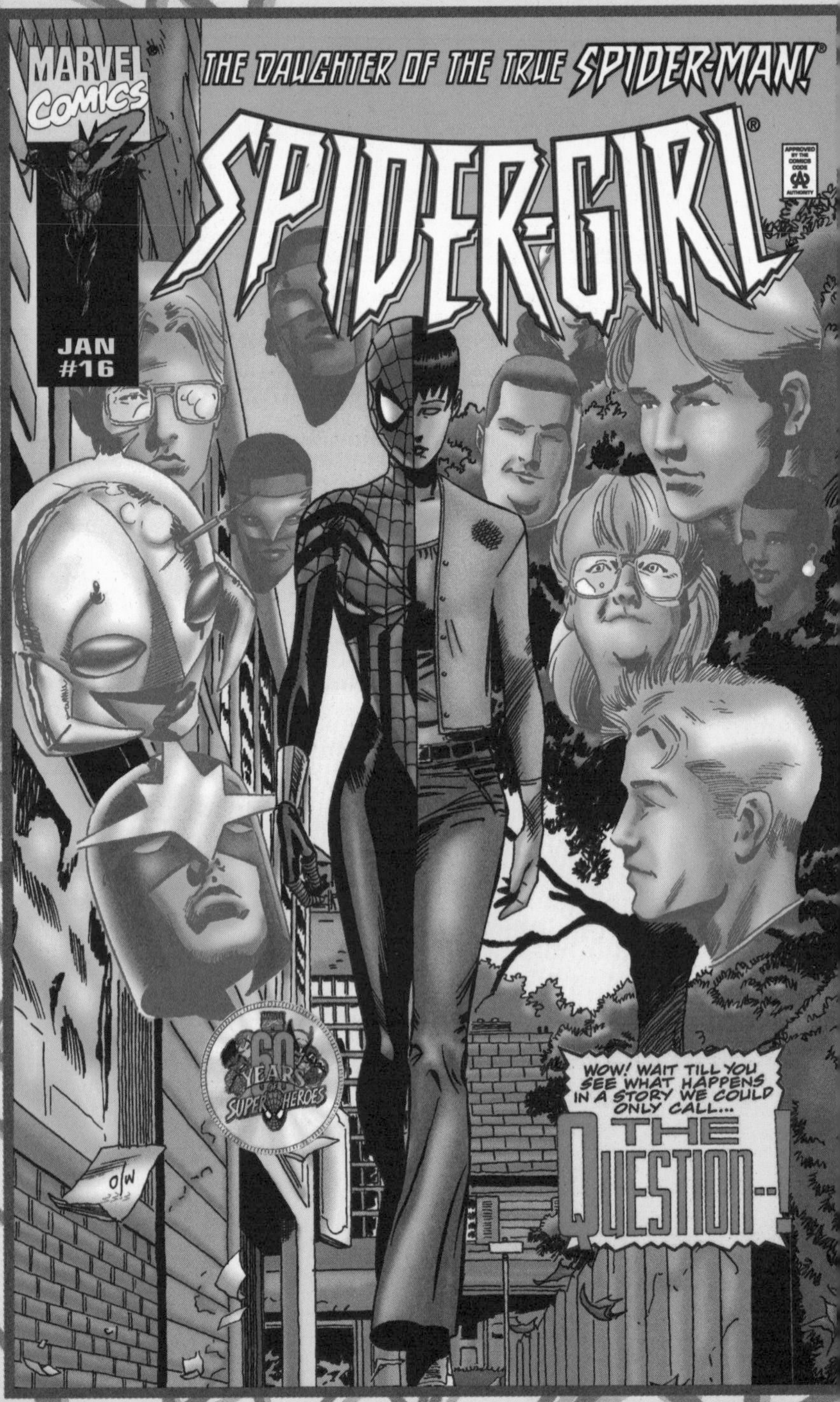
MARVEL COMICS
THE DAUGHTER OF THE TRUE SPIDER-MAN!
SPIDER-GIRL
JAN #16
60 YEARS OF SUPER HEROES
WOW! WAIT TILL YOU SEE WHAT HAPPENS IN A STORY WE COULD ONLY CALL...
THE QUESTION--!

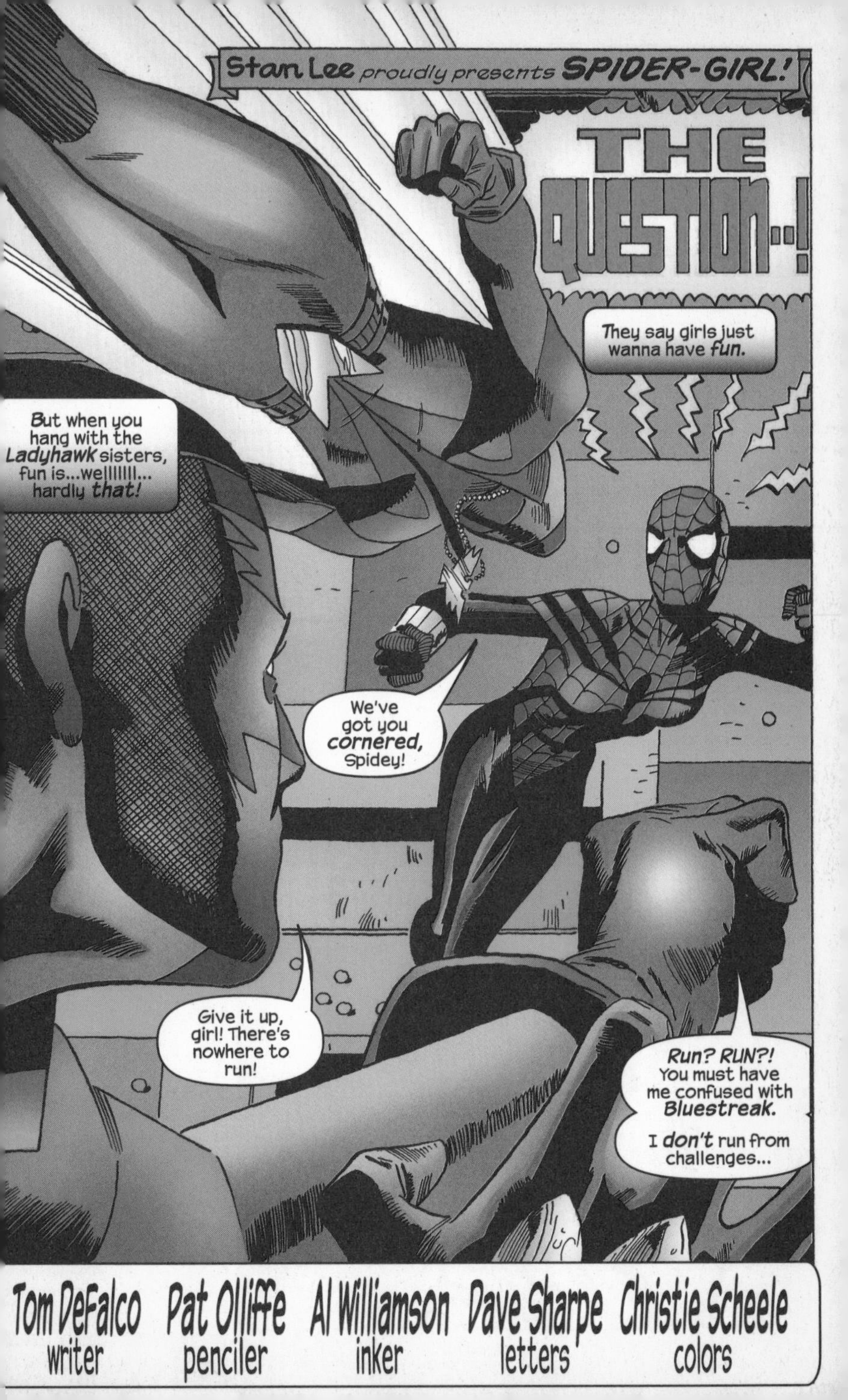
Stan Lee proudly presents SPIDER-GIRL!
THE QUESTION..!
They say girls just wanna have fun.
But when you hang with the Ladyhawk sisters, fun is...wellllllll... hardly that!
We've got you cornered, Spidey!
Give it up, girl! There's nowhere to run!
Run? RUN?! You must have me confused with Bluestreak.
I don't run from challenges...
Tom DeFalco writer
Pat Olliffe penciler
Al Williamson inker
Dave Sharpe letters
Christie Scheele colors

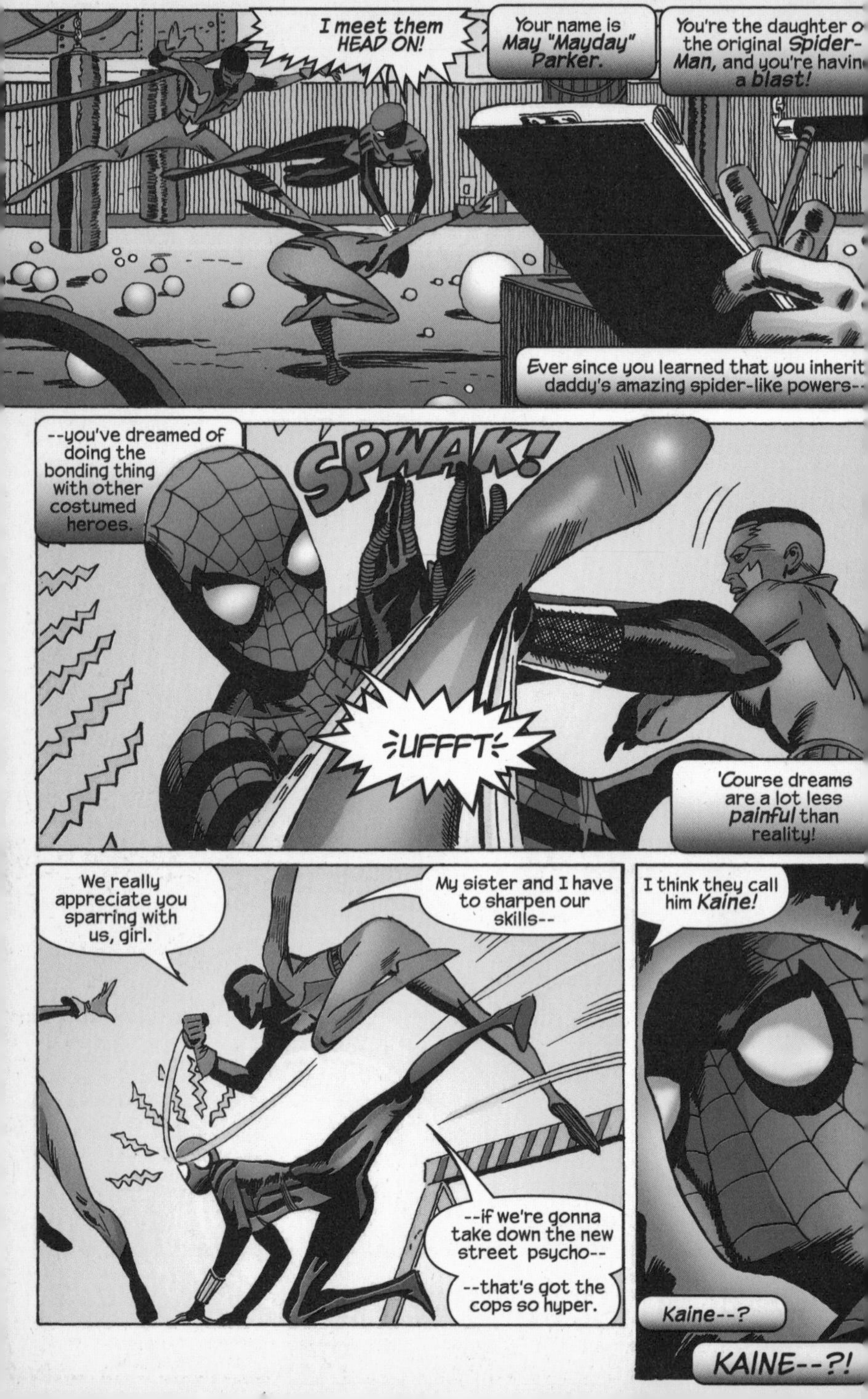

I meet them HEAD ON!
Your name is May "Mayday" Parker.
You're the daughter o the original Spider-Man, and you're havin a blast!
Ever since you learned that you inherit daddy's amazing spider-like powers--
--you've dreamed of doing the bonding thing with other costumed heroes.
SPWAK!
UFFFT
'Course dreams are a lot less painful than reality!
We really appreciate you sparring with us, girl.
My sister and I have to sharpen our skills--
--if we're gonna take down the new street psycho--
--that's got the cops so hyper.
I think they call him Kaine!
Kaine--?
KAINE--?!

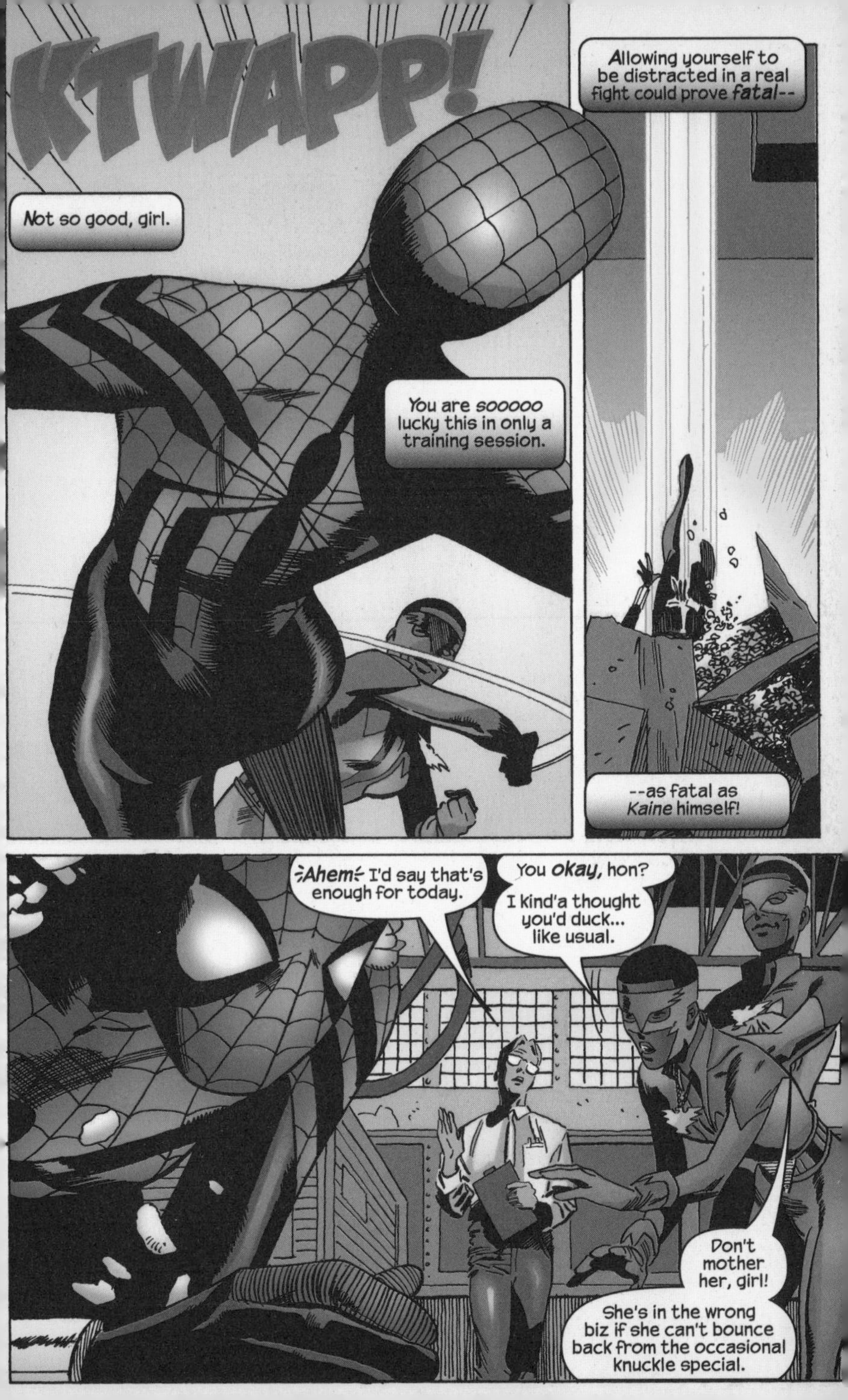
KTWAPP!
Not so good, girl.
You are sooooo lucky this in only a training session.
Allowing yourself to be distracted in a real fight could prove fatal--
--as fatal as Kaine himself!
Ahem I'd say that's enough for today.
You okay, hon?
I kind'a thought you'd duck... like usual.
Don't mother her, girl!
She's in the wrong biz if she can't bounce back from the occasional knuckle special.

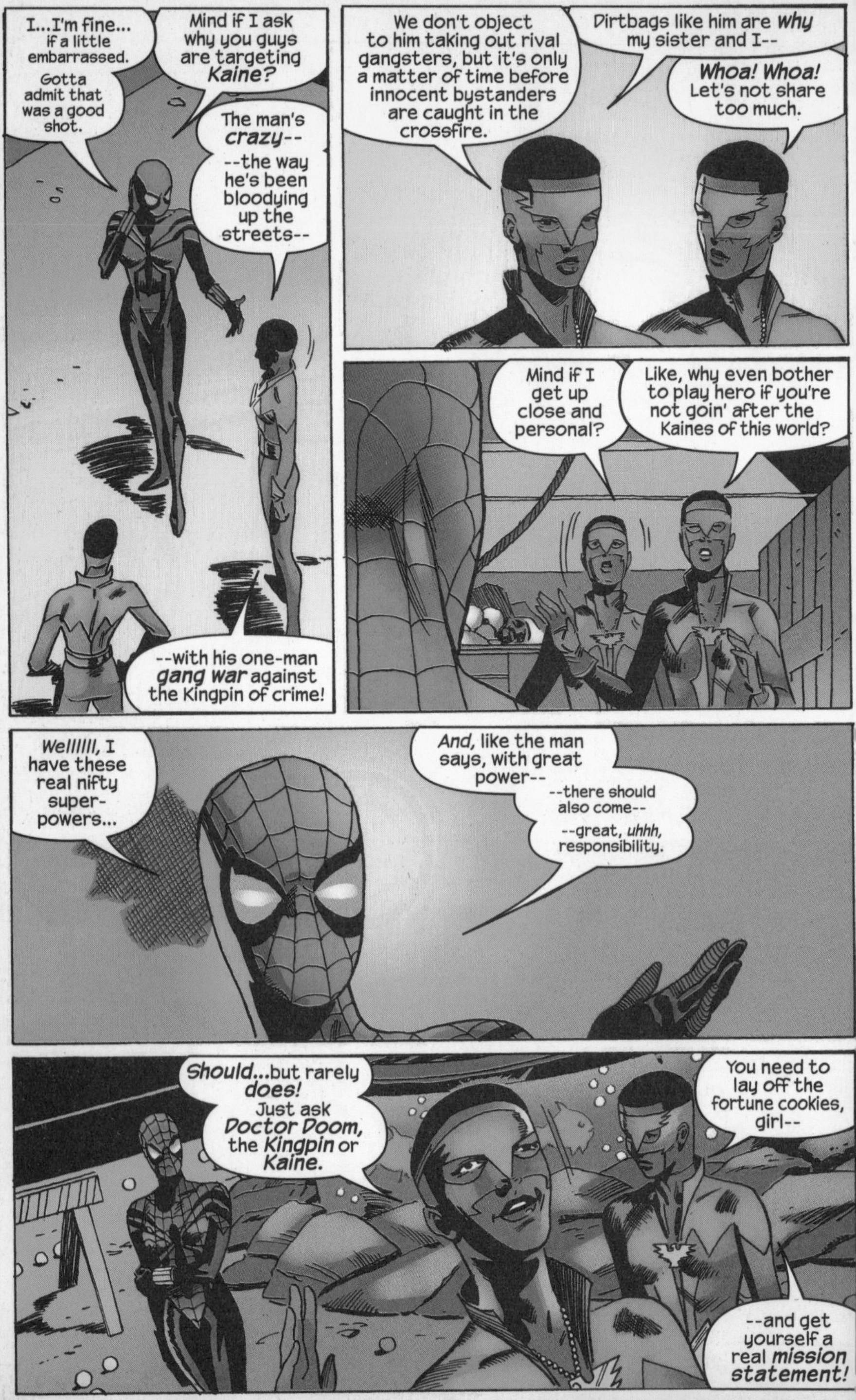
I...I'm fine... if a little embarrassed.
Gotta admit that was a good shot.
Mind if I ask why you guys are targeting *Kaine?*
The man's *crazy*--
--the way he's been bloodying up the streets--
--with his one-man *gang war* against the Kingpin of crime!
We don't object to him taking out rival gangsters, but it's only a matter of time before innocent bystanders are caught in the crossfire.
Dirtbags like him are *why* my sister and I--
Whoa! Whoa! Let's not share too much.
Mind if I get up close and personal?
Like, why even bother to play hero if you're not goin' after the Kaines of this world?
Welllll, I have these real nifty super-powers...
And, like the man says, with great power--
--there should also come--
--great, *uhhh,* responsibility.
Should...but rarely *does!* Just ask *Doctor Doom,* the *Kingpin* or *Kaine.*
You need to lay off the fortune cookies, girl--
--and get yourself a real *mission statement!*

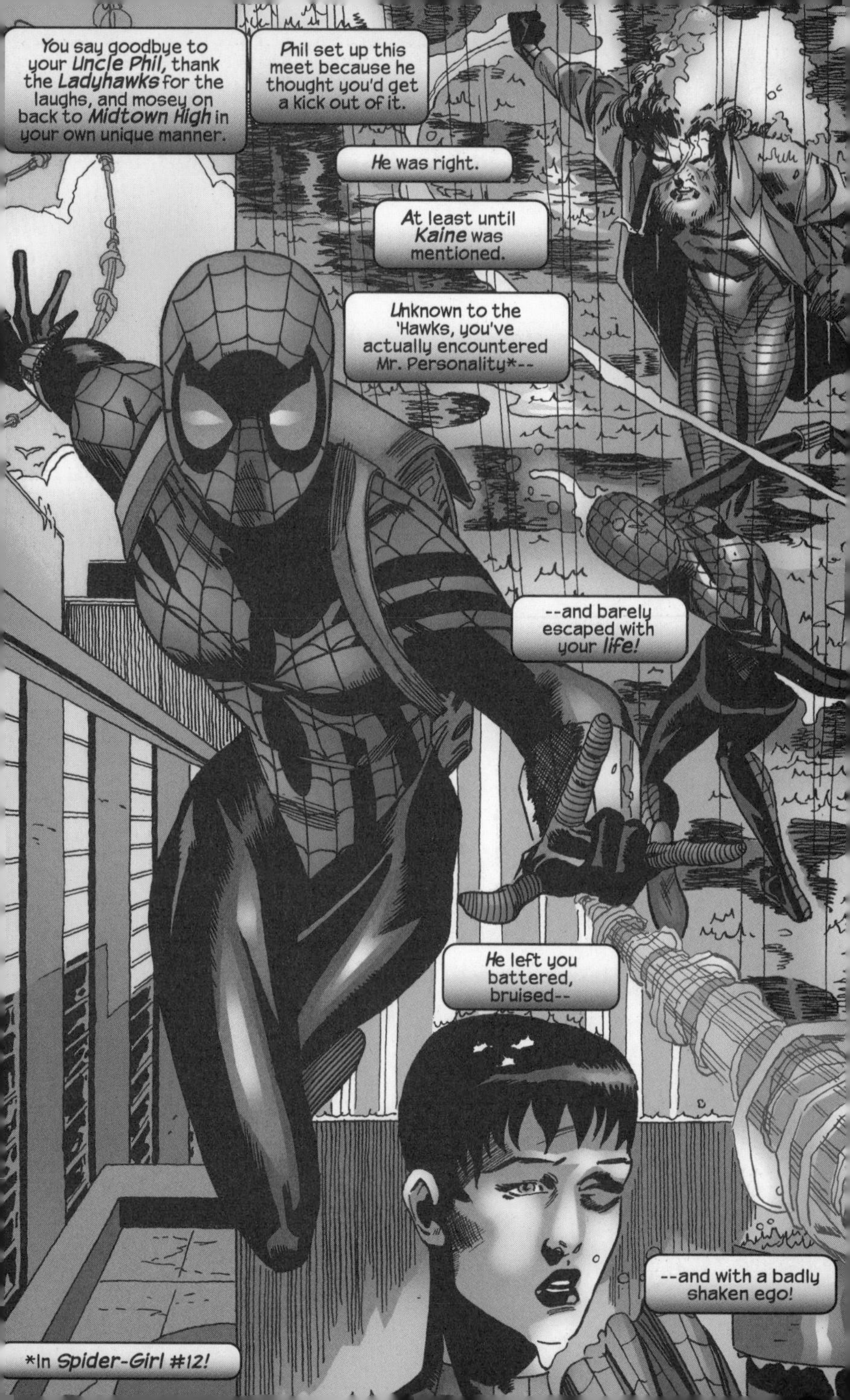
You say goodbye to your Uncle Phil, thank the Ladyhawks for the laughs, and mosey on back to Midtown High in your own unique manner.
Phil set up this meet because he thought you'd get a kick out of it.
He was right.
At least until Kaine was mentioned.
Unknown to the 'Hawks, you've actually encountered Mr. Personality*--
--and barely escaped with your life!
He left you battered, bruised--
--and with a badly shaken ego!
*In Spider-Girl #12!

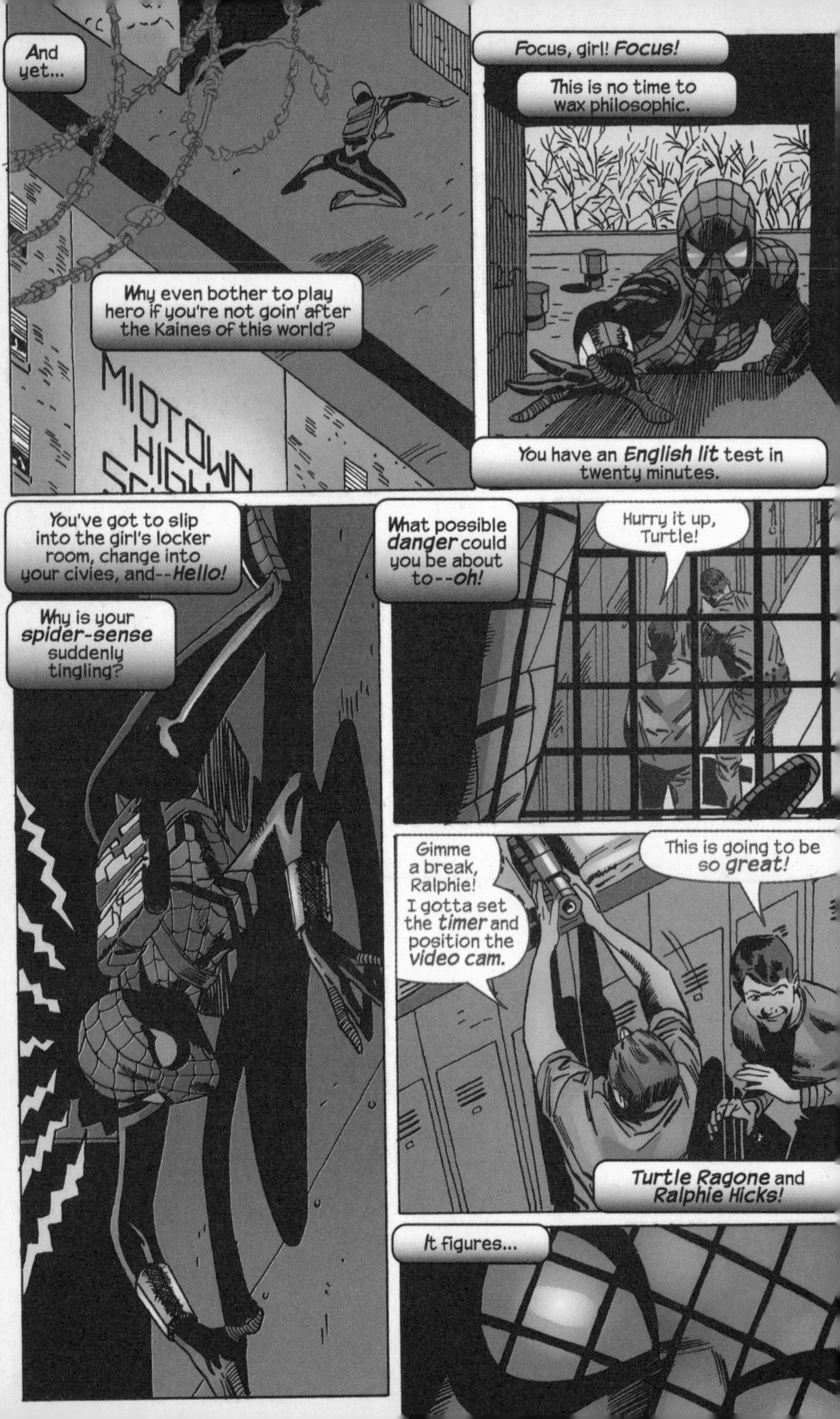
And yet...
Why even bother to play hero if you're not goin' after the Kaines of this world?
MIDTOWN HIGH
Focus, girl! Focus!
This is no time to wax philosophic.
You have an English lit test in twenty minutes.
You've got to slip into the girl's locker room, change into your civies, and--Hello!
Why is your spider-sense suddenly tingling?
What possible danger could you be about to--oh!
Hurry it up, Turtle!
Gimme a break, Ralphie! I gotta set the timer and position the video cam.
This is going to be so great!
Turtle Ragone and Ralphie Hicks!
It figures...

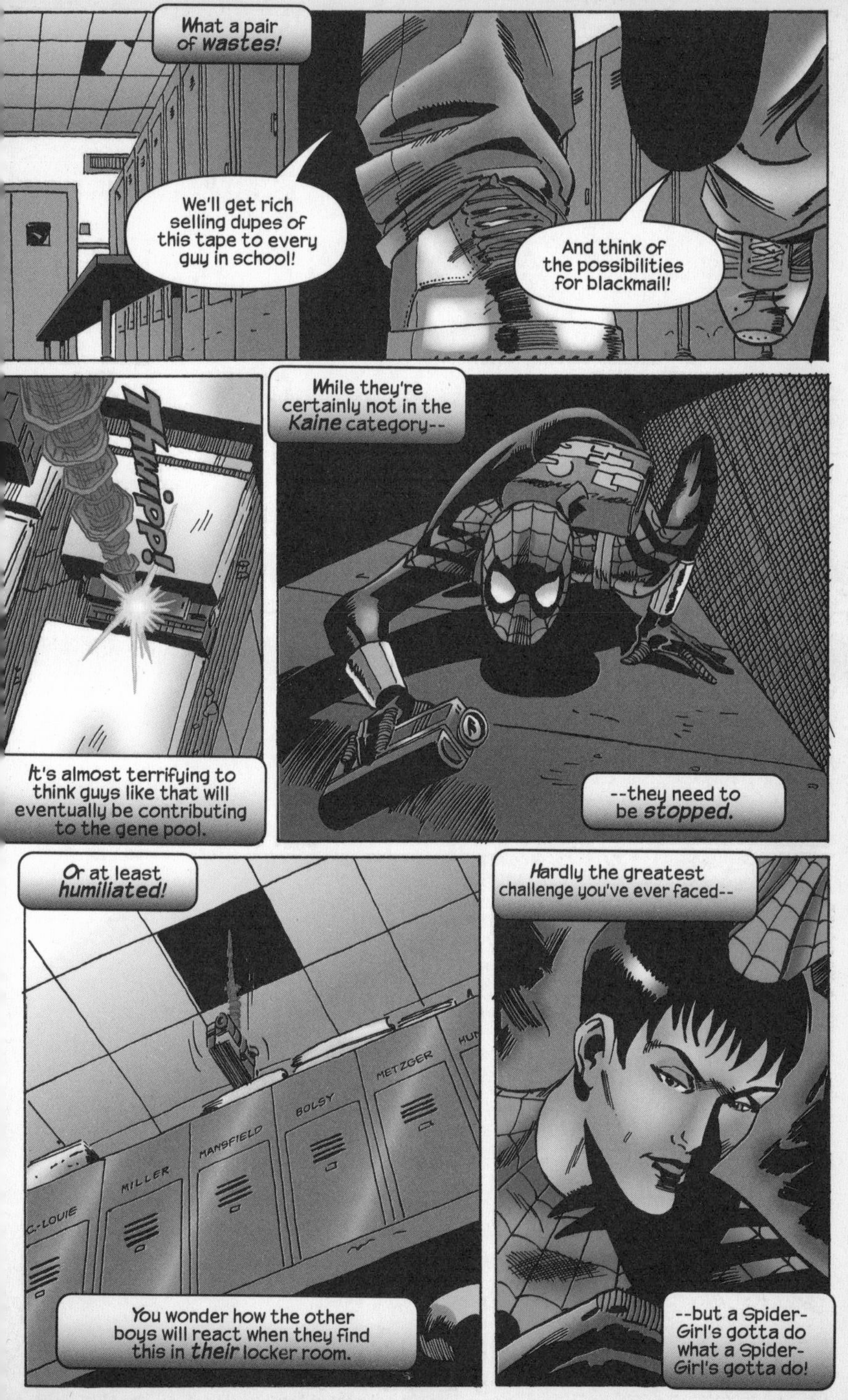
What a pair of wastes!
We'll get rich selling dupes of this tape to every guy in school!
And think of the possibilities for blackmail!
THWIPP!
It's almost terrifying to think guys like that will eventually be contributing to the gene pool.
While they're certainly not in the Kaine category--
--they need to be stopped.
Or at least humiliated!
C-LOUIE
MILLER
MANSFIELD
BOLSY
METZGER
You wonder how the other boys will react when they find this in their locker room.
Hardly the greatest challenge you've ever faced--
--but a Spider-Girl's gotta do what a Spider-Girl's gotta do!

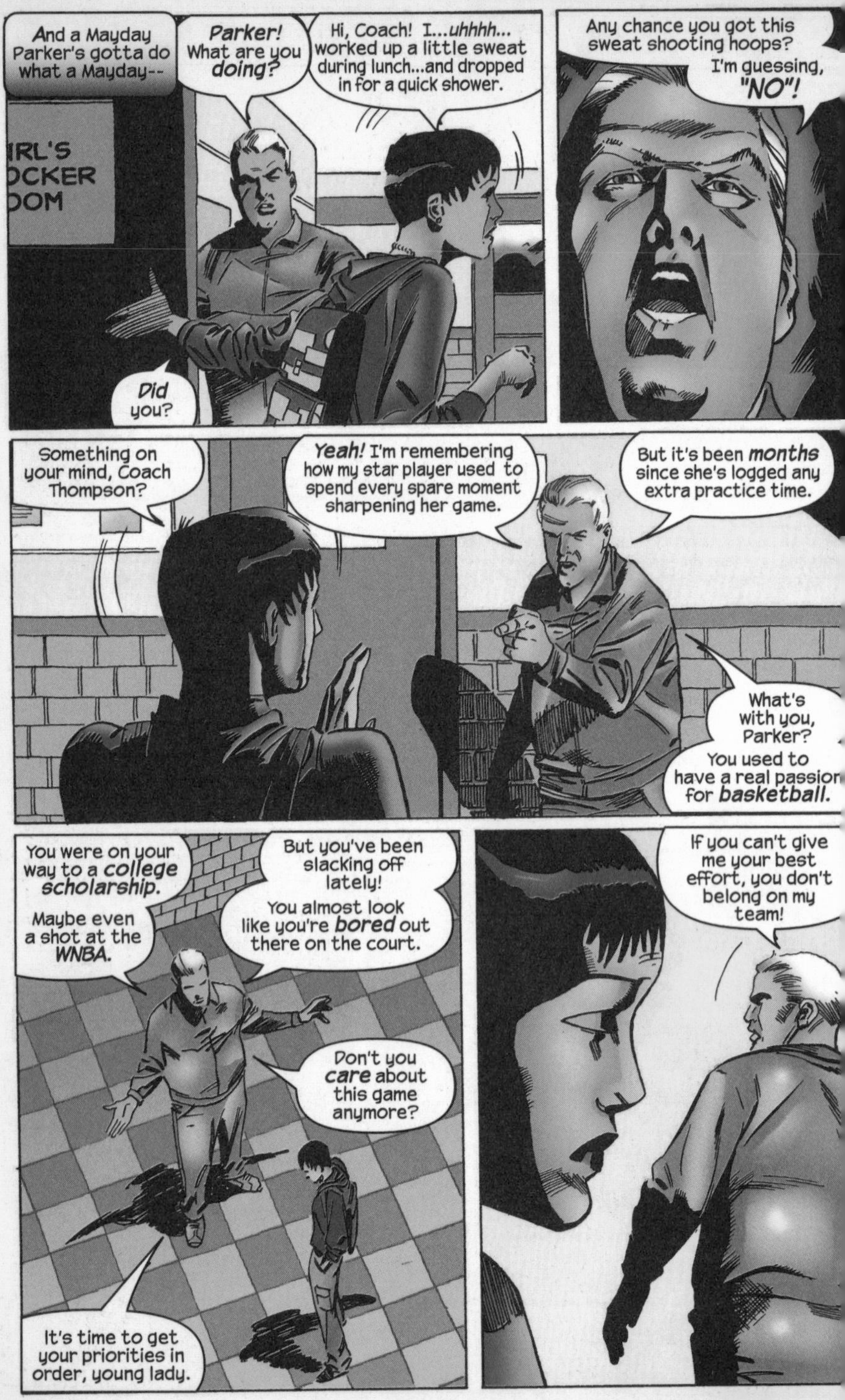
And a Mayday Parker's gotta do what a Mayday--
Parker! What are you doing?
Hi, Coach! I...uhhhh... worked up a little sweat during lunch...and dropped in for a quick shower.
IRL'S
OCKER
OOM
Did you?
Any chance you got this sweat shooting hoops?
I'm guessing, "NO"!
Something on your mind, Coach Thompson?
Yeah! I'm remembering how my star player used to spend every spare moment sharpening her game.
But it's been months since she's logged any extra practice time.
What's with you, Parker?
You used to have a real passion for basketball.
You were on your way to a college scholarship.
Maybe even a shot at the WNBA.
But you've been slacking off lately!
You almost look like you're bored out there on the court.
Don't you care about this game anymore?
It's time to get your priorities in order, young lady.
If you can't give me your best effort, you don't belong on my team!

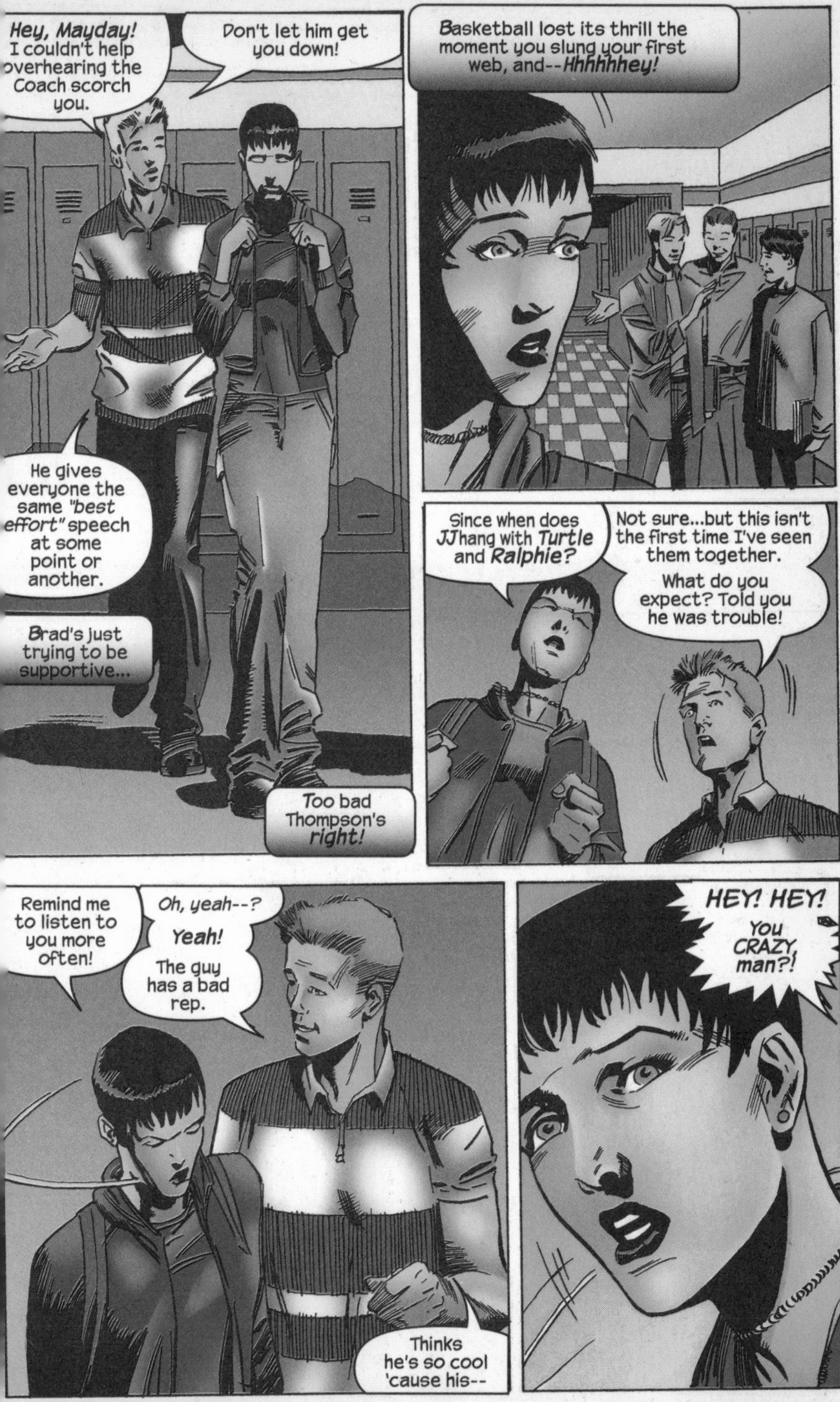

Hey, Mayday! I couldn't help overhearing the Coach scorch you.
Don't let him get you down!
He gives everyone the same "best effort" speech at some point or another.
Brad's just trying to be supportive...
Too bad Thompson's right!
Basketball lost its thrill the moment you slung your first web, and--Hhhhhhey!
Since when does JJ hang with Turtle and Ralphie?
Not sure...but this isn't the first time I've seen them together.
What do you expect? Told you he was trouble!
Remind me to listen to you more often!
Oh, yeah--?
Yeah!
The guy has a bad rep.
Thinks he's so cool 'cause his--
HEY! HEY!
You CRAZY, man?!

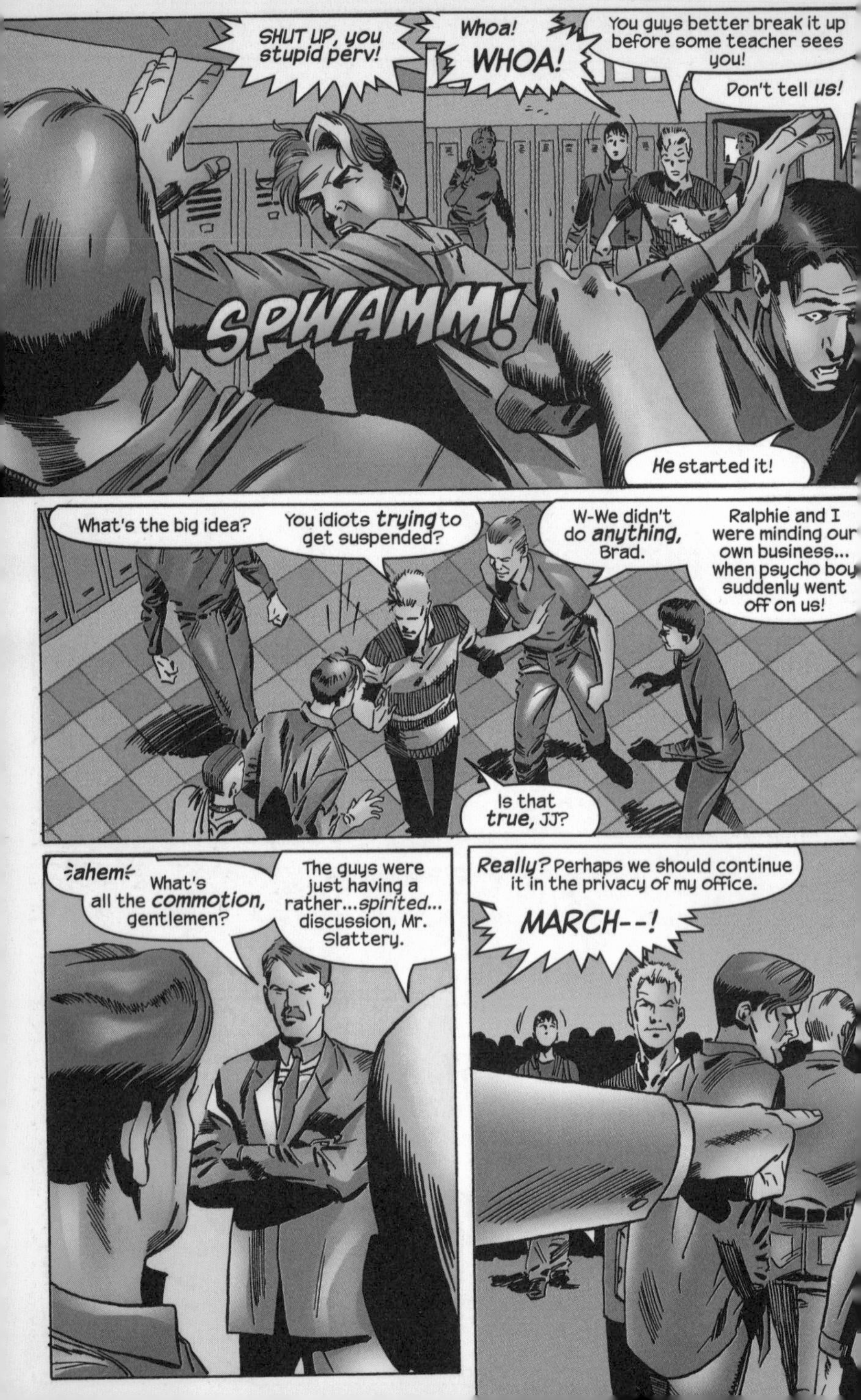
SHUT UP, you stupid perv!
Whoa! WHOA!
You guys better break it up before some teacher sees you!
Don't tell us!
SPWAMM!
He started it!
What's the big idea?
You idiots trying to get suspended?
W-We didn't do anything, Brad.
Ralphie and I were minding our own business... when psycho boy suddenly went off on us!
Is that true, JJ?
ahem What's all the commotion, gentlemen?
The guys were just having a rather...spirited... discussion, Mr. Slattery.
Really? Perhaps we should continue it in the privacy of my office.
MARCH--!

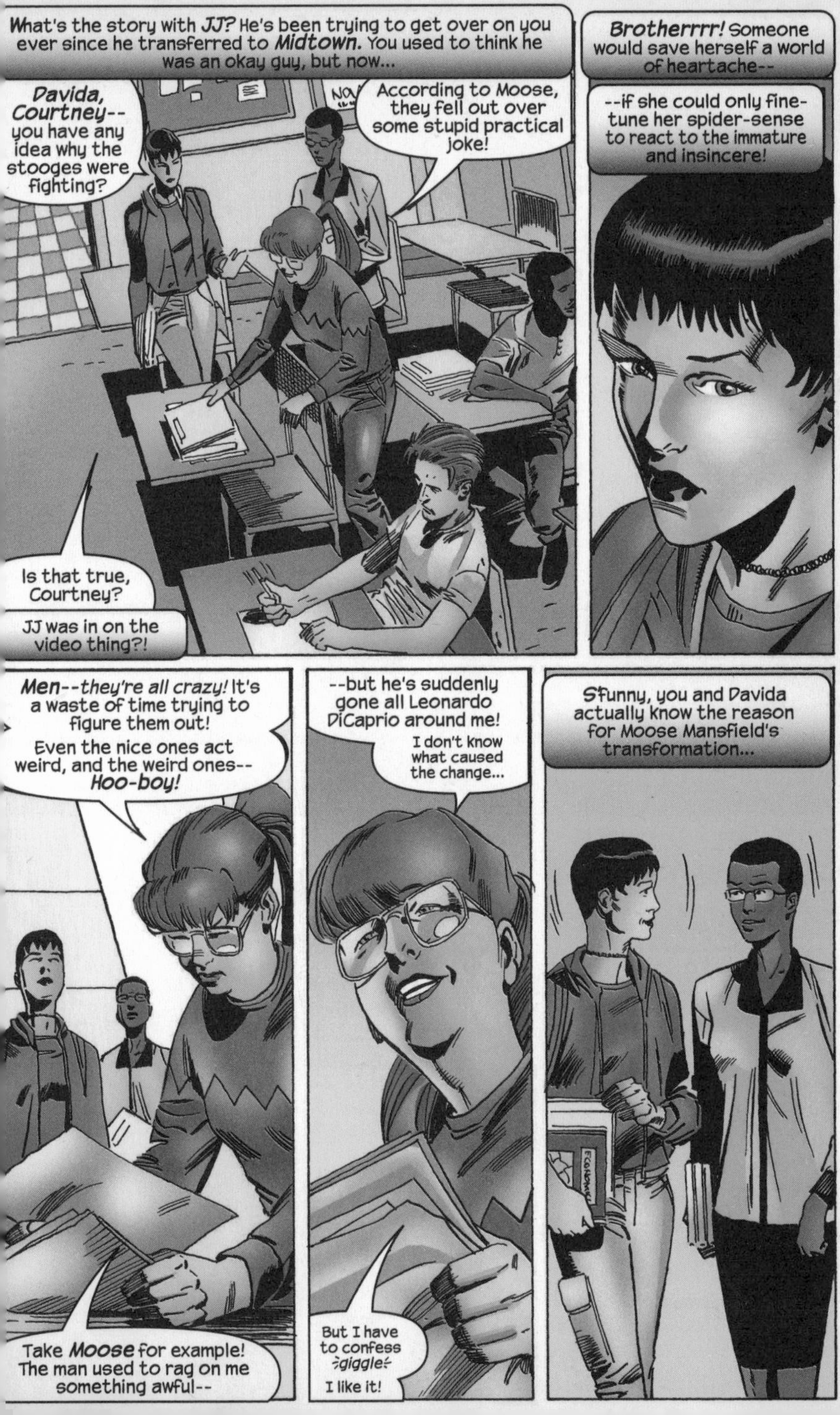
What's the story with JJ? He's been trying to get over on you ever since he transferred to Midtown. You used to think he was an okay guy, but now...
Davida, Courtney-- you have any idea why the stooges were fighting?
According to Moose, they fell out over some stupid practical joke!
Is that true, Courtney?
JJ was in on the video thing?!
Brotherrrr! Someone would save herself a world of heartache--
--if she could only fine-tune her spider-sense to react to the immature and insincere!
Men--they're all crazy! It's a waste of time trying to figure them out!
Even the nice ones act weird, and the weird ones-- Hoo-boy!
Take Moose for example! The man used to rag on me something awful--
--but he's suddenly gone all Leonardo DiCaprio around me!
I don't know what caused the change...
But I have to confess ≈giggle≈ I like it!
S'funny, you and Davida actually know the reason for Moose Mansfield's transformation...

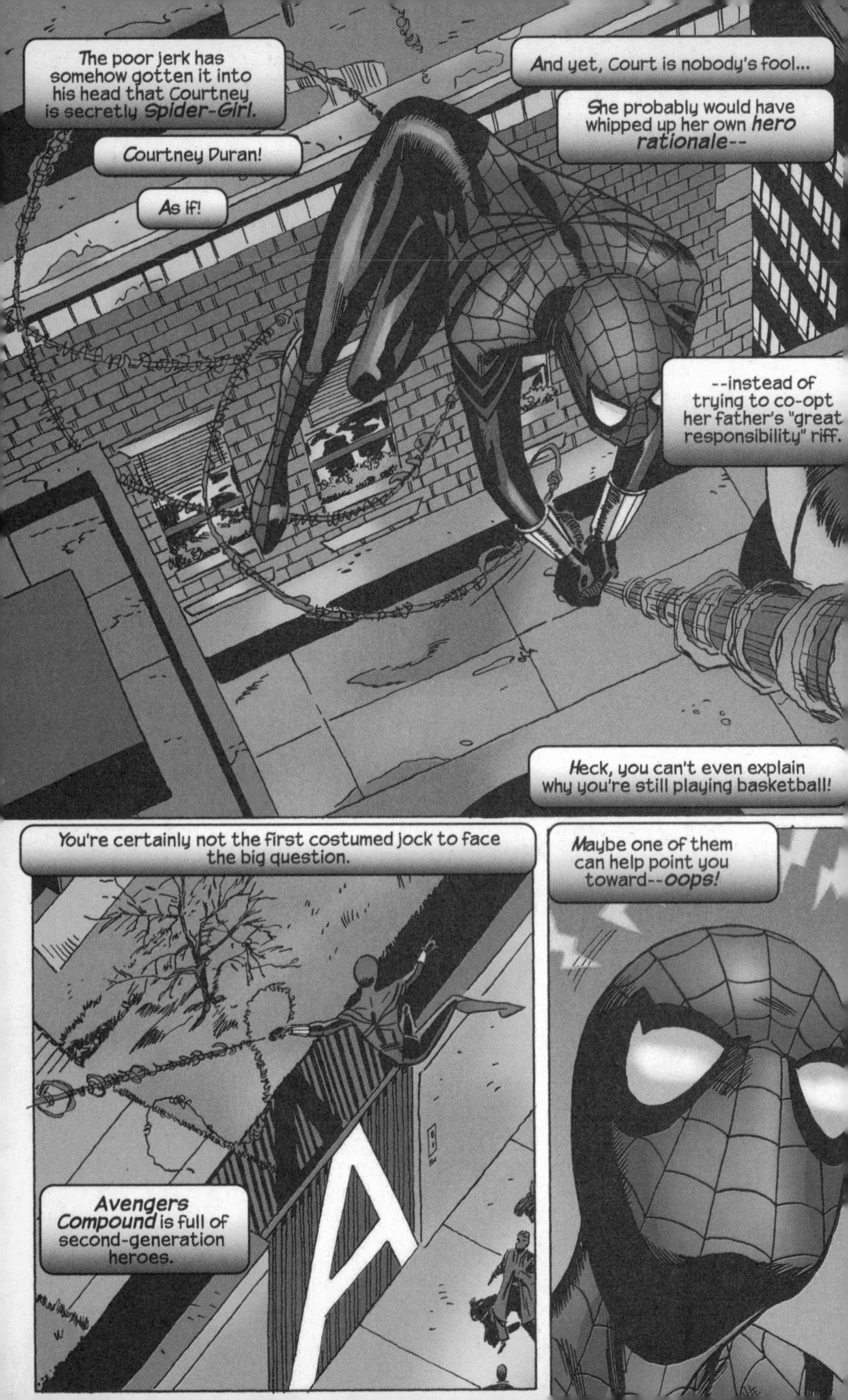

The poor jerk has somehow gotten it into his head that Courtney is secretly Spider-Girl.
Courtney Duran!
As if!
And yet, Court is nobody's fool...
She probably would have whipped up her own hero rationale--
--instead of trying to co-opt her father's "great responsibility" riff.
Heck, you can't even explain why you're still playing basketball!
You're certainly not the first costumed jock to face the big question.
Avengers Compound is full of second-generation heroes.
Maybe one of them can help point you toward--oops!

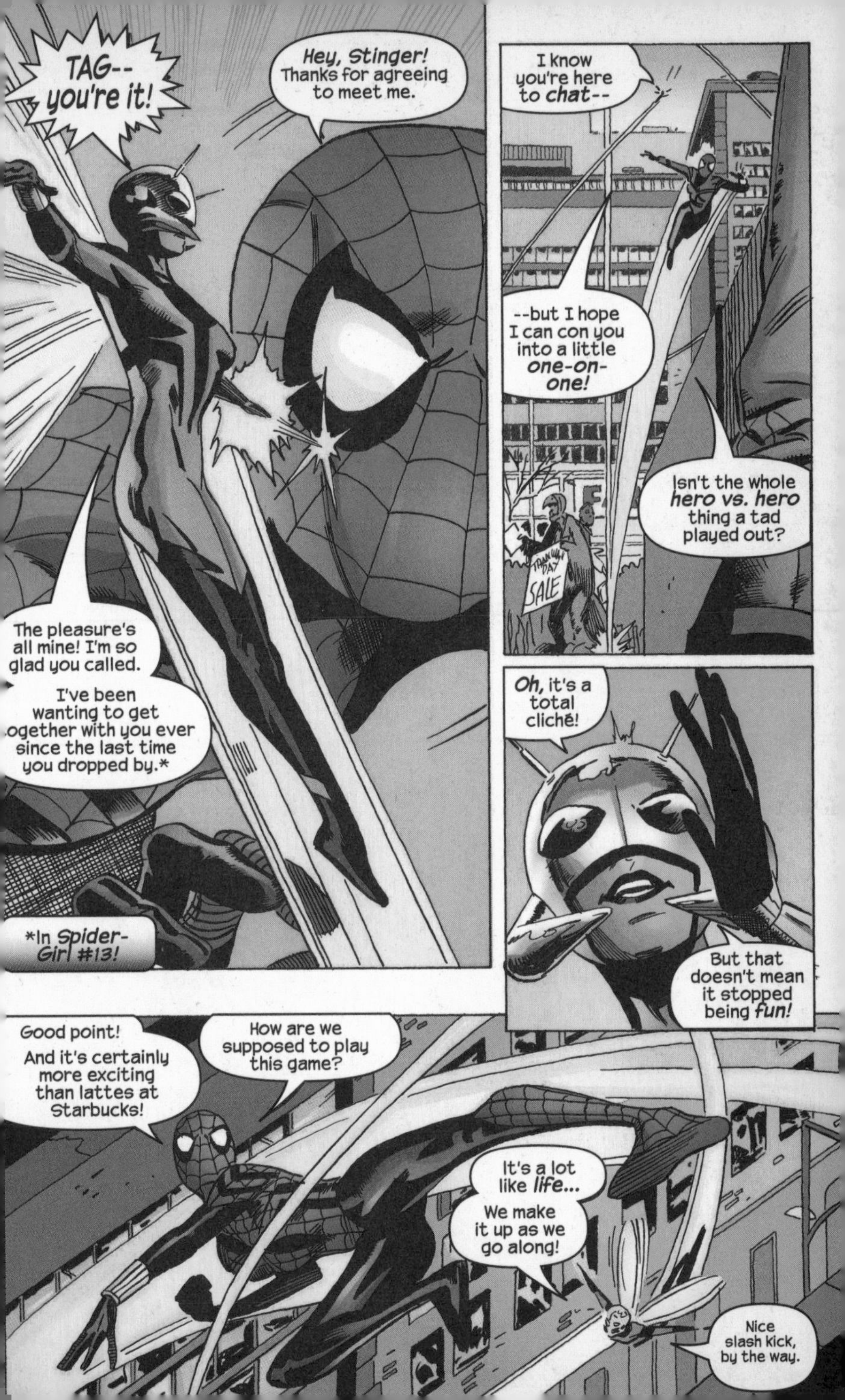
TAG--
you're it!
Hey, Stinger! Thanks for agreeing to meet me.
The pleasure's all mine! I'm so glad you called.
I've been wanting to get together with you ever since the last time you dropped by.*
*In Spider-Girl #13!
I know you're here to chat--
--but I hope I can con you into a little one-on-one!
Isn't the whole hero vs. hero thing a tad played out?
SALE
Oh, it's a total cliché!
But that doesn't mean it stopped being fun!
Good point!
And it's certainly more exciting than lattes at Starbucks!
How are we supposed to play this game?
It's a lot like life...
We make it up as we go along!
Nice slash kick, by the way.

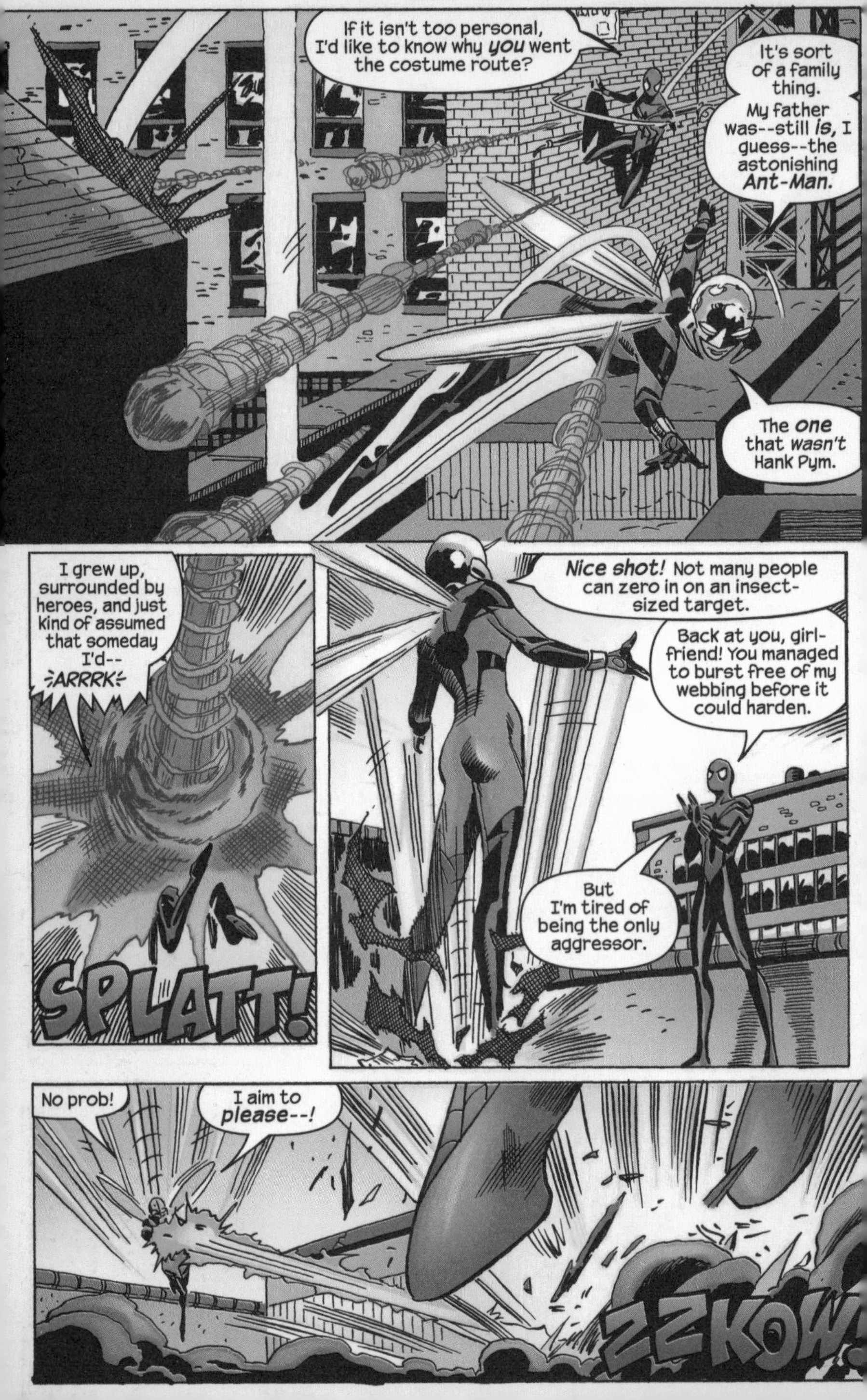

If it isn't too personal, I'd like to know why *you* went the costume route?
It's sort of a family thing.
My father was--still *is,* I guess--the astonishing ***Ant-Man.***
The ***one*** that *wasn't* Hank Pym.
I grew up, surrounded by heroes, and just kind of assumed that someday I'd--
ARRRK
SPLATT!
Nice shot! Not many people can zero in on an insect-sized target.
Back at you, girl-friend! You managed to burst free of my webbing before it could harden.
But I'm tired of being the only aggressor.
No prob!
I aim to ***please--!***
ZZKOW

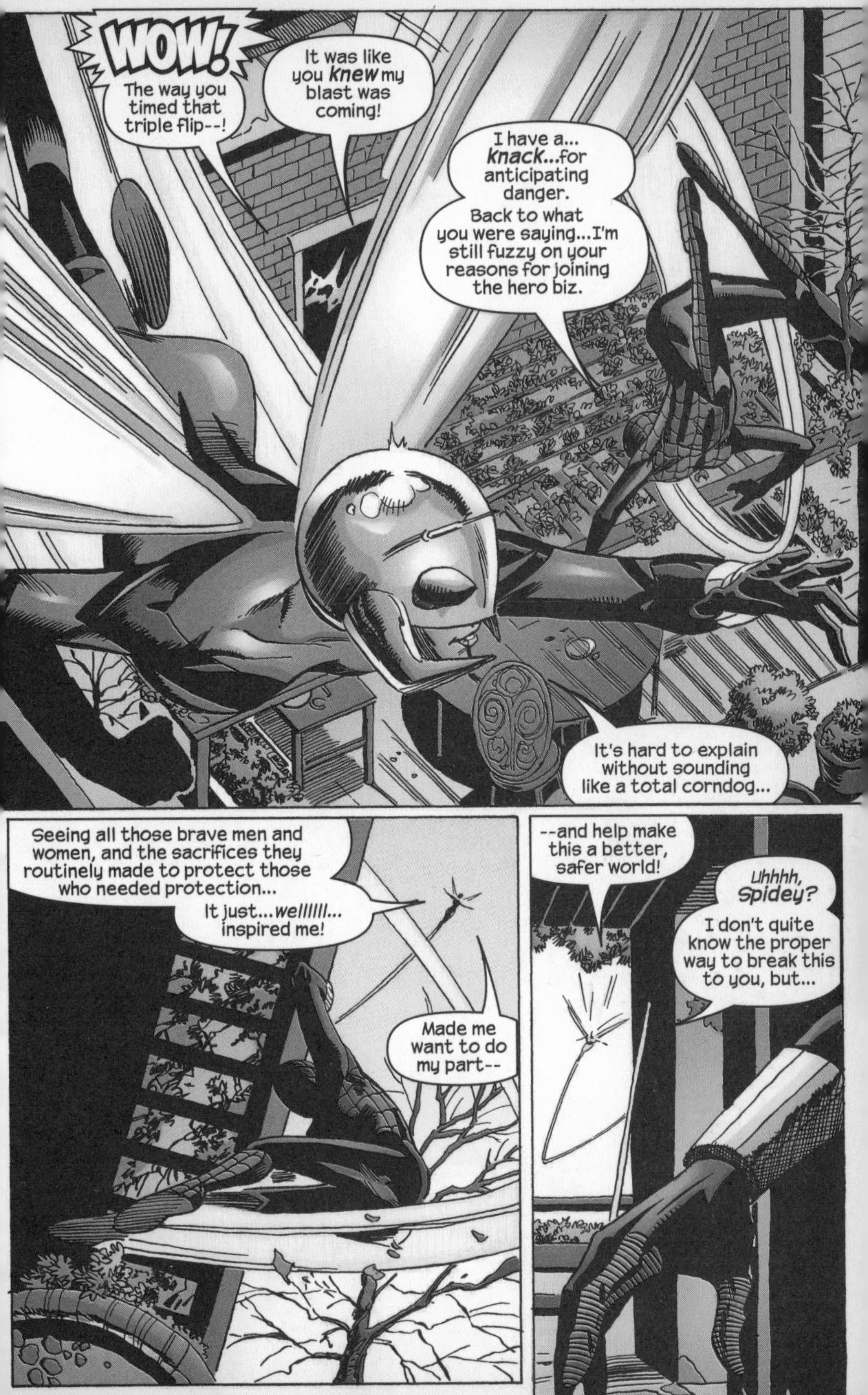
WOW!
The way you timed that triple flip--!
It was like you *knew* my blast was coming!
I have a... *knack*...for anticipating danger.
Back to what you were saying...I'm still fuzzy on your reasons for joining the hero biz.
It's hard to explain without sounding like a total corndog...
Seeing all those brave men and women, and the sacrifices they routinely made to protect those who needed protection...
It just...*wellllll*... inspired me!
Made me want to do my part--
--and help make this a better, safer world!
Uhhhh, Spidey?
I don't quite know the proper way to break this to you, but...

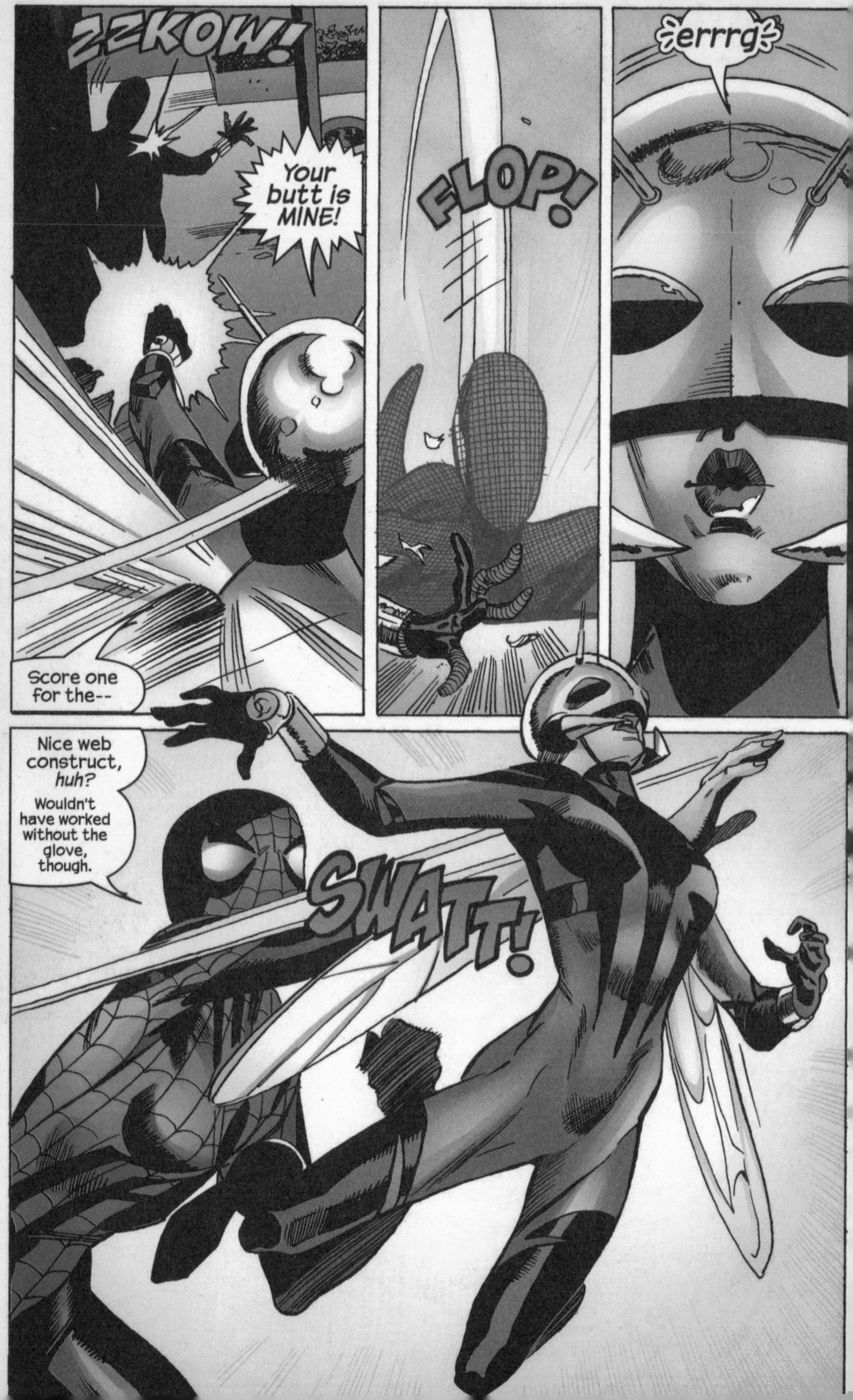
ZZKOW!
Your butt is MINE!
FLOP!
errrg
Score one for the--
Nice web construct, huh?
Wouldn't have worked without the glove, though.
SWATT!

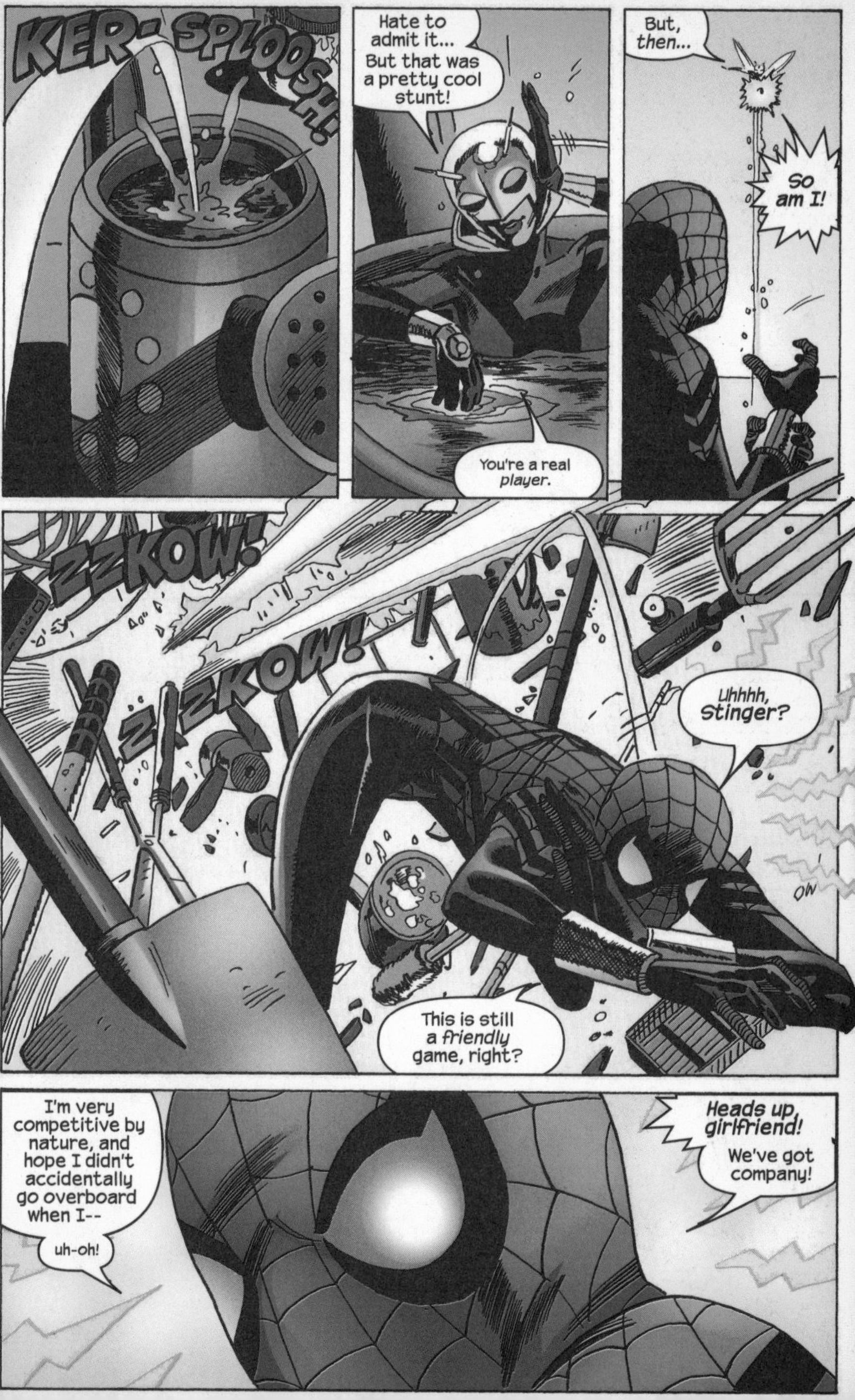
KER-SPLOOSH!
Hate to admit it... But that was a pretty cool stunt!
You're a real *player*.
But, then...
So am I!
ZZKOW!
ZZKOW!
Uhhhh, Stinger?
This is still a *friendly* game, right?
I'm very competitive by nature, and hope I didn't accidentally go overboard when I--
uh-oh!
Heads up, girlfriend!
We've got company!

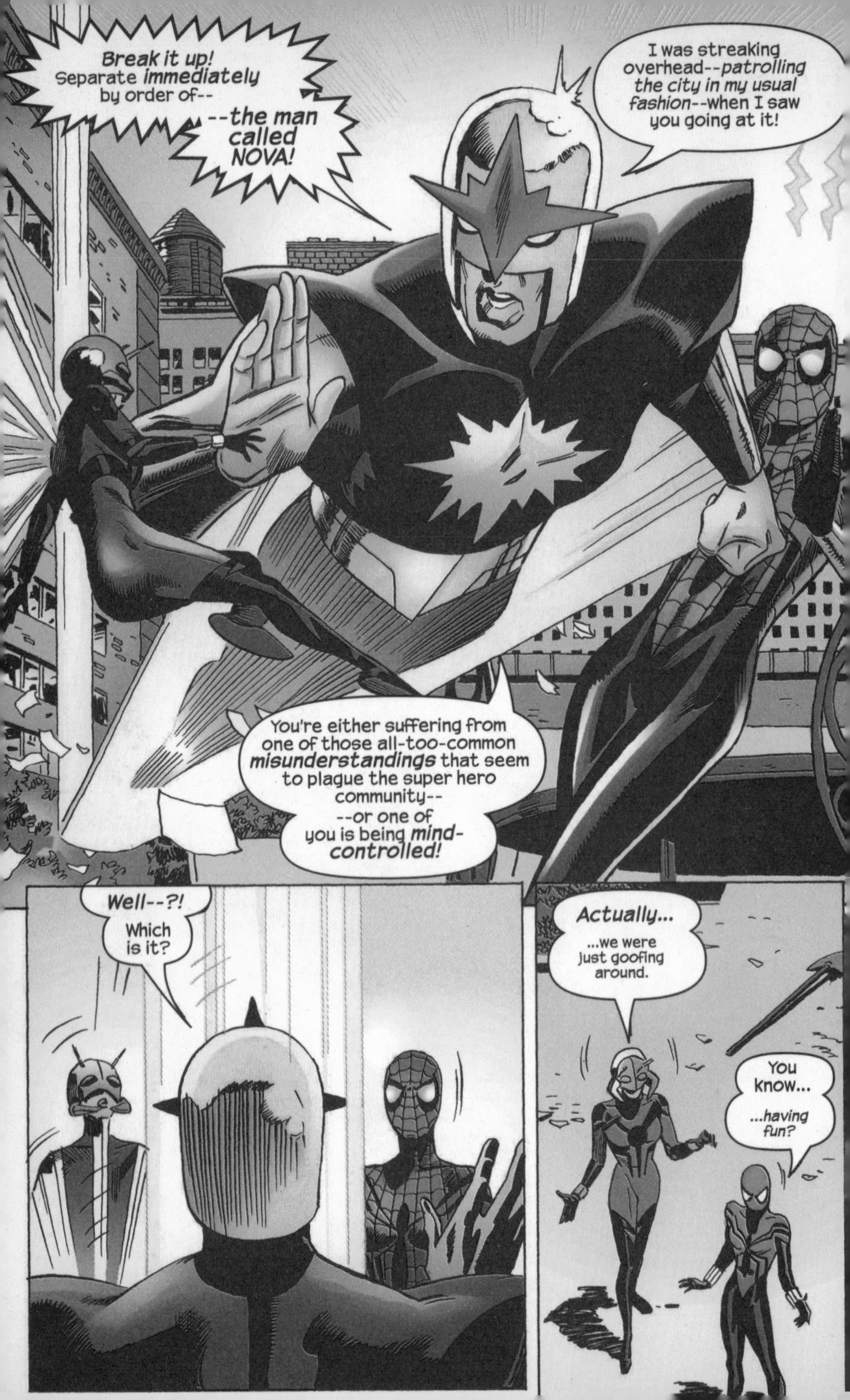
Break it up! Separate immediately by order of--
--the man called NOVA!
I was streaking overhead--patrolling the city in my usual fashion--when I saw you going at it!
You're either suffering from one of those all-too-common misunderstandings that seem to plague the super hero community--
--or one of you is being mind-controlled!
Well--?!
Which is it?
Actually...
...we were just goofing around.
You know...
...having fun?

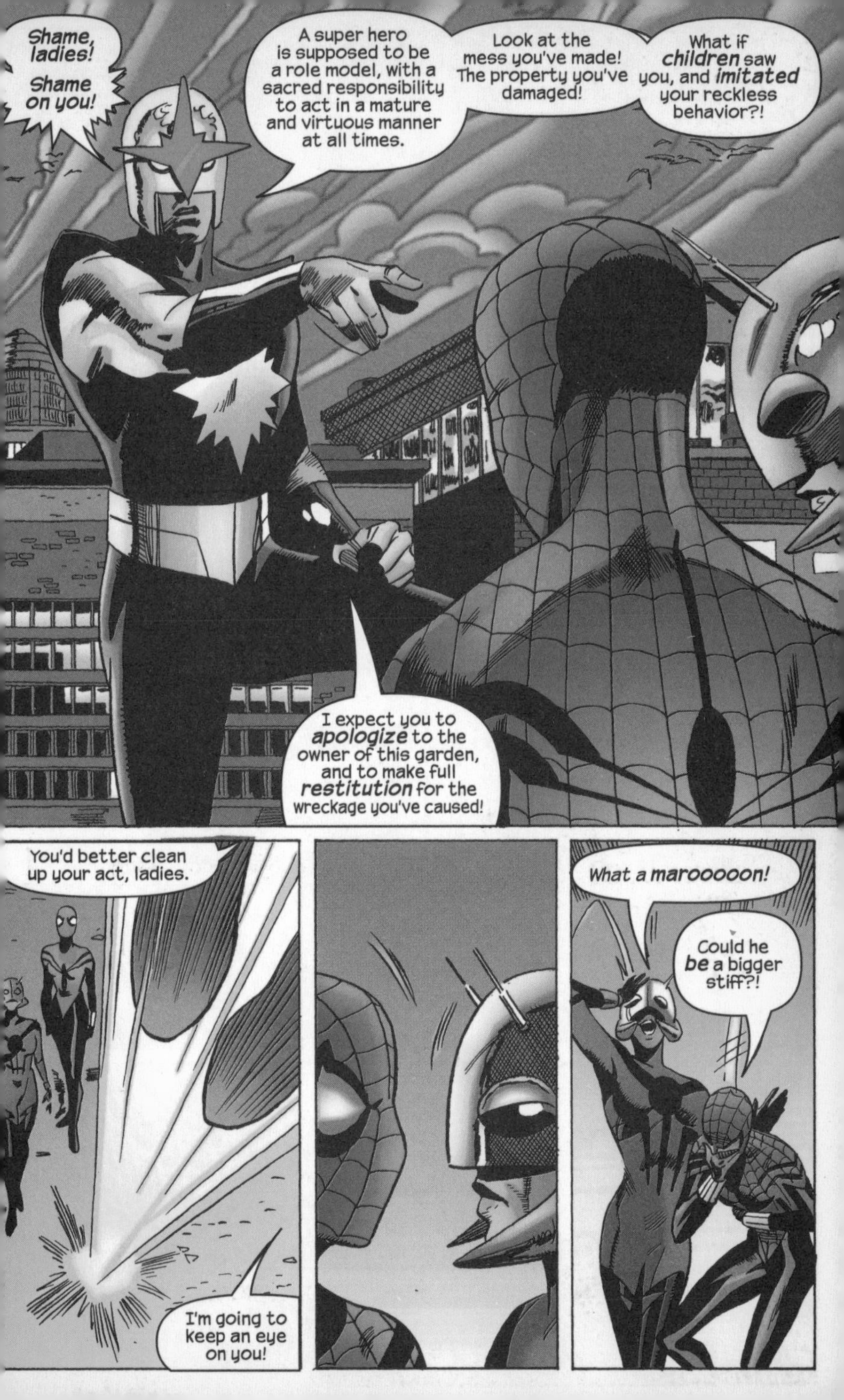
Shame, ladies!
Shame on you!
A super hero is supposed to be a role model, with a sacred responsibility to act in a mature and virtuous manner at all times.
Look at the mess you've made! The property you've damaged!
What if *children* saw you, and *imitated* your reckless behavior?!
I expect you to *apologize* to the owner of this garden, and to make full *restitution* for the wreckage you've caused!
You'd better clean up your act, ladies.
I'm going to keep an eye on you!
What a *marooooon!*
Could he *be* a bigger stiff?!

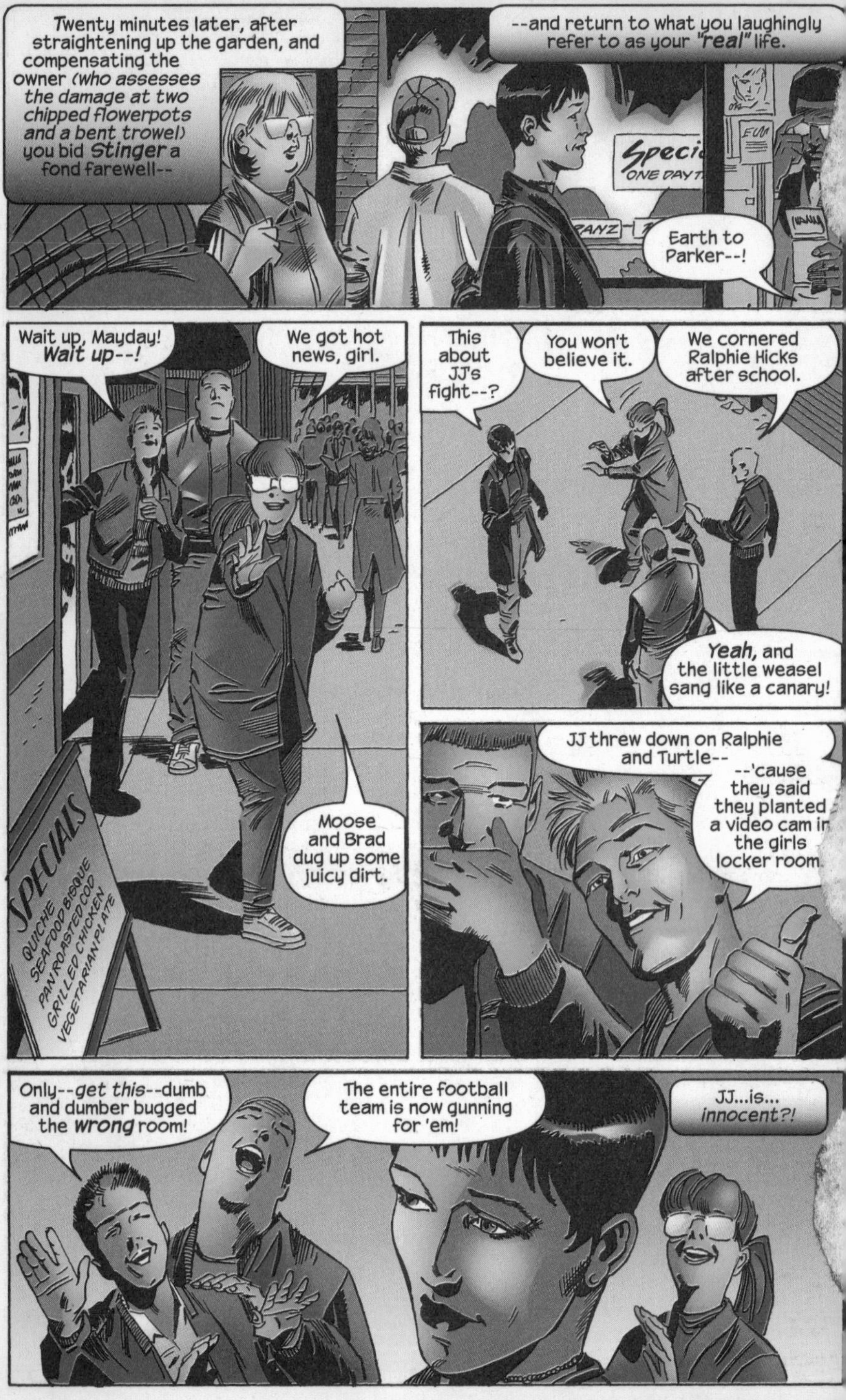
Twenty minutes later, after straightening up the garden, and compensating the owner (who assesses the damage at two chipped flowerpots and a bent trowel) you bid Stinger a fond farewell--
--and return to what you laughingly refer to as your "real" life.
Earth to Parker--!
Wait up, Mayday! Wait up--!
We got hot news, girl.
Moose and Brad dug up some juicy dirt.
SPECIALS
QUICHE
SEAFOOD BISQUE
PAN ROASTED COD
GRILLED CHICKEN
VEGETARIAN PLATE
This about JJ's fight--?
You won't believe it.
We cornered Ralphie Hicks after school.
Yeah, and the little weasel sang like a canary!
JJ threw down on Ralphie and Turtle--
--'cause they said they planted a video cam in the girls locker room.
Only--get this--dumb and dumber bugged the wrong room!
The entire football team is now gunning for 'em!
JJ...is... innocent?!

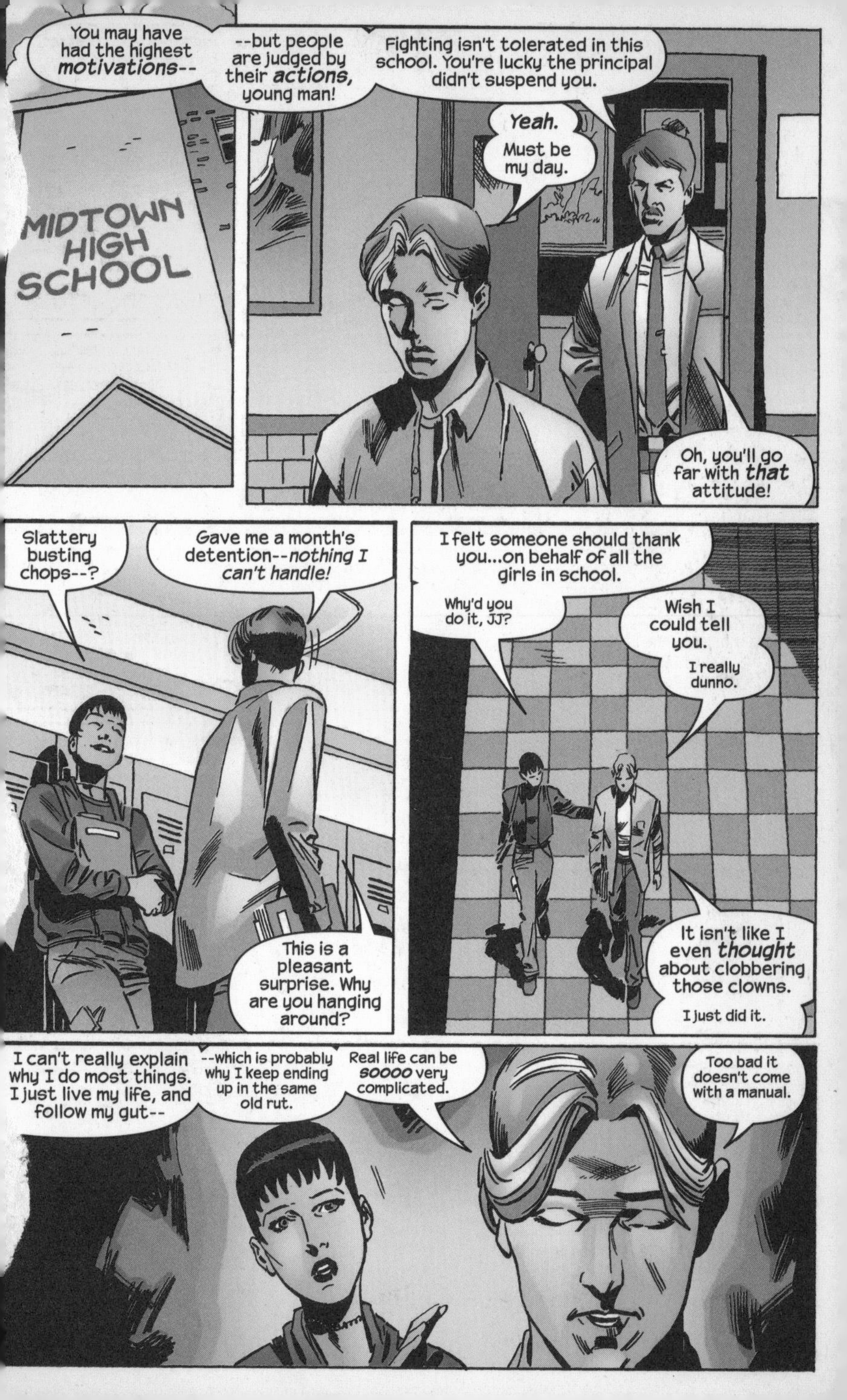

You may have had the highest motivations--
--but people are judged by their actions, young man!
Fighting isn't tolerated in this school. You're lucky the principal didn't suspend you.
MIDTOWN HIGH SCHOOL
Yeah.
Must be my day.
Oh, you'll go far with that attitude!
Slattery busting chops--?
Gave me a month's detention--nothing I can't handle!
This is a pleasant surprise. Why are you hanging around?
I felt someone should thank you...on behalf of all the girls in school.
Why'd you do it, JJ?
Wish I could tell you.
I really dunno.
It isn't like I even thought about clobbering those clowns.
I just did it.
I can't really explain why I do most things. I just live my life, and follow my gut--
--which is probably why I keep ending up in the same old rut.
Real life can be soooo very complicated.
Too bad it doesn't come with a manual.

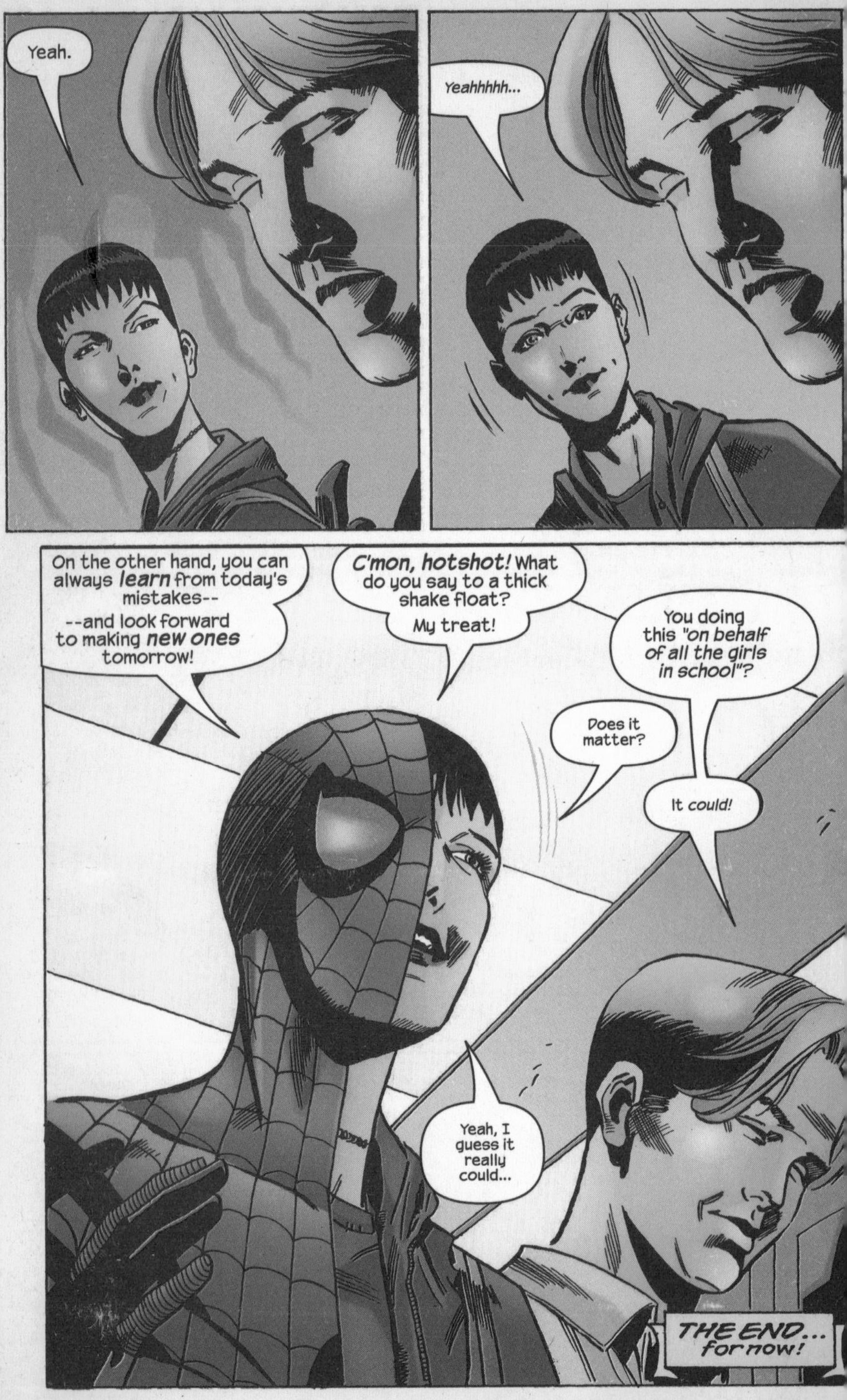
Yeah.
Yeahhhhh...
On the other hand, you can always learn from today's mistakes--
--and look forward to making new ones tomorrow!
C'mon, hotshot! What do you say to a thick shake float?
My treat!
You doing this "on behalf of all the girls in school"?
Does it matter?
It could!
Yeah, I guess it really could...
THE END... for now!